Samuel Longfellow

Life Of Henry Wadsworth Longfellow

Vol. III

Samuel Longfellow

Life Of Henry Wadsworth Longfellow
Vol. III

ISBN/EAN: 9783348009263

Printed in Europe, USA, Canada, Australia, Japan

Cover: Foto ©ninafisch / pixelio.de

More available books at **www.hansebooks.com**

LIFE OF
HENRY WADSWORTH LONGFELLOW

WITH EXTRACTS FROM HIS JOURNALS AND CORRESPONDENCE

EDITED BY

SAMUEL LONGFELLOW

IN THREE VOLUMES

VOLUME III.

BOSTON AND NEW YORK
HOUGHTON, MIFFLIN AND COMPANY
The Riverside Press, Cambridge

The Riverside Press, Cambridge, Mass., U. S. A.
Electrotyped and Printed by H. O. Houghton & Co.

CONTENTS OF VOLUME III.

APPENDIX.

LIST OF ILLUSTRATIONS.

The wood-cuts are printed on Imperial Japanese paper.

[1] Copyrighted and published by Benjamin F. Mills, Cambridge, Mass.

HENRY WADSWORTH LONGFELLOW.

VOLUME III.

CHAPTER I.

JOURNAL AND LETTERS.

1862.

January 8. Bright, — not with the enamelled cold of the last week, but a certain vapory softness in the air. I have letters to write; but nevertheless, I will first go and walk. Walk to Mt. Auburn.

9th. Beautiful description of a heron and a gerfalcon in Calderon's *El Mayor Encanto*, jornada ii. I am trying to bring myself to a little more systematic course of reading.

To Charles Sumner.

January 15, 1862.

It is hard for me not to write to you, and still harder to write. I have no heart for anything. There is only one thought in my mind. You know what that is. . . . So we will not speak of it, but rather of your admirable speech on the Trent affair. It is very clear and thorough and statesmanlike. Everybody reads it; and none reads it but to praise. Curtis was here yesterday, and thinks it admirable; so does Norton; so does T.; so does Mrs. Kemble, who says she likes it best of all your speeches. And these, with one or two newspaper writers, are my "everybody." When you add to these everybody else's everybody, you will have a grand aggregate.

How busy and overburdened you must be! Felton says we owe it to you that we have no war with England; and I have no doubt it is so.

16th. I hardly know how these weary winter days creep along. Newspapers, Calderon, Michael Angelo's Sonnets, *Fioretti di San Francesco;* Woods and Waters, by Street; letters, talk with friends, walks through the snow; so one after another the heavy days are rolled over the horizon and disappear in the abyss.

29th. Kept in-doors [by a lame knee]. Read Vapereau's *Année Littéraire,* which gives a sketch of everything published in France during the year; endless poems, plays, and novels. Very clever critics are the French, with their easy, subtle analysis of everything. We and the English have nothing of the kind.

30th. Read newspapers, wrote letters, and mused unprofitably by the fireside. Tried a walk. In the twilight Miss C. comes and sings to the children, accompanying herself on her guitar; strange Spanish and Indian songs from New Mexico.

31st. Read the inevitable newspapers, hoping for something, longing for something; finding nothing, except a little poem by Tennyson, — 'The Sailor Boy.'

February 3. In the morning, Michael Angelo's *Sonnetti.* In the evening, read Dante, Purgatory, with the children. C. has taken up this idea from attending Lowell's lectures in college.

4th. Newspapers take up much time, — too much by a great deal; but one can hardly help it now when any moment may bring the greatest tidings. Visit from Curtis.

5th. A visit from my classmate, J. S. C. Abbott, author of the Life of Napoleon. Still amiable and joyous, as of old.

6th. An hour at the Nortons'. Borrow the splendid illustrated Dante of Gustave Doré, which is very imaginative, wild, and vigorous.

8th. Look over Doré's illustrations of the *Inferno.* They leave on the mind an idea of vastness and lurid sublimity, greater than that produced by Flaxman. A prodigality of horrors. "Soleva dire Michel Angelo Buonarotti quelle sole figure esser buone delli quali *era cavata la fatica,"* — only those figures were good from which the *fatigue* was taken out. This is not always the case with Doré's.

10th. Wrote a long letter to Paul Blier, the French translator of The Golden Legend; answering sundry questions, to hunt up which answers took me all day long. Then walked up to the Nortons'.

12th. The days pass in dull monotony, and having nothing to record, I record nothing. A newspaper, a novel, a vain attempt at more serious study, and weariness, — that is all.

13th. The war goes on. The North is in motion at last; and great results are looked for.

14th. The little girls sending and receiving Valentines. Well, it is something to busy one's self with their business, and partake their joy.

15th. A week of victories all along the line, East and West.[1]

20th. Translated the beautiful Canto xxv. of the *Paradiso.*

21st. To-day Captain Gordon, the slaver, is to be hanged. It seems to me very illogical to hang him, and yet to protect by the Constitution all our internal slave-traders.

24th. Translate Canto xxx. of the *Paradiso.* In the evening a great fire in Boston, flushing the whole heavens.

[1] Springfield, Fort Henry, Roanoke Island, Elizabeth City.

A wonderful scene from the windows. The sheeted snow, and lights from houses gleaming through the red flush of the air; the wind blowing like a trumpet.

25th. Translated part of *Paradiso* xxvii.; St. Peter's wrath, and the angry glow of the air, which I thought of last night as I looked from the window.

27th. My birthday. Translated Canto xxiii. of *Paradiso.* News comes of Felton's death at his brother's, in Chester, near Philadelphia. I go down to see Agassiz, and find him in great distress. Dear, good Felton! how much he is beloved!

28th. I keep mostly in-doors, translating. Snow-drifts are piled about, and the month ends with the blast of windy trumpets over the chimney-tops, — melancholy enough to a melancholy man.

March 3. Finished *Paradiso* xxiv. Went to town. At the publisher's, met Mr. Trollope, who has just returned from the West.

4th. A cheerless, gray March day, — the streets flooded with snow and water. Felton's funeral, from the college chapel. So passes away the learned scholar, the genial companion, the affectionate, faithful friend!

5th. Went to the greenhouse to get flowers for Miss W——'s funeral. The funeral in the afternoon. Ah, what sorrow and what loveliness united! Painter never painted death in lovelier shape than this young girl. "Dear, beauteous death!"

6th. C. has been asked to go to Ship Island. Drive to town with him to see him on board. It is a great tug at the heart-strings, this parting with a son for the first time.

10th. See Fields, who wants some cantos of the *Paradiso* for the Atlantic. He gives me a picture of Stradivarius in his workship among his violins. I feel as if I should like to make musical instruments and could do it, if my head were not full of other things, — as Don Quixote thought he could have made good toothpicks and bird-cages, if his head had not been full of adventures.

18th. All the past week I have been pretty busy upon Dante, — quite absorbed.

25th. Another week gone. All given to Dante. I have now completed twelve cantos of the *Paradiso*, — xxii.–xxxiii. Sit an hour with Lowell in his study. Go up to the Nortons'.

26th. Meet Sophocles in the street. He has written an epitaph in Greek for Felton's gravestone, which he wishes me to translate. A strange, eccentric man is Sophocles, with his blue cloak and wild gray beard, his learning and his silence. He makes Diogenes a possibility.

April 2. Walk to town. Then hurry home to read the first volume of Irving's Life and Letters. Very interesting.

9th. Great battles, and great victories for Freedom.

11th. Bought a set of the British Essayists, in forty-five volumes; beginning with The Tatler, the first number of which was published April 12, 1709.

12th. Walking in the pleasant sunset, I met Richard Dana, and shortly afterward his father, the old essayist, author of The Idle Man; a courteous gentleman, who has somewhat outlived his fame, and to whom the present generation does not pay the honor which is due to him. We had some pleasant chat about the British essayists, and the charm that still lingers round their memory. As we walked we met Lowell and Norton; and I felt that we belonged to the "Old-Guard."

14th. Letters, letters, letters! How they come, and how they consume one's time! Not those from friends, — I do not mean that, for it is always a pleasure to hear from them, — but the "perfect stranger," as he is fond of calling himself, who always wants you to turn his grindstone. A charming essay might be written on the Perfect Stranger.

20th. Easter Sunday. Keep in-doors with heavy cold. The sickly sunshine streams through the windows. The dust flies. Heavy in heart and head.

To Charles Sumner.

April 20, 1862.

Here is a photograph of Felton, which is pretty good. Dexter has made a bust of him, a most agreeable likeness; an admirable head, like one of the Roman Emperors. It is not yet in marble, so that one cannot pronounce a final judgment.

You are hard at work; and God bless you in it. In every country the "dangerous classes" are those who do no work; for instance, the nobility in Europe and the slave-holders here. It is evident that the world needs a new nobility, — not of the gold medal and *sangre azul* order; not of the blood that is blue because it stagnates; but of the red arterial blood, that circulates, and has heart in it, and life, and labor.

I am writing you on Easter Sunday. What an Easter this is for the negroes in the District of Columbia![1] I rejoice, with you and with all true men, on this Easter of Africa.

To ——.

April 23, 1862.

Your letter and your poems have touched me very much. Tears fell down my cheeks as I read them, and I

[1] Congress had just passed a bill emancipating the slaves in the District; "the first instalment" said Mr. Sumner, "of the great debt we owe an enslaved race."

think them very true and tender expressions of your sense of loss.

So the little ones fade and fall, like blossoms wafted away by the wind! But the wind is the breath of God, and the falling blossoms perfume the air, and the remembrance of them is sweet and sacred.

In our greatest sorrows we must not forget that there is always some one who has a greater sorrow, or at all events a more recent one; and that may give us courage, though it cannot give us comfort.

To Miss F——.

April 28, 1862.

Your letter from Seaforth last summer comforted me in a very dark hour, and I should not have left it so long unanswered if I had had the heart to write to any one. Even now I can do little more than thank you for it. I cannot speak of the desolation of this house, and the sorrow which overwhelms and crushes me. I must be patient and silent. My children are all well, and good; and that is a great comfort to me. . . .

I can hardly tell you how changed Cambridge has become to me. Felton, too, is gone; one of my oldest and dearest friends. It seems indeed as if the world were reeling and sinking under my feet. He died of heart disease, and is buried here at Mt. Auburn, the crests of whose trees I can see from this window where I write. A truly noble, sweet nature!

To Ferdinand Freiligrath.

April 28, 1862.

Pardon me for not having answered your letter of last summer, which comforted and strengthened me with its words of sympathy. I have not had the heart to write; nor have I now, save my thanks and my affectionate remembrances to you and your dear wife. It makes my fatal wound ache and bleed too much. So forgive me if I say no more than that I am still overwhelmed and crushed.

I have no definite plans for the future, but drift along from day to day through these bitter waters. It is very difficult to build up again such a shattered life. It crumbled away like sand. But I try, and am patient; though, having seen what I have seen, I wonder I am still alive. My children are all well, and that comforts me, and gives me courage.

Thanks for the *Skizzen aus Nord America*. Do you know the author, Dr. Kohl? He is a very admirable excellent man.

I hope that you and yours are all well and happy. God bless you and guard you!

29th. Lowell comes to hear some cantos of my translation of the *Paradiso*. Then Fields; and I walk with him on his way to town.

May 1. A lovely May-day. A procession of girls and boys has just gone by with banners and wreaths of flowers.

To Miss F——.

May 8, 1862.

As I was passing down the village street yesterday, I saw at a shop window, directly opposite Felton's study, a beautiful orange-tree, having upon it six oranges and a hundred buds and blossoms. I could not resist the temptation of buying it; and it is now flourishing in my own window and filling the room with fragrance. . . . It stands under the shelter of a lemon-tree ten feet high, which for the last ten years has kept up a make-believe summer all winter long in my study.[1]

Felton is universally regretted. He had thousands of friends and not one enemy. What Burke (or some other friend) said at Johnson's death may be said of Felton's: "It has made a chasm which not only nothing can fill up, but which nothing has a tendency to fill up. Johnson is dead: let us go to the next best. There is nobody. No man can be said to put you in mind of Johnson."[2]

This is equally true of Felton. He had a wider range of scholarship than any of us; and his nature to the last was pure, genial, and sympathetic. Strangely enough, I was not much shocked at the tidings of his death. I suppose I was too benumbed with suffering to feel anything very keenly at that time. But I feel his loss all the more perhaps. His epitaph has been written in Greek, by Sophocles, himself a Greek, and Professor of Greek in the University. I send you a literal translation; like the original, it is in the elegiac, or hexameter and pentameter, metre.

Felton, dearest of friends, to the land unseen thou departest;
  Snatched away, thou hast left sorrow and sighing behind!
On thy companions, the dear ones, alas! the affliction has fallen;
  Hellas, of thee beloved, misses thy beautiful life!

Of the civil war I say only this. It is not a revolution, but a Catalinian conspiracy. It is Slavery against Freedom; the north wind against the southern pestilence. I saw lately, at a jeweller's, a slave's collar of iron, with an iron tongue as large as a spoon, to go into the mouth.

1 The lemon-tree is gone, but the orange-tree still adorns and perfumes the study.

2 It was William Gerrard Hamilton, who said this. See Croker's Boswell, v. 353.

Every drop of blood in me quivered! The world forgets what Slavery really is!

10th. I send you a photograph of my little Saxon E., eight years old. I am very fond of photographs. Did you ever examine what the photographers call the *negative*, in which all that is to be light is dark, and the reverse? If so, you will feel how beautiful was the remark made by a brother-in-law of mine that "this world is only the *negative* of the world to come, and what is dark here will be light hereafter."

I wonder what you are doing on this beautiful day. My little girls are flitting about my study, as blithe as two birds. They are preparing to celebrate the birthday of one of their dolls; and on the table I find this programme, in E.'s handwriting, which I purloin and send to you, thinking it may amuse you. What a beautiful world this child's world is! So instinct with life, so illuminated with imagination! I take infinite delight in seeing it go on around me, and feel all the tenderness of the words that fell from the blessed lips, — "Suffer the little children to come unto me." After that benediction how can any one dare to deal harshly with a child!

E. occupies her leisure in a correspondence with me. Her post-office is under her pillow, where she expects to find a letter in the morning.

9th. On my way out from town, met John Dwight, and asked him to dinner. Pleasant chat about music and musical people in Germany and Italy. He is translating Mendelssohn's letters, for his Journal of Music. They are very interesting.

11th. News to-day of the surrender of Norfolk, and the destruction, by the Rebels, of the iron ship Merrimac.

12th. Begin sitting to Healy for portrait.

17th. Drove with my little girls through the budding, blossoming roads of Watertown, under Wellington's Hill, and home by Mr. Cushing's. Here is one of the best things the war has yet given us. [A newspaper paragraph containing General Hunter's Order, declaring the military department of the South under martial law, and all persons held as slaves therein, free.] All hail to General Hunter.

22d. Emerson and Lowell call.

In the month of June Mr. Longfellow joined a party of friends in a visit to Niagara Falls, which he had never seen, — taking his boys with him.

June 4. A rainy day to begin the Niagara journey. On, on, on, all day long. Reach Albany at five.

5th. To Utica by rail. There we take a carriage to Trenton Falls. Dine, and then go down the steep steps to the lovely river, rushing, roaring along its banks of stone, through a deep wooded ravine. We follow it up for miles; all loveliness, and a little spice of danger from a slip on the narrow ledges. A nice hotel, and a good host, fond of music and of art, and possessing two parlor organs and a piano, and rooms full of pictures. Go down to the river at night. Black and fearful is it in the deep ravine, with flashes of white foam, and the waterfalls calling and beckoning.

6th. Down at the river before breakfast. In the afternoon another ramble up the beautiful river. It is very lovely.

7th. Reach Niagara at nine, and stop at the Cataract House impending over the Rapids. After supper go with E. and Miss S. to Goat Island, lovely in the moonlight, and get our first glimpse of the Falls.

8th. A bright, beautiful day. Pass all the morning

alone, on Goat Island and a smaller one, just on the western brink of the American Fall. What a lovely spot! Better than a church for me to-day. Go up the stone tower in the midst of the English Fall. It drives me frantic with excitement. In the afternoon, go over the suspension bridge to Table Rock, on the Canada side. It is the finest view of the English Fall. In every other particular the American side is preferable.

9th. Niagara is too much for me; my nerves shake like a bridge of wire; a vague sense of terror and unrest haunts me all the time. My head swims and reels with the ceaseless motion of the water.

10th. Last night we took a farewell ramble on Goat Island, Luna Island, and the Three Sisters. Leave Niagara for Toronto after dinner to-day. After supper, took a stroll through the main street of Toronto with E.; then to bed in our gloomy Castle of Otranto, called the Rossin House.

12th. From Kingston, down the St. Lawrence in the steamboat; first, among the "Thousand Islands," then down the rapids, which is exciting. But in the afternoon we ran aground in Lake St. Francis, where we remained fast, till two steam-tugs got us off in the evening and conveyed us to the shore. We passed the night snugly at the landing-place.

From ——.

VICTORIA, VANCOUVER ISLAND,
June 12, 1862.

DEAR MR. LONGFELLOW,—A few days ago I was told an Indian legend, genuine Chimsean (the Chimseans are a tribe living close to Victoria), related by very old Chimsean lips to an English clergyman here,—a bit of theology which instantly put me in mind of the beautiful legends you have so gracefully rendered into poetry, and which, in the hope of its being new to you, I cannot resist sending. One feature in it has so strong an affinity with the story of Eve and the tree of knowledge as to be really striking.

In starting, I must remind you that the Olympian range of mountains is on the opposite side the straits of Fula, in Washington Territory, and is so grand and Alpine-like a chain, the many-peaked summit crowned with eternal snow, that no one knowing it can wonder that it should have figured in the legend which embodies the Chimsean belief as to the peopling of our globe. It is as follows:

Afar off in the land of Nokun, there beyond the Olympian mountains, years and years ago, dwelt two women, the only beings on earth. As they lay side by side upon the ground one starlight night, the one said to the other, pointing to the heavens above: "Oh, how I should like that pale-faced star for my husband!" And said the other: "Oh, how I should like that red-faced star for mine!" And they were the two brightest stars in heaven. The women fell into a deep sleep, awoke, and found themselves in the sky amid the stars; and all took place as they had wished. They were very happy in heaven, the one with her pale-faced and the other with her red-faced husband, and they had plenty of fine things, and lots of beds of onions (the Chimsean gourmand's especial weakness); but in the middle of the largest bed grew an immensely large onion, which the pale-face and the red-face told them they were on no account to touch.

But one day, when the pale-face and the red-face were away hunting, the two women went straight to the great onion-bed and pulled at the great onion. They pulled and pulled and pulled, till they pulled it right up. And below there was a great hole; and peeping through the hole, they saw beneath them the world they had left, looking far, far away, and very green and beautiful. And straightway they longed to return home. Rolling the great onion back into its hole, in secret and whenever the pale-face and the red-face were safely away hunting, they began to plait what in course of time became a long, stout rope of grass and rushes and whatever else they could find; and as they made it they carefully hid it out of sight. One day when they had plaited a great quantity, and the pale-face and the red-face were safely away hunting, the women pulled up the great onion again, and let the rope fall down toward the earth below. But, alas! it was too short. So they pulled it up again as fast as ever they could, and plaited a piece more to it, and let it down again; and this time it touched the earth below. Then one of the women slid down upon it; and when she was safely landed on the earth she gave the rope a shake, to signify that all was right, and then the other woman slid down. And then they gave the rope a good pull, and pulled it right down, so that the pale-face and the red-face might not come after them to punish them; and the many coils of the rope in falling made the long line of the Olympian mountains as they stand to this day. And the children born of the two women grew and filled the earth with people. And, as the children say, that is all.

13th. Started early, and passed through the lake, and down the Coteau, Cedar, and Cascade Rapids, and across Lake St. Louis. At a wretched little Indian village of huts, with moss-covered roofs, Caughnawaga, the Indian pilot Baptiste came on board and steered us down the last and most dangerous of the rapids, the Lachine. We reached Montreal for breakfast, at the St. Lawrence hotel. A day in Montreal is not much time for so nice a place. We all like it. Pass the forenoon in rambling through the streets, and the afternoon in a drive round the mountain.

16th. From Burlington to Boston, by Bellow's Falls, a pleasant route. Reached home at dark, and found the house deserted.

22d. Bright, melancholy day. It is too terrible to bear! This utter loneliness!

24th. Begin to get ready for Nahant. Afternoon, go to the college chapel to hear Mr. Paine, on the organ. Some of Sebastian Bach's fugues. Mr. P. is a Portlander, just returned from Germany, and now musical instructor in the college. A fine organist, young and full of promise. He and Dwight at tea.

July 8. Afternoon hazy and hot. A bath, and a soft hazy evening, with a copper moon, rayless and ominous, hanging over the motionless sea.

10th. I can make no record of these days. Better leave them wrapped in silence. Perhaps some day God will give me peace.

To James T. Fields.

NAHANT, July 16, 1862.

Your second note, "to remind," shows me how the days pass. A terrible week this last has been. So pardon the neglect. Thanks for the offer of books. Trollope I have, and Winthrop's last novel I should like very much. I began copying 'The Cumberland' for you the other day; but gave it up in disgust at the end of the second stanza. I have found the seven volumes of Mme. D'Arblay, very pleasant seaside reading. They have helped me over some dreary hours. I find Nahant very sad this summer; "remote, unfriended, melancholy, slow." But I fancy place makes no great difference. Change of place does. That is the best thing, if one were only free to take it, or make it.

19th. Nahant is very solitary and deserted this year. I stood looking down at the steamboat-landing opposite. Not a fishing-boat; not a human being in sight. Then the ghostly little steamer comes in, and the phantoms go over the hill toward the ruins of the burned hotel, and all is still and lonely again.

31st. A visit from Sumner, and long political talk.

August 2. A bath at noon, with the children. Try to write. Splendid mirage.

4th. Reading a very clever French book, with a very foolish title, *Dick Moon en France.* A beautiful description of Paris, *prise du Pont des Arts,* on the sixty-seventh page.

. . . . . .

The rest of August a blank. War and rumors of war; and a sense of apprehension in the air, and sadness and general discomfort; no heart to write down the record of the passing day.

September 1. Yesterday we had report of a great battle at Manassas, ending in defeat of the Rebels. The moon set red and lowering; and I thought in the night of the pale, upturned faces of young men on the battle-field, and the agonies of the wounded; and my wretchedness was very great. Every shell from the cannon's mouth bursts not only on the battle-field, but in far-away homes, North or South, carrying dismay and death. What an infernal thing war is! Woe to him by whom it cometh! We are waiting this morning with greatest anxiety for news.

3d. Field, of Philadelphia, and Wild, the painter, dine with us. After dinner, Agassiz comes in. He is at his wit's end about the Scientific School. Want of funds to go on with, and so forth.

5th. Read Voltaire's Charles XII., whom he considers "l'homme le plus remarquable qui ait existé," — though I believe he throws in a *peut-être* somewhere. Elsewhere, he calls him an "homme unique, plutôt que grand homme."

14th. Sumner comes to dinner. He is very gloomy and desponding; and sighs out every now and then, "Poor country! poor, poor country!"

23d. Good news this morning. Emancipation of the slaves! On and after January 1, 1863, "all persons held as slaves within any State, or designated part of a State, the people whereof shall then be in rebellion against the United States, shall be then and thenceforward and forever free."

October 11. Write a little upon the Wayside Inn, — a beginning, only.

31st. October ends with a delicious Indian-summer day. Drive with Fields to the old Red Horse Tavern in Sudbury, — alas, no longer an inn! A lovely valley; the winding road shaded by grand old oaks before the house. A rambling, tumble-down old building, two hundred years old; and till now in the family of the Howes, who have kept an inn for one hundred and seventy-five years. In the old time, it was a house of call for all travellers from Boston westward.

To James T. Fields.

November 11, 1862.

To the best of my recollection, Miss Procter's Poems was returned long and long ago, — a belief in which I am confirmed by an old habit of having a place apart for borrowed books, and of returning them as soon as read, — and sometimes sooner. Still, I will make diligent search; and if I find the books, I promise to — well, say *blush unseen.*

The breakfast was very charming. You and your

wife understand the divine art of entertaining as few people do.

The Sudbury Tales go on famously. I have now five complete, with a great part of the 'Prelude.'

November 18. A lovely day, — the latest Indian summer. Finished the 'Prelude' to the Wayside Inn.

28th. See in the paper that "Professor F. Newman has produced in England a Latin translation of Longfellow's Hiawatha."

29th. Received a copy of this translation, from the author, — *Carmen Hiawathæ.* It is in prose, though printed as verse; and begins: —

> Si rogitas unde hæc fabulæ,
> Unde vagus carminis mei rumor,
> Odorem secum vehens silvestrem
> Roreisque et nebulas pratorum.

At work on a tale called 'Torquemada,' for the Sudbury Tales.

December 5. [At midnight.] Finished 'Torquemada,' — a dismal story of fanaticism; but in its main points historic. See De Castro, *Protestantes Españolas,* page 310.

13th. Fredericksburg is taken; a great battle is going on to-day. Went to South Boston, with S., C., and E., to see the Nahant, — an ironclad with revolving turret, like the Monitor. A curious sight. How ingenious men are in the ways of destruction! In the evening, Fields came out, and I read to him 'Torquemada.'

14th. The new President, Dr. Hill, at chapel. He thinks Liberal Christians do not lay emphasis enough upon the "fear of God."

25th. "A merry Christmas," say the children; but that is no more, for me. Last night the little girls had a pretty Christmas-tree.

CHAPTER II.

JOURNAL AND LETTERS.

1863.

January 1. A great day. The President's Proclamation for Emancipation of Slaves in the rebel States, goes into effect. A beautiful day, full of sunshine, ending in a tranquil moonlight night. May it be symbolical of the Emancipation. There was a grand meeting in Boston, at which Emerson recited a poem. I was not there.

2d. Beautiful as yesterday. I read in C. T. Brooks's translation of Richter's *Titan*. Wrote letters. R. H. Dana came in the evening, and talked of the President's Proclamation, in his own clear way.

3d. Still the same soft weather, suggesting Spring, Italy, Youth. Read *Titan;* very cleverly done into English.

7th. Looked at engravings at the Library. A portfolio of Nanteuil's and Masson's and other French engravers; subjects not interesting, but the engraving fine.

9th. Very dark and dreary within me. I am ashamed to lead so useless and listless a life.

11th. After chapel walk home with Agassiz. Ill all day. In the evening my old friend George W. Greene comes. He is here to give a course of Lowell lectures.

12th. Rembrandt's etchings (at the Library), — a beautiful and interesting portfolio. What homely women! and yet how true to nature. The "Three Trees" and "Three Cottages" and the "Burgomaster Six" are charming etchings. Greene comes out to dine and passes the afternoon and evening.

14th. Read *Titan;* a splendid book, wild and wonderful. I have not read it since I was in Heidelberg.

19th. Our last session with the engravings. We went over a portfolio of Schöngauer and Albrecht Durer.

21st. A dinner for Thies, to close up our engraving class.

22d. In-doors all day, reading *Jean Valjean,* the close of Victor Hugo's *Misérables.*

26th. A divine morning, lovely as Italy. The hoar frost, the haze, the genial sun,—all are beautiful. In the evening Greene reads to me his fourth lecture, and I read to him some cantos of the *Paradiso.*

February 19. If you want to enliven a dull dinner table you have only to ask the question, "To which century does the year 1800 belong?" I tried it to-day with success.

28th. Went to town. At Fields's saw Hawthorne, whom I have not met for months. He looks gray and grand, with something very pathetic about him.

To James T. Fields.

March 3, 1863.

I was ashamed this morning to send the expressman to your door in quest of an old umbrella, not unlike that which accompanied and consoled the exiled king of France in his flight to England. Nevertheless, I did send; for it is a lineal descendant of King Cotton, and is of that particularly audacious kind that never says "Lost." In the hands of a modern "sensuous" poet the handle would become pearl (daughter, not mother of) and the rest would be of a "tissue from the looms of Samarcand." Finally, it is the one I keep to lend to lecturers at the Lowell Institute, and the like; and, though very dissipated, is worth reclaiming.

Accept my apology and believe me, or not,

Yours truly.

March 14. This has been a sad week to me. To-day I began the *Inferno.* I mean to take a canto a day till it is finished.

16th. A letter from Captain McCartney, of Battery A. Mass. Artillery, says Charles is with him on the Rappahannock. He is where he wants to be, in the midst of it all. General Hooker is a fighting general, and will soon be moving.

30th. On recommendation of Colonel Sargent, C. has received a commission as second lieutenant of cavalry. In town all the morning getting his outfit.

To James T. Fields.

——, 1863.

If it is not too late to say so, I had rather not be voted for at the Club just yet.[1] If I were a member I should not go there once a year. Then what is the use of being a member? I do not feel at all up to it Strange as you may think it, I find no longer any pleasure in such things. nor take any interest in going about among men. Whenever I try it I fail utterly. I had rather be here at my work as long as the day continues; for the night cometh wherein no man can work.

April 16. Finish the translation of the *Inferno.* So the whole work is done; the *Purgatorio* and *Paradiso* having

[1] Probably the Union Club.

been finished before. I have written a canto a day, thirty-four days in succession, with many anxieties and interruptions. Now I must make some Notes. Meanwhile the Sudbury Tales are in press.

18th. A troubled day. It always makes me unhappy to go to town now. See Fields, and hear report of the taking of Gordonsville by our troops.

30th. Charles Norton tells me that in 1865 the six-hundredth anniversary of the birth-day of Dante is to be celebrated in Florence. He wants me to keep back my translation of the *Divina Commedia* for that occasion.

May 10. Beautiful, after a week of rain. A day full of sunshine, blossoms, and song of birds; and of tender memories!

28th. In town saw the first regiment of blacks march through Beacon Street. An imposing sight, with something wild and strange about it, like a dream. At last the North consents to let the negro fight for freedom.

June 1. Sat an hour with poor George Sumner at the Hospital (in that cheerful No. 10 looking out on the Charles River bridge). T. came to dinner and we went to see Agassiz, who is not well.

2d. Great gusts of wind shaking the heavy tree-tops. Go to the Port to get a license for Trap. Met Thies, who tells me of the Memoirs of Varnhagen von Ense and his day-books, just published [in Germany] and likely to make a sensation. Made up a box of birthday presents for C. in camp on the Potomac.

4th. How sad to me are these beautiful summer days. The burden seems too great for me to bear.

5th. Pass the morning listlessly and wearily. T. comes to dine. And so goes the day; ended by a chapter of Jane Austen's Mansfield Park.

6th. I grow more and more restless. I need change of scene.

To James T. Fields.

NAHANT, August 25, 1863.

A youth in the West, a farmer's boy, sends me these two poems, the one in manuscript for the Atlantic. There are good touches in them. "The cloudy gloom under the moon," I have often noticed, but have never before seen it in print. Perhaps you may foster a new poet.

I am afraid we have made a mistake in calling the new volume, "The Sudbury Tales." Now that I see it announced I do not like the title. Sumner cries out against it and has persuaded me, as I think he will you, to come back to "The Wayside Inn." Pray think as we do.

October 3. Call on my neighbor Worcester, the lexicographer; an old man, nearly eighty.

6th. Went again to the Hospital. A man met us at the gate and said, "Mr. Sumner is dead." We found his brother Charles in the room.

To George W. Curtis.

November 19, 1863.

I have just been reading your very generous, and more than generous, article in the Atlantic. If it were not written about myself I should say it is beautifully done. As it is I must say nothing of the kind, but only think it.

Let us make believe that you were writing about somebody else. Then I can tell you what a charming piece of criticism this is, and how delicately and skilfully wrought out. All this in a merely literary point of view. But the good-will, the sympathy, the tenderness of the article, I cannot make believe about those; nor can I adequately tell you how much I feel and value them. You will find out some day, when you are among the afternoon shadows, and hear the same call from some one who has the shadows still under his feet. Till then you must try to imagine it.

We are all well here in this old house; mainly waiting and watching the tides of the great war. This morning's paper brings the report of Lincoln's brief speech at Gettysburg, which seems to me admirable.

I am also rejoicing in the new editors of the North American; as you are, I am sure.[1]

November 25. Published to-day by Ticknor and Fields Tales of a Wayside Inn; fifteen thousand copies. The publishers dined with me; also Sumner and Greene.

26th. Thanksgiving Day; ushered in with news of a victory of Grant in Tennessee. Mrs. Appleton and T. dined with us, and we drank the health of "all the lieutenants in the Army of the Potomac."

27th. I have begun to have [the translation of] Dante put in type; so as to have a clear copy to work upon, in making the Notes.

28th. The Army of the Potomac advancing.

December 1. At dinner received a telegram from Washington stating that Charles had been severely wounded. Left for Washington with Ernest at five o'clock. Stormy night, and severe gale on the Sound.

3d. *Washington.* Engaged rooms at the Ebbitt House. Then went in pursuit of C. Find he has not been sent up yet. Go down to Alexandria in steamboat, passing through the Russian fleet. Find Colonel Devereaux, who telegraphs for news. Wait all the afternoon for answer, but get none. Go back to Washington in last boat. At

[1] Mr. Norton and Mr. Lowell had taken the editorship.

midnight, a knock at my chamber-door. Telegram from Colonel D.: "Wounded will be sent up to-morrow."

4th. No wounded arrive; will not be up till to-morrow noon.

5th. Drive to station at noon. While I am waiting, a person steps up to me dressed in military overcoat, high boots, and corduroys. He says, "Are you Professor Longfellow? Give me your hand. I am Dr. B—— of Riga; have translated your Hiawatha into Russian. When I came to this country there were three men I wanted to see, — Agassiz, Emerson, and yourself. I am glad to see you here on this business. I am glad to see you are a *man*. I saw your portrait once in an English paper and it looked like a ——. I have been a colonel in the army; am now director of the flying ambulance. etc., etc." The train came in from Alexandria, — only a baggage-car. But in it were sixteen wounded officers, and among them were Charles and Captain Bowditch. Take them to the Ebbitt House, and soon have them snug in bed. Bowditch is wounded through the arm; C. through both shoulders, — an Enfield ball entering under the left shoulder-blade and passing directly through the back, taking off one of the spinal processes and passing out under the right shoulder-blade. A wonderful escape. Both doing well. I watch with them all night.

6th. The army surgeon who came with the wounded alarmed me by saying that his duty to himself and to me required him to say that the wound was a very serious one and paralysis might ensue. In the evening three surgeons came. One of them, Dr. McGill, evidently an able man, gives favorable report, but says the wound will be long in healing, — "he will not be fit for service under six months."

7th. Enter Gurowski, full of sympathy. Dr. Bates, surgeon of this district, takes charge, — a modest, deft little man, kind and obliging. He makes out certificate for leave of absence. Go with Sumner to the Senate-chamber to see the opening of Congress. See Fessenden, Hale, Dixon, and others. Also Mr. Lyon, of Lyonsdale, who was so kind when I was here last summer. Mr. and Mrs. Bowditch arrive.

8th. Leave for home with the two wounded officers. A very comfortable night journey.

9th. Reach New York at half-past seven. Stop at the Fifth Avenue Hotel. Dr. Van Buren dresses C.'s wounds. He refuses any fee, saying, "I am not often sentimental, but feel disposed to be so this morning." Reach home at ten; Dr. Wyman comes; wounds dressed; patient in bed by midnight.

16th. The girls all go to the great "Sanitary" Fair with Miss Davie.

To Miss F——.

December 28, 1863.

It is so long since I wrote you last that I am heartily ashamed to think of it. So I will not think of it. Let us make believe that I have been a good and punctual correspondent, and then I shall have courage to proceed. . . .

Since I wrote you, I have been through a great deal of trouble and anxiety. My oldest boy, not yet twenty, is a lieutenant of cavalry in the Army of the Potomac. Early in the summer he was taken down with camp fever, and did not rejoin his regiment till September. In the last battle on the Rapidan he was shot through both shoulders with a rifle-ball, and had a very narrow escape of it. He is now at home, and doing very well. The two anxious journeys to the army to bring him back, together with the waiting and the watching, have not done me much good, nor left me much time for other things. However, I have contrived to get a volume of poems through the press, and have requested the London publishers to send you a copy.

The Wayside Inn has more foundation in fact than you may suppose. The town of Sudbury is about twenty miles from Cambridge. Some two hundred years ago, an English family, by the name of Howe, built there a country house, which has remained in the family down to the present time, the last of the race dying but two years ago. Losing their fortune, they became inn-keepers; and for a century the Red-Horse Inn has flourished, going down from father to son. The place is just as I have described it, though no longer an inn. All this will account for the landlord's coat-of-arms, and his being a justice of the peace, and his being known as "the Squire," — things that must sound strange in English ears. All the characters are real. The musician is Ole Bull; the Spanish Jew, Israel Edrehi, whom I have seen as I have painted him, etc., etc.[1]

Your lotus-leaf pillow is now giving comfort to a younger head than mine, — the wounded officer's. He comes down into my study every day, and is propped up with it in a great chair. How brave these boys are! Not a single murmur or complaint, though he has a wound through him a foot long. He pretends it does not hurt him.

[1] All the characters were real, but they were not really at the Sudbury Inn. The poet was T. W. Parsons, the translator of Dante; the Sicilian, Luigi Monti; the theologian, Professor Treadwell, of Harvard; the student, Henry Ware Wales. Parsons, Monti, and Treadwell were in the habit of spending the summer months at the Sudbury Inn. On this very slender thread of fact, the fiction is woven. The tales are drawn from various sources. To Mr. Longfellow belongs the charm of the telling; often with much amplification and adornment. In perhaps only one instance, 'The Birds of Killingworth,' is the story of his own invention.

CHAPTER III.

JOURNAL AND LETTERS.

1864.

January 1. We all dined in town at 39. Even C. went in. To me it was very sad; well nigh insupportable.

2d. Look over Mr. Ticknor's Life of Prescott. Very interesting. Also the North American Review, — the first number of the new editors, Lowell and Norton. A new life is infused into it.

From Nathaniel Hawthorne.

CONCORD, January 2, 1864.

DEAR LONGFELLOW, — It seems idle to tell you that I have read the Wayside Inn with great comfort and delight. I take vast satisfaction in your poetry, and take very little in most other men's, except it be the grand old strains that have been sounding on through all my life. Nothing can be better than these tales of yours, one and all. I was especially charmed with the description of an old Scandinavian ship-of-war,[1] with her officers and crew; in which, by some inscrutable magic, you contrive to suggest a parallel picture of a modern frigate.

It gratifies my mind to find my own name shining in your verse,[2] — even as if I had been gazing up at the moon and detected my own features in its profile.

[1] 'The Building of the Long Serpent.'

[2] In the 'Prelude.'

I have been much out of sorts of late, and do not well know what is the matter with me; but am inclined to draw the conclusion that I shall have little more to do with pen and ink. One more book I should like well enough to write, and have indeed begun it, but with no assurance of ever bringing it to an end. As is always the case, I have a notion that the last book would be my best, and full of wisdom about matters of life and death, — and yet it will be no deadly disappointment if I am compelled to drop it. You can tell, far better than I, whether there is anything worth having in literary reputation; and whether the best achievements seem to have any substance after they grow cold.

Your friend, NATH. HAWTHORNE.

4th. A letter from Hawthorne. He says he is not well, and is evidently out of spirits. He is busy with a new book. Write to Bryant, thanking him for his new volume of poems.[1] In the evening, finish the Life of Prescott.

To William C. Bryant.

January 4, 1864.

I was much gratified to receive on New Year's Day your kind remembrance in your new volume of poems, which I have read with great sympathy and delight, and find very consoling, both in its music and its meaning. I most heartily congratulate you on this new success. Have you looked at the January number of the North American Review, the first under the new management? Some of the articles, I think, will please you; particularly 'Immorality in Politics,' by Mr. Norton, and 'The President's Policy,' by Mr. Lowell.

[1] This was the Thirty Poems, containing among others, 'The Future Life.'

5th. A cloudy day and gentle fall of snow. Such winter days have a peculiar charm. I like them better than the usual glare and glitter of the New England winter.

7th. 'St. Distaff's day; so says the Old Farmer's Almanac, which I bought this morning to see "when there is a moon," as the *bourgeois gentilhomme* says; and because I saw as the motto for each month a stanza of my own verses!

10th. Wrote to M. Brunel, who has been translating Evangeline into French.

To Mrs. James T. Fields.

January 18, 1864.

I am much obliged to you for your charming note. It certainly is a great pleasure to give pleasure to others, and particularly to those whom we wish to please. Though one may sing for the mere delight of singing, I think it increases the delight to know that the song has been heard and liked. Especially if one sings from the corner of School and Washington streets!

I send you, with this, *Jean Paul's Geist,* in the fourth volume of which apparition you will find [some pieces] which Mr. Fields wanted you to see. It has no index, and no references to the volumes from which the extracts are made,—a great drawback, in my opinion. Glancing over it, you will find many things already familiar, perhaps something new; certainly much that is beautiful.

19th. A misty morning; a twilight such as the "Spiritualists" delight in. And I have a strong impression that a letter from a particular person is lying in the post-office, or is on its way from town, though I have not heard of the arrival of a steamer, and do not know that any is due to-day. No letter came!

26th. Read over a part of Hyperion, to prepare for a new edition. Ah, me! how many graves I dug open! When it is once revised, I shall never dare look into the book again.

28th. The letter looked for on the 19th arrived.

February 2. Went to town, which devastated the day. After dinner, letters, and autographs for fairs.

From Ralph Waldo Emerson.

CONCORD, February 24, 1864.

MY DEAR LONGFELLOW, — What a rusty place is the country to live in, where a man loses his manners, — or never attains to them! What a fat and sleepy air is this, that I have never thanked you for the New Year's poems,[1] — chiefly, the 'Birds,' which is serene, happy, and immortal as Chaucer, and speaks to all conditions! And now you punish me for my ingratitude by new cares for me, and send me word of a new horizon for me in Sweden. Was it you who sent me, a week earlier (the envelope was stamped Cambridge), a Brussels publisher's list, announcing the French translation of Representative Men as *défendu* in France? — of which too much honor I am curious to know the cause.[2] Have you read Elliot Cabot's paper on Art? How dangerously subtile! One would say it must be the epitaph of existing Art, if the artists once read and understand him. And yet, of course, he will say, — only to begin a new creation. But I am very proud of Boston when it turns out such a Greek as Cabot.

[1] Tales of a Wayside Inn, containing 'The Birds of Killingworth.' This poem Mr. Emerson put into his Parnassus.

[2] One might suggest the chapter on Napoleon.

When will you come back to the Saturdays, which want their ancient lustre? I hope the evil symptoms I heard of months ago have disappeared. I have often in these solitudes questions to ask you; but, at such distant meetings, they have no answers.

R. W. EMERSON.

March 10. Wrote a poem, 'The Bridge in the Air,' — a little 'Bird of Passage.'[1]

To James T. Fields.

March 13, 1864.

I send you herewith the proof of 'Kambalu.' I think "Mahomed" will do. He evidently did not know how to write his own name, any more than Shakspeare did his, and indulged in variations. Let it pass, — a poetic license. I send also 'The Bridge of Cloud,' or 'Bridge in the Air,' — which shall it be? — enlarged, and more fully expressing the thought in my mind. I should like to consult you also about the passages marked in pencil. Read by candle-light, if you can, and not by the broad daylight of office hours. In the last stanza of 'Palingenesis,' I come back to the old reading, — "nor will I vainly question." That is better, on the whole; and I do not mean to tamper with it any more.

17th. Finished to-day the revision and copying, or rewriting, the translation of the *Purgatorio*, so as to have it all of one piece with the rest; it having been made at different times, long, long ago, and never revised. Now I have the whole before me, of uniform style and workmanship.

23d. Began the notes to the *Inferno*.

[1] Printed with the Wayside Inn as 'The Bridge of Cloud.'

24th. Finished notes on canto i. Norton came in, and we had a long Dantesque talk. I wish I could hope to get my translation ready for next year's celebration. I am afraid it cannot be.

25th. The dates and days of this year 1864 correspond with those of the Dantesque year 1300.

To George W. Greene.

March 25, 1864.

This is a lovely day, as you are well aware. Moreover, it is Good Friday, as you are equally well aware; and leaving aside the deeper meaning of the day, I will tell you something of which I suspect you are not aware. Have you remembered, or noticed, that the days and dates of 1864 correspond with those of the Dantesque 1300?— so that in both years Good Friday falls on the 25th of March. Five hundred and sixty-four years ago to-day, Dante descended to the *città dolente;* and to-day, with the first two cantos of the *Inferno* in my hand, I descended among the printers' devils, — the *malebolge* of the University Press. Is it a good omen? I know not. But something urges me on and on and on with this work, and will not let me rest; though I often hear the warning voice from within, —

Me degno a ciò nè io nè altri crede.

Did you ever notice the beautiful and endless aspiration so artistically and silently suggested by Dante in closing each part of his poem with the word *stelle?* Did any Italian commentator ever find it out? Among English translators, I believe Cayley was the first to remark it.

April 9. In the afternoon I received a copy of *La Legende Dorée* from the translators [Paul Blier and Edward

Macdonnel], — a handsome octavo. In the preface, mention is made of a French translation of Hiawatha as already existing. Hyperion, Kavanagh, and Evangeline have already been translated into French. This translation of the Legend is in prose, and is admirable.

11th. Read in the morning paper of the sudden death of W. D. Ticknor [the publisher] in Philadelphia, whither he had gone with Hawthorne, who is ill. Ticknor published my first volume, the *Coplas de Manrique,* in 1833, — more than thirty years ago. I saw him the day before he went away, merry and rejoicing in the prospect of a pleasant journey, — he knew not whither; but hoping to go from New York to Havana, and by New Orleans homeward.

To George W. Greene.

April 20, 1864.

Walking the other day along the accustomed townward walk, made pleasanter by remembrances of you, I met the East Wind, blowing, blowing; and I said, "This will never do for Greene." And the day after, in the same place, I met the West Wind, and said, "O Mudjekeewis, you are worse than your brother Wabun!" But I hope next week this will all be over, and spring begin as if it were giving some attention to its business, and not going into hopeless bankruptcy.

To my great surprise, I find the making of Notes to Dante very pleasant work. I wish somebody would pour a barrel of something into the grave of the commentators, as the bridegroom in the old Icelandic tale did into the grave of his friend the toper, to moisten the dry bones. I shall not be able to do that; but something like it, perhaps. I have begun already to light up these footlights of the great Comedy, and am not wholly dissatisfied with the effect. Will the oil hold out? I hope so. I have three introductory sonnets for fly-leaves of the three parts, — Boccaccio's, Michael Angelo's, and a new one of my own.[1]

To Charles Sumner.

April 30, 1864.

Is this which you send me the Gorgon's head on the shield of Minerva, or is it Minerva herself behind the shield, chiding Telemachus?

Your report on the rejection of colored testimony I read with a kind of agony, to think what we had been inflicting on those "whose despair is dumb."[2] This dreadful stone of Slavery! — whenever you lift it, what reptiles crawl out from under it!

Your speech on the Abolition of Slavery came this morning. I shall read it at once. It is enough for me that you have made it.

Ever truly, upholding your hands.

P. S. Many thanks for the Duchess's letter. There is no Gorgon in that.

May 7. In translating Dante, something must be relinquished. Shall it be the beautiful rhyme that blossoms all along the lines like a honeysuckle on a hedge? It must be, in order to retain something more precious than rhyme; namely, fidelity, truth, — the life of the hedge itself.

8th. News of battles, and victories of General Grant over General Lee in Virginia. If fully confirmed, it is the beginning of the end.

[1] He afterwards wrote five more of his own, and prefixed them to the volumes, omitting the others.

[2] In no court of the District of Columbia or any Slave-State could the testimony of a black man be received.

19th. Drove with Greene to Lee's Headquarters and "Hobgoblin Hall." On our return, found this upon my desk: —

"Mr. Fields asked me to call and tell you the sad news of the death of Mr. Hawthorne. The telegram has just reached us from Plymouth, N. H.

A. F."

To Charles Sumner.

May 23, 1864.

And Hawthorne, too, is gone! I am waiting for the carriage which is to take Greene, Agassiz, and myself to Concord this bright spring morning, to his funeral.

But do not be disheartened. You have much work of the noble kind to do yet. Let us die standing. Your Report on the old French claims is complete and unanswerable. I breathe more freely when I read such papers!

I am full of faith, hope, and good heart!

25th. You have doubtless read some description of Hawthorne's funeral. It was a lovely day; the village all sunshine and blossoms and the song of birds. You cannot imagine anything at once more sad and beautiful. He is buried on a hill-top under the pines. I saw your portrait at Emerson's; so in a certain sense you were present.

To James T. Fields.

May 30, 1864.

Hawthorne's copy of Goldsmith has just reached me, saddening me with the thought that I shall see his beautiful face no more. I shall place it among my treasures as one of the most dear to me.

Do, if possible, get one of ——'s articles in type so that he can read the proof-sheets here. It would comfort him greatly.

From James T. Fields.

CAMPTON VILLAGE, June 19, 1864.

MY DEAR LONGFELLOW, — We are here among the serenities and the fresh eggs. Would that you were near, to feel with us the wonderful beauty of the hills! Do come, and go over the Willy acres, and drive down into the comforting valleys by the lovely river, and eat wild strawberries, and rattle over the hills in our old wagon. In one week of this life I have grown as rusty as an old nail. I have lost all care; and the bundles of business have dropped clean off my shoulders and gone into the Pemigewasset. All the *buzziness* here is done by the bees; and the only active people are the birds, who sing all day long about our old dwelling by the roadside. Such a careless, good-for-nothing peaceful old life as this is well worth trying. A great and glorious laziness creeps up and takes possession of you the moment you arrive, and never lets go its hold as long as you stay. You loaf about in dell and hollow, and lie down on the hillside and let the slugs crawl over you without a shake. In the "broad orchards resonant with bees" you go to sleep, and only wake up when the horn blows for dinner. We know nothing of the weather in these parts.

"It may blow North, it still is warm,
Or South, it still is clear;
Or East, it smells like a clover farm,
Or West, no thunder fear."

Will you not come? . . .

I hope 'Palingenesis' will be well launched when the July Atlantic is ready. I left directions to have it properly put in the papers, but I have small faith in editors when I am out of the way. I am sure nothing finer has been printed for years.

"Suns rise and set in Saadi's speech."

My wife sends kindest regards and hopes you will make your way to our roadside perch in New Hampshire.

Yours ever, J. T. F.

To James T. Fields.

June 23, 1864.

I have received your pleasant letter. It reads like one of Virgil's Eclogues; or the second stanza of Gray's Elegy; or an article in the Gentleman's Magazine signed Sylvanus Urban; or Don Quixote's discourse to the goat-herds; or Guarini's Pastor Fido. And yet I cannot come.

In return I send you a poem ['Hawthorne'], premising that I have not seen Holmes's article in the Atlantic. I hope we have not been singing and saying the same things. I have only tried to describe the state of mind I was in on that day. Did you not feel so likewise?

On the first day of July, — so my daughter informs me — we take our departure for Nahant. That is one week from to-day. It makes me think of General Grant's movement across the James.

To Mrs. Nathaniel Hawthorne.

June 23, 1864.

I have long been wishing to write you, to thank you for your kind remembrance in sending me the volume of Goldsmith; but I have not had the heart to do it. There are some things that one cannot say; and I hardly need tell you how much I value your gift, and how often I shall look at the familiar name on the blank leaf, — a name which more than any other links me to my youth.

I have written a few lines trying to express the impressions of May 23, and I venture to send you a copy of them. I had rather no one should see them but yourself; as I have also sent them to Mr. Fields for the Atlantic.

I feel how imperfect and inadequate they are; but I trust you will pardon their deficiencies for the love I bear his memory.

More than ever I now regret that I postponed from day to day coming to see you in Concord, and that at last I should have seen your house only on the outside!

From T. G. Appleton.

LONDON, June 28, 1864.

. . . We congratulated each other on the ruin of the wicked "Alabama." The Vice-Consul was in, the day before, to see us, and he told me that only three men were wounded in the "Kearsarge," none killed; that shells struck the chains without penetrating. The whole thing has produced much effect here, and our splendid firing sounds uncomfortable so near these shores. There is much feeling among the Americans and their friends here at the carrying off the enemy after she had surrendered. The "Alabama" intended to try boarding, but could not make it out, the "Kearsarge" being the better sailor.

A splendid dinner the other day at the Benzons'; a better I never ate. I sat between Browning and young Lytton, and had Ernst, the composer, and Louis Blanc opposite. It was very pleasant. Browning asked after you and George Curtis, and spoke with much feeling of Hawthorne, whom he knew well. He evidently has the very highest opinion of his abilities. The Storys are here, and a great comfort to me. We went to Walton and spent a day. It was extremely pleasant, and like the old times. We recalled a thousand past pleasant moments, and refurbished all our old jokes. Colonel Hamley, of Lady Lee's Widowhood, was there, and vowed I was an old friend, so much had he heard me talked of. —— looked well; all the better for having tried "Banting," — a system of thinning introduced here by an upholsterer, whose pamphlet I have read. They have added a rose-bed to their pretty lawn, and it reminded me of the old pictures in Beauty and the Beast, — only so far as the roses are concerned, however. I was yesterday at the Crystal Palace to see a flower-show. How I wish A. and the lads could see that "Versailles of the people," as Victor Hugo calls it in his new rhapsody about Shakspeare, — a book you might glance at. I have seen Fechter in Hamlet. Superbly got up, and Hamlet new and good. Very swift and colloquial in the dialogue; and, but for a kind of whine, the best, on the whole, I have seen. Great talk of war here; look out for squalls. There is much notion that England should not allow the Danes to go to the wall. A war would leave us still freer to finish our own. The Lyells went last Sunday to hear [M. D.] Conway, and were loud in his praise. I went to hear Martineau in his new church. He is refined and agreeable. There is no great show of carriages at his door, as is the case always with the Unitarians.

From Mrs. Hawthorne.

CONCORD, July 24, 1864.

MY DEAR MR. LONGFELLOW, — Your kind note and profoundly affecting poem moved me so much that it has been very difficult for me to reply. This you will entirely understand. We are both now entered fully into the worship of sorrow, and comprehend all its conditions.

It is impossible for me to express the emotion with which I saw you, — on that wonderful day, that was made to seem to me a festival of life, — at the head of the line of loving friends, going up to the Mount of Vision. I had not seen you since the dread epoch of God's mysterious dispensation to you. As it was, I did not see your face, but only the form and the white hair waving in the wind. I thought I had always sympathized with you; but that day I first knew what you had suffered. I understood the depths and heights of bereavement. Remembering also my husband's most affectionate regard for you, it was very sweet and grateful to see you there. I earnestly wished that I could convey to you my sense of these things.

My dear Mr. Longfellow, the last Sunday Mr. Hawthorne was at home, he was sitting in this little library with Julian; and I, in another room, suddenly heard J. begin to read aloud a passage from Evangeline beginning

> "Suddenly, as if arrested by fear or a feeling of wonder,"

and ending with the end of the poem. It broke on the perfect silence with singular power. At the close, Mr. Hawthorne said, "I like that,"—and then there was again silence. We have often recalled that incident since. With Evangeline we have been enabled to "murmur, Father I thank Thee." I suppose you know how very much Mr. Hawthorne loved this poem; and it was remarkable that Julian should happen to open to it on that last day he saw his father, and read that particular passage, with no forethought.

The poem that you send me has such an Eolian delicacy, sweetness, and pathos, that it seems a strain of music rather than written words. It has in an eminent degree the unbroken melody of your verse. The picture of the scene you have now made immortal.

> "Its monument shall be your gentle verse."

I cannot suppose that you would wish, now that All is gone, to come to this house, no longer a palace since the king has left it. But if you are ever in Concord, and would not feel too much saddened to enter these deserted halls, I should most gladly welcome you as one of his chief friends, tenderly valued. His visits to you in Cambridge used to be a great enjoyment to him. He always spoke of them as peculiarly agreeable. For the last years he had stood reverent, silent, and appalled before your unspeakable sorrow.

With great regard, sincerely yours,

SOPHIA HAWTHORNE.

September 1. I hope this absolute rest from all labor will not be without good effect in the long run. But I am getting rather too much of it, and would willingly be in Cambridge again. Correct some proof-sheets of a new edition of Hyperion.

10th. Sundry people came. The Hon. E. Lyulph Stanley of England, a pleasant gentleman, Fellow of Baliol, Oxford, brings me a letter from Mr. Adams, our Minister in London, and stays to dine.

27th. Mr. Robert Ferguson [of Carlisle, England] brings me a letter of introduction. I invite him to stay with me.

Mr. Ferguson has given this pleasant account of his visit, in his volume, America During and After the War: —

"Here, clustered together under the shadow of the oldest university of the New World, dwell many of the men whose names America most justly cherishes. And here, just landed from Boston by the horse-cars, I found myself inquiring the way to the residence of the poet Longfellow. . . .

"I found him in his study, — an elegant and cheerful room, in one corner of which a fine orange-tree, with its golden fruit, keeps green the memory of a departed friend, — the late Professor Felton. The table is strewn with books and presentation copies in various languages, — ay, even in Chinese. But the ways of the Chinese are not as our ways; and this presentation copy was in the shape of a fan, on which a poet of the Flowery Land had written a translation of the Psalm of Life; and if the translation were only as good as the writing, assuredly the work was well done. Though the features of the poet have been made familiar to us by many pictures and photographs, yet no one can see him for the first time without being struck with his appearance. His expression of mingled dignity and gentleness has been fairly presented to us; but the peculiar sweetness of his smile, and the touch of spiritual beauty which often plays upon his features, cannot be rendered in a likeness. Before him lies the ever-open Dante, his translation of which — a labor of love, which has occupied him for some years — now approaches to completion. But Dante has not his undivided regard, and hardly would the picture of Longfellow in his study be complete without, ever and anon, through one of the 'three doors left unguarded,' a little figure stealing gently in, laying an arm around his neck as he bends over his work, and softly whispering some childish secret in his ear.

"Then, too, his work is interrupted by frequent visitors of another sort; for among the travellers of all nations the tour of America would hardly be considered complete without a visit to Craigie House. And speaking fluently French, German, Italian, Spanish, and Portuguese, having also a knowledge of Danish, and of Dutch, it may well be supposed that there seldom comes a traveller with whom the poet cannot, if need be, hold converse in his own tongue. And sometimes there come other visitors too, self-introduced, — a class to whom the customs of America show more tolerance than they do with us. I remember, during the period of my stay, a Western man, comically quaint and cool, who came with a request to see the pictures at Craigie House. On two successive days he came, and for three or four good hours was Dante thrown aside while, with an amused good-humor, the poet answered all his odd questions, and showed him everything there was to be seen. Then there came very many others, craving assistance in sickness or sorrow, and to these a deaf ear is never turned. No man's income can be a secret in America; the income-tax returns are open to public inspection; and the newspapers amuse their readers by classified lists of the incomes of prominent merchants, literary men, politicians, and others. Mr. Longfellow is endowed with an income far exceeding that which is generally supposed to fall to the lot of poets, and as he never refuses to listen to any tale of distress, the number of applicants, worthy and unworthy, who find their way to his gate, is by no means small. The airs which some of the American beggars give themselves are very amusing. I remember the case of a man who came with his arm in a sling, representing himself to have been wounded in the service of his country. Mr. Longfellow, having some suspicion, asked to be allowed to look at the wounded arm. 'It is not a pleasant sight to show a gentleman,' said the man. 'Perhaps not, but we are obliged sometimes to look at unpleasant things.' 'Well, sir!' said the man, drawing himself up, 'if that is the light in which you look at the matter, I would rather not be beholden to you for assistance, and so I wish you good morning.' Then there was another man upon whom, in response to his tale of hunger and distress, there was bestowed a handsome loaf. Now, the least that any English beggar would have done under the circumstances would have been to have taken the loaf and converted it into gin. But this would have been beneath the spirit of an American beggar; and so he resented the insult to his dignity by depositing the loaf as he passed out, like an ornament, on the top of the gate-post. . . .

"A frequent visitor at Craigie House, when Congress is not sitting, is Charles Sumner, the scholarly Senator for Massachusetts, and the representative man of New England politics. And an interesting sight it was to see these two men, Longfellow and Sumner, so kindred and yet so different, sitting together on the eve of the great contest which was to decide the place of America in the world's history; Sumner, with the poet's little daughter nestling in his lap, — for he is a man to whom all children come, — calmly discussing some question of European literature. Mr. Sumner seemed to feel deeply the defection of certain of the old anti-slavery leaders of England from the Northern cause in the great crisis of the struggle; and all the more because New England had always been a link, by this common sympathy, between the old country and the new.

"A frequent guest, too, is James Russell Lowell, who succeeded to the professorship formerly held by Mr. Longfellow. In conversation brilliant and amusing, Mr. Lowell is one of the persons in whose company one can scarcely be without carrying away something worthy to be remembered.

"And often, too, comes Agassiz, with his gentle and genial spirit, his child-like devotion to science, and — or he would not be a true son of his adopted country — his eager interests in the politics of the day. We went to hear one of his lectures at the University, — not one of what are considered the popular lectures, but one of a special course to a small class. Yet it was deeply interesting. He wound up with some general remarks, in the course of which he exhorted his hearers to strive to take the same pleasure in the scientific discoveries of others as in their own, — a noble aim, yet, ah! how difficult to attain. I believe, however, that if there are any persons capable of so much single-mindedness, Agassiz is one of them. Between the Poet and the Naturalist there exists a very warm friendship, and among other poetical tributes, Mr. Longfellow has achieved the feat — for so it must seem to us, with our rigid English tongues — of addressing to his friend, in the October number of the Atlantic Monthly, a gay and graceful *chanson* in his native language.

"And often, too, comes Dana, one of the most charming of talkers, and, more especially with his sea-stories, enthralling the circle of young and old. . . .

"It was my privilege, on the occasion of both my visits to America, to spend my parting days at Craigie House. And as the traveller, after his weary journey through the desert, rests at eventide by the still waters under the shadow of the palm-trees, so from the keen, anxious life of the West, from the strife and bitterness of the South, did I come back to the calm, beautiful life of the poet's household. The last day of all was a Christmas Day, — kept up in the good old style. The yule-log sparkled on the hearth; the plum-pudding smoked upon the board; with his prettiest offerings did the good Saint fill the stockings of the little girls by night; and all day long did the presents come pouring in to the children of a much-loved household, till the drawing-room table on the following morning looked like the stall of a fancy fair. Even the passing guest came in for some tokens, not needed to remind him of that day. And he left the house wherein the presence of the Master is a perpetual sunshine — where never a peremptory word is spoken, and yet there is a perfect, loving obedience —

with the feeling that it was good for a man to have been there."

October 1. Call on Theodore Fay at Parker's. We go to Milmore's studio to see Sumner's bust. Bring Mr. Fay out to tea. A very sweet and elevated nature. He has lived abroad for twenty, thirty, years. In the evening read North American Review. Good articles are 'Modern Italian Comedy,' by Howells; 'Hawthorne,' by G. W. Curtis; and 'The next Election,' by Lowell.

3d. In the car met Miss Harriet Hosmer, the sculptor, full of spirit and energy.

6th. Go down to the printer's with a sonnet, 'On translating Dante.' Meet Fields. He wants it for the Atlantic.

7th. A warm bright day with open windows, and the fireless grate heaped with autumnal leaves that imitate a flame. Greene arrives. Walk with him to the Riverside Press. See a little steam-tug passing the bridge; we get on board and go down the Charles to the lowest bridge. Land, and cross over to Mr. Alvan Clark's observatory. He showed us his great telescope, and the largest lens ever made.

November 10. Lincoln re-elected beyond a doubt. We breathe freer. The country will be saved.

13th. Stay at home and ponder upon Dante. I am frequently tempted to write upon my work the inscription found upon an oar cast on the coast of Iceland, —

Oft war ek dasa dur ek dro thick.
"Oft was I weary when I tugged at thee."

24th. I cut this from to-day's paper: "A new edition of Longfellow's Hyperion, illustrated with photographs, by Francis Frith, has just been issued in London."

From Louis Agassiz.

[The original is in French.]

December 24, 1864.

MY DEAR LONGFELLOW, — I was on my way to your house when, thinking of my mother, great tears began to fill my eyes, and fearing to be taken for an idiot, I returned home. You, then, were thinking of me at that moment; I have just received the proof of it, only an hour ago. Thanks, a thousand times, dear friend. I am as proud as happy for your present. Proud, because it comes from Longfellow, whom I admire; happy, because it comes from Longfellow, whom I love. And then also I can let my good mother *read* my wine, if I cannot let her taste it.

Adieu, dear friend. Accept the good wishes of *Noël* which I make for you. May your *quintette* give you as much happiness as my *trio*. Hoping soon to see you,

Tout à vous,

L. AGASSIZ.[1]

29th. T. came out to dine, with M. Laugel, a writer in the *Revue des Deux Mondes*, and secretary to the Duc d'Aumale; and M. Duvergier d'Hauranne, a young Paris-

[1] Mrs. Agassiz also wrote, "Your birthday poem I do not read to this day without emotion, and this 'Noël' touches the same chord. For, witty and gay and graceful as it is, a loving sympathy for Agassiz pervades every line. We read it together, not without tears as well as laughter; for its affectionate tone moved us both. Then it came as if in answer to a thought which Agassiz had just expressed, — that it seemed so sad to him that his mother should never share in our enjoyment. Hardly five minutes after, your note was handed him with the verses, all in French; and our first exclamation was, 'And the best and loveliest of all our Christmas gifts can be fully shared by her.'"

ian, just past twenty-one, — the most youthful French traveller I ever met with.

To George W. Greene.

December 27, 1864.

I have just received your letter, and am thinking with pain what a sad Christmas you must have had, with your darlings so ill. I hope and trust that the danger is now past, and that you are relieved from all apprehension. I sympathize with all your anxieties.

To-day I have been making Notes on *Inferno*, canto six. In spite of Ginguené's abuse, I have always taken an interest in that poor old diner-out, Ciacco; and I shall quote the whole of Boccaccio's tale of him and Filippo Argenti. It is like looking out of a window on the piazza in Florence, — a curious glimpse into the days of old. What fools some critics make of themselves by insisting that Dante ought to keep himself up to his highest level. As if he did not know best what he was about. Sometimes the sock, sometimes the buskin; the final result a real *commedia.* Ginguené wants it all buskin. That would be *tragedia.* Now, I think canto six peculiarly felicitous. The outer darkness, the rain "eternal, maledict, and cold, and heavy;" the mire and the stench, and the being bitten now and then by the dog in the yard, contrast so admirably with the warmth and light and perfume of a banquet, that perhaps we could have better spared a better canto, if all were not necessary to the completeness of the work.

I send you to-day the Evening Post, that you may not lose the remarks of the literary critic therein contained, and other things marked. I send you also a 'Noël,' which I wrote the other day, to go with some bottles of wine to Agassiz. As they tell their own story, I will not tell it for them here. I hope it will amuse you as much in reading as it did me in writing.

December 31. I looked out of the window at night and saw the trees all covered and bent down with snow, and thought of Richter's "New Year's Eve of an Unhappy Man," and knew that I should *not* "wake and find it a dream."

CHAPTER IV.

JOURNAL AND LETTERS.

1865.

January 1. I was up at two o'clock this morning. I placed a candle at one window, and looked out of another on the lovely trees, all feathered and plumed with snow. The air was motionless, and in their illumination they looked like one great aerial Christmas-tree.

To —— ——.

January 30, 1865.

I have had the pleasure of receiving your letter and your poems, which I have read with much interest and sympathy. You must excuse me if I do not give you any opinion of their merits in detail, nor offer any criticism. I never sit in judgment upon the writings of others; and therefore beg you to be satisfied with my saying that the pieces found in me a friendly reader, and not a Rhadamanthus.

February 10. Received from the binder, volume one of my translation of the *Divina Commedia;* a copy, to be sent to Italy, "*In Commemorazione del Seccentesimo Anniversario della Nascita di Dante Alighieri.*"[1]

[1] This was the inscription printed upon a blank leaf of the copy.

To Charles Sumner.

February 10, 1865.

To-morrow, I shall send you by post, a copy of the first volume of my translation of the Divine Comedy, to be handed to the Italian minister, and by him forwarded to Italy. You may make, if you like, a small speech on the occasion, expressing my regret that it was impossible to get the other two volumes printed in season. They will follow later.

I want you and the Minister to look at the volume. It is beautiful, and worthy of the Italian press; all written, printed, bound, in Cambridge, Middlesex County, Massachusetts!

The grand event of the century — the Anti-Slavery Enactment — has been as silent as the daybreak, or the coming of a new year. And yet this year will always be the Year of Jubilee in our history.

Find time to write me a line to say you are well.

12th. Trying hard to snow. Lowell read to me a new poem, 'The Gold Egg.'

To Henry Bright (in Liverpool).

February 14, 1865.

I should have written you by the last steamer, but missed it, somehow or other; and so this will come to you as a valentine. The pheasants and the grouse, I am most happy to say, arrived without accident and in excellent condition. They were delicious, particularly the pheasants, and furnished two or three dinners; at one of which I had *to meet them,* — Agassiz, Lowell, and Appleton. They praised, and the dinner was not cold; and I think the birds, could they have foreseen their meeting with such illustrious shades in this *other world*, would have been willing to die.

Our united thanks to you for this banquet, and mine for the gift and the kind remembrance. I regretted only that Charles Norton was not with us; he was not to be had on that day. He is not the "student" of the Wayside Inn; that was a Mr. Wales, now dead.

To G. W. Greene.

February 26, 1865.

Now is a good time to come to Cambridge. Do not procrastinate in the coming; but in the going as much as you like. The weather, to be sure, is not much better than Catawba wine, with a certain exaggerated flavor of something very fine. But we can turn the world outside in, and so be pretty comfortable. . . . To-morrow I shall be fifty-eight years old. I wish you were here to celebrate the day. I will postpone the celebration till you come.

The *Inferno* is a very handsome book.[1] I have a copy for you.

27th. Somebody is fifty-eight years old to-day. E. and A. insist upon it that I am the guilty man, and I cannot deny it.

28th. At Fields's, met Alcott, the philosopher, — a prose Wordsworth; and, I fancy, much like him personally.

March 1. March begins with Ash Wednesday; and the day seems clothed in sackcloth and ashes, so gray is it everywhere. Go to Charles Norton's, to bespeak a

[1] The first edition of his Translation, published in 1867; but a few copies were printed in 1865.

favorable notice of Miss Booth's translation of Martin's History of France. Found him writing one, with the original and translation before him.

5th. Called on Agassiz. He has decided to go to Brazil and the Amazons this spring.

6th. Mr. Fletcher brings me some Portuguese translations of 'The Children's Hour' and 'Daybreak,' by Da Silva, President of the *Gymnase* at Rio. He says that Lisboa (the Portuguese Minister at Washington) has translated 'King Robert of Sicily,' as well as the Emperor. In the evening, read a French comedy, *Le Voyage de M. Perrichon*, — very clever and amusing.

7th. Another French comedy, — *Par Droit de Conquête*, by Legouvé; in a lighter vein, but not so funny.

8th. In an English paper, an excellent lecture on American affairs, by Mr. Stanley. Also a second lecture by Mr. Ferguson, with beautiful bits of landscape.

9th. As one grows older, the wheels move slower. The day goes by, and the result is small. Go up to Lowell's and read to him canto x. of 'Purgatory,' — one of the beautiful. Dante looks out for his perfect number, ten, and takes care that it shall have a perfect canto, — in the *Inferno*, Farinata; in the *Purgatorio*, the bas-reliefs on the wall; in the *Paradiso*, the celestial horologe.

11th. A doleful day. T. comes out to dinner; the only cheer I had.

13th. How slowly the printers get on with my work! It is discouraging. We shall not have the 'Purgatory' finished before summer.

14th. Fields comes out, with the proposition to publish a selection from my poems, in a cheap form.[1] Begins with twenty thousand.

21st. Walked into town with Lowell, to see some

[1] Household Poems.

billiard-playing by "professionals." Lieutenant Cushing of the Navy was there, — he who destroyed the Rebel ironclad Albemarle. A handsome, intrepid-looking youth of twenty. His profile is very like the portraits of Count Rumford.

23d. A parting dinner to Agassiz [on his departure for Brazil] at the Union Club. A dozen guests. Holmes read a witty poem.

29th. Reading Sainte-Beuve's *Nouveaux Lundis.* He is a fascinating critic.

April 2. Sunshine, and song of birds. An afternoon walk with E. to the old Fort Putnam, on Dana Hill, overlooking the Charles.

3d. Great news to-day, of the evacuation of Richmond.

To George W. Greene.

April 4, 1865.

Make all haste you can conveniently to come on. The weather is fine, the walking good. But I begin to find that it takes two to take a walk; yes, and a *dog.* Trap has tried me several times lately, but single-handed he cannot succeed. And then, the great events that are taking place almost every hour! Really, you ought to be here.

The printing of the Dante is such slow work that Fields has almost persuaded me to publish the volumes separately. What do you think? Sumner sends me a note on the *gran rifiuto,* from the N. British Review. The writer thinks the person in question was not Pope Celestine V., but the "young man" in Matthew. But how would Dante recognize him?

The town is all illuminated to-night, and the bells ringing for the great victory!

5th. Grant in pursuit of Lee, who is "turned into the bitter passes of flight."

7th. In the afternoon comes news that Lee has surrendered. So ends the Rebellion of the slave-owners!

8th. How I am weary of correcting and weighing, and criticising my translation! It takes more time than it did to make it.

14th. The hideous news comes this morning of the assassination of President Lincoln, and attempt to assassinate Secretary Seward.

From G. P. Marsh.[1]

TURIN, May 15, 1865.

DEAR SIR, — Two or three days after mine of the 2d was posted I received your favor of April 8, and I now have the pleasure of enclosing herewith the official acknowledgment of the receipt of the volume presented by you to the Dante *Centenario*, together with a copy of a letter with which I had accompanied your donation. As I had the translation in my hands only a very few hours, I could only examine at a hurried moment, here and

[1] Mr. Marsh, the accomplished philological scholar, was the American Minister in Italy at the time of the celebration of the six hundredth anniversary of Dante's birth, to which Mr. Longfellow had sent a copy of his translation of the *Inferno*, in advance of its publication (followed, of course, by the other volumes). In forwarding it Mr. Marsh had written: "I am persuaded that the Committee will receive this first American reproduction of the great poem — a translation most valuable as well for its felicity of expression as for the exactness with which my distinguished compatriot has had the ability to render, in a language so foreign to that of the original, the thought of Dante's sovereign genius — as a contribution most fitting the solemnity of the Centenary, and at the same time as a worthy homage from the New World to one of the chief glories of the country of its discoverer."

there, a passage which occurred to me; but I can truly say that the expressions I used concerning it, in writing to Signor Corsini, fall short of what I should very conscientiously have said if I had been addressing an American or English scholar. I was unable to attend the *festa*, but shall go to Florence in a week. I am, dear sir,

Very faithfully yours,

GEORGE P. MARSH.

To George W. Greene.

June 7, 1865.

As I was sitting at dinner to-day, with an open window at my back, Mudjekeewis, the Northwest Wind, shot me in the back with an arrow so keen that I lost my evening walk, and am bent just in the proper attitude for writing a letter. You know those treacherous dining-room windows, and how often you have shut them. Thank them, this time, else instead of writing to you I might be wasting my time on Notes to Dante!

My little girls have gone to Portland, and I am silent and solitary here.

8th. Here I was interrupted. *Dico continuando* that it is an intensely hot day, but I have been nevertheless at Lowell's, and at Norton's, on Dantesque matters. I am afraid you will find it very hot work moving your household. Courage!

Sumner is in very good spirits. His Eulogy [on Lincoln] was a success, though he read it, which diminished its effect.

To George W. Greene.

June 11, 1865.

Lord Derby in his preface, ridicules [English] hexameters, and thinks there is no salvation outside of blank verse. He translates the last line of the Iliad thus. —

"Such were the rites to glorious Hector paid."

For the one characteristic Homeric epithet there was not room enough in the line. In an hexameter line there is: —

Such were the funeral rites of Hector, the Tamer of Horses.

It is odd enough that a man who had the "Derby" named after him, or his, should have omitted the stable so completely in his version.

The Senator [Sumner] has dined with me to-day, satisfactorily, I hope, as he is now asleep in the great arm-chair, with a white handkerchief thrown over his head. He is now meditating two speeches, — one on the importance of negro suffrage, and another on our foreign relations, — particularly our English cousins. For my part I have been meditating on the great importance it is to a literary man to remain unknown till he gets his work fairly done. It can hardly be overstated.

If Sumner were not sound asleep he would send his love.

To James T. Fields.

June 16, 1865.

Among the fifty-two impossible weeks in the year, you have chosen the most impossible for my imaginary visit to the mountains. For next week I expect C., and I must be at home to receive him. Besides, the Dantesque Notes move along so slowly that I cannot bear to put any impediment in their way. We have just reached the twentieth canto, and fourteen more remain! I must be satisfied with looking at the blue hills from my window, instead of the White Mountains from yours. Yet what would I not give for the sight of a brook brawling through a wood, and the sound thereof. Give my best regards and worst regrets to your wife, and tell her how sorry I am that so cordial an invitation must be declined.

I am also looking over my poems for the new edition. They remind me almost too keenly of the days that are no more. "There is no greater grief than to be mindful of the happy days in misery,"—so says Boethius in his Consolations of Philosophy, and one Dante, in a curious book, so tragic that he calls it a comedy.

To G. W. Greene.

June 25, 1865.

Two days ago I sent you some reviews of the new translations of Dante. Mr. Ford's I have not seen. To-day I send you a curious paragraph about Dante's bones.[1] Can it be true? The same thing happened to Shakespeare, and pretty much in the same way. Irving mentions it in the Sketch-book; though the old sexton who looked into the hole "could see neither coffin nor bones, only dust."

We shall soon be going to Nahant, and when once there I become as fixed as the rocks themselves. I should like to visit you at East Greenwich, but am afraid to promise.

To James T. Fields.

Nahant, August —, 1865.

I do not know what day of the month it is, but I know that it is Friday, and just twelve o'clock, for the village bell is ringing. I shall not write you a long letter; the weather is too hot. But I must thank you for your kind invitation to Manchester and the Isles of Shoals. It will

[1] In some reparations which were making about the Braccioforte Chapel at Ravenna, in the month of May of this year, the workmen came upon a coffin containing bones which were identified as those of Dante.

give me great pleasure to promise to come, — with the understanding that you do not expect me to keep my promise. It is so pleasant to make plans, and then not carry them out! You have only to sit still and imagine the thing done, and it is done, without fatigue or expense.

Dante is going on as fast as the printers please, and every day I do something in the way of correcting copy, so as to have no delay when I get back to Cambridge. Please send me Botta's book on Dante. I see it advertised.

As you have not promised to come to Nahant, I hope you will come soon and dine, at half-past two.

To G. W. Greene.

September 20, 1865.

I was just leaving Nahant when I received your last sorrowful letter, and have not found a moment to answer it. I am now going down to the Library to consult "Livy, who errs not," about that famous Battle of the Rings, and scribble this to post on the way. I am most truly grieved to hear of your illness, and that of your household. It must be very distressing to you. But married men must have courage, and always courage. I know too well what it is to carry my heart in my mouth not to sympathize deeply with you. Thinking of you in my dressing-room last night, where we have so often discussed passages of Dante while sharing the hot and cold water between us, it came into my mind that a translation of Dante's letters would make a good paper for the Atlantic, and that yours is the pen to do it. It would not take you more than a week, if I correctly estimate the amount of matter from memory, and would be an agreeable change. I have this morning written to Fields about it. Be of good cheer!

September 20. At the college library, verifying facts and dates for Dante Notes. Take the last thirteen cantos of the Purgatory to the printer. The new University Press is the old Brattle House, or hotel, which makes a spacious and commodious printing-office.

21st. Mr. M., a Frenchman of the old school, who used to live in the Place Royale, No. 6, where also Victor Hugo lived, came with his daughter, and a letter from Chief Justice Chase, and I kept them to dinner, and showed them the college library.

To James T. Fields.

[Enclosing a poem.]

September 21, 1865.

Listen to the bells of Lynn, Lynn, Lynn!

What a pleasant glimpse I had of you yesterday. That corner room is charming as anything can be. Everything will prosper with you, till the Park Street steeple falls.

There are still extant four or five letters of Dante, which have never been translated entire. They would make a capital article for the Atlantic, and Greene is the man to do it.

Would you be kind enough to pay for me in New York the enclosed bill, through B. Ticknor, and pass to my account. If you are weak enough to do me this favor, you will much oblige me. It is not the amount of the bill which staggers me, but the amount of arithmetic involved in doing the sum; for if I get it right here, it would be wrong the next day in New York.[1]

October 9. Walked to the Port, to pay my taxes. Returning, overtook Sam. Ward and took him home to dinner. T. also came. We talked of spiritual manifestations, and

[1] Presumably on account of the fluctuations in the value of the paper currency of the time.

of the Fox girls. There was a knock at the door, and cards were brought in, "Mr. and Mrs. T——," and "Miss Katie Fox"! Went into the library to see them, and had some rappings, — knocks on the door, on the table, on the floor. In the evening Professor Nichol returned from New York and the Hudson.

11th. We were all up at six o'clock. Drove E., S., and Professor N. to East Boston to take the steamer Cuba for Liverpool. So E. departs on his travels. We shall miss him sorely. On reaching home find a note from Mr. Robert Ferguson, saying he has just arrived in the China.

12th. Mr. Ferguson comes to stay with me. We go in the evening to a supper at Dr. Gould's, where we meet Señor Sarmiento, Minister of the Argentine Republic; and I have a chance to try my Spanish, the first time for six years or more.

13th. The printers get on slowly with the *Dante*, which puts me quite in despair. The task seems endless; but will nevertheless come to an end some time or other.

To Charles Sumner.

October 24, 1865.

I found it impossible to engage "Smith and his men" [the caterers] for to-morrow; consequently I must postpone the great Mandarin Fan dinner until Friday. Will that suit you as well? I hope so; as the zig-zag of one who can, and one who cannot, makes life difficult.

25th. Lowell, Norton, and myself had the first meeting of our Dante Club. We read the xxv. *Purgatorio;* and then had a little supper. We are to meet every Wednesday evening at my house.[1]

[1] These meetings were held for the final revision of the Translation, which was going through the press. There was the fullest and

29th. Sumner brought out the agreeable Marquis de Chambrun to dinner; very pleasant and full of conversation.

frankest criticism. Mr. Longfellow noted upon the printed sheets before him the various suggestions of his friends, both Dantean experts; and the next day carefully weighed them, finally accepting or rejecting. Mr. Norton has given in the first Report of the Dante Society the following interesting account of these meetings, which were continued through this and the following winter: —

"In 1863, when Mr. Longfellow was experiencing a deeper need than at any other period of his life of occupation that should be of a nature congenial with his mood, and which should at least give him tranquil and regular employment, he was led, partly by his own impulse, partly by friendly urgency, to resume the work long laid aside, and to engage in the restorative labor of translating the whole of the Divine Comedy. The work was steadily pursued, and with increasing interest. In the course of the year the greater part of the *Inferno* was finished. The sixth centenary of Dante's birth was approaching. Florence was about to celebrate the anniversary with unusual observances. She invited the lovers of her poet, wherever they might be, to unite with her in doing honor to his memory. Mr. Longfellow determined to send his translation to her, as a tribute from America. But master as he was of his own language and of that of Dante, and thorough as was his knowledge of the substance and significance of the poem, he was too modest to rely wholly upon his own judgment and genius in the performance of his work, and he called upon two of his friends to sit with him in the final revision of it.

"In 1865, the manuscript was put in the printers' hands, and every Wednesday evening Mr. Lowell and I met in Mr. Longfellow's study to listen while he read a canto of his translation from the proof-sheet. We paused over every doubtful passage, discussed the various readings, considered the true meaning of obscure words and phrases, sought for the most exact equivalent of Dante's expression, objected, criticised, praised, with a freedom that was made perfect by Mr. Longfellow's absolute sweetness, simplicity, and modesty, and by the entire confidence that existed between us. Witte's text was always before us, and of the early commentators Buti was the one to whom we had most frequent and most serviceable recourse. They were delightful evenings; there could be no pleasanter occupation; the spirits of poetry, of learning, of friendship, were with us. Now and then some

30th. I gave a dinner to Mr. and Mrs. Burlingame, in honor of the Chinese Fan sent me by a mandarin, with the "Psalm of Life" written upon it in Chinese. Burlingame, Palfrey, Sumner, and Richard Dana, — all original Free-soilers.

To Ernest Longfellow.

November 17, 1865.

We were all delighted last night by the arrival of your interesting letter from London and Paris. It is pleasant to know that you are seeing and enjoying so much. Your account of the Horse-Guardsman is very comic, and that of Carlyle very amusing. . . . Mr. Greene is here, and takes great interest in your travels. He is particularly glad that you climbed the Côte d'Ingouville at Havre; and so am I. The view repays one for the toil, as I remember well. We are now in the midst of the hottest of Indian summers. I only hope you are having as pleasant weather amid the gardens and groves in the environs of Paris. Is it not a splendid city? . . .

There is nothing new here in the old house except a cuckoo-clock, which when it strikes in the night alarms

other friend or acquaintance would join us for the hours of study. Almost always one or two guests would come in at ten o'clock, when the work ended, and sit down with us to a supper, with which the evening closed. Mr. Longfellow had a special charm as a host, the charm of social grace and humor, by which his guests were brought into congenial disposition. His delicate and refined taste, his cheerful enjoyment of good things, showed themselves in the arrangement and order of the table, no less than in the talk that went on round about it. He was in truth

'A man of such a genial mood
The heart of all things he embraced,
And yet of such fastidious taste
He never found the best too good.'"

the household. Mr. Greene started up, thinking one of the children had the croup. It is very droll. The Cambridge Assemblies have begun, and you are wanted. To enliven the winter, I have formed a Dante Club, consisting of Lowell, Norton, and myself, meeting here every Wednesday evening, with a good deal of talk and a little supper. So we try to get along without you and your uncle; but we miss you nevertheless. Trap [the Scotch terrier] sends his regards. His last misdemeanor was stealing a partridge from the supper-table of the Club. That was his view of the Divine Comedy! Of your other friends in Cambridge I see nothing. Nobody comes to play billiards. Your room is now occupied by E., as the office of The Secret.[1] On the door is "No Ad*d*mittance."

November 30. Dante Club. Lowell did not come. Greene was here. Read the first canto of the *Paradiso*. My brother A. came in to supper.

December 1. A gentle rain and mist covering the whole landscape. The river changed to a lake. Not a breath of wind. The brown leafless branches all at rest. A day of quiet and seclusion.

5th. Went to town; to the new "Corner."[2] Fields has hung Healy's portrait of me in his room. After dinner Captain Norris, of Sherman's army, now in the Law school, came with a letter from Sumner. Also Mr. Thomas, reporter for the Manchester Times.

[1] A manuscript monthly, carried on by the little girls of the family.

[2] The firm of Ticknor and Fields for many years had occupied the old gambrel-roofed building on the corner of Washington and School streets, well known as "The Old Corner." They had now removed to Tremont Street and Hamilton Place.

To George W. Greene.

December 29, 1865.

If you wish to contemplate the virtuous man, think of me on an allowance of one cigar a day! But if you wish to see the just man made perfect, wait till I give up that one!

Your letter has just come, with the extract from Vico, for which a thousand thanks. What a lucky escape you have had! A little harder blow and all your fine fancies in this world would have been ended. What a shame it is that these accidents are always happening! The locomotive is the American Juggernaut; I am glad you were not made one of its victims. We miss you at the Dante Club; and I am sorry you are not here to-day to dine with "The Saturday." Here comes your second letter and second extract from Vico, and again I thank you.

CHAPTER V.

JOURNAL AND LETTERS.

1866.

To G. W. Greene.

January 7, 1866.

I sent you the History some days ago; but not the fenders. When I looked at them I saw all your darlings tumbling over them into the fire, and determined to have nothing to do with such a Slaughter of the Innocents. Altogether too low and unsafe. You can do better in the *Judenstrasse*, when you come. Meanwhile I will tell the little man here to be on the lookout. Let me advise you also to take an arm-chair instead of the lounge, which is an ugly and inconvenient piece of furniture.

The little girls are highly delighted with your contribution to The Secret; and a special extra number of that popular journal is to be devoted to it. Not every contributor is treated with such distinguished regard.

Dante moves slowly, but surely. Next Wednesday we have canto ix. and perhaps x. I have just got, of Norton, Covino's *Descrizione Geographica dell' Italia, ad Illustrazione della Divina Commedia.* It is difficult to navigate Dante's rivers and harbors without some such pilot.

January 9. At Dante Club, only Norton and myself. Lowell excuses himself.

10th. Went up to see Lowell. He read me a beautiful poem, 'What Rabbi Jehosha said,' — a Rabbinical legend, which he was just sending to the Nation. After dinner, a grazier, from Springfield, Illinois, President Lincoln's town, called to see Washington's headquarters.

12th. Cogswell and T. at dinner. Lowell could not come, on account of his sore throat, but writes his excuse in some funny verses on a claret gargle which I had recommended to him.

To G. W. Greene.

January 15, 1866.

As Kiernan has no good arm-chair, nor any prospect of one, I told him this morning to send you the green lounge, that you may lie down and meditate on the fenders, of which he is in hot pursuit. For the lounge, you are to pay nothing but the freight, which I forgot.

We miss you at the Dante Club, which goes singing on its way, though diminished in numbers. Last Wednesday only Charles Norton and myself were present, Lowell being kept at home by a sore throat. Whereupon I sent him the enclosed prescription in Italian. The lines will amuse you if you like nonsense verses. [See p. 442.]

To Charles Sumner.

January 17, 1866.

I hardly know which is most revolting, — the article sent you in a box, or that served up for you on the dirty Round Table. Each shows about the same amount of barbarism, and each is equally harmless to yourself and discreditable to the author. So let them pass away, among the things forgotten.

Meanwhile, it grows more and more evident that we shall have no peace in the country till your doctrines prevail. All accounts from the South betray a deplorable state of feeling toward the negro.

I have nothing new to write you, not having been in town since the day of the "Tattered Flags," — which was a most impressive occasion, — a month ago, or more.

Dante marches on slowly, and with decorum. In printing, — or rather, stereotyping, — I have now reached the tenth canto of *Paradiso.* A little club meets here every Wednesday evening, — Lowell, Norton, and myself; with sometimes an outsider or two. We go over a canto critically, and then have a supper. I wish we could have you with us. Take down your Dante, and read the beginning of *Paradiso* xi.

17th. Dante Club. Lowell, Norton, Fields, T. *Paradiso* xi. Great discussion about the meaning of *in basso* in the third line, etc.

To Ernest Longfellow.

January 17, 1866.

In Dante's *Paradiso,* canto x., a French professor is spoken of thus: —

> "This is the light eternal of Sigier,
> Who, reading lectures in the Street of Straw,
> Did syllogize invidious verities."

The "Street of Straw" is the Rue du Fouarre, near the Place Maubert, and got its name from the fact that the students used to sit on bundles of straw at their lectures, or because it was a hay-market, or probably from both. I want you and your uncle to hunt up this old street and tell me how it looks now; I want something to make a note of.[1] Look up also the Hôtel Carnavalet, in the Rue

[1] See note to Paradise, canto x., line 137, in Mr. Longfellow's translation.

Culture-St. Catherine. That is where Mme. de Sévigné lived and wrote her famous letters. In fine, I advise you to buy a book called *Les Rues de Paris*, by Louis Lurine. You will find a good deal of curious matter and curious illustration in it.

It would be rather difficult to say what books I should like, not having a peep at the bookstalls. But I will name two, — Quérard, all his bibliographical works; and Vapereau, who publishes every year a review of the literature of the previous years. These you may get, at all events. As soon as the first flower blooms and the first bird sings, if not sooner, you will no doubt break up your winter quarters and move southward to meet the spring. That will be pleasant, and make up for the dull weather of Paris.

I have kept this page for Cambridge news, and none comes to hand. Now that you have gone away, nothing happens; and I have not been much in the way if it did. I send you, therefore, now and then a newspaper; and by to-day's mail the Advertiser, with an article by "Tom Brown" (Mr. Hughes), on American affairs, which will interest you, as he makes honorable mention of Charles. C. got back to-day from Montreal. He has brought home blanket-coats and moccasins enough to furnish a small shop. What a time the moths will have next summer! I have just stopped to do a deed of charity for you; namely, to give a pair of your shoes to a handsome Italian boy who came here barefoot in the ice and snow. He says he has had no shoes all winter.

To G. W. Greene.

January 18, 1866.

In *Paradiso* xi., line 3, does *in basso* imply motion downward, or simply motion below? Is it to be rendered "downward beat your wings," or "beat your wings below"? This is one of the points we discussed last night. Another was, adopting the reading *ricerna*, not *discerna*, in line 22, — whether he sifted it fine or coarse. A third was, *per diritto segno*, line 120, — whether it refers to the stars he steered by, or simply means "straight upon its course," or "in the right course." And fourthly, and finally, in line 138 shall one read *il Correggier*, "the Dominican," or *il correger*, "the reproof"? Do not give yourself the trouble to hunt these matters through various editions; but if one rendering strikes you as more simple and natural than another, please answer as follows, without giving any reasons, or even filling out the sentences: —

1. Downward. 2. Sift fine. 3. Right course. 4. Reproof. Or the reverse, as the case may be. This is criticism made easy.

In a paper which I send you to-day, you will find some of your own views pretty vigorously stated, on the subject of reprints of English notices. The abuse of Sumner is simply atrocious; it must come from a very vulgar mind. Burn it.

22d. Note from Fields, who likes the new sonnets ii. and iii., 'On Translating Dante,' and wishes to print them in the Atlantic.

28th. Dante Club; *Paradiso* xxii. Norton, Lowell, Fields, Akers, and Mr. Howells, — formerly consul at Venice, poet and prose-writer; a very clever and cultivated young man.[1]

To G. W. Greene.

February 9, 1866.

This is a lovely winter morning. I cannot tire looking out of the window at the brown branches against the

[1] But lately come to Cambridge, as will be inferred.

colorless gray sky. The air is windless, and the snow falling gently; the nearest glimpse we can have of *creation*, the beautiful something that comes from nothing, — the crystallization of air!

Please read this as a sonnet, and pass on.

I wish all things would go on smoothly in this world. Now, here is our good Fields frightened at the length of the Dante letters. But at the last Dante Club, Lowell and Norton, as well as myself, were so positive that they ought to go into the Magazine, that he seemed to take heart. I confess it is a quality of food not adapted to the great mass of Magazine readers. But I trust the Atlantic has some judicious readers who like to have some timber in the building, and not all clapboards. Norton has translated the *Vita Nuova*, and is translating the *Convito*.

To G. W. Greene.

February 18, 1866.

"The airy tongues that syllable men's names" begin again to cry with constant iteration, "When is Mr. Greene coming?" I am then reminded that you promised to be here on my birthday. Moreover, Howe has just asked me to dine with him on the convenient "some day" to be appointed by the guest. ("*Vinum non habeo*," he says, "but a warm welcome.") Whereupon I make answer and say, "I am expecting Greene; wait a little, and we will come together." This pleases him, and he writes you the enclosed. Then there is the Dante meeting on Wednesday evening, and the Saturday Club dinner close upon us; and, putting all things together, now is the time to come. I want you also to sign a petition for an international copyright, which is lying on my desk, and which I will keep as long as possible.

Have you read Sumner's speech? I have not, except

in part, from newspapers. I do not know about the details, but I am sure of his fidelity.

To G. W. Greene.

March 20, 1866.

You will certainly think that this is the land of funerals. We have just buried our old and dear friend Sparks, and now another friend, whom I saw at Sparks's funeral full of life and strength, is dead.[1] Vespasian died standing; Dr. Beck died on horseback. Yesterday afternoon, as he was riding with a party of friends, he reeled in the saddle. He was caught by some one of the party, carried home, and died in the course of the evening without any consciousness after the attack. It was apoplexy. He is a great loss to us, — a man of convictions, and who had the courage of his convictions and always acted up to them; a most excellent, sincere, just, charitable, good man; and a thoroughly loyal man in every sense of the word; who, in the Rebellion, wished to serve as a foot-soldier, — to his honor be it remembered, — and was only refused on account of his age. Cambridge will soon be stripped of all the Old Guard. When Sumner returns he will find it more of "a shell" than ever, — a flattering phrase which he sometimes uses in speaking to me.

To H. I. Bowditch.

March 23, 1866.

. . . The poem you speak of was not a record of any one event which came to my knowledge, but of many which came to my imagination. It is an attempt to express something of the inexpressible sympathy which I

[1] Charles Beck, Ph. D., for many years Professor of Latin in Harvard College.

feel for the death of the young men in the war, which makes my heart bleed whenever I think of it.[1]

How much I have felt for *you* I cannot tell you, particularly on that cold December night when I came back with my son, and saw you at the station and knew that yours would come back to you no more.

Pardon me for touching that wound; it is only that I may tell you how deep the impression is. It was from such impressions that the poem came to my mind.

April 1. Easter Sunday. I always think, in connection with its greater significance, of Virgil and Dante emerging on the shores of Purgatory.

To G. W. Greene.

April 1, 1866.

This is Easter morning, with all its

"Dolce color d'oriental zaffiro;"

and I send you the salutation and benediction of the day.

In worldly matters, I send you Deeds, not words; or, better to speak, good deed and word intermingled. On account of the weather, I could not go to the Notary Public (in this case the Recording *Angell* of Rhode Island, as you will see by his signature) until yesterday, when the whole matter was settled, signed, sealed, and delivered. And if you have as much pleasure in having it done as I have in doing it, this will be a pleasant Easter.[2]

[1] In answer to a letter from him asking whether the poem 'Killed at the Ford' referred to any particular person.

[2] Mr. Longfellow had purchased and presented to his friend a house in East Greenwich.

I must go out and breathe the beautiful air and "expatiate," like Milton's bees and Dante's lark.

Where shall I find the best account of Monte Cassino?

2d. I meet in the street some young ladies, who ask if "they may shake hands with" me. Bring them in, with a gentleman and lady who seem to have charge of the party, to see the house. They are from Philadelphia; but I do not learn their names.

3d. I have to go to town on business, and hope it may not happen again for a long while. Loring Moody [a philanthropist and philozoist] calls, — the man with the beautiful soul and beautiful face.

May 1. A bright, warm, lovely May-day. The children have a May-pole in the garden; and are busy putting up a tent. It is half-past twelve o'clock, and I have just finished the Notes to the *Purgatorio.*

10th. "Sleep, sleep to-day, tormenting cares
Of earth and folly born;
Ye shall not dim the light that streams
From this celestial morn."

31st. Dined at Mr. Forceythe Wilson's with Emerson and Rev. Dr. Bartol.[1] In the afternoon took to the printer the last canto of *Paradiso.*

June 1. A lovely, sad day.

2d. Darley has made some illustrations for 'Evangeline.'

13th. The last Dante reading. Lowell, Greene, Holmes, Howells, Furness, and F. Wilson. *Paradiso* xxxiii. A very pleasant supper, which did not break

[1] Mr. Wilson was a young poet of promise then in Cambridge, who died soon after.

up till two o'clock in the morning. After it Greene and I sat talking in the study till three. The day was dawning and the birds singing when we went to bed.

To G. W. Greene.

July 1, 1866.

Your letter reached me yesterday; and I am glad to hear that you are surrounded with the pleasant sounds of building a home. Nest-building, ship-building, bridge-building, house-building, — all pleasant, though sometimes noisy!

I have left the little girls in Portland, where I passed a day or two with them; and, among other things, had a sail down Casco Bay through the wooded islands, and wished you there. We go to Nahant on the fifth; and if you find the hammering about your ears too bad you must take your carpet-bag in hand and run down to see us. Bring Fields with you.

Sumner has gone back to Washington and is now simmering in the dust and heat of that incipient city. I wish he were free. This relapse is a warning that he can no longer work day and night.

July 11. *Nahant.* Charles sailed from here in the yacht "Alice," with Clark and Stanfield [for a voyage across the Atlantic in a vessel of fifty tons].

August 5. A message by Atlantic cable. The "Alice" reached the Isle of Wight in nineteen days.

To G. W. Greene.

NAHANT, July 23, 1866.

It is rather dreary and doleful at Nahant this year, and I hope you will soon show yourself. I do not get much work out of myself here, and enjoy talking on the windy verandas more than writing.

I have been in Portland, since the fire.[1] Desolation, desolation, desolation! It reminded me of Pompeii, "that sepult city." The old family house was not burned, the track of the fire passing just below it.

To G. W. Greene.

NAHANT, July 29, 1866.

I wish it were possible for you to come now. After the middle of August, A. is expecting four of her school-girl friends, and we shall be crowded. Bring some new chapters of the Biography,[2] and we will have a quiet and delightful interchange of thought on this and many other matters; and I will do my best to make you like Nahant; and, as Chaucer says, —

"And ded and quicke be ever yours
Late, erly and at alle houres."

My house is only five minutes walk from the steam-boat-landing, and on the same southern shore. Another reason for coming soon is the moon! The nights are divine.

Have you Scipio's Dream in English? If so, bring it.

September 14. Returned from Nahant. Find on my table two books of poems by H. A. Rawes of Trinity, Cambridge, intensely Roman Catholic. Also a volume of poems by Robert Leighton of Liverpool, very liberal and Unitarian.

[1] A fire which on the 4th of July devastated a large part of the city.

[2] Mr. Greene was engaged upon a Life of his grandfather, General Nathaniel Greene of the army of the Revolution.

16th. After chapel, went to Lowell's. He has nothing to do in college now but to lecture. He is at work on a political article for the North American.

18th. In town. Bought sundry articles for Christmas presents. There is nothing like being in season.

19th. Corrected proofs and wrote letters. Dined at Mr. Hooper's, to meet Baron Gerolt, the Prussian Minister, a precise old gentleman with a good deal of Prussian rigidity.

To G. W. Greene.

September 28, 1866.

For the first time in my life I was this morning stung by a wasp. He alighted on my fore-finger, and without provocation whipped out his rapier and gave me such a thrust that it has almost paralyzed my hand. The pain went to my elbow, and I had a taste of galvanism on the tip of my tongue. This being a new experience and a new sensation, I record it here, and proceed.

Your entanglement in the thickets of 1778 is not unlike mine at this moment in the tenth canto of *Paradiso*, among the innumerable saints. My Notes on that canto will amaze you. They are almost as voluminous as the writings of Albertus Magnus, which fill twenty-one volumes folio. However, I have got through, or nearly so; but have found it pretty hard work to compress Thomas Aquinas, St. Francis, and the rest, into their several nutshells.

Sumner is busy, at work on a lecture which he is to deliver on Tuesday next, — and on Tuesday last had only begun. What confidence Sumner has in Sumner! I would not trust H. W. L. to that amount, nor would you, G. W. G.

Ernest will be back in November, for his twenty-first birth-day. I hope you will be able to combine that with Ristori.

Let me close with a blossom from St. Bonaventura. "The best perfection of a religious man is to do common things in a perfect manner. A constant fidelity in small things is a great and heroic virtue."

October 6. Parmenides and Brissus [*Paradiso* xiii.] must wait. Instead of writing of them I was obliged to go to town. This evening I expect Carl Rosa, Hatton, and Mr. Mills to make some music, and one or two friends to hear them.

17th. A beautiful day it is; full of sunshine, and all the trees lighted like torches. A stranger called here to-day, to see Washington's Headquarters. He asked me if Shakespeare did not live somewhere about here. I told him I knew no such person in this neighborhood.[1]

19th. Warm and splendid; all the fields and roads bordered with red and gold, like an illuminated missal.

28th. Hepworth Dixon called, and passed an hour this afternoon. An ardent temperament and a great talker. He is editor of the London Athenæum, which has been too full of sneers at us poor outsiders.

30th. Rain at last, and it seems to enjoy itself greatly.

November 30. The south wind whistling through the keyhole, and roaring over the chimney. I have just finished the last Note to Dante; eleven in the forenoon.

December 16. Bayard Taylor came to dinner, and the young Comte de Lubersac. After dinner, Norton came in

[1] At another time, a man who came to the house in Portland to make some repairs, inquired "if a Mr. Shakespeare, or some such name, was not born there." It would appear that to some persons, as to Sir Topas, "a poet is — a poet."

with Baron M——, a young Hollander, who brings me an introduction.

To Charles Sumner.

December 18, 1866.

This is a business letter. I want you to take up the *copyright* question, and to introduce a Bill in the Senate, providing "that any copyright hereafter taken out in England or in any of her colonies, shall be valid in the United States, on condition that England will pass a similar law in reference to copyright taken out in the United States." This seems to me to cover the whole ground, and to be simple and practicable. I wish you would consult Sir Frederick Bruce on the subject; and if you are too busy, or have no inclination to move in the matter, can you tell me of any one who will? If I were a senator, there is no measure with which I should be more eager to associate my name. Think upon it and reply. As to limitation of time, when any copyright expired in the country in which it was taken out, it should expire in the other. This is the best plan I can think of, and I hope you will be interested in it.[1]

19th. First of the Dante Club meetings for the winter. Lowell, Norton, Baron M——, Fields. Discussed various points in *Inferno* i. ii. The Baron is an intelligent and agreeable young man, of Scotch ancestry.

25th. All holidays and anniversaries are so sad to me. I almost sink under the burden.

26th. Dante Club. Lowell, Norton, Howells, and Fields.

[1] Mr. Sumner answered that the subject of copyright was before the Committee on Foreign Relations, of which he was chairman, and that he hoped to do something for it. Sir Frederick Bruce was then English minister at Washington. He died the next year, in Boston.

To Romeo Cantagalli.[1]

1866.

Dear Sir, — I have had the honor of receiving your letter of the 18th inst., with the Diploma and Cross of the Order of SS. Maurizio and Lazzaro.

If, as an American citizen, a Protestant, and Republican, I could consistently accept such an Order of Knighthood, there is no one from whom I would more willingly receive it than from the Restorer of the Unity of Italy,—a sacred cause, which has, and always has had, my most sincere and fervent sympathy.

I trust, therefore, that you will not regard it as the slightest disrespect either to your Sovereign or to yourself if, under these circumstances, I feel myself constrained to decline the honor proposed.

With expressions of great regard and consideration, I remain your obedient servant.

[1] Signor Cantagalli, the Italian *Chargé d'affaires* in Washington, had written Mr. Longfellow: "It is my agreeable duty to announce to you that his Majesty the King, my Sovereign, has deigned to confer upon you, in token of the high esteem in which he holds your talents, the grade of *Cavaliere* in his Order of SS. Maurizio and Lazzaro." To Mr. Sumner Mr. Longfellow wrote that he "did not think it appropriate to a Republican and a Protestant to receive a Catholic Order of Knighthood;" and added, "I wonder how this matter has found vent; I have tried to keep it secret."

CHAPTER VI.

JOURNAL AND LETTERS.

1867–1868.

January 1. Corrected the last proof-sheets of the Notes to Dante; and the long labor is done. What next?

To Charles Sumner.

January 1, 1867.

Agassiz has just left me. He goes to Washington next week or the week after; but I must stay here and finish my work.

Pray do not let the matter of international copyright fade out of sight. Now is the time. A week hence may be too late. I hope it may take the shape of a treaty. Probably in that shape it would pass more readily than in any other.

I have just received a letter from Tennyson, in which he says: "We English and Americans should all be brothers as none other among the nations can be; and some of us, come what may, will always be so, I trust."

To George W. Greene.

February 1, 1867.

In order to satisfy you and Sumner, I yesterday had a consultation with Dr. Brown Séquard. He says I am perfectly sound from attic to underpinning, — only my bell-wires a little jangled and out of order. Brain in good working condition; heart perfect in every pulsation; lungs equally so in every respiration. Nothing in the world the matter but nerves. This agrees precisely with Dr. Longfellow's opinion; though Dr. Sumner thought the brain was overworked, and Dr. Greene that there was trouble in the heart! But the remedy is severe. "Positively no smoking allowed here!" Only think of it!

To G. W. Greene.

February 7, 1867.

I fear you must decide the matter for yourself; no one can decide for you. For myself, I think I should not send the letter. Forbearance brings a certain comfort with it. Anything like vengeance brings dissatisfaction. You have been harshly treated. —— is in the wrong; and I think he feels it. Wait!

I have been working very hard this last week, and have almost re-written the New England Tragedy in verse. Only two or three scenes remain. It is greatly improved, though it is not yet what I mean it shall be. This has absorbed me day and night, and put me into better spirits. Happy the man who has something to do — and does it!

February 18.

A month ago I felt as if I should never write another line. And lo! since then I have written a Tragedy, and am half way through with another. That is the reason I have not written you. I have written two whole scenes to-day; one of them the most important of all.

February 27. My sixtieth birthday. Sundry bouquets, and presents from the children. Ernest presented me with his charming portrait of his sister, reading. In the Advertiser came this poem by Lowell:[1] —

TO H. W. L.

(On his birthday, 27th February, 1867.)

I need not praise the sweetness of his song,
  Where limpid verse to limpid verse succeeds
Smooth as our Charles, when, fearing lest he wrong
The new moon's mirrored skiff, he slides along,
  Full without noise, and whispers in his reeds.

With loving breath of all the winds, his name
  Is blown about the world; but to his friends
A sweeter secret hides behind his fame,
And Love steals shyly through the loud acclaim
  To murmur a *God bless you!* and there ends.

As I muse backward up the checkered years
  Wherein so much was given, so much was lost,
Blessings in both kinds, such as cheapen tears, —
But, hush! this is not for profaner ears:
  Let them drink molten pearls, nor dream the cost.

Some suck up poison from a sorrow's core,
  As nought but nightshade grew upon earth's ground:
Love turned all his to heart's-ease; and the more
Fate tried his bastions, she but forced a door
  Leading to sweeter manhood and more sound.

Even as a wind-waved fountain's swaying shade
  Seems of mixed race, a gray wraith shot with sun,

[1] In the copy of these verses sent by Mr. Lowell to his friend was added this stanza: —

"A gift of symbol-flowers I meant to bring,
White for thy candor, for thy kindness red;
But Nature here denies them to the Spring,
And in forced blooms an odorous warmth will cling
Not artless: take this bunch of verse instead."

So through his trial faith translucent rayed,
Till darkness, half disnatured so, betrayed
  A heart of sunshine that would fain o'errun.

Surely, if skill in song the shears may stay
  And of its purpose cheat the charmed abyss,
If our poor life be lengthened by a lay,
He shall not go, although his presence may,
  And the next age in praise shall double this.

Long days be his, and each as lusty-sweet
  As gracious natures find his song to be!
May Age steal on with softly-cadenced feet,
Falling in music as for him were meet
  Whose choicest verse is harsher-toned than he!

J. R. L.

In the afternoon Greene came on from Rhode Island, and in the evening we had our usual Dante Club. At supper Holmes read these lines:—

In gentle bosoms tried and true
  How oft the thought will be,
"Dear friend, shall I remember you
  Or you remember me?"

But thou, sweet singer of the West,
  Whose song in every zone
Has soothed some aching grief to rest
  And made some heart thine own,

Whene'er thy tranquil sun descends,—
  Far, far that evening be!—
What mortal tongue may count the friends
  That shall remember thee?

To Mrs. James T. Fields.

February 28, 1867.

I am very much obliged to you for your kind remembrance yesterday, and for sending such messengers to tell it to me. Their "voiceless lips" delivered the message of good-will, and sang it to the eye all supper-time, as your husband will bear witness. Many thanks — say sixty — for these lovely flowers.

From Henry Hart Milman.

DEANERY, ST. PAUL'S, April 18, 1867.

MY DEAR MR. LONGFELLOW, — I am delighted to hear that my History has been of service to you in the illustration of Dante. The more extracts you make the more flattering to me; as no one can judge so well as a translator what throws the best and clearest light on his original. I have from my youth been a great worshipper of Dante, and from an accomplished Italian friend have received the high praise of having fairly comprehended the relation of the great poet to his time. I write this rather as a testimony to the accuracy of my observations than to any merit of my own.

I shall look with the utmost interest for the copy of your translation, which you are so kind as to promise me. We may expect great things from one who has added so much to our English poetry, and has such varied command of our language.

You have, I trust, not recently visited England. I hope, if you think of doing so, that you will *make haste;* for, at my age, I have not long to wait; and I should be most glad to be able to show in how high respect and esteem you are held by men of letters in your mother country.

Believe me, dear Mr. Longfellow, with much regard,

Faithfully yours,

H. H. MILMAN.

From Victor Hugo.

HAUTEVILLE HOUSE, 22 avril, 1867.

MONSIEUR ET CHER CONFRÈRE, — J'ai reçu le beau livre que vous m'envoyez. Vous êtes un des hommes qui honorent la grande Amérique. Vous donnez la poésie à cette terre qui a la liberté. Je vous remercie, et je suis heureux de serrer dans ma vieille main française la jeune main américaine.

Croyez à ma vive cordialité,

VICTOR HUGO.

May 1. Dante Club; the last of the season. Norton, Greene, Howells, Fields, and Whipple.

4th. Heard Agassiz lecture. He had an introduction on the duties of teacher and taught; and made a strong protest against the pupil's running off with the master's ideas and publishing them as his own. Evening, at Norton's. *Vita Nuova.* A very pleasant evening and supper.

5th. On my walk met Henry James, who said some pleasant words about the translation of Dante; and afterwards Cogswell, who did the same.

6th. Showed Fields a new sonnet which I wrote last night, and which is to go into the Purgatory. The Dante work is now all done, — the last word, and the final corrections, all in the printer's hands.

To J. T. Fields.

May 6, 1867.

I believe you have my copy of Flaxman's Dante. Please tell me if it be so; for I cannot find it, and must have lent it, and I may as well begin with you as with any other friend.

Notwithstanding what you say, the sonnet is poor and feeble. It stands well enough upon its *feet,* but it has no legs, no body, no soul.

Poor ——! You must try to get some people to take tickets, whether they go to the lectures or not. This is a real tragedy, and a real charity.

To Robert Ferguson.

May 8, 1867.

It was only yesterday that I had the pleasure of receiving your charming birthday present, the Della Crusca edition of the *Commedia.* It is a *cara gioia,* a precious jewel of a book, which I value very highly, for its own sake and for yours. You could not have thought of a more acceptable gift; and I am very much obliged to you for it, and for the kind remembrance.

I suppose that before this time you have received a copy of my translation of the *Inferno.* The second volume will be out this month, and the third in June. They will be duly sent you, with copies for Miss F—— and Mr. Dayman, which I took the liberty of having directed to your care. The only merit my book has is that it is exactly what Dante says, and not what the translator imagines he might have said if he had been an Englishman. In other words, while making it rhythmic, I have endeavored to make it also as literal as a prose translation.

We are all well at the Craigie House, and are beginning to think what we shall do this summer. The great point is, shall it be Nahant or England? How it will be settled I do not know; perhaps, by accident or fate, — certainly, by Providence.

11th. Went with the girls down the harbor in the steam revenue cutter Pawtuxet, to the outer light, and the outer islands — the Brewsters. Professors Peirce, Agassiz, and Goodwin were of the party; Judge Russell the Collector, and Captain Hockley, of the China, the English steamer. Returning, we stopped near the school-ship, which was crowded with boys, all singing an evening hymn. Then they manned the yards and gave us three cheers, which we returned. A very striking sight. Then we went on board the China; and so ended a day of great delight to the girls, which they will not soon forget, — particularly the jolly captain's cry for beer: "Steward, some *beah;* I'm dying for some *beah.*"

To Ferdinand Freiligrath.

May 24, 1867.

Of late years I have almost given up writing letters; and when one gets out of the habit of doing a thing, it becomes difficult.

From time to time, as I have published a book in London, I have never failed to tell Routledge to send a copy to you. I hope he has always done so; and that you have received the Wayside Inn, the Flower de Luce, and lastly, the translation of the *Divina Commedia,* of which two volumes have been published, and the third will appear in June.

I hope, my dear Freiligrath, that we shall some day meet again; and I wish it could be on the Rhine. I always remember our last evening at St. Goar, when we paced to and fro on the banks of the river till near midnight; and all that we said. I have always loved you, and never for a moment has my feeling abated or changed. I beg you to write me about yourself, about your dear wife, about your dear children.

Of what I have been through, during the last six years, I dare not venture to write even to you; it is almost too much for any man to bear and live. I have taken refuge in this translation of the Divine Comedy, and this may give it perhaps an added interest in your sight.

28th. Agassiz's birthday. Pass the evening with him. He is sixty years old.

From George Ticknor.

PARK STREET, June 1, 1867.

MY DEAR SIR, — When I received the first volume of your translation of Dante, I thought I should not acknowledge your kindness in sending it until I had received the remainder. But I will wait no longer. The second volume has come out; and not only the main principles of the great work, but the details and finish are as plain as they ever will be.

There can be, I think, no doubt that you have done something astonishing. I should not have thought it possible beforehand, and do not altogether comprehend now how you have accomplished it. I was led on, canto by canto, wondering all the time whether you would give out or stumble; but you never did, so far as I could observe, and I meant to be watchful. The movement of your verse — its cadence and rhythm, I mean — explain, perhaps, a good deal of your power, or rather conceal it; although I confess I do not, after some consideration, understand how you make us feel a sort of presence of the *terza rima*, in a measure so different. But you do; at least to me. Whether you have not encumbered yourself with heavier and more embarrassing conditions [1] than permit the free poetical movement which an absolutely Eng-

[1] The translation follows the original line for line, and almost word for word.

lish reader covets, is a question that must be settled by the popular voice, as separate from that of scholastic lovers of Dante. On that bench of judges I can never be competent to sit; I shall always read your translation with the original ringing in my ears.

I know nothing like it; *nil simile aut secundum.* It reminds me, however, of a few lines — not above ten or twelve — translated from the Odyssey by Wolf, which I read half a century ago, done with the most extraordinary strictness, and at the same time with grace and fluency. But I remember thinking, as I read them, that Wolf, with all his genius and pluck, could not in the same way make a translation of Homer, if he should have a thousand years given him for the task.

I did not receive the first volume of your Dante without many thoughts and recollections running far back into the darkening past. I shall gratefully keep the entire work, with such memories always legible to me between the lines.

Yours with much regard,

GEO. TICKNOR.

June 1. Went with Fields to see Story's bust of Browning the poet, at Mr. Dana's in Arlington Street. Very good; but not so good as that of Mrs. Browning by the same artist. In the evening went to hear some music at the Music Hall. Mr. Thayer played. We sat in the twilight, some fifty of us, on the platform, under Beethoven's statue, without lights in the gathering darkness, and listened for an hour or two. It was very impressive.

2d. Another lovely day; the lilacs all in bloom and tossing in the wind. Agassiz calls and sits half an hour. In the afternoon, Parsons the poet and translator of Dante. We have a talk about theories of translation.

4th. I met in the street an Irish mason, whom I have seen now and then about new houses. I wished him good morning, and joining me he said, "I am glad to speak to a poet. I have meself a brother in the Port, who is a drunkard and a poet."

5th. Bought books; some for the Portland Library, some for myself. In the afternoon Captain Dixon from Kidderminster called with a letter from Elihu Burritt. Then Dana, with Mr. Jennings, the New York correspondent of the London Times, and his wife, a beautiful young American.

6th. A perfect day. An excellent lecture from Lowell, on Shakespeare. Then Sophocles calls to say that he would to-morrow bring out Mr. Rangebé, the Greek Envoy, to see me.

8th. Read Sumner's speech on Alaska, or Russian America; and Calderon's *La Vida es Sueño.*

To G. W. Curtis.

June 13, 1867.

It was very pleasant to see your handwriting last evening; the next best thing to seeing yourself. At T.'s dinner we missed you very much; the only skeleton there was your vacant chair. Kensett I found quite unchanged after so many years that I have not met him; just as sweet and sound as ever; and his voice murmuring on in its old pleasant undertone, like a hidden brook.

Perhaps you will infer from this last elaborate sentence that my letter is meant for an autograph, and that I have Mrs. —— in my eye. Not in the least. I have this morning made my peace with her, or hope I have, by writing to her in answer to a note received some time ago, and by me neglected. Therefore you need not send this.

We are all well here, and begin to think of Nahant.

I wish there were any chance of seeing you there this summer. Could we persuade you to come, if we tried?

18th. Mr. Routledge, my London publisher, came to lunch. A sturdy, blue-eyed, North Country gentleman. We had much talk of books and the book-trade. Dined with Agassiz, to meet Senhor Azumbaja, the Brazilian Minister.

19th. Sumner dined with me; and we went to the Palfreys'; then strolled through the college grounds and sentimentalized.

To G. W. Greene.

NAHANT, June 19, 1867.

. . . I had got thus far when Senator Sumner came to dinner, in the quiet old way. After dinner we went to see Palfrey, and then loitered through the College grounds and looked at old familiar windows painted with sunset and memories of youth; and the senator moralized thereupon and sighed. . . . Come for a day or two — next week, say. You need not lose much time by the movement, and we will discuss "a good many things besides the Rhenish." I am reading Walpole's Letters. The clever wag! how pleasantly he writes, though rather self-conscious in style.

20th. There was a beautiful wedding to-day; the chimes ringing, as if Cambridge were still a village. This and the lovely June weather made a very pleasant occasion.

26th. The Paradise published to-day. And so endeth the Divine Comedy! Greene arrives in the evening, and we celebrate the occasion with a little supper.

27th. A rainy day. Read Mrs. Radcliffe's novel, the Romance of the Forest. Was this the sensation novel of the last generation? How feeble it seems!

July 1. Greene departs for home, and so ends a short but pleasant visit. What cheer there is in the face of an old friend!

8th. *Nahant.* Read Erckmann-Chatrian's pretty novel, *Le Blocus.* There is a great charm about the style; very simple and sweet in tone. Always, even in depicting war, he preaches the gospel of peace.

9th. Reading over Ariosto's *Orlando Furioso.* Easy, elegant narrative, and prodigality of strange adventure; but it is verse rather than poetry, after all.

14th. The Rev. Mr. —— preached a sermon against Liberal Christianity. He seems to prefer the illiberal.

18th. Dip into the Greek Anthology; the most melancholy of books, with an odor of dead garlands about it. Voices from the grave, cymbals of Bacchantes, songs of love, sighs, groans, prayers,—all mingled together. I never read a book that made me sadder.

August 1. Fields and Mrs F. came with Mr. White, President of the new Cornell University, to dine.

2d. A foggy morning; and the lazy sea heaving in with a low wash, wash, on the rocks. The sun begins to break through the mist. There are few things so beautiful as the clearing of the fog. I will go down and watch it.

To John Neal.

August 2, 1867.

I had the pleasure of receiving your letter yesterday, and am very happy to get your hearty approval of my attempt to tell the exact truth of Dante. A great many people think that a translation ought not to be too faithful; that the writer should put *himself* into it as well as his original; that it should be Homer and Co., or Dante and Co.; and that what the foreign author really says should be falsified or modified, if thereby the smoothness of the verse can be improved. On the contrary I maintain — and am delighted that you agree with me — that a translator, like a witness on the stand, should hold up his right hand and swear to "tell the truth, the whole truth, and nothing but the truth." You, who all your life long have been fighting for the truth in all things, without fear or favor, could not, I am sure, think otherwise.

To Ferdinand Freiligrath.

NAHANT, August 12, 1867.

I have received and read with great eagerness and pleasure your three letters, in which you give me exactly the kind of information I wanted about yourself and your family; so that I feel now as if I really knew your children as well as you and your wife. I have read also with the deepest interest the several accounts, in the paper and pamphlet you were so kind as to send, of the honors done you in your native country.

The whole movement seems to be a national one; and I am delighted to see the German heart thus warm towards you. I can well imagine that some indiscreet individual may do or say something now and then which will not be exactly pleasant; but the whole movement is so honorable to you and to all concerned in it, and so spontaneous and universal that you ought to accept it with joy.

You are called back to your country as Dante wished to be to his, — by acclamation. It is your coronation. How well you deserved it, it is not needful for me to say. . . .

Very curious and interesting is your discussion of that favorite metre of Burns; and your conclusion is doubtless perfectly correct. It came into Scotland with French claret, and both became equally popular. Very amusing and cleverly done are those lines on cleaning your study. I sympathize with you, as I suppose every bookish man must. But not every one gets his sorrows so well sung.

No doubt, after a while you will gravitate back to the Continent.

I do not wholly despair of meeting you again on the Rhine, though I confess the chances at present are somewhat against it.

22d. Called on Agassiz, and found him busy dissecting a huge skate. Intolerable fishy odor in his room.

23d. Wakened at six by singing of sailors, and looking out of the window saw the Alice [1] at her moorings. All landed safe for breakfast.

26th. Sail down to Manchester in the Alice, with all the family, to visit the Danas. Pace the sands with the old poet. Leave E. and A. behind to make a visit.

28th. I miss the little girls very much; though W. and his sister are here to take their place.

30th. Went down to Manchester with Fields. Oh, quaint, quiet little sea-side village! Rambled through its streets with Mr. and Mrs. F., and climbed the rocks, and then home to dinner at their pleasant house, where I found Dr. Bartol and his wife, and Johnson the artist, and others. Drove to Dana's for the children.

September 2. A bright morning. The sea very calm, sending up along the rocks and beaches a long, low respiration: —

[1] Mr. T. G. Appleton's yacht.

"secondo che per ascoltare
Non avea pianto, ma che di sospiri
Che l'aura eterna facevan tremare."[1]

To G. W. Greene.

NAHANT, September 4, 1867.

I have this morning received your letter, which says so much in so few words. It is very sad. Knowing what that sorrow is, I deeply sympathize with you and your wife. No one who has not undergone such a bereavement can have any idea of the keenness of the affliction that has fallen upon you. I cannot console you, I can only feel for you and with you. Such ploughshares do not go over us for naught; they turn up the deepest parts of our natures, and make us more akin to all who have suffered. I hope you will all have strength to bear it; but it is hard to bear.

20th. Return home. Sail up to Boston in the "Alice," and walk out to Cambridge in the evening.

24th. Forenoon, attended the funeral of Sir Frederick Bruce, the British Minister. In the afternoon go to Portland.

29th. Mr. Macmillan, the English publisher, and Professor Child dine with me. After dinner Lowell and Fields come in. We sit out, in the lovely weather, till sunset.

October 1. Give the morning to business. In the evening, go to hear Emerson lecture on "Eloquence." Then a

[1] There, in so far as I had power to hear,
Were lamentations none, but only sighs
That tremulous made the everlasting air.

Inferno iv. 25.

supper at Fields's, where Mr. Macmillan is staying. Mr. and Mrs. Emerson, Agassiz, Dr. Holmes, Lowell, Wendell Phillips.

2d. Dine with Sumner for the last time in the old house (in Hancock Street, Boston). At sunset, walk across the bridge with Sumner, and take leave of him at the end of it.

13th. Had good Mr. Folsom to dine with us. He grows old; it is like a summer sunset fading away.

14th. Rev. E. Hale came out with Newman Hall, the popular preacher. Go into town in the evening to hear him speak at the Music Hall, on "The Relations between England and America during the Late War." He made out a very good case for England, and kept his immense audience interested for two hours.

From A. P. Stanley.

DEANERY, WESTMINSTER, Oct. 15, 1867.

MY DEAR SIR, — You will pardon me, although a stranger personally, in writing to express to you, in case it has not already been said by some other and nearer member of the family, how deeply was valued and felt your last tribute to the memory of Sir Frederick Bruce in attending the funeral ceremony in Boston. We had heard from him how much he had enjoyed his intercourse with you. We little thought that the next time we should hear of you in connection with him would be in the tidings that your venerable presence would be honoring his memory in death. It is the hardest of all tasks to believe at such a moment that "celestial benedictions assume this dark disguise." Yet as we stood in Dunfermline Abbey, where his remains are laid beside his brother Robert's, and within the same walls that contain the burial-place of his royal ancestors, I would fain hope that

"Amid these earthly damps,
What seem to us but sad, funereal tapers
May be Heaven's distant lamps."

My dear wife, his beloved sister, begs me to ask you to accept the enclosed likeness of that old church, so dear to her race. He lies under the projecting transept which has been built against the ancient edifice.

Once more let me ask you to forgive this intrusion, and to receive this assurance of gratitude for this last service from one who has often felt how much he owed to you for the expression of thoughts which bind together our two countries by the best of all possible bonds.

Yours sincerely,

ARTHUR P. STANLEY.

17th Walk up to Norton's. He shows me some of Turner's sketches, — originals, which he has just received from Ruskin.

26th. At the Club dinner, many strangers. Among them, Lord Amberley, Mr. Hamilton, Mr. Vogeli. Lord A. is son of Earl Russell. Mr. H. is in the Colonial Office; I asked him to dinner to-morrow. Mr. V. is a Frenchman, living in Brazil, who has come to Cambridge to translate Agassiz's new book on Brazil.

November 2. The funeral of Governor Andrew, whom all men delight to honor.

6th. Ticknor and Fields give a beautiful banquet at the Union Club, in honor of the *Divina Commedia* translation. Among other guests, R. H. Dana, of the Old Guard of literature; Dr. Hayes, the Arctic explorer; Lord Amberley, etc.[1]

[1] During dinner, a lovely wreath of choice flowers was brought him, from Mrs. Fields, Mrs. Stowe, and Lady Amberley.

14th. Lord and Lady Amberley dined with me. Had Agassiz to meet them. In the evening, drove to the Observatory.

20th. Dined with Dr. Holmes. On my way, stopped at the Parker House to see Dickens [just arrived from England], whom I found very well and most cordial. It was right pleasant to see him again, after so many years, — twenty-five! He looks somewhat older, but is as elastic and quick in his movement as ever. At Holmes's we had the Earl of Camperdown, Lord Morley, and Mr. Cowper; all very agreeable gentlemen.

21st. Young Holmes called with Lord C., who brings me a letter from Motley, and whom I like very much. Dined with Fields, — a dinner of welcome to Dickens.

22d. In town. Passed through the Public Garden, and saw Story's statue of Everett, which is good. In the evening Dickens came out to a little supper.

28th. Thanksgiving-day. Dickens came out to a quiet family dinner.

29th. In the afternoon Agassiz came to read us the sheets of his closing chapters on Brazil.

December 2. A snow-storm, stopping at noon. Dickens's first Reading. We all went; a pleasant moonlight drive. A triumph for Dickens. It is not reading exactly, but acting; and quite wonderful in its way. He gave the Christmas Carol and the "Trial," from Pickwick. The old judge was equal to Dogberry.

5th and 6th. Dickens's Readings.

January 1, 1868. The new year begins with a snow-storm. E. had, in the evening, a girl and boy party, with music, and dancing, and supper; very charming.

2d. A call from my old pupil and successor at Brunswick, Professor Goodwin, now of Philadelphia. A pleasant talk of old times.

To Charles Sumner.

January 12, 1868.

What a beautiful thing is silence! and yet one may carry it a great deal too far. For instance, I have not yet answered your Christmas greeting, and it is past Twelfth-night! I will not wish you a happy New Year; only a *happier* one. That, I am sure, is possible; and from the depth of my heart I wish it may be yours.

I am seriously meditating a flight to Europe in the spring or early summer. First to England, then to the Continent. I think I can accomplish it; and it would do me great good, mentally and bodily.

Dickens has been, and is still, triumphant. His readings — or recitations, rather — are wonderful to hear and see. Sergeant Buzfuz's argument to the jury in "Bardell vs. Pickwick," would delight you. In what raptures our dear Felton would be, were he now alive!

To Miss F——.

January 24, 1868.

Your letters about the Dante were altogether the pleasantest that have come to me from England on the subject. I am indeed very glad that you liked the translation. I hold that the primary object of all translation is to tell us exactly what a foreign author says; while many others think that a translator may take all kinds of liberties with his original.

. . . Our winter here has been rather cold and solitary, and quite uneventful, save in the advent of Mr. Dickens. His readings have enlivened us; and are, as you know, wonderful in their way, and very interesting. I presume you have heard him, and it is not necessary to enlarge upon that topic.

When the weather is dull and cold, we talk of going to Europe in the spring. When it grows milder, we are content to stay at home and avoid the troubles of travelling, repeating the German proverb,—

"Osten und Westen,
Zu Haus am besten."

A fortnight on board an Atlantic steamer is not an exhilarating subject of contemplation.

In speaking of Dickens, I ought to have added that in all the cities where he has read, he has been received with great enthusiasm; and the popularity of his works was never greater in America than now. This puts to flight the fears and surmises of those who thought there was still some lurking grudge against him here, on account of his American Notes and Martin Chuzzlewit. The result of his coming here is a great triumph. When I listen to Dickens, I always think how Felton would have enjoyed these readings; for he was one of the most constant and ardent admirers of the great novelist; and his wide sympathies made it possible for him to appreciate and enjoy all varieties of character. We still mourn for Felton.

I hope you have no brother nor friend in the Abyssinian expedition. From this distance it looks like a forlorn piece of work, which one would like to see well ended.

29th. Took up my New England Tragedy, to remodel it.[1] Wrote a fresh scene.

30th. Remodelled and versified the first scene of act i. of the Tragedy. There is good material in it, if I can fashion it.

February 4. I have worked pretty steadily on the Tragedy; rewriting it from the beginning. Owen came

[1] It was at first written in prose, and a few copies were printed.

in the afternoon, bringing Mr. M. of Salem, Mr. Fry of England, — descended from the Quakeress, Mrs. Fry. He gave me a photograph of her, — from a portrait, of course.

10th. Went to town, for the first time for a fortnight. The Tragedy is finished. I have worked steadily on it, for it took hold of me, — a kind of *possession*. Evening at Professor Horsford's, to meet Senator Morgan of New York, who is versed in Indian affairs.

11th. The day is dark and dreary. A letter from Sumner, which is also dark and dreary. Evening at T.'s, where were some beautiful *tableaux*; and the most beautiful was M. L—— as a "portrait by Copley."

12th. Having finished the Tragedy of the Quakers, I now design another, on Witchcraft.

14th. Read John Neal's Rachel Dyer, a tale of Witchcraft. Some parts very powerful. I am overwhelmed with unanswered letters.

15th. Wrote a scene of the new tragedy. I think I shall call it 'Giles Corey of the Salem Farms.' A homely name; so is the subject. It is taking hold of me powerfully.

18th. Wrote two scenes, — one of them the trial scene. If this possession lasts, I shall soon finish the work.

19th. 'Cotton Mather in his Study;' mostly in his own words.[1]

To J. T. Fields.

February 19, 1868.

I am delighted with Mrs. Fields's kind remembrance and invitation for the 27th. And if I have not accepted it sooner, attribute it only to one thing; namely, that since I saw you I have been possessed by an angel — or a demon — to write another tragedy, which has absorbed

[1] This scene was omitted in printing.

me for a time, and is now half finished. So I have two to show you instead of one, — an awful consideration!

Tom Appleton has been here to-day, and tells me that you are expecting Dickens this evening. I shall be delighted to sup with you, as I always am. To have a Dickens Reading, and a supper too, will make a great holiday.

Please do not say a word to anybody about the Tragedies. I want that kept a secret for the present.

21st. There seems to be a witch element in the air. As I walked down to the Square this morning, I saw a great placard on a fence, with a picture. It was the advertisement of a new sensation-story, — The Witch Proof; or, the Hunted Maid of Salem

24th, 25th. Dickens Reading [the second series].

27th. My birthday Evening, Dickens read the Carol, and "Boots at the Holly-Tree Inn." Then there was a supper at Fields's, in honor of the day! Dickens wrote me a nice letter on the occasion.

From Charles Dickens.

BOSTON, February 27, 1868.

MY DEAR LONGFELLOW, — I wish you from my deepest heart many, many happy returns of this day, — a precious one to the civilized world, — and all earthly happiness and prosperity. God bless you, my dear friend! I hope to welcome you at Gad's Hill this next summer, and to give you the heartiest reception that the undersigned village blacksmith can strike out of his domestic anvil.

Dolby will report that I have been terrifying him by sneezing melodiously for the last half-hour. The moment there is a fall from the sky, this national catarrh gives me an extra grip. I dare not come to Fields's to-night, having to read to-morrow; but you shall in my flowing cups (or sneezes) be especially remembered after to-night's reading.

Even your imagination cannot conceive how admiringly, tenderly, and truly,

Ever your affectionate CHARLES DICKENS.

From R. H. Dana, Jr.

February 28, 1868.

MY DEAR MR. LONGFELLOW, — I regretted extremely that I could not join the circle that honored your birthday last night at Fields's. It was in my heart to go, but Dr. Langmaid tells me that I have a little bronchitis; and as I must speak in the House, I must not expose myself, and must keep early hours, and the like. . . .

Mrs. Dana and I regretted my hard fate, at home, and thought what your birthday had been for letters, for American letters, and especially for your friends, — among whom we hope always to be.

With the best wishes for the year to come,

Yours faithfully, RICHARD H. DANA, JR.

29th. All this week, have done little or nothing on the Tragedy. And I hoped to have finished it before my birthday. A. and I dined with Dickens at the Parker House, — a grand banquet given by him to Mrs. F——. We were eighteen in all.

March 2. At the rooms of the Historical Society, to look over King James's Dæmonologie. After my return I finished the Tragedy.

3d. Retouch it here and there, and fill up gaps.

4th. Gave a dinner to Dickens.

To Charles Sumner.

March 9, 1868.

I have been so very busy, and so much driven to and fro by visitors and various things, that I have not had time to write you for a long while.

In the month of February I wrote two tragedies in verse, — one on the persecution of the Quakers in Boston, which I had sketched out before [and indeed written and printed in prose]; and another, entirely new, on the Salem Witchcraft. Please say nothing of this; as I may never publish them, and can hardly yet form an opinion of them, they are so fresh from my mind.

The European expedition is taking shape. We are going at the end of May, — probably in the "Russia," on the 27th. I do not like the breaking up of home and drifting about the Old World; but I suppose it is for the best. I hope to come back better in body and mind. I need a good shaking up, and expect to get it.

I am sorry, very sorry, that I cannot run on to Washington to see you before I go; but there is no chance of that, I fear.

Thanks for your Speech. I liked it greatly.

Good-night. God bless you.

April 6, 1868. The printers get on slowly with the New England Tragedies.[1] The printing-office is a kind of court of chancery, — once in and you can never get out.

8th. In town. Muddy, sloppy, drippy. Dickens's last Reading, and a triumphant one, with abundant flowers and a "little speech."

[1] Only ten copies were printed at this time.

16th. A whole week of aches and pains and influenza. A young Prussian from Berlin, a pleasant youth, well read in German and English literature, and professing himself a firm believer in the Divine Right of Kings.

30th. Mr. and Mrs. Waterston came out, with Mr. Ernst Perabo, the young musician; and we had a charming musical evening. He played Beethoven divinely. I never heard such expression given to the music of the great master. My old schoolmate and classmate, Patrick Henry Greenleaf, was here, and we were all delighted.

To G. W. Greene.

May 5, 1868.

I am sorry that you are not here this week, as it presents unusual attractions in the way of moonlight, mist, and music. Every day an oratorio, and every night a concert. On Friday afternoon Beethoven's Ninth Symphony!

All my preparations are completed for the voyage; and, strange to say, I begin to think the life at sea will be very agreeable. Come as soon as you can.

May 17. Suddenly, with a gush of song and sunshine, after long days of rain and dreary weather, spring and summer come together, bride and bridegroom, — blush of youth, and heat of passion.

23d. Rain like the deluge. A parting dinner at the Fields's. Very beautiful with flowers and all pleasant things. The guests were Greene, Holmes, Agassiz, Dana, Lowell, Norton, and Whipple. Holmes read a charming poem, and we enjoyed ourselves extremely.

27th. Sailed from New York for Liverpool in the steamer Russia.

These were the verses read by Dr. Holmes at the farewell dinner: —

Our Poet, who has taught the Western breeze
To waft his songs before him o'er the seas,
Will find them wheresoe'er his wanderings reach,
Borne on the spreading tide of English speech,
Twin with the rhythmic waves that kiss the farthest beach.

Where shall the singing bird a stranger be
That finds a nest for him in every tree?
How shall he travel, who can never go
Where his own voice the echoes do not know,
Where his own garden-flowers no longer learn to grow?

Ah, gentlest soul! how gracious, how benign
Breathes through our troubled life that voice of thine,
Filled with a sweetness born of happier spheres,
That wins and warms, that kindles, softens, cheers,
That calms the wildest woe, and stays the bitterest tears!

Forgive the simple words that sound like praise;
The mist before me dims my gilded phrase;
Our speech at best is half alive and cold,
And save that tenderer moments make us bold
Our whitening lips would close, their truest truth untold.

We who behold our autumn sun below
The Scorpion's sign, against the Archer's bow,
Know well what parting means of friend from friend;
After the snows no freshening dews descend,
And what the frost has marred, the sunshine will not mend.

So we all count the months, the weeks, the days
That keep thee from us in unwonted ways,
Grudging to alien hearths our widowed time;
And one unwinds a clew of artless rhyme
To track thee, following still through each remotest clime.

What wishes, longings, blessings, prayers shall be
The more than golden freight that floats with thee!
And know, whatever welcome thou shalt find,—
Thou who hast won the hearts of half mankind,—
The proudest, fondest love thou leavest still behind!

CHAPTER VII.

LAST VISIT IN EUROPE.

1868–1869.

MR. LONGFELLOW was now to carry out the long contemplated plan of another visit to Europe, to which his travelled heart had so often and so fondly turned. His son, just married, was about to make the tour, and he decided to accompany him, taking his three young daughters. The party was increased by his two sisters and a brother, and Mr. T. G. Appleton added his lively companionship. From Liverpool the party went at once to the English Lakes, a thing by all means to be done by American travellers arriving in June; for then the shores of Windermere, besides their constant beauty, are glorified by the great plantations of blooming rhododendrons which embellish the grounds about them. Mr. Longfellow especially enjoyed the brief visit at Bowness and its neighborhood, including the trip to Furness Abbey. From Keswick he went with his daughters to visit his friend Mr. Robert Ferguson, at Morton near Carlisle. Here he received a public address of

Flow on, fair stream! that dream is o'er;
He stands upon another shore;
A vaster river near him flows,
And still he follows where it goes.

– Henry W. Longfellow.

compliment and welcome, to which he replied.[1] And from here he visited Corby Castle and Eden Hall, where he saw the famous goblet still entirely unshattered, spite of Uhland's ballad which he had translated in former years. Returning to Lowood on Windermere, he set out for Cambridge, to be the guest of the Master of Gonville and Caius College. And here, in the Senate-House, "at the Congregation on Tuesday, June 16th," he was publicly admitted to the honorary degree of Doctor of Laws, "in the presence of a large concourse of spectators." One of these gave to the press this description of the scene: —

"Amid a score or so of Heads of Houses and other Academic dignitaries conspicuous by their scarlet robes, the one on whom all eyes were turned was Henry Wadsworth Longfellow. The face was one which would have caught the spectator's glance, even if not called to it

[1] Mr. Longfellow, upon receiving the address, said: —

MR. PRESIDENT and GENTLEMEN, — Being more accustomed to speak with the pen than with the tongue, it is somewhat difficult for me to find appropriate words now to thank you for the honor you have done me, and the very kind expressions you have used. Coming here as a stranger, this welcome makes me feel that I am not a stranger; for how can a man be a stranger in a country where he finds all doors and all hearts open to him? Besides, I myself am a Cumberland man, — I was born in the County of Cumberland, in the State of Maine, three thousand miles from here, — and you all know that the familiar name of a town or country has a home-like sound to our ears. . . . You can think then how very grateful it is to me — how very pleasant — to find my name has a place in your memories and your affections. For this kindness I most heartily thank you, and I reciprocate all the good wishes which you have expressed for perpetual peace and amity between our two nations. — *Carlisle Paper.*

by the cheers which greeted his appearance in the red robes of an LL.D. Long, white, silken hair and a beard of patriarchal whiteness enclosed a fresh-colored countenance, with fine-cut features and deep-sunken eyes, overshadowed by massive eyebrows. In a few well-rounded Latin sentences, Mr. Clark, the Public Orator, recited the claims of the distinguished visitor to the privilege of an honorary degree. The names of *Hiawatha* and *Evangeline* sounded strangely amid the sonorous periods." "In one portion [wrote another correspondent] he drew a picture of the function of poetry to solace the ills of life and draw men from its low cares *ad excelsiora.* This point was caught at once by the undergraduates, and drew forth hearty cheering. The degree was then conferred; after which Mr. Longfellow took his place upon the dais."

The English papers very generally gave a paragraph to Mr. Longfellow's arrival, usually with some criticism upon his poetry, in which the phrase, "household words" largely figured. The Daily News, in an elaborate article, said: —

"He is the familiar friend, who has sung to every household, and set to music their aspirations and their affections. He is the poet of our sober English nature, with its deep undercurrent of earnestness and enthusiasm, yet with its dislike of extravagance, and its joy in the tender relations of life. He shows us the poetic side of ordinary events."

The Spectator, after some satirical qualifications of his earlier and more popular poems, such as the 'Psalm of Life,' and 'Excelsior,' regrets that he should be known and loved for these rather than for —

"the sweet and limpid purity, the shy and graceful humor, the cool and perfectly natural colors and forms, and the thoroughly original conception and treatment, of his later poems, especially that which will doubtless live as long as the English language, Hiawatha. For playful and tender interpretation of the way in which the child-like tribes measure themselves against the powers and the creatures by which they are surrounded, there is not anything like it in any language." And after a column given to Hiawatha it adds: "It seems to us that the poem of which we have ventured to say so much, — not the only poem in which Mr. Longfellow's true genius is shown, — is one of the really permanent contributions to modern literature, and that no other genius known to us would have been in any way equal to the work. We wish that England could be as grateful to Mr. Longfellow for this as we think she ought to be."

Arrived in London on the 26th of June, Mr. Longfellow with his party took rooms in the Langham Hotel. Immediately a flood of hospitality flowed in upon him, — calls, cards, invitations, letters of welcome. He breakfasted with Mr. Gladstone, Sir Henry Holland, the Duke of Argyll; lunched with Lord John Russell at Richmond, dined with various hosts, received midnight calls from Bulwer and Aubrey de Vere. Through Lady Augusta Stanley came an intimation that the Queen would be sorry to have Mr. Longfellow pass through England without her meeting him, and a day was named for his visit to Windsor. The Queen received him cordially and without ceremony in one of the galleries of the Castle. He also called, by request, upon the Prince of Wales. With his daughters he spent a Sunday at Gadshill. By invitation of Dean Stanley he attended the evening service at Westminster Abbey to hear a sermon from Dr. Jowett, and took tea afterward at the Deanery; and there was a visit to the Archbishop of Canterbury at Lambeth Palace. His countryman, Mr. Bierstadt, the landscape painter, gave in his honor a great dinner, at the Langham Hotel, where were met several hundred of the celebrities in literature and art, science and politics. Mr. Longfellow had stipulated for "no speeches." But at the close of the dinner there were loud calls for Mr. Gladstone, in response to which he said, as reported, that

"they must be permitted to break through the restrictions which the authority of their respected host had imposed upon them, and to give expression to the feelings which one and all entertained on this occasion. After all, it was simply impossible to sit at the social board with a man of Mr. Longfellow's world-wide fame, without offering him some tribute of their admiration. There was perhaps no class of persons less fitted to do justice to an occasion of this character than those who were destined to tread the toilsome and dusty road of politics. Nevertheless, he was glad to render his tribute of hearty admiration to one whom they were glad to welcome not only as a poet but as a citizen of America."

Mr. Longfellow replied, in a few words, that

"they had taken him by surprise, a traveller but just landed and with Bradshaw still undigested upon his brain, and they would not expect him to make a speech. There were times, indeed, when it was easier to speak than to act; but it was not so with him, now. He would, however, be strangely constituted if he did not in his heart respond to their kind and generous welcome. In the longest speech he could make, he could but say in many phrases what he now said in a few sincere words,—that he was deeply grateful for the kindness which had been shown him."[1]

After a fortnight in London, the party journeyed by Salisbury to the Isle of Wight, where was a pleasant visit of two days with Mr. Tennyson. From thence they went by way of Dover to the Continent, going up the Rhine to Switzerland. There the summer was spent, with a charming parenthesis of a trip over the St. Gothard pass to Lugano and Cadenabbia on the Lake of Como,—a delicious bit of Italy, long after embalmed in a poem. The autumn found the party in Paris. The Paris of the Second Empire had little in its literature to interest Mr. Longfellow. He was most interested in hearing Molière at the Théâtre Français, in exploring what remained of the old localities of literary history, or in haunting the booksellers and the stalls of the *quais*, in the company of M. Marmier, afterward Member of the

[1] Mr. R. C. Winthrop relates an incident of the London visit. As he was leaving the House of Lords in company with Mr. Longfellow, from out of a group of people upon the sidewalk a laboring man came forward, and asking if it were the poet, begged to be allowed to shake hands with him. This, of course, was willingly granted; but when he proceeded to recite a verse of 'Excelsior,' its author was glad to make his escape.

Academy, whose acquaintance he then made. At the close of the autumn, travel was resumed, southward, through Arles, with its Dantean *Aliscamps*; and then along the Cornice into Italy. This last journey was made in carriages,—the young people of the party finding endless pleasure in repeating Tennyson's poem, 'The Daisy,' which, stanza by stanza, paints in delicious vignettes every step of that lovely way.

After a few weeks' stay in Florence, the wings of travel were folded for the winter in Rome,—in the Hotel Costanzi, above the Piazza Barberini, whose windows command so fine a view over the whole city to where St. Peter's dome darkens against the sunset. Here Mr. Longfellow became for the season the centre of the group of American visitors and resident artists, whose well-known names need not be recounted. Here he made, also, acquaintances among the Italians,—especially the Duke of Sermoneta, the Dantean scholar, and Monsignore Nardi, of the papal court. The Pope himself he did not visit. An interesting acquaintance was that made with the Abbé Liszt, who was spending the winter in Rome, having rooms in the abandoned Convent of Santa Francesca, in the Forum. Calling there one evening, in company with Mr. Healy the artist, the inner door of the apartment was opened to them by Liszt himself, holding high in his hand a candle which illuminated his fine face. The picture was so striking that Mr. Longfellow begged his companion to put it upon canvas, — which he did; and the painting now hangs in the library of Craigie House. At a morning visit, Liszt delighted the party with a performance upon his Chickering piano-forte.[1]

To "see Rome," as all travellers know, is a work for many months; and it was pursued with tolerable diligence. But Mr. Longfellow was never a good sight-seer. He was impatient of lingering in picture-galleries, churches, or ruins. He saw quickly the essential points, and soon tired of any minuter examination.

With the spring, travel was renewed, — still southward, to Naples and its environs.[2] There was a night with the Benedictines at Monte Casino, and a trip to Amalfi, both of which he afterwards sang in verse; an excursion to Pœstum; and a stay amid the siren charms of Sorrento. Then the party went northward to Venice, and over the Brenner to Innspruck, Munich, Nuremberg, and Dresden; and across Switzerland to

[1] Liszt afterward set to characteristic music the introduction to The Golden Legend.

[2] Soon after Mr. Longfellow's death, there appeared in the London Times a letter, purporting to give an account of the writer's acquaintance with the poet while in Naples. There was a detailed story of an ascent of Vesuvius, in which Mr. Longfellow insisted upon being left to spend the night alone upon the mountain, "to gain inspiration;" and a still more detailed report of his conversation on the return journey the next day. The whole is pure fiction. Mr. Longfellow did not visit, much less ascend, Vesuvius; least of all did he spend the night there, for "inspiration" or any other purpose. With this story, of course, the pretended conversation also falls to the ground It is possible that some one may have passed himself off, in jest or otherwise, as the American poet.

Paris. A few days again in London, a day at Oxford where he received the degree of D. C. L., a tour through Devonshire, and then to Edinburgh, the Scottish lakes, and the Burns region, completed the European journey.

During this crowded eighteen months of travel, Mr. Longfellow had little time for journalizing, or even for letter-writing. There were two bits of diary, written in the days of quiet at Sorrento, and by the Lake of Como, — the two most enchanting spots of Italy, — and a few letters.

To Robert Ferguson.

STATION HOTEL, YORK, June 19, 1868.

We reached York with great comfort, at 5.35 to the minute. I hope you were as fortunate in reaching Carlisle. We had not left the station when the train came in from Leeds, bringing all the rest of the party. Ernest came yesterday. We all stop at this hotel, which is a very good one; even more, — an excellent one. Our drawing-room window looks out upon the cathedral.

That cathedral! If I said my say about it, you would think me sixteen, instead of sixty. So I will be silent.

To-morrow we go to Matlock and Rowsley, where we pass Sunday. On Monday or Tuesday, to Malvern; and trust to meet you there, to make the tour of Stratford, Kenilworth, etc.

In great haste, with much love from my darlings.

To Mrs. J. T. Fields.

BONCHURCH, July 19, 1868.

This letter is dated from your favorite hotel in the Isle of Wight, and from parlor No. 4, with a glimpse of flowers.

hedges, and tops of trees in the hollow, and of the blue sea beyond. This is literally my first day of rest; and I, as you see, have not gone to church with all the others of my party, but am here writing with hotel ink and a barbarous pen.

We came last night from Freshwater, where we had passed two happy days with Tennyson, — not at his house, but mostly with him. He was very cordial, and very amiable; and gave up his whole time to us. At Farringford your memory is fresh and fragrant.

Since landing in England I have not had one leisure moment. I cannot describe to you the overwhelming hospitality with which I have been greeted, and will not attempt it. From Liverpool we went to the Lakes; then to Carlisle. Then I swooped down to Cambridge, where I had a scarlet gown put upon me, and the students shouted "Three cheers for the red man of the West." Then I went to York, and down through Derbyshire to London, where I stayed a fortnight and saw everybody, from the Archbishop of Canterbury to —— ——.

I do not mean to palm this off upon you as a letter. It is only a word to tell you where I am, and to thank you for your and Fields's joint letter, duly received in London.

I and my girls passed a pleasant Sunday at Gad's Hill.

To G. W. Greene.

Shanklin, Isle of Wight, July 21, 1868.

I write you this from a lovely little thatch-roofed inn, all covered with ivy, and extremely desirable to the tired American traveller. Opposite the door is a new fountain, for which I have been requested to write an inscription; and our windows look down upon the quaintest little village you ever saw. It is all like a scene on the stage.

The landlady is a portly dame; the head-waiter, a red-faced Alsatian; and when the chambermaid appears, you expect she will sing instead of speak.

Such are our surroundings. We are all well, and all hot, the thermometer being at 84° in the shade. To-morrow we take steamer from Dover to the Continent.

In England I have been most heartily welcomed; and in London almost killed with kindness. The number of letters I have had to answer is incredible, which is the reason I have not written you sooner. I have seen almost everybody I most cared to see in England, and now am quite ready for the Continent. I think of you often, and often envy you your quiet study, while I am so banged about in the heat.

To Charles Sumner.

SHANKLIN, July 21, 1868.

If you have been in Shanklin, and stopped at Hollier's, you will know exactly where we are, and how we are. Last night I slept for the first time under a roof of thatch. It is very rural, and extremely pleasant. In fine, this is one of the quietest and loveliest places in the kingdom; and at last I get a moment of leisure to write to you, which I have not had before.

And now I know hardly where to begin, or what to say. London was very hot, and very hurried. I was whirled about from morning to night, without rest. You remember how it is, in the season. The Argylls were most kind, in all ways. From the Duchess I received a very cordial letter at Malvern, and I had my first London breakfast with them. I need not say that of you they retain the most affectionate remembrance.

I cannot tell you of all the people I lunched and dined with. Lord Stanhope and all his family were particularly kind. So were the Gladstones, — so was everybody.

To James R. Lowell.

INTERLAKEN, August 14, 1868.

I fear I am a restless and uncomfortable kind of traveller. I no sooner reach a place than, like the character in the Vicar of Wakefield, who was collecting materials for the Life of the celebrated Mr. Trip, I "exhibit a great desire to be gone again." The truth is, I believe in rapid travelling, with one's eyes open; and I observe that people who stay long in places always waste their time in lounging about the hotels.

All summer long the heat has been almost intolerable and incessant, and I have oftener longed for Nahant than I confess to anybody. There is very little snow on the mountains, and the Jungfrau looks wrinkled, and brown, and old. Nevertheless, there is no disappointment in Switzerland. It outbids the imagination with its grandeurs and perpetual surprises.

The memory of my welcome in England is very pleasant to me. It was most cordial and sincere in every way. It was only by dint of great resolution that I escaped a dozen public and semi-public dinners. The private hospitalities were more to my taste, and were endless.

I passed a couple of delightful days with Tennyson at the Isle of Wight, though I insisted on sleeping at my own inn. If two men should try to look alike, they could not do it better than he and Professor Lovering do without trying.

I write this in heat and weariness. My hand trembles; but it shall not tremble when I say how affectionately I am always yours.

To J. T. Fields.

LUGANO, August 23, 1868.

I write you, much to my own surprise (not to mention yours), from this lovely lake. We came here by one of those lucky accidents of travel into which unseen postilions drive us. We went to Hospenthal, meaning to cross the Furca and go down the valley of the Rhone to Vevey. But finding the road over the Furca broken by rain and river, we came over the St. Gothard, and through Bellinzona to this place, — a beautiful two days' drive through the valley of the Ticino, the Val Tremola, Val Levantina, Val d'Agno. Ah, me, how charming it was, and is, and ever will be!

Delightful it is to be once more in Italy. I already feel the fascination of the old Siren; and if it were later in the season I would not turn back. As it is, in a day or two we are going over the Simplon to resume the broken route of the Rhone valley. But it is really too pleasant here to think of going anywhere else. You remember this Hôtel du Parc, once a convent. The very chambermaids look like nuns, or the ghosts of nuns. The lapping of the water under the windows, and the view of lake and mountains, will make the "charges moderate," whatever they may be.

To make you more unhappy than you already are, I must not forget to mention a dish of fresh figs beside the inkstand as I write, and a boat with an awning, full in sight, waiting under a willow-tree to take us across the lake. It is such a surprise to me to be here that I enjoy it more than anything else we have seen. The old familiar places saddened me.

And now for business. Please publish the New England Tragedies on Saturday, October 10. That is the day

I have agreed upon with Routledge, with whom I have made a very good arrangement. Tauchnitz will publish on the same day.

I have so many, many things to tell you that there would be no end; therefore there shall be no beginning. Among them is Tennyson's reading 'Boadicea' to me at midnight. A memorable night!

To J. T. Fields.

VEVEY, September 5, 1868.

I do not like your idea of calling the Tragedies "sketches." They are not sketches, and only seem so at first because I have studiously left out all that could impede the action. I have purposely made them simple and direct. [John] Forster, with whom I left the proof-sheets in London, to be made over to Routledge, writes as follows: —

"Your Tragedies are very beautiful, — beauty everywhere subduing and chastening the sadness; the pictures of nature in delightful contrast to the sorrowful and tragic violence of the laws; truth and unaffectedness everywhere. I hardly know which I like best; but there are things in 'Giles Corey' that have a strange attractiveness for me." This to encourage you.

It is a novel and pleasant sensation to publish a book and be so far away from all comment and criticism of newspapers. As to anybody's "adapting" these Tragedies for the stage, I do not like the idea of it at all. Prevent this, if possible. I should, however, like to have the opinion of some good actor — not a sensational actor — on that point. I should like to have Booth look at them.

I wrote you last from Lugano. From that pleasant place we went to one still pleasanter; namely, Cadenabbia on the Lake of Como. That was Italy! and as lovely as

Italy can be when she tries. The climate is delicious; neither hot nor cold, but delightfully tempered with all the elements necessary to make a climate perfect. Not an insect to be seen or heard! and a gentle breath of air stirring up or down the lake all day long, — no more than a large fan would make. No carriage-road leads to Cadenabbia,[1] — only a foot-way, along the borders of the lake, between it and many villas. It is directly opposite Bellagio, but is more beautiful and more desirable. It was very difficult to get away. Going there for one night, we stayed a week. From there we went to the Villa d'Este, near Como; thence across to Luino on Lago Maggiore, and by steamer to Baveno. From Baveno to Duomo d'Ossola; and over the Simplon, through the valley of the Rhone, to this place. You know the road, and you know Vevey and the Hôtel Monnet. But do you know Cadenabbia?

After all, nothing quite equals the sea-breeze of Nahant and Manchester in the heat of summer. This to comfort you.

To J. T. Fields.

Hôtel Windsor, Rue de Rivoli, Paris, October 18, 1868.

When in London, last week, I sent from the Langham Hotel a box of books and papers to your care. I hope they will pass the custom-house without duty, being only presentation copies of books, and odds and ends which accumulated on my hands in London and were left there. Here in Paris, I have made a pretty large collection of books.

I was three days in London.[2] I saw Burlingame, who was looking well, and took a quiet view of the opposition

[1] One has since been made from Menaggio.

[2] He had run over to secure the copyright on the New England Tragedies.

to his mission manifested by the English papers. I saw also Bandmann the tragedian, who expressed the liveliest interest in what I told him of the Tragedies.

20th. Bandmann writes me a nice letter about the Tragedies, but says they are not adapted to the stage. So we will say no more about that for the present.

21st. I have left my letter open for a day, in the hope of finding time to write more. But the busy idleness of Paris is too much for me; and "days are lost lamenting o'er lost days." Yesterday I went to visit the old Rue du Fouarre (*Paradiso* x., note 137). When you come to Paris you must not fail to see it, as it is one of the oldest streets. I shall bring home a picture of it, as an illustration to our Landscape Dante.

I have seen Charles Brunel, the translator of 'Evangeline;' and Prévost Paradol, a good writer on politics; and Sainte-Beuve. My visit to him I shall give you in detail when we meet. Lamartine I have not seen. He is ill, and failing fast, they say. My chief amusement in Paris is buying books and seeing some comedy of Molière at the Théâtre Français. We have very pleasant rooms, looking upon the Tuileries gardens,—airy and sunny.

To J. R. Lowell.

Hôtel dell' Arno, Florence, November 29, 1868.

My first act in Florence was to read your letter; my second is to answer it and return the petition signed. I will write to Sumner to-day.

We arrived last night from Bologna, by the railway over and through the Apennines, with forty-five tunnels. A soft moonlight night, with glimpses of valley and river and town; very beautiful.

We are sumptuously lodged in a palace on the Lung' Arno, within a stone's throw of the Ponte Vecchio. My bedroom, looking over the river, is thirty-three feet by thirty, and high in proportion. I feel as if I were sleeping in some public square, — that of the Gran Duca, for instance, with the David and the Perseus looking at me. I was there this morning before breakfast; so that I fairly woke up there, and rubbed my eyes and wondered if I were awake or dreaming.

I congratulate you upon having passed the fever of a Presidential election. But this was one in which I should like to have had a hand. I am sorry not to have voted.

Appleton left us at Genoa, and went with Ernest to Naples by sea, in search of the eruption of Vesuvius. I hope they got there in season, but doubt it. We came on by Piacenza, Parma, and Bologna. Ah, how I wish we could have a Memorial Hall [in Cambridge] after the model of the old University at Bologna! If we built only one side of the quadrangle at first, it would be enough for our day. Do you remember it? A noble building, with all its memorials of professors and students.

To George W. Greene.

ROME, January 30, 1869.

I have just received your letter, the second I have had from you, and hasten to answer it; for, as you suggest, my conscience *da delle calcagne;* particularly for not writing from Genoa. But what with the shortness of the days there and the dim lamps at night, it was impossible. *Perdonate e compatite.*

In that quaint and ever-charming city I did not stop at our old hotel, but at a newer and better one, close by. I often took my girls to walk on the sea-wall, and pointed out to them our old terrace with its flower-pots and statues; though I confess that it had grown smaller and somewhat shorn of its former splendors. Still, it was a sweet memory, and I always thought of you, even if I did not write to you. Ah, if you were here!

Florence was charming. We were there only three weeks, but are going back again. We had a beautiful apartment close by the Ponte Vecchio, and right in the heart of the mediæval town. Close by, too, was the little church of San Stefano, where Boccaccio read his Comment on Dante; and the Uffizi and the Palazzo Vecchio and Giotto's tower and *il mio bel San Giovanni* [were near]. It was delightful to be there. Ah, if you were here!

Here in Rome we are at a new hotel built in the gardens of Sallust's villa; on a spur of the Quirinal, back of the Barberini palace. In the rear the windows look across the Campagna to the Alban hills. In front we have all Rome, unrolled like a panorama, and crowned by St. Peter's. But with all this, I find Rome very depressing. It is a death-in-life incredible, surprising beyond descrip- tion,—a beleaguered city, bombarded by public opini and the new ideas; still holding out, ringing its alai bells and living on old shoes.[1] It is quite unchange since you and I were here forty years ago. I said so t Cardinal Antonelli the other day; and he answered, takin a pinch of snuff, "Yes, thank God!"

I look out of the window this gray, rainy day, an see the streets all mud and the roofs all green mould, a the mist lying like a pall over the lower town, and R- seems to me like king Lear staggering in the storm. crowned with weeds. od-

But this is altogether too fine writing. Let ueead to prose. Prose is disillusion. But as a chibf her century, I infinitely prefer our American pr kind of European poetry. And, as the Rom te cloud sings,—

Vesuvius,
the wind,
h snow.

[1] In 1869, it will be remembered, Rome was still government.

> Se il Papa mi donasse Campidoglio
> E mi dicesse, "lascia andar sta figlia" (*America*)
> Quella che amava prima, quella voglio.

A Roman gentleman said to me a few days ago, "You as a stranger cannot conceive what an oppression comes over me here in Rome. I have to go out of town to breathe.' The *life* of Italy is in the North, as it is in all countries The Roman poets publish their books in Florence. Milan has become a great, roaring, industrial city. The port of Genoa is as busy as that of Boston.

The most sympathetic and cultivated man I have found here is the Duca di Sermoneta; about my age, but totally blind. He can repeat the *Divina Commedia* from beginning to end. We have long conferences together. I have broached here my idea of a landscape edition of Dante, which meets with great approval. But who will do it?

oı
fo
w

To George W. Greene.

ROME, February 7, 1869.

The carnival has begun, and is a pretty heavy kind of 'un; quite fallen away from its pristine glory. I am ›nging to get off to Naples.

February 9. Yesterday I dined with the Dominican frars at their convent of San Clemente. Archbishop my ning was there, and the chief of the Sant' Offizio, write name I do not remember. We had a jovial dinner, the good wine, and every dish Italian, not to say *Italian*-sible. After dinner, we went into a small coffee-room,

In the inquisitor tried to light a fire, with small suc-at our olde one cried out, "Ah, Padre! the days have I often too hen fires can be lighted by inquisitors!" and out to the great roar of laughter, in which the Padre statues; thed heartily.

and somewh

Journal.

Sorrento, March 25, 1869. Six sunless windows looking out on a sunless sea, — such is our welcome at *La Sirena.* I remember the old English song, —

> " He that the Siren's hair would win
> Is mostly strangled in the tide."

But the Siren sings sweetly at dinner. The dining-room is like a vast bird-cage. There is a marvellous clock in it, and the dinner excellent.

26th. We walk between the showers through the narrow streets of this picturesque old town. In the market-place "Antonio della piccola Marina" smiles upon us and offers his boat for Capri; and in competition Salvatore suggests donkeys for Massa. The rain answers, No! This is no weather for Capri or for Massa. In the evening, a gloomy procession with torches, and a wonderful wooden image of Christ carried on a bier. The Sorrentines are very fond of this image. It was made by an unknown stranger, who took refuge in the church, having committed some unknown crime. "No one," say the Sorrentines, "not even the most learned lawyers in Naples, can tell of what wood it is made."

27th. A brighter day. We change our quarters from the Sirena to the Villa Nardi, which has ample garden-terraces overlooking the sea, hundreds of feet plumb down. Part of the morning we give to buying the beautiful wood-work, the *legni intarsi* of Sorrento. In the evening read in Miss Kavanagh's Two Sicilies, the description of her stay in Sorrento.

29th. After a night of storm, a day of alternate cloud and sunshine. The sea blue, and across the sea Vesuvius, with his white plume of smoke flattened by the wind, and behind Vesuvius the Appenines covered with snow.

"Even as the snow among the living rafters
Upon the back of Italy congeals,
Blown on and drifted by Sclavonian winds."

After breakfast made an excursion to Conti Fontanella on the mountain-ridge back of the town, — Ernest and I on foot, and five of our ladies on five donkeys, named respectively Monaca, Maccaroni, Masantonio, Cardinale, and Secatella. From the summit a fine view. A good three hours' walk.

30th. The terrace of the Villa Nardi, hanging over the sea, is protected by a parapet breast-high, with frequent embrasures or openings with iron railings, like balconies. The parapet is adorned with painted busts of terra cotta. A stairway of stone, partly under the terrace, partly on the face of the cliff, leads down to the beach; and from windows in the covered gallery painted terra-cotta heads lean out, as if enjoying the view and conversing together. I should like to note down their imaginary conversations.

31st. A bright, beautiful day which we devote to the Island of Capri, going merrily over in a six-oared galley under the guidance of "Antonio della piccola Marina." The words of cheer uttered by the boatmen were alternately *Sant' Anton' !* and *Maccaroni !* We went first to the *Grotta Azurra*, the Blue Grotto, which was strange and beautiful. Then we landed at the Marina, amid a noisy crowd of men, women, and donkeys, and climbed the steep hillside to the Albergo Tiberio, once a convent. We lunched in the refectory, with its huge fireplace and Latin inscription.

To Mr. and Mrs. Fields.

VILLA NARDI, SORRENTO, ITALY, April 2, 1869.

MY DEAR FIELDS, OR MRS. FIELDS, — I do not know whether I am writing to you or to your wife or your husband, so intermingled was your last letter, and so like one of those Italian words that have a masculine singular and a feminine plural. No matter; whatever there is of business in my answer goes by right to Mr. F., and all the rest to Mrs. F.; the whole to each and both.

It is something to have such a place to date from as the Villa Nardi, Sorrento. Incessant oranges and lemons, and also incessant rains, — like an endless shower of lemonade ready iced by the snow on the Apennines. As you have already been in Sorrento, and as I am sixty-two and not sixteen, I will spare you all description of scenery. Having one pleasant day this week, we went to Capri and saw the *Grotta Azurra* and the ruins of the Palace of Tiberias, — the *Salto di Timberio* as the Capriotes call it, instead of *Tiberio.* On the way home six lusty oarsmen sang at the top of their voices the song *O Pescator dell' onda;* but they sang it *O Pescator di Londra,* — as if invoking the ancient guild of the Fishmongers.

In Naples I saw the banished partner of the vanished house of Ticknor and Fields. Banishment does not seem to disagree with him; and he, no doubt, owes this to receiving regularly the Atlantic Monthly. I have signed the document you sent me, and will hand it to you when we meet. You see there is no lost letter after all. Alas, for the lost *Château Yquem!* Never mind, I will send home some Capri almost as good.

I am very glad you are coming so soon. Do join us in the north of Italy in May.

April 7. Went to an orange orchard where we ate our fill of oranges from the trees.

8th. In the afternoon went to see the orange and lemon packing in an old dilapidated palace; afterward to see a bust of Tasso in the house of Signor Annuvola; then to what remains of the house in which he was born. In the garden is a laurel-tree.

10th. The Signor Gargiullo is all politeness and hospitality. From the terrace of his house at Capo di Massa is a splendid view of Capri. East and west of Sorrento runs a deep ravine or *burrone* opening on the sea and forming the natural fortification of the town. These are crossed by bridges, and formerly there were lofty stone gates; but these, alas! the Syndic of Sorrento in his rage for modern improvements has taken down, to the great loss of picturesqueness.

11th. This is the loveliest of the lovely days by the sea. A white cloud hovers above Vesuvius, and the snow on the Apennines gleams with a rosy hue. A thin, tender haze lies along the horizon, a sail or two, here and there, and dolphins disport themselves in the water. This is more like the home of the Sirens than anything we have seen. Looking at this, we pass hours on the terrace, till idleness becomes almost oppressive. Our stay at Sorrento is drawing to a close. I am not very sorry. I do not like to stay so long in a place as to have regrets at leaving it. And I am afraid that I am growing a little weary of this *vita beata* of the sea-side, with nothing to do. Or am I hurried by what still remains to be done?

12th. The weather has become enchanting. At sunrise this morning the lemon gardens about the house rang with the song of the birds. As the Scotch poet Dunbar says so poetically, —

> "The sky was full of shoutings of the larks."

13th. This morning at eight we leave Sorrento for Amalfi.

May 16. We reached Cadenabbia and this pleasant Hôtel Belle Vue yesterday afternoon. We find everything as lovely as we left it in August. This is a silent, sunny Sunday. Only the soft bells from the distant villages on the lake chiming a while, then all is still again, save the birds singing in the woods; as when the organ ceases, but the choir sings on. It is Whitsunday. Before dinner, a walk down the lake, past the Villa Somariva to Tremezzo. After dinner a walk up the lake, half-way to Menaggio.

19th. The whole valley of the lake full of the sound of bells and the songs of birds. After breakfast, a row; then reading till dinner. Cadenabbia is a handful of houses on the western shore, opposite Bellagio, its rival as a place of summer resort. No carriage road leads to it, and there is no sound of wheels or hoofs to break the stillness. All round rise the beautiful green, folded hills. In the morning the cool north wind blows down the lake; in the afternoon the "Brera" springs up from the south.[1]

20th. The girls go to row and I take a solitary walk

[1] No sound of wheels or hoof-beats breaks
The silence of the summer day,
As by the loveliest of all lakes
I while the idle hours away.

. . . . . .

By Somariva's garden gate
I make the marble stairs my seat,
And hear the water, as I wait,
Lapping the steps beneath my feet.

. . . . . .

The hills sweep upward from the shore,
With villas scattered one by one
Upon their wooded spurs, and lower,
Bellagio blazing in the sun.

And dimly seen, a tangled mass
Of walls and wood, of light and shade,
Stands beckoning up the Stelvio Pass
Varenna with its white cascade.

Cadenabbia.

along the lake to Tremezzo and beyond,—mile after mile of villas and villages, with gardens and flights of stone steps leading down into the lake or up among the gardens. A lovely walk for a cloudy day, having roses for sunshine. In the afternoon we rowed across the lake to the village and waterfall of Fiume-Latte, the River of Milk, just below Varenna. On the hillside above the village it hangs like a fleece. We climbed to where it springs full-grown out of a cavern in the rock.

To Mrs. J. T. Fields.

CADENABBIA, May 20, 1869.

I was delighted, yesterday, to receive your bit of a note and to know that you are all safe in London. We find it hard to get out of Italy or any other country. There never was a family that dragged along like this. Every town seems a quicksand in which we sink to the knees. On Saturday, or Monday, or some other day of the week, or of next month, we are going to Venice, to sink in the mud for an unknown length of time. Then to Verona, Innsbruck, Nuremberg, Dresden, Paris. And there we shall hope to meet you, as it may not be sooner.

22d. A thistle-down of cloud trailing along the mountains. A visit to the silkworms. Then a row to the beautiful Villa Giulia on the Lecco branch of the lake. Lovely terraces, full of roses of all kinds.

23d. The walk along the lake under the plane-trees from the hotel to the Villa Carlotta (or Somariva) ever beautiful. A merle in a cage is singing gayly; the voice of the English clergyman comes up from the reading-room below. All else is silent as silent as can be.

Farewell, Cadenabbia! Farewell the dancing boats

Pepina and Sylphide; farewell the jolly boatmen Francesco and Achille; farewell the venders of olive-wood under the plane-trees, Marianna and pretty Lucia of Tremezzo!

From Mrs. F—— (in England).

July 21, 1869.

DEAR MR. LONGFELLOW,—At the risk of being thought troublesome, I venture to forward a note from E. J. Reed, C. B., the Chief Constructor to our Navy, and one of the greatest ship-builders the world ever produced, in which he speaks most highly of your poem, 'The Building of the Ship.'

As Apelles liked the sandal-maker's criticism on the sandal of one of his figures, so you may approve of Mr. Reed's testimony in favor of the truth of your poem.

[*From Mr. Reed's Note.*]

ADMIRALTY, July 20.

I should have been so pleased to meet, and pay my profound respects to, the author of the finest poem on ship-building that ever was, or probably ever will be, written,—a poem which I often read with the truest pleasure.

August 31. Arrived in New York from Liverpool.
September 1. Reached Cambridge at sunset.

To George W. Greene.

CRAIGIE HOUSE, September 1, 1869.

Here I am, once more at my desk, under the evening lamp; but there is not a drop of ink in my inkstand, and no bottle can be found. Still, I must write you one word to say that we are all safe again at home.

How strange and how familiar it all seems! And how thankful I am to have brought my little flock back to the fold. The young voices and little feet are musical overhead; and the Year of Travel floats away and dissolves like a *Fata Morgana.*

Do come as soon as you can, before I grow vapid by being too long uncorked. I have seen no one, and want to see you among the first. Jump into the train and speed hitherward. I have brought across the sea a famous game-pie, to make merry with you and Sumner, and it will not keep. Write and say when you will come; or still better, come without writing.

We reached home to-day at sunset, and found Cambridge in all its beauty; not a leaf faded.

How glad I am to be at home! The quiet and rest are welcome after the surly sea. But there is a tinge of sadness in it, also.

13th. Paid my taxes, which gives one a home feeling. Met Dr. Holmes, also Lowell, and Cranch; and finally Agassiz, full of the discourse he is to make at the centennial celebration of Humboldt's birth, to-morrow. Go with him to the printing-office, where they are putting it in type.

15th. In town on business; boxes and custom-house duties. I mean to become a free-trader as soon as possible.

18th. At the custom-house for a long while. Healy's picture of Liszt has arrived. The Collector gives a free pass for it, and for my books (as professional).

To G. W. Curtis.

September 19, 1869.

I thank you most heartily for your pleasant words of welcome home. As we steamed up the beautiful harbor of New York and passed your green island, I tried to catch a glimpse of your roof and chimneys; but I saw only those of a neighbor of yours, who stood at my side on deck and pointed them out to me in triumph. I warmed towards him when he said that he knew you, and sent you a message by him as he departed in the tug of the Port physician.

And so, here we are again safe and sound in the Craigie House, which had begun to grow vapory and hazy in the splendors of great towns across the sea. It is pleasant to get back to it, and yet sad. I do not know whether to laugh or cry.

T. came back with us; but is rather restless, I think.

October 2. In the afternoon Greene departs for home, and I drive over to Brookline to meet Sir Henry Holland at dinner, at Mr. Winthrop's. Sir Henry is Dr. Holland. He said he had known Wordsworth, Byron, Moore, Coleridge, and Campbell, as their medical attendant. A curious experience. He said also that he attended Mme. D'Arblay in the last years of her life; that she had a great aversion to water, and had not washed for fifteen years.

7th. Full of cares of many kinds, and memories of the past; but I will not record them.

8th. The world without is splendid in its autumnal glories. It is darker within. To-day has been a day of many vexations; but they will soon be forgotten. Went to town. Saw Sumner, busy on his lecture, "Caste." Called on Mr. Ticknor, who is very cordial and kind.

From R. W. Emerson.

CONCORD, October 10, 1869.

MY DEAR LONGFELLOW, — First, I rejoice that you are safe at home; and, as all mankind know, full of happy experiences, of which I wished to gather some scraps at the Club of Saturday. To my dismay, at midnight I discovered that I had utterly forgotten the existence of the Club. Yesterday I met Appleton, who ludicrously consoled me by affirming that yourself, and himself, had made the same slip. I entreat you not to fail on the thirtieth of October.

Next, I have to thank you for your punctual remembrance of Admiral Brown's commission, — though a slight failure of memory here would perhaps cost fewer sighs than the alarming ones above-mentioned.

With all kind regards,

R. W. EMERSON.

To Robert Ferguson.

October 15, 1869.

It is high time that I gave you tidings of Craigie House and its inhabitants. I should have done so sooner but for all kinds of interruptions and occupations. *Apenas llego, cuando llego à penas,*[1] says some forlorn punster in some Spanish play; and it is pretty true of every one who has been away from home for a year and a day, as we have.

Alas for the Lagrima! When Scala bottled it, he cast an Evil Eye upon it, because I did not buy it of him. Owing to this and to bad corks, it came to grief and is as sour as the Saturday Review. I have also three paintings soaked in bilge-water; but, to make amends, my books

[1] Hardly do I come back when I come back to hardships.

have thus far come safe and dry. The beautiful and valuable ones which you gave me adorn my study table, and are a constant reminder of you and all your kindness.[1]

My girls are well and happy. I think they miss now and then the excitement of travel; and who does not? Even the undersigned pleads guilty to an occasional sigh for the far away.

17th. I am as good as ever at forgetting my journal. But who wants to be a Crabbe Robinson? What have I done the past week? Finished the revision of the Divine Comedy for a new edition, and translated a lyric of Mercantini, *La Spigolatrice di Sapri.*[2] Also have unpacked endless boxes, attended a meeting of the Historical Society, and run to and fro about the Brighton meadows. This evening I read John Neal's autobiography, — a curious book, interesting to me from personal recollections.

[1] Among these books was a copy of the first edition of the Sibylline Leaves, — Coleridge's own copy, with notes in his handwriting. 'The Ancient Mariner' in this volume contains the following verse, noted in the margin — "to be struck out, S. T. C."

> "A gust of wind sterte up behind
> And whistled through his bones;
> Through the holes of his eyes and the hole of his mouth,
> Half whistles and half groans."

It follows the verse beginning "The naked hulk alongside came." Mr. Longfellow's study-table already held an inkstand which had belonged to Coleridge, a gift from Mr. S. C. Hall, who also gave him the inkstand which had belonged to George Crabbe and afterward to Thomas Moore. Showing the Coleridge inkstand to a rustic visitor one day, Mr. Longfellow said "Perhaps the 'Ancient Mariner' was written from this." The stranger looked blank for a moment and then said, "And the 'Old Oaken Bucket,' who done that?"

[2] 'The Gleaner of Sapri.'

> "They were three hundred, they were young and strong,
> And they are dead!"

Poets and Poetry of Europe, 1871; p. 885.

18th. The Brighton meadows are as good as saved for the University, though not yet bought. Got Parsons the carpenter to make book-shelves in the attic. Talked with Parsons the Professor about ——'s strange will. T. at dinner.

November 1. Got out my Bodonis from their box.[1] All in good order.

6th. Mr. Clarke at dinner, — "Conversation Clarke," he is sometimes called, from his powers in that way. In the evening read *Il Podere*, of Tansillo, — a very clever, if not very poetic, poem.

20th. Dined with Mr. Winthrop, to meet Père Hyacinthe, the preacher of Notre Dame, Paris. I had seen him in Paris, in his Carmelite dress. He has now laid it aside, being excommunicated, and wears only the *petit collet*. A quiet, pleasant man, with soft, low voice.

22d. Père Hyacinthe dined with us quietly. We had Agassiz, T., and S. to meet him.[2]

To J. T. Fields.

November 30, 1869.

Have the goodness to look over this poem, for the sake of the lady who wrote it. Like it, if possible, and keep it. If impossible, send it back to me by Sawin, and I will do my best to console her.

Hoping that you have accepted Miss B——'s lines, I remain yours truly (otherwise quite the reverse).

P. S. I enclose a note for Aldrich. What a clever story he has written!

[1] Some fine vellum-bound folios from the famous press in Parma.

[2] M. Loyson afterward wrote to his host, "Je garde la noble devise que vous m' avez fait l' honneur de me donner :

Libertà va cercando, ch' è si cara,
Come sa chi per lei vita rifiuta."

December 1. December begins with a warm, spring-like day. There is no snow, and there are buds on the honeysuckles. Wasted the day in arranging book-cases.

4th. Dined with T., to meet George Curtis; the other guests, Agassiz, Lowell, and Dana. Afterwards, late at night, I read Lowell's new poem, 'The Cathedral.' It is very beautiful, and more than that.

5th. Read again 'The Cathedral,' and like it better even than at first.

7th. Snowing still. We are beleaguered by winter. I feel the cold very much, in contrast with last year in Rome.

8th. Bright and cold. But why keep a journal of the weather? It is very lonely here in Cambridge. Nothing seems to move.

17th. All the morning at the custom-house, plagued with red tape. If I went in a Protectionist, I came out a Free-trader.

An old Italian woman came here to-day and brought me a Christmas-tree as a present; a Christmas-tree full of little wax birds, — red, green, and white. She said it was made by her son, who "has a great talent for music." I asked her if he played any instrument. "Oh, yes," she said; "he goes round with a hand-organ and a little monkey."

To James T. Fields.

December 24, 1869.

A merry Christmas to the house of Fields!

What dusky splendors of song there are in King Alfred's new volume. It is always a delight to get anything from him. His 'Holy Grail' and Lowell's 'Cathedral' are enough for a holiday, and make this one notable. With such "good works," you can go forward to meet the New Year with a conscience void of reproach.

CHAPTER VIII.

JOURNAL AND LETTERS.

1870.

January 1. A lovely morning; the warm sun shining through a soft haze. As beautiful as Italy.

2d. A pouring rain, but not cold; reminding one of Rome and Naples. I stay at home and read, and feel protected from external annoyances.

5th. All the morning interrupted by callers. The door-bell ringing incessantly.

6th. Flying cloud-rack. At two o'clock I saw what I never saw before, — a rainbow above the sun, like a garland hung in the sky, not like the arch of a bridge.

9th. A letter from Sam Ward, with some of his clever French poems.

10th. Walked. Read Crabbe Robinson, and Grimm's Correspondence. A young poet called.

13th. Passed the day in putting up books and pictures. Where I shall find room for them all I really do not know; but they cannot be left piled upon the floor.

14th. Called upon Palfrey, and Agassiz, who has had for a week no return of his malady. Palfrey dined with me.

17th. Have been reading lately some of Victor Hugo's dramas. Great power of all kinds, and great extravagance. Perhaps exaggeration is necessary for the stage; I am inclined to think it is. A play, like a bust or statue destined for a large room, must be a little larger than life.

24th. Go to the Harvard Musical Association supper, and carry as a present to their library a *Canon Missæ Pontificalis*, printed in 1725.

To Charles Sumner.

January 25, 1870.

My opinion very decidedly is, that the passage from Leibnitz should stand on the title-page. It is dignified and appropriate. For the other motto there seems to be no place, and therefore I should omit it.

I have just been looking over the Table of Contents in the three volumes of your first edition: each title a round in the ladder by which you mounted, and reaching from 1845 to 1855. What a noble decade, and what a noble record! I say the "rounds of a ladder;" let me rather say steps hewn in the rock, one after the other, as you toiled upward.

This is a dark, rainy day, and to-night T. gives a ball at Papanti's. I shall go, but you can imagine with what heart. The waters of Lethe are a fable; there is no nepenthe.

To Charles Sumner.

January 27, 1870.

Never having dealt with any other figures than figures of speech; never having known the difference between a bank-note and a greenback; never having suspected that there was any difference between them, — you can imagine with what a dark-lantern I have read your speech on the Refunding and Consolidation of the National Debt.

I am as capable of forming an idea of it as a gentleman was the other day of estimating a lovely little Albani's "Europa" which I showed him, when he said, "A *chromolithograph*, I presume."

However, I have faith in you; and faith is "the evidence of things unseen," — though I think that before having it, one must have seen something or other which inspires it. This is just my case. Having known you so wise and far-seeing in other matters, I believe you to be in this. And I am confirmed in my belief by a Boston merchant who was here a few days ago, and desired me to say to you how much he admired this speech, and how entirely he agreed with it.

31st. Breakfasted at six. Walked to the Square with Greene, on his way to Providence. A calm, peaceful, overclouded, winter day. In the evening began a story in verse, 'The Bell of Atri,' for a second day of the Wayside Inn.

February 21. I like all kinds of weather, except cold weather.

22d. A day of disagreeable sensations, Washington's birthday though it be. A northwest wind blowing, and dust flying. A northwest newspaper, in which I have been "interviewed," and private conversation reported to the public. The income-tax bill presented, and hours occupied in going over my accounts, to have everything right.

25th. Lunched with Fields, to meet Fechter, the tragedian, — an agreeable man, and not at all stagey.

To James R. Lowell.

N'oubliez pas demain,
À une heure et demie,
Je vous en prie ;
Huîtres et vin du Rhin,
Salade de homard,
Volnay et venaison,
Don, Don,
N'arrivez pas trop tard !

Ce Lundi, 28 Février, 1870.

March 1. Fechter comes to lunch with me. Fields, Lowell, and Henry James the other guests. Fechter is very amiable and natural, and has a good deal to say.

2d. Call from young ——, who has sent me some verses of no particular merit. I like him much better than his poems. I advised him not to think of poetry as a profession, as he evidently wanted my opinion on that point. An interesting youth, with a clear, frank look in his eyes.

3d. Saw Fechter's Hamlet. Very unconventional,—Hamlet in a flaxen wig. It is pleasant to see anything so like nature on the stage; not the everlasting mouthing and ranting.

5th. Here I am, scribbling, and reading Hans Andersen's Wonder Stories, and wondering whether I shall ever write anything more.

To Charles Sumner.

[With a newspaper scrap: "Fechter dined with Longfellow yesterday."]

March 12, 1870.

We live in nests, and not in houses. The penny-a-liner, the *Diable Boiteux* of the Press, has unroofed all our habitations. Shall Fechter dine with Longfellow on Tuesday, and shall it be a secret in Chicago on Wednesday? No! let it be proclaimed by telegraph,—

> "And let the kettle to the trumpet speak,
> The trumpet to the cannoneer without,
> The cannons to the heavens, the heavens to earth,
> 'Now the King drinks to *Hamlet.*'"

Owen was here all yesterday forenoon, and we thoroughly searched the five great folios of the Florentine Museum, looking among the antique gems for something fitting to adorn the cover of your works. The nearest was not a gem, but an initial letter,—a female figure holding an olive-branch. There is another with a torch. Which do you prefer? I prefer the torch. J. O. has more time to spare than anybody I ever knew. His day has twenty-six hours in it.

How are you in body and mind? Well, I hope; working hard, I know.

Agassiz is no better, though he goes out. He sees no one.

To Charles Sumner.

March 17, 1870.

I do not hear from you, but I hear of you. One returning traveller reports that you are the leader of the Senate, and have more influence than any man there. Another reports that you have the best cook in Washington! The view becomes stereoscopic. Being taken from two points of sight, it rounds and completes the portrait.

A pretty dull winter this has been in Cambridge. I see no one, or hardly any one but my own household. Agassiz is no better. For nearly three months now he has been disabled; receives no visits; cannot read or write a letter. I greatly fear he will never be himself again; never the old strength and the old power of work. Cogswell seldom goes out of the house; Palfrey is far away; Lowell is busy. Not a very lively picture. But it is incredible how much one can do without, in this world.

Have you seen Bryant's Homer, or Emerson's new book, or Lowell's? All good reading.

March 19.

Io dico seguitando, that is, continuing my letter of yesterday, that Winter has come back upon us like Napoleon from Elba; but I hope not for a hundred days. We are beleaguered by snow-storms and shut up in our castles. You remember what Cambridge is in such weather.

Writing from America, De Tocqueville says in one of his letters, "On jouit ici du plus pâle bonheur qu'on puisse imaginer." I have been trying to-day to heighten the color of my pale happiness by reading Michelet's *Précis de l'Histoire de France*, a compendium of his large work, and as dry as the pressed meats put up for the French army. One sentence made me think of you. "Les Romains virent avec honte et douleur des sénateurs gaulois siégeant entre Cicéron et Brutus." For *Gaulois* read *Illinois*, and I fancy you have sometimes felt as the Romans did.

I have also been trying to follow Dante in his exile, — a hopeless task. One gets easily as far as Arezzo; then all is confusion as to dates.

18th. A gentleman in Maine wants me to read and criticise "an Epic Poem," which he has written on the Creation, "the six days' work," which, he says, is "done up in about six hundred lines."

21st. Go to the Library with Greene, through mud and mire. Then home, and read to him Miss Horner's Life and Times of Giusti, the Tuscan poet. He departs homeward, and I give the rest of the afternoon to Miss Frothingham's translation of *Hermann und Dorothea.*

29th. For the last few days I have read nothing but the Comedies of Plautús, translated by Thornton. Very interesting reading. This morning Prior's Danish Ballads fell in my way, and the misty world of the North, weird and wonderful, rose before me in place of the Mediterranean shore.

April 1. I have been reading, through the past week, nearly all of Plautus, and am rather tired of pimps, parasites, and debauchery in general. What a state of society he depicts!

3d. A stormy Sunday. Keep in doors mostly; getting, for air and exercise, only a tramp on the veranda. Read in the old monkish story-book, the *Gesta Romanorum*.

5th. In the evening read 'The Legend of Jubal,' by Mrs. Lewes, — a poem of a good deal of power, but in parts rather confused, as the "new style" poetry often is to me.

6th. Tom Taylor's Ballads and Songs of Brittany, — a charming book.

To J. T. Fields.

April 20, 1870.

Some English poet has said or sung, —

> "At the close of the day, when the hamlet is still,
> And mortals the sweets of forgetfulness prove."

I wish Hamlet would be still! I wish I could prove the sweets of forgetfulness! I wish Fechter would depart into infinite space, and "leave, oh, leave me to repose!" When will this disturbing star disappear, and suffer the domestic planetary system to move on in its ordinary course, and keep time with the old clock in the corner?

I return the volume you sent with many thanks for your kindness. I found in it what I wanted. I never thought that I should come back to this kind of work.[1] It transports me to my happiest years, and the contrast is too painful to think of.

May 1. For the last week or two I have been at work upon a Supplement to the Poets and Poetry of Europe, and have made several translations for it, — such as 'Remorse,' from Platen, 'The Angel and Child,' from Reboul, 'Consolation,' from Malherbe.

[1] He was engaged upon a new edition of the Poets and Poetry of Europe. The original edition was prepared just after his marriage, in 1843.

25th. This has been to me a day of indescribable mental suffering. I have given great pain to others; but I could not do otherwise and be true to myself. God grant it may be for the best!

June 3. Read Disraeli's new novel, Lothair. It is decidedly clever, and refreshing in its coolness after the hot breath of most modern novels. Still the old love of dukes and duchesses, and the light touch as of old.

5th. Read Hawthorne's English Notebooks. Charmingly written. If he had prepared them for printing, they could hardly have been better.

6th. Howells's lecture on Modern Italian Poets. In the evening read an English version of Mistral's Provençal poem *Mireio*, — very striking, and full of strong, simple poetry; but too tragic, and encumbered with irrelevant materials which destroy its simplicity as a tale.

14th. Heard of the sudden death of Charles Dickens. I can think of nothing else, but see him lying there dead in his house at Gad's Hill.

16th. Went with President Eliot to look at marshland on Mount Auburn Street; then called on Professor Fisher of Yale; and in the afternoon heard him lecture on the various philosophic views of the existence of evil in the world, — the Stoic, the Mediæval, and the Modern.

July 3. It is as much trouble to go to Nahant as to Europe. What an absurdity to break up one's life into fragments in this way!

4th. Execute the deed of the Brighton Meadows for the College. Write to the President and Fellows.[1]

[1] Receiving this acknowledgment: "The President and Fellows of Harvard College thank you very heartily for the valuable gift of land in Brighton which they have received from you and other friends of the College. They have observed how large is the share which you and your family have in the subscription, and they know

10th. *Nahant.* In the new church, which is quaint and village-like. Mr. Morison preaches, — mild, and yet fervent.

To G. W. Greene.

NAHANT, July 10, 1870.

I am glad you have finished your Siege of Ninety-Six, and that you can perfume its pages with a remembrance of Alba Longa. Bitter-sweet memories! They have a taste of the rind of life in them, but nevertheless are sweet with the sweetness of youth.

We have been here now nearly a week. The air is delightful, and most things unchanged;

The same wind blowing,
The same sea flowing;
Only the beholder
Grown three years older.

We have a new church and a new steamboat-landing, and little else that is not as old as the oldest inhabitant.

I wish this *fainéant* Congress would rise, and let Sumner loose. I agree with him about the Chinese, and about striking the word *white* out of every law of the land. Of course *you* do.

To Charles Sumner.

NAHANT, July 18, 1870.

I have just received your letter, and deplore with you the removal of Motley.[1] It is a gross insult to him, and a very disreputable act to all concerned in it. And now, it seems, the office is to go a-begging, like the Spanish

that they are indebted exclusively to your exertions for this large and promising addition to their territory." There were some seventy acres.

[1] Mr. Lothrop Motley had just been recalled from the English Mission.

throne, and finally we shall have some —— sent out to disgrace us!

I am glad you are released, and hope that as soon as possible you will come to me. I have a room for you, and all things necessary for your comfort in a small way; and in a large way, gladness to see you. I never knew Nahant in finer flavor than this year. It is a delight to look at the sea; and as for the air, none is so good for me. Thalatta! Thalatta!

And then to think of the daily chowder! Why, no *bouillabaisse* of Arles or Marseilles can compare with it! So make all the speed you can, and make glad my heart.

To J. T. Fields.

NAHANT, July 29, 1870.

You see by the spreading of the ink that this is a soft, misty day. Life by the seaside becomes a dream. I only dream that I am writing to you to say that I shall not be able to go to town to-morrow for the Club dinner, as Mr. C. A. L., of the yacht "Dauntless," is expected here, and I cannot be absent on such an occasion.

I have dreamed also several times that you came here to dine; but I believe we have only made believe eat and drink together, like the Barmecide and the barber's sixth brother, and that the real dinner is yet to come. I have dreamed, moreover, that I went to Portland last week, and on arriving walked two miles into the country after sunset, and came to a cottage[1] and saw through the open door Perabo sitting at a pianoforte, playing to a company of girls; that the next day we went down the harbor in a vessel belonging to the Coast Survey; that I became so nautical that, on our safe return to port, I bought a barometer and a chronometer, and that the merchant threw

[1] His brother Alexander's, at Highfield, in Westbrook.

into the bargain a Nautical Almanac, from which I learned that —

"A mackerel sky and mares' tails
Make tall ships carry low sails."

Then I dreamed about coming back to Nahant; and that the weather was very hot (which I knew could not possibly be true, because I was by the seaside!); and that I went to a "spiritual séance," and saw the "medium" elongated, — which I knew was true, because he was lifting his shoulders and standing on his toes. He said he felt his ribs drawn apart. I asked him how it was with his back-bone and spinal marrow. He modestly answered that he did not know; he had not thought of that. He was pleased at being called Count Cagliostro; and many in the audience considered the performance very wonderful. But nothing seems strange in a dream.

And now I dream that I am sitting in an upper room by an open window, and have just received a poem called 'Ramon's Bride' from a young lady in New South Wales, and that you are going to publish it in the Atlantic, and send the authoress an independent fortune!

Yours always, dreaming or waking.

30th. A whole fortnight of idleness. Read Curtis's Nile-Notes, and the Arabian Nights, and the newspapers. C. is in New York, just from England in the yacht "Dauntless,"—beaten by the English yacht "Cambria" one hour and a few minutes only, in a race of three thousand miles!

August 1. Sumner lying all the morning in a hammock reading Lothair. Dine with him and T. at Mr. George James's.

There is nothing more disagreeable than long-continued and enforced idleness. That is the only drawback of

Nahant in summer. One becomes too listless and lazy, and, though free to come and go, feels a sense of imprisonment. All summer I have done nothing but lounge and read. I have read *Wilhelm Meister*, and Dino Compagni's *Cronica di Firenze*, and one volume of Lecky, and a good deal of Sainte-Beuve's *Causeries de Lundi*. I have thought of translating Dino Compagni, by way of illustration to the *Divina Commedia;* but it will be better to make extracts only.

From Samuel Ward.

BASLE, SWITZERLAND, August 26, 1870.

MY DEAR HEINRICH VON OFTERDINGEN, — When I passed through Andernach last Sunday, on my way hither, dear Paul Flemming rose up before me as he used to emerge from his bath and bedroom on those blessed Sunday mornings of yore, and after lighting his spirit-lamp under the Mocha, to walk up to the standing-desk near the window and sew an English button upon Alighieri's tattered gabardine.[1] I then vowed that I would, in Europe as in Nicaragua, devote the first spare half-hour to you. For you are more or less a child of mine, — at least I have been the family physician of some of your bairns; notably 'The Skeleton in Armor,' 'The Children of the Lord's Supper,' 'The Two Locks of Hair,' and Hyperion. To-morrow I start for Schaffhausen, thence to Zurich, and so on through all the mazes of that dance, with mountains and glaciers for partners, which seems by foretaste worthy to be called the "Swiss Lancers." I got here last evening, and felt like a *grand seigneur*

[1] In 1843 Mr. Longfellow translated some portions of the *Divina Commedia*, in the fashion here noted, while his morning coffee was making.

when the blue-and-gold-bedizened *chasseur* of the Trois Couronnes ushered me up the tiled steps, on the lowest of which "Salve!" is inscribed in mosaics. I don't know whether it is Paul Flemming or Vivian Grey who calls the Aar "arrowy;" but the epithet is certainly deserved by the rushing river, which, flowing through this bridge,

"Labitur, et labetur in omne volubilis ævum."

The view from the dining-room terrace at night-fall, with the swift intermingling and passing "of woven paces and of waving hands," reminded me of the lovely bridge at Lima, which I often saw at the same semi-nebulous hour, and was more moved by than by any scene I had then known, — in 1849. This morning at six, as I was dreaming "memories of the Middle Ages," a blast of trumpets awoke me, and I rushed to the window and beheld a troop of cavalry majestically crossing the bridge. The morning sun flashed upon their morions, and I was transported at least two centuries back, and felt that glorious *chair de poule* which in me is inseparable from genuine emotion. I pulled my right ear and asked myself: "Am I that same poor old weather-beaten Bohemian who four weeks ago was perspiring his sixth summer in Washington, and who am here realizing at fifty-six my boyish dream of seeing Switzerland?" . . . I saw at Liverpool a glorious life-sized portrait of you in a picture-dealer's window. I mean to buy it if it is there when I return in November. And now, while the majestic river is passing the lights of Kleiner Basel, opposite my window, I will say good-night in a scene so suggestive of our lives from 1836 to 1843. I send you a leaf from the grave of Charras which I plucked this afternoon in the cemetery where a bronze bas-relief perpetuates in the wall a typical Garibaldian head. Poor France! Wretched Napoleon! Ruthless Bismarck!

September 1. Mr. Bryce and Mr. Dicey, English lawyers with letters from Professor Nichol, pass the day with us.

5th. C. and W. set sail in the "Wyvern" for a run down the coast. Go to town. News of the surrender of Napoleon and his army to the Prussians. Mrs. Hamilton reads me some part of her novel, Woven of Many Threads.

7th. The Republic proclaimed in France!

8th. Another perfect autumn day. It is enough to sit still and look at it and admire its beauty, and not attempt to describe it, even in verse.

To C. E. Norton (in Italy).

NAHANT, September 8, 1870.

You will see by the date of this that we are still lingering by the sea-side. The autumnal weather is in all its splendor. You cannot beat us there, though I confess that the Villa Spanocchi is larger than the Wetmore Cottage. So far as I am personally concerned, I am satisfied that I made a great mistake in not staying longer in Europe. You were wiser, and have your reward. I am still hungry for more. Enough is decidedly *not* as good as a feast. No one is ever satisfied till he gets too much.

Your opinion of France and Prussia is also mine and that of most Americans. Now that the Empire is no more, let there be war no more, and *Vive la République!* for, as Emerson sings, "God said, I am tired of kings."

Agassiz is still among the White Mountains. I hear reports of his being better, but none of his being *well*. I am afraid, I am afraid! What Lowell is doing, I do not know. He has had Tom Hughes with him; but I did not succeed in getting them here to dine, and have not seen the "Rugby boy." The University is flourishing under its young President to one's heart's content. A few of us have just presented [to it] seventy acres of the Brighton meadows, with your namesake flowing through it and making its favorite flourish of the letter S. During the progress of this transaction I was assailed in the Legislature by an irate member, who accused me of a plot to buy up lands adjoining the projected Park, to sell to the city at great advance! So I was ranked among the speculators! My vulnerable point was not this, but another; namely, that I wanted to keep the land open in front of my own house. It is as good as five hundred dollars in your pocket that you were not here; for you would have been unable to resist my blandishments.

I wish we had Ruskin here to lecture on art, and stir people up a little upon the subject. The last time I saw him was at Verona, perched upon a ladder, copying some detail of the tomb of Can Grande over the church door; thus representing the coat-of-arms of the Scala family in his own person. I admired his enthusiasm and singleness of purpose. How good his description of the "democratic fly" in his last book! Yet he belongs to the working-class, if ever man did. Appleton is well and thriving. He has to-day taken all my girls and boys in the "Alice" to the yacht-races at Swampscott. We are not without our amusements also!

12th. T. went in his yacht to dine at Shirley Point. I declined, not liking raw birds, which is the epicurean fashion of eating them, — an abominable fashion, it seems to me.

15th. Despatch boxes and trunks by land, and come home in the "Alice," — A most pleasant sail up the harbor, and the Craigie House charming.

To G. W. Greene.

September 16, 1870.

We returned yesterday from Nahant all in good condition, sailing up the harbor in a yacht in the lovely September day. Entering the old house again was like coming back from Europe. I had a kind of dazed feeling, a kind of familiar, unfamiliar sense of place. But in the evening one of my most intimate bores came in, saying, "I did not know that you had got back, but thought I would come up and see." So he came up and saw, and — I knew that I was in Cambridge.

This fact was still further confirmed to-day; for immediately after breakfast came one of my crazy women, and I had no sooner disposed of her than there appeared another bore, who occasionally frequents these forests, — huge, Hyrcanian, hopeless! There can be no doubt of the fact, I am certainly in Cambridge.

Come to me as soon as you can, and we will talk over your summer's work and my summer's idleness, and pass some Autumnal Hours a good deal more agreeable than Drake's.

While I was writing the last line an Irishwoman called with a petition to the Governor to pardon her son, in prison for theft, "that he may become what he is capable of being, — an honor to his family and the community."

17th. In town on business. See at Doll's some good pictures, — a Farm by Daubigny, and Beech-trees at Fontainebleau by Diaz.

18th. No news but war news. The horrible war in France going on. The Prussians closing in on Paris.

21st. Greene arrives, looking well after his summer work. He has finished the Biography of General Greene, and is now free.

25th. A young man from Horton, the Grand Pré of Acadie, comes to see me. He is a printer, and is going back to his province to be editor of "Pancuramata," — whatever that may mean, — a weekly newspaper.

28th. Greene finishes reading to me his Biography [of General Greene], which is more than a biography, — a noble historical work.

30th. Heard the introductory lecture of Professor Sophocles on "Pagan Views of the Christians." In the College yard met Dr. Hoppin, with the Rev. Edward Henry Bickersteth and his son, of Pembroke College, Cambridge, England. Brought them home to lunch.

October 3. Hear Lowell's introductory on Old French Poets, and William Everett's on Virgil.

6th. Laying of the corner-stone of Memorial Hall.[1] Dine with Lowell, to meet Mr. Tom Hughes, of Rugby memory.

To H. C. Lukens.

October 6, 1870.

I hope you will pardon my long delay in answering yours of August 4th, and thanking you for the handsome volume that came with it.[2] My excuse is that I was absent from Cambridge when the parcel came, and did not return until a few days ago.

I wish I could sympathize more fully than I do with this kind of writing, and consequently enjoy it more; but I confess that I have rather a dislike to it. A parody or travesty of a poem is apt to throw an air of ridicule about the original, though made with no such intention, and on that account they are unpleasant to me, however well

[1] A Memorial to the students who had died in the War for the Union. Under the same roof are the academic theatre and the dining-hall.

[2] Containing a travesty of Bürger's *Lenora.*

they may be done. In fact, the better they are done, the worse they are in their effects; for one cannot get rid of them, but ever after sees them making faces behind the original.

Excuse this dissertation, and accept my thanks all the same.

8th. Thomas's concert. Miss Anna Mehlig plays beautifully on the pianoforte. Zerdahelyi introduces me to her.

11th. In the evening go to town to hear Mr. Hughes in the Music Hall,—"John to Jonathan;" a very good, straightforward description of England's position during our Civil War, from the English point of view. After the lecture, a supper at Fields's.

13th. At luncheon Mr. W., a London barrister, and his son from Oxford; also Mr. Hughes. Took them to see the College Library; then to Everett's lecture on Virgil,—a capital lecture on the various editions; and brought them home to dine.

14th. Dined at the Somerset Club to meet Mr. Mundella, Member of Parliament.

18th. Reading a Swedish novel, *Den Rätte,* by Marie Schwartz. Very clever, with all the minuteness of detail which the Northern novelists delight in.

25th. Went to Plymouth with Judge Russel, Fields, and Greene. Saw the Plymouth Rock, and drew the sword of Miles Standish, and read the old Records. Then drove through the Plymouth woods of oak to Billington Sea,—a beautiful drive, and along the valley by the brook. Plymouth is a charming town, with over two hundred little lakes in it. From the Burial Hill is a charming view,—westward across a rolling country red with oak-leaves, and eastward over the harbor, the sandy headlands, and the sea. On our way back we had all kinds of adventures, being detained by a schooner that stuck in the drawbridge at Neponset and blocked all passage. We had a long foot-tramp over unknown roads in the night, and did not reach home till eleven.

November 4. In the evening at a political caucus; the only one I ever attended, I believe. I did not like it.

9th. Lunched with Fields to meet the beautiful Nilsson, who is as charming in her manners as in her voice. Another "Swedish nightingale," Jenny Lind being the first.

10th. Professor Washburn's funeral at the Shepard Church, with three clergymen of three different sects officiating, — a Unitarian, a Congregationalist, and a Baptist.

13th. Went to Mount Auburn and found it desolated and ruined; trees cut down, irregularities levelled, and nothing to be seen but granite, granite, granite. It is shocking! Sat an hour with Lowell. We talked over the proposed widening of Brattle Street, which will also be the destruction of a number of trees.

To Charles Sumner.

November 14, 1870.

These are happy days at Argyll Lodge and at Inverary; and well they may be, for the Princess is a lovely woman in her own right, and quite apart from her royal birth.

Where are you now? In what remote and comfortless "best chamber" are you this moment undergoing your lecturer's purgatory?[1]

Miss Nilsson is now stirring the hearts of the Bostonians. She is a charming person, as well as a beautiful singer, — a true daughter of the North. She dines with me on Thursday, and I wish you could be with us. Far-

[1] Mr. Sumner was on a "lecturing tour" through the West.

ther than this, I have no news to send you. So good-night, and God bless you!

17th. Miss Nilsson dined with us. She is charming; sunny, fresh, and beautiful, with the beauty of the North. I like herself even better than her singing, delightful as that is.

29th. [Mr. W. Everett's] lecture on Virgil; excellent. In the evening I tried to render the First Eclogue into English hexameters, but did not write it down.

To G. W. Greene.

November 29, 1870.

I have this morning received from the author a poem, in twenty-eight cantos, on an Indian subject, filling an octavo volume of 446 pages. It begins:—

> "My gentle Muse! Awake and sing
> Of wigwam, tomahawk, and quiver;"

and ends:—

> "We love thee, happy home, we love thee still,
> And loud respond again to Whippoorwill."

The best lines I have found in it are these:—

> "Such were the solemn rites the throng displayed,
> And peaceful slept the pious Vareau's shade,"—

which prove that the author has read the last lines of Pope's Iliad, if nothing more.

I enclose a cheque, and wish you joy of your windmill.[1] Of the Sumner testimonial I know nothing, never having heard of it before,—unless it be the fund raised to defray the expense of publishing his Works, which I supposed to be a secret.

[1] Mr. Longfellow purchased for his friend a windmill, which was moved and attached as a library tower to his house in East Greenwich, giving it the name of Windmill Cottage.

To G. W. Curtis.

December 10, 1870.

I am delighted that you can come to me on the 20th. Come to dinner at five o'clock, and stay all night if you can. Such is the programme, not to be changed except by dire necessity!

The moon is still shining. I looked out of the window just now, and there it was, making my neighbor's house beautiful, — which is more than the architect did. I begin to think that the moon never sets in Cambridge.

Your lecture leaves behind pleasant reverberations. Mr. Houghton (who shall be mayor hereafter, though we did not succeed in getting him into the gilded coach this year) was here this morning, and was loud in its praises. But what I value most was the exclamation of the old lady in coming out: "Oh, dear! what a splendid lecture!" Like Madelon in the *Précieuses Ridicules*, "Je trouve ce oh! oh! admirable. J'aimerais mieux avoir fait ce oh! oh! qu'un poème épique."

December 14. Dined with Fields to meet Bayard Taylor, in honor of the publication of his translation of *Faust*. The guests were Lowell, Dana, Howells, Holmes, Aldrich, and Osgood.

19th. In town. Went to a meeting of the —— Company, which is utterly ruined, and my loss several thousand dollars; then to a Beethoven concert, which was beautiful, particularly the overture to *Egmont*. In the evening numerous callers. Notwithstanding all these interruptions I contrived to write a part of 'Herod's Banquet' [for the Divine Tragedy].

20th. Finished 'Herod's Banquet.' Gave a little dinner to Curtis.

22d. The cares and vexations of daily life, letters, and manifold interruptions, have driven away my poetic mood, of which I was making such diligent use and hoping so much.

23d. A letter from Collector Russel, in which occurs this appalling sentence: "Remembering your interest in the stray volume of Lamartine which was imported as paper stock, I write to say that Mr. B., of Washington Street, has three hundred tons of Lamartine's works now on their way to this port."

To Charles Sumner.

Christmas, 1870.

I wish you "a Merry Christmas!" As I write the word "merry," the two *aruspices* look at each other, not having been merry for some time past!

Well, then, a Happy Christmas, or a Tolerable Christmas, or any unobjectionable adjective you may prefer.

What shameful assaults your colleagues are making upon you in the Senate, if I may judge from the garbled newspaper accounts. I need not say to you, "Stand firm," because you cannot stand in any other way. *Non ragionam di lor.*

Sam Ward is to dine with me on Friday.

I need not say that this is not a letter, only a salutation. I am so driven by angels and demons, — by books, bores, and beggars, — that I can never achieve anything that shall rise to the dignity of a letter.

31st. The year ends with a Club dinner.[1] Agassiz is not well enough to be there. But Emerson and Holmes of the older set were; and so I was not quite alone.

[1] The "Saturday Club," so often alluded to. It met on the last Saturday of each month at Parker's, in School Street.

CHAPTER IX.

JOURNAL AND LETTERS.

1871.

January 6. The subject of the Divine Tragedy has taken entire possession of me, so that I can think of nothing else. All day pondering upon and arranging it.[1]

7th. I find all hospitalities and social gatherings just now great interruptions. But perhaps it is for the best [that I have them]. I should work too hard, and perhaps not so well.

8th. During the last week I have written [five scenes in the Tragedy].

10th. Cold, hard, and steel-bright. I can hardly hold a pen to write. Thermometer here in my study only 58° with a fire. And I have so many letters to answer!

11th. In town at a meeting of stockholders of a coal-mine company that has come to nought through the fraud or mismanagement of the directors. A poor widow was weeping, and saying that her son was dying, and all her property was in this mine. It was a sad sight. "And there is the man sitting in that corner who has defrauded you," said a free-spoken stockholder. In the afternoon went to a concert and heard Miss Mehlig.

13th. Wrote 'Gamaliel the Scribe' and part of the 'Porch of Solomon.' [After this, each day records the writing of a scene, often two, of the Tragedy.]

[1] The Divine Tragedy, it may be remembered, was the Gospel Story, which was to form the first part of the Trilogy, Christus.

17th. Agassiz comes. It is very sad to see the strong man weakened. He said, "I cannot work," and put his face in his hands and wept. I comforted him, as well as I could, with the thought that at sixty we must work more slowly and more calmly; that old age is better than youth for system and supervision, though not for swift execution of details.

25th. A continued series of interruptions, from breakfast till dinner. I could not get half an hour to myself all day long. Oh, for a good snow-storm to block the door!

27th. Wrote 'The Three Crosses' and 'The Two Maries.' And now the Divine Tragedy is finished, in its first shape, and needs only revision, and perhaps amplification, here and there.

30th. The weather moderates. G —— goes to Riverside, and comes back saying that he "feels as weak as a rat." Why do we say "weak as a rat?" That little animal seems to me uncommonly strong, when I hear him at night trundling great weights between the walls.

From Samuel Ward.

WASHINGTON, January 31, 1871.

MI QUERIDO DUEÑO, — Your charming letter half consoled me for my great disappointment at missing your genial hospitality and the wedding. I unfortunately am a brick — a small one — in a pile, and I could not be pulled out, at the time in question, without disturbing the equilibrium of other and more important incumbents. The idea was to bring together my friend General Schenck and my friend Mr. Evarts, who, having been sent to England twice by Mr. Lincoln, at a great professional sacrifice, about the "Alabama" and British and French neutrality, was in a condition to furnish the

General with points and details of value to his mission. . . . I thus did good service, at a sacrifice of my own enjoyment, in a matter wherein I had no other than a friendly and patriotic interest. This little incident is a fair illustration of my daily life. So many of my years have been wasted in misfortunes and uncongenialities that the only stimulus that keeps me up to the work is contracting no end of benevolent obligations and endeavoring to fulfil them.

I completed last Friday my fifty-seventh birthday, — ever memorable to me as the future anniversary of the capitulation of Paris. Poor Béranger died before the evil day which gave such awful contradiction to his patriotic songs. As for J. J., he has the melancholy comfort of the annihilation of a dynasty he detested. The days of "mimae, balatrones, et hoc genus omne" are numbered. Tigellius is no more emperor. To tell you the truth, this fearful war-symphony has saddened the last six months of my life. The dead-march in Beethoven's Heroic Symphony has pervaded my ears to the exclusion of all cheerful melodies. Baron Rumohr, in his charming Cookery-book, says that all the great wars in the world have been between the *butter countries* and the *oil countries*, and have resulted in the triumph of the former. So in the recent disasters of France we find History again repeating herself. Does it not remind you of Jean Paul's phrase: "Eternity sat upon chaos and gnawed it and spat it out again"? The parallel holds good if you let Bismarck, as the Eternity of Despotism, and France, as the Chaos of Revolutions, personify Jean Paul's ideas.

I was dreaming the other night of your lovely 'Oliver Basselin,' which I consider inimitable. Do you remember my sending it to Morpeth in the green cover of Putnam's Magazine in 1855, and his letter of thanks which you gave to Mrs. R. at Newport? I accept the prophet's chamber in the spring, and enclose a lovely poem I found in the Post.

Affectionately thine,

S. W.

February 2. Read some of Browning's Ring and Book He is very powerful, but very obscure.

3d. Begin 'Fra Joachim,' which is to be an interlude between parts i. and ii. of Christus.

4th. Read and pondered on many things. Continued 'Fra Joachim.'

8th. Began the second interlude, 'Luther in the Wartburg,' to come after the Golden Legend.

9th. Read in Luther's Life, by Michelet, and his Table-Talk. Translated *Ein' feste Burg.* Mr. P., of Philadelphia, a very cultivated and agreeable young man, at dinner.

12th. Began 'St. John,' to serve as prologue to the third part of Christus.

To Miss E. C——.

[With some autographs for a Fair.]

February 15, 1871.

I send you half a dozen autographs, and would send you more if I were not ashamed. But I am ashamed. And so will you be, when you find you have more than are wanted.

But it is never too late to mend, — particularly a pen. So if you find *more* than half a dozen lunatics who are willing to take this paper currency, be kind enough to let me know it.

February 20.

How charming it is to be able to help you in so good a cause by using my pen for a sword, and shedding the blue blood of my ink, instead of my own!

I send you twelve more mercenaries to serve in the ranks, and am always, with best wishes, yours.

17th. Field called in the afternoon. We went to hear a lecture by Emerson in Boylston Hall. It was on Unity, as applied to the outer and the inner world, the physical and intellectual; the same universal law governing both.

18th. A driving storm from the South. Key-holes whistling and chimneys roaring. Amuse myself with White's Selborne.

20th. Read Lowell's new book, and heard him lecture on 'Reynard the Fox.' In the afternoon read over some passages in the poem, and also Chaucer's 'Nonne's Priest's Tale,' which is taken from Reynard and idealized.

24th. Read Shelley's 'Epipsichidion.' In the afternoon Lowell came and sat an hour, and then we walked in the mud another hour.

To Charles Sumner.

February 24, 1871.

Your letter has just come, and I am delighted beyond measure at having a word from you, showing the danger to be past. I am glad, too, that my medicine agrees with you, and I forthwith prescribe again.

Prescription: Come on to Cambridge at once, and take possession of the southwest chamber, looking over the meadows and at the sunset. There you shall have uninterrupted quiet, and Dr. Brown-Séquard within reasonable distance. If you stay in Washington you cannot have quiet, you know you cannot. So leave the plough in the furrow and come.

Let Santo Domingo go, as any ordinary echo would tell

you if you asked it.[1] Above all things, do not think of making another speech at present.

I wish you were here now, and going down with me to hear Emerson lecture on the Natural History of the Intellect.[2] These lectures would be a cordial to you; and there are others which would interest you.

25th. Saturday Club dinner. Agassiz reappeared, after an absence of more than a year. We had among our guests Mr. Bret Harte, from California, who has made his mark in literature by tales and poems.

27th. My sixty-fourth birthday. I hoped no one would remember it; but a great many people did, and sent me flowers, etc.

To Mrs. J. T. Fields.

February 28, 1871.

A benediction on the Benedictines!

I knew they were great lovers of literature, but I did not know that they were also distillers of herbs and manufacturers of exquisite *liqueurs!*

Your charming remembrance of me on my birthday, — the jolly, round, and happy little monk bedded in flowers, came safely in his wooden cradle. A thousand and a thousand thanks!

I am ashamed to send back the basket, or bucket, empty; but I look round in vain for something to fill it. What shall I do?

After all, the greatest grace of a gift, perhaps, is that it anticipates and admits of no return. I therefore accept

[1] Mr. Sumner was throwing himself with ardor against the President's project of annexing Santo Domingo.

[2] Mr. Emerson was giving a course at the University under this title.

yours, pure and simple; and on the whole am glad that I have nothing to send back in the basket.

Still, *empty* is a horrid word. I try in vain to comfort myself. I make believe it is the best thing to do, and do it, knowing all the while that it is not the best thing.

March 1. Bret Harte dined with me; the other guests Lowell, Howells, Henry James; S. and A.

19th. My brother Alexander came in the morning; and in the afternoon Professor Horsford and Ole Bull, who is staying with him. Dined at Horsford's, and after dinner Ole Bull played to us for an hour or two.

To J. T. Fields.

March 19, 1871.

CARO SIGNÒR CAMPI, — I beg you not to eat much dinner to-morrow, because I propose to give you a little supper with my brother Alexander, commander of the "Meredith," U. S. Coast Survey.

I dined this evening with Professor Horsford, to meet your friend Ole Bull. After dinner he played divinely on the violin, and told some amusing stories, — for which I promised to pardon him, on condition of his dining with me when he comes back to Boston.

He also described to me his improvement of the pianoforte. I thought it was the Marquis of Worcester reading from his Century of Inventions.

What a child of Nature, and how very agreeable he is!

To Charles Sumner.

March 22, 1871.

I have just received three volumes of the new edition of your Works, beautifully printed and beautifully bound; and

Mr. Butler says that my functions as subscriber are no longer to be exercised, but that I am to look upon these volumes and the rest as a gift from you.

I was just taking up my pen to thank you for this munificence, when I took up the first volume and began to read at the beginning, "The True Grandeur of Nations." How it took me back to the days of youth! How it recalled the whole scene, — the crowd, the hot summer day, the dismay of the military men in their uniforms, the delight and applause of the audience!

Then I went on with the Phi Beta Kappa oration and the Prison Discipline discussion, — each bringing up very vividly a scene of the past. To-night I have been living your life over again, and mine in part.

I have also looked over the Contents of the other volumes, and remembering that seven more are to come, I am amazed and delighted.

This is a noble monument of a noble life! God bless you! No statesman in any age or country has a better or a nobler.

23d. Harvard Association Concert. Mostly Beethoven's music, upon which the grand bronze statue of the great master, by Crawford, looked down well pleased.

To Miss P——.

March 30, 1871.

I have had the great pleasure of receiving the silver spoon made by Paul Revere which you have been so kind and generous as to send me by the hand of our highly esteemed friend Miss M. C. I beg you to accept my most cordial thanks. It is a gift which I shall highly prize and cherish.

When I received it, I felt as if I had been christened over again, and had an "apostle spoon" sent me as a present. Paul Revere was an apostle of liberty, if not of religion.

In a narrow street in Florence is still to be seen the humble shop in which Benvenuto Cellini worked. But alas! in Boston there is no longer any trace of the workshop of Paul Revere. All the more shall I value this little relic of him.

April 3. Went to see J. O., whose place by the river has been sold. They are stripping it of its fruit and forest trees. In the afternoon Emerson's lecture on the Will. He did not once quote Jonathan Edwards, whose work I never read, but mean now to read it.

To G. W. Greene.

April 3, 1871.

I send you one or two advertisements of a certain book which may interest you. Keep the long one, as it may be interesting hereafter to see what books came out with yours, and what their fortunes were. I wish I had the original advertisement of all my books; I have not one.

The weather to-day has been like midsummer; the thermometer in my study has stood at eighty. I have kept indoors all day, and have written a new scene that occurred to me for the Divine Tragedy. The danger is that I shall make it too long.

The girls have a musical party to-night. The pianoforte is going on one side of me, and the venerable, historic door-knocker on the other. Some bashful juvenile is even now timidly applying his hand to it. A confused murmur of voices comes from the library; and I sit here like a sphinx who has had a riddle proposed to her, instead of proposing one to other people.

The door again!

5th. Transplanted from Owen's an elm-tree, a seedling from the Washington elm, and placed it between me and my neighbor Hastings, on the east side of the house.

10th. Meditating a third play, to complete the third part of Christus. The scene to be among the Moravians at Bethlehem, Pennsylvania.

11th. Happy to-day in the new poetic idea which begins to germinate and develop itself in my mind. I hope I shall be able to harmonize in it the discord of the New England Tragedies, and thus give a not unfitting close to the work.[1]

13th. Wrote 'At Bethany,' for the Divine Tragedy, — a very short scene; but it would be no better for being longer.

14th. A call from Mrs. Julia Howe and her brother, Sam Ward. He looks like a prime minister or European diplomat. I was very glad to see him.

To Mrs. J. T. Fields.

April 25, 1871.

We accept, Greene and myself, your kind invitation to dinner on Thursday, and will present ourselves in proper uniform at six o'clock.

Do not give yourself any further trouble about the notices of Greene's book. Several papers have been sent by the publishers. Already I notice something like peacock's feathers growing upon my friend, and have to spread my own very wide to show that I still exist and

[1] This was never written.

am still respectable, though tarnished. It is a very comical sight to see two authors shut up in one room together!

However, we will be serious on Thursday.

30th. A gap in my Journal. I have been busy helping Greene with the Index to his biography of his grandfather.

May 1. C. leaves us for his long journey to San Francisco, Japan, and China. In the afternoon heard Dr. Hedge's lecture on Spinoza.

5th. Read *Liza*, by Tourgénief, the Russian novelist, translated by Ralston, of the British Museum. Very interesting, and the descriptions of Nature fresh and sweet. Dine with Mrs. Howe.

12th. A call from Dana, bringing Lord Tenterden and Professor Bernard, of "Her Majesty's High Commission" on the "Alabama" claims.

15th. Agassiz called, and talked about his expedition round the Cape to California, upon which he starts this summer.

24th. Finished a new Tale for the second day of the Wayside Inn, — a New England story, 'Lady Wentworth.'

31st. Read Johnson's Life of Dryden, and Dryden's 'Hind and Panther.' Not much edified by either. A theological discussion in verse is not redeemed by the splendor of single lines. The 'Religio Laici' is far superior. But in reading Dryden one always feels that he is breathing a strong, deep-sea atmosphere.

June 1. Went with Fields to Portsmouth to see old houses. Mr. Haven received us at the station and entertained us most hospitably. First, lunch; then drive to Little Harbor to see the Wentworth house, — a quaint, irregular pile of buildings hidden from the road by rising ground, though close upon it, with lilac hedges, and looking seaward; not unlike my description of it.[1] We went all over the lower part of the house, and saw the present owner, a sprightly old lady of ninety, and her daughter. Then we drove to Newcastle, — an island reached by bridges over arms of the sea, — and went to Mr. Albee's cottage. He was away; but we saw his wife, whom I remember as Miss R., of Boston, a young Catholic, full of charitable works. Then back to town and visited the beautiful Barrows house, the Wentworth town house, and the Warner house. Dined with Mr. Haven and the Unitarian clergyman Mr. De Normandie, who had been the companion of our drive. Home by the evening train.

3d. Excessively hot; nevertheless drove in to the opera in the afternoon. Gounod's *Faust;* Miss Kellogg as Margaret, and Castelmary as Mephisto.

To J. T. Fields.

Three-fifths of twelve
  Are $7.20.
This may appear
To be somewhat dear;
  But wherefore went he?

The Faust of Goúnod
Is an opera, *you* know,
In which Castelmary
Plays the Old Harry, —
  Therefore spent he
  His $7.20.

June 4, 1871.

[1] He wrote to Mr. Greene: "I had a most successful day with Fields at his native town, and saw sundry curious old houses, — among them the Wentworth house, which I was anxious to see, having already described it in a poem. I found it necessary to change only a single line, — which was lucky. We saw also some very interesting old people, with the grand manners of other days, — always so attractive."

5th. Read Dryden's Songs and Elegies. He is pretty tame sometimes; and then will come a line which flashes across the page like a train of powder.

6th. Walked to Riverside to see Mr. Houghton about Mr. Kroeger's Specimens of the Minnesingers, which I want him to publish. A cool wind blowing over the river and the salt-marshes. In the afternoon Signor Corti, the Italian minister, calls with S. Eliot and Signor Bragiotti.

7th. Sirocco very oppressive. Began the poem of 'Carmilhan.'

10th. Finished 'Carmilhan.' Only two more stories are wanted to complete the Second Day of the Wayside Inn.

12th. Looking for the theme of another story. Fix upon the 'Legend Beautiful,' and begin it.

13th. Went with A. to "Shark's Mouth," H.'s seaside place at Manchester. A lovely stone house, with lofty terraces, and splendid outlook over the sea and rocky islands. I do not believe there is a more beautiful seaside place in New England; it is all one could ask.

17th. Lowell, Cranch, and Fields dined with me. After dinner C. sang two songs with great effect.

23d. Class-day; and a very delightful day for the collegians and the young ladies.

25th. Mr. Haliburton, of Nova Scotia, dined with me, son of Judge Haliburton. He is much interested in certain abstruse speculations about the symbolism of the Cross.

July 1. A day of affairs preparatory to Nahant. In the afternoon Mrs. B. called for flowers to make button-hole bouquets for the convicts in the State Prison. Mr. Zerdahelyi came to dinner, and played in the evening some beautiful things from Chopin.

3d. In the afternoon Mr. and Mrs. Stillman. She is like Rossetti's "Blessed Damosel." There is something pre-Raphaelite about her.

6th. *Nahant.* The low wash of the sea very soothing. Last night was lovely, — a tropical night, with dreamy stars, and phosphorescent waves rolling up the beach.

To J. T. Fields.

NAHANT, July 7, 1871.

A thousand thanks for your note and its enclosure. There goes a gleam of sunshine into a dark house, which is always pleasant to think of. I have not yet got the senator's sunbeam to add to it, but as soon as I do, both shall go shining on their way.

I come back to my old wish and intention of leaving the [Atlantic] Magazine when you do. This is the wisest course, as I could easily persuade you, if I had you alone here by the seaside. But I do not like to write about it, for you see how the paper blots and the ink spreads with the damp.

I am curious to hear of the effect of your reading at the Island. When you come to the lines about the Spring, read as follows: —

"The robin, the forerunner of the Spring,
The blue-bird with his jocund carolling."

The robin is more familiar, and belongs more to New England than the oriole, and must take his place.

I hear the steamboat's whistle below. I wish you were coming to dinner; but I know you are not.

13th. Ah, these melancholy anniversaries! [his wedding day and his wife's funeral.] I was awakened this morning about sunrise by the singing of a bird inside my room. I looked up and saw it perched on the window-blind. It then hopped into the room, — a little yellow bird with brown wings. After singing awhile, it perched on the rounds of a chair, then flew out of the other window.

16th. Dr. —— was very long and very ardent and very Scotch. The doctrine I did not agree with, but liked parts of the sermon, notwithstanding.

18th. Too cold to sit still, too hot to walk in the sun. That is the peculiar character of Nahant. T. returned in his yacht from Portland this morning. After dinner the S——s called. They are here for an hour or two in a beautiful yacht, — the "Palmer," — bound for the coast of Maine.

To Charles Sumner.

NAHANT, July 19, 1871.

Your working on so steadily through the hot weather fills me with wonder and envy. I cannot do it even here at the seaside. In fact I find that being by the sea is as bad as being *on* the sea, for any kind of intellectual work. It is a good place to read newspapers and Reviews; and that is about all. This year I brought down with me Plutarch's Morals, — a charming book for town or country. Here I cannot take the slightest interest in it. It seems prolix and ponderous.

Come and see if the briny atmosphere does not lay a wet cloth on your brain and cool it down to the average human speed. That is why I do not like to stay here so long. But in summer would it be different elsewhere? No; it is the season, not the place, after all.

Cogswell is coming to us on Saturday for a few days. After that, this whole house is *á su disposicion de Vmd.*[1]

[1] "At your Grace's disposal," the customary Spanish courtesy.

You who speak all modern languages "in a calm and measured tone," will understand the Spanish. But I do not mean the words in the Spanish complimentary sense, but literally, — as you well know.

20th. Behold the virtuous man, who answers all letters as soon as they are received! If I can only keep up this habit it will save me great annoyance.

22d. Cogswell comes down in the boat. Dear old man, how glad I am to see him! In the evening I call on the Rev. Dr. Potter, of Grace Church, New York, who is to preach to-morrow. He comes home with me and sits an hour in pleasant talk.

To J. R. Lowell.

NAHANT, July 25, 1871.

I am very sorry to hear such a story of poor ——, and will to-day send my contribution.

I shall not be able to go to the Club on Saturday, having, in forgetfulness of its being the last Saturday [of the month], invited a gentleman to come down to Nahant that day. Besides, the uncertainty of getting back here at night intimidates me.

Is there any chance of your coming down to dine with us? Choose your own day, — the brightest and hottest you can find, — and we shall be only too glad to see you. We dine at five, and you can return by the boat at quarter past six. On Sunday we dine at two, — from a vague notion that somebody wants to go to church in the afternoon. Therefore do not choose Sunday, if you please.

Mr. Cogswell is passing a few days with us, and is very pleasant company; otherwise Nahant is unusually dull this year.

27th. Read some articles in the Journal of Speculative Philosophy; wrote some letters; and that is the record of the day.

28th. Being troubled with sleeplessness, I determined last night to go to sleep by force of will. It succeeded perfectly. A thunder-storm waked me in the night. As soon as it was over, I was asleep again. If this always succeeds, I shall be a happy man.

29th. Read Ginx's Baby, — a clever book on pauperism in England; very tragic, and I suppose true.

From H. C. Andersen.

COPENHAGEN, July, 1871.

MY DEAR SIR, — A talented young Dane, Mr. W., is going to visit America for the first time. I send you, through him, my kindest regards. He will be happy in making your acquaintance, and I shall be so by hearing news from you when he returns. I hope that you have a copy of my Collected Works, and that you will have a spare moment to glance at them. My latest story, *Lykke Peer*, you will not find there; but it is in Scribner's Magazine.

If the great rolling Ocean were not between us, and I were not sixty-seven years old, then I should arrive in your mighty country some pleasant summer day. As it is, I can only send a letter and the kind regards of your friend and admirer,

HANS CHRISTIAN ANDERSEN.

August 1. A splendid sunset, with a thunder-storm passing over Boston seaward, — a sight of surpassing beauty.

2d. M. Auguste Bartholdi, French sculptor, calls with a letter from Agassiz. A pleasant, lively, intelligent man, a Republican and an Alsatian. He has a plan for erecting a bronze Colossus on Bedloe's Island, in New York harbor, — a statue of Liberty, to serve at night as a lighthouse. It is a grand plan; I hope it will strike the New Yorkers.

3d. A youth in England, of the Swinburne-Rossetti school, sends me three volumes of verse, mostly love-sonnets. In one of them he says: —

"We see no longer what of old we *saw*,
Nor is the vision present any *more*."

To G. W. Greene.

NAHANT, August 3, 1871.

Shall I lie down and sleep, on this sultry summer noon, or sit here and write to you? The question is answered as soon as asked. You smile, and think I cannot sleep when I will. You are mistaken; I can. After so many sleepless nights, — so many years of sleepless nights, — I have made a great discovery, and to me of infinite value. I can put myself to sleep by an effort of the will. When I go to bed at night, I will myself to sleep; and the next thing I am conscious of is that it is morning, and the birds are singing. Congratulate me!

Sumner has not yet made his appearance, though I look for him daily. I have had a letter from Lord Stanhope, and an invitation, couched in the most flattering terms, to preside at the Royal Literary Fund Society. Shall I go? Rhyme and Reason answer, "No!"

August 5.

I dreamed of you last night. You got home very late, and came up by the dumb-waiter into the dining-room closet, in a dress-coat and a white hat very much crushed. You said you had been out to drive with a Spanish lady. It seemed in the dream all very natural; but a sudden rush of rain on the roof woke me, and I laughed aloud at the absurdity of the vision, — as you will probably do when you read this account of it.

Allow me to offer you, for your future guidance, Alderman G——'s views on public libraries: —

"Alderman G—— has not a doubt that the library would hold all the books actually required, — such works as were likely to be in demand by the reading public, and would do any good. He believed in casting off a great deal of superfluous matter that he had reason to think was already there. The works of nearly every writer in the world were fast finding their way into the library, and were stored there at great expense. He asked if there were not a hundred thousand volumes on the shelves that were never called for."

A gentleman who has been trying to get a Lowell course writes to me: "As for lectures at the Lowell next season, there has been such an overflow of applications that it was impossible for me to obtain a course. . . . Sometimes applicants have to wait three or four years."

No Sumner yet. He leaves Washington on Monday the 7th, but stops in Philadelphia and New York.

4th. Write, declining the honor of presiding at the Literary Fund dinner. I cannot cross the ocean again so soon.

6th. Mr. McKenzie preached a good sermon on Rest, — Christ sitting by Jacob's well, being weary.

7th. Read a little in Michelet's French Revolution, — a pictorial style, the style of romance rather than history.

8th. Read, in Hedge's Prose Writers of Germany, an essay on the supposed origin of Man [by Kant], — an interesting interpretation of Genesis.

12th. A man with a divining-rod points out a place where we may dig a well. I am curious to see if we shall find water there. Sumner arrives.

14th. Go with Sumner to Mr. James's to see the regatta. A pretty sight,—all those towering white sails in the distance; and then a slow and scattered flight, as of sea-birds, south toward Minot's Ledge.

15th. Went to town to attend the meeting of the Historical Society in celebration of Walter Scott's birthday. Remarks by Winthrop, Emerson, Hillard, Quincy, and Waterston, and letters from Holmes and Bryant.

17th. The senator brings a perfect avalanche of newspapers with him from all quarters of the Union; and I see what unwholesome food for the million they furnish.

From Louis Agassiz.

CAMBRIDGE, August 18, 1871.

MY DEAR LONGFELLOW,—You are so lovable that I should like to have you all to myself; and yet my necessities are such, on the eve of a long journey, that I hardly know how to enjoy what is actually offered me. Mrs. A., too, would gladly join me on a day's visit to you at Nahant. I had hoped to accompany her this morning when she went to see her mother, and had intended to call upon you to agree for a day; but the Museum has kept me prisoner, and I must postpone my visit to next week. Meanwhile believe me

Ever truly your friend,

L.[s] AGASSIZ.

22d. The steam-tug comes for us, and Sumner, Mr. James, Ernest, and myself go to meet the revenue-cutter in the harbor. Find on board the Collector, with Agassiz and a young Japanese prince; and we steam away for Minot's Ledge. Dinner (on board) ended, we find ourselves at the base of the lighthouse, rising sheer out of the sea like a huge stone cannon, mouth upward. We are hoisted up forty feet in a chair, some of us; others go up by an iron ladder,—all but the young Japanese, who refuses to go up at all. Whether he was afraid, or thought it only a trick to imprison him, will remain a mystery till his Travels are published.

23d. Sumner departs, and we are left quite lonely. Read Scott's Rokeby. In the evening see the half-moon sailing through broken clouds, white and black, like a ship making her way through fields of ice.

25th. Mr. [F. H.] Underwood calls to talk about some literary matters.

To G. W. Greene.

NAHANT, August 25, 1871.

The senator [Sumner] has departed; he comes back to Nahant on Sunday, but not to me, having another friend to visit here, who insists upon having his share. I am sorry to say that the violent attack of *angina pectoris* which he had last winter has left some traces. He complains that I walk too fast, and is averse to walking at all. The air of Nahant is just the thing for him, and he means to stay a week or two longer,—about as long as we do.

Thanks for the gondolier's pamphlet on Dante; I dare say it is very curious: but did you find in it any valuable hint or suggestion? On Tuesday we made our expedition to Minot's Ledge; it was every way pleasant and successful. We wished you could have been with us; but it was impossible to notify you in season. The lighthouse rises out of the sea like a beautiful stone cannon, mouth upward, belching forth only friendly fires. We went up into it,—even into the lantern itself, the glass of which (beautiful plate-glass) cost ten thousand dollars. I can believe this, having seen it, and knowing what telescopic lenses cost. The lantern will hold six people easily.

The days grow shorter; the trees begin to scatter their curl-papers about the grass; there is a touch of autumn in the air; and the swift summer is gone.

September 1. Everything alive with sunshine, and the sea grinding its curved battle-axe on the beach. Read in Plutarch's Morals and in Tyndall's Swiss Sketches, — climbing the Matterhorn and other perilous peaks. His descriptions of sky-effects are very beautiful.

2d. Receive from Mr. Henry Gersoni a Hebrew translation of 'Excelsior.'

4th. Call on Dr. Holmes at Mr. James's. Sumner still there. We discuss the new poets.

7th. I begin to grow restless, and want to get back to Cambridge.

11th. Begin to pack. I wish it were over, and I in Cambridge. I am impatient to send the Divine Tragedy to the printers.

25th, *Cambridge*. Begin the printing of the Tragedy. In the evening look over Weber's Metrical Romances.

28th. Sophocles passed a couple of hours with me talking about Homer, and the convents in the East, in one of which he was educated.

29th. Read Strodtman's Life of Heine.

30th. Dinner at the Club. Among other guests M. Coquerel, the Protestant liberal clergyman from Paris. A very agreeable man, speaking English with the greatest fluency.

October 11. In the evening take the girls to see Miss Nilsson in *Lucia*. Her singing and acting both superb. Brignoli, with his pathetic tenor, as Edgardo.

12th. Corrected manuscript and proofs. Strodtman's Heine; rather long-winded.

15th. Drove Agassiz in to dine with Mr. Hooper, to meet

President Grant and some of his Secretaries. The President is a quiet, unostentatious man, with a soft, pleasant voice.

18th. The delays of printers are a great worry to authors.

20th. A call from the son of the late Archbishop of Canterbury, whom I saw at Lambeth Palace in 1868. Went with him to the Library and to the Museum.

21st. Go to see Prescott's library, which is to be sold by auction; then to Music Hall to hear the organ.

25th. At the Prescott sale. A great sacrifice.[1] Get the last proof-sheet of the Divine Tragedy.

28th. Dinner at Club. The British Parliament was well represented.

29th. Heard M. Coquerel, the French clergyman, preach in English, which he did astonishingly well. The choir sang Luther's hymn, *Ein' feste Burg*, in Dr. Hedge's translation, which I thought very good.

30th. Read over proofs of the Interludes and Finale and am doubtful and perplexed.

31st. Mr. Samuelson, M.P., came out to dine. We took a walk to see the Colleges and the Observatory. Lowell dined with us, and was very gay and agreeable.

November 2. Walked to Riverside, and bought Pictures in Black, by Paul Konewka, — books for children, but with beautiful "scissor-pictures," silhouettes of great artistic skill; I never tire of them, they are so natural.

8th. M. Coquerel, Professor Child, and S. at our family dinner to-day. Coquerel is a great talker, and talks well.

15th. All the last week perplexed and busy with final correction of the Tragedy.

[1] Mr. Prescott's copies of Irving — nine volumes — are in the library of Craigie House.

16th. Went down to the Riverside Press with a manuscript novel sent by a lady to find a publisher, and bespeak for it an early and friendly reading. Call on Mountford, who has taken the old Winthrop house for the winter.[1]

17th. Two editions of the Divine Tragedy will be published at the same time, — a dear one and a cheap one. I never had so many doubts and hesitations about any book as about this.

18th. Went with Fields to the Globe to see Miss Cushman as Katharine in Henry VIII.

19th. Wrote a great many letters. Sumner at dinner. He seemed weary of work.

To Florence A-

November 20, 1871.

I have put off answering your nice little note from day to day; but, as you see, I have not forgotten it. I have been hoping all along that some lines of poetry, such as you ask for, would come into my mind. But they would not, and so I have to write you in prose, not to keep you waiting any longer.

If you will ask your papa, who knows all about it, he will tell you that good poems do not always come to one's mind when wanted. Verses — yes, one can write those at any time; but real poetry — that is another matter. I think good prose is better than bad verse. I do not say bad *poetry*, because when it is bad, it is no longer poetry.

And so I send you this little note instead of a little song; and with it good wishes for your birthday, and kind remembrances for your father.

[1] William Mountford, author of Euthanasy, and Thorpe.

26th. Drove over to the Navy Yard in the afternoon with my girls to see the little steamer (the "Hassler") in which Agassiz is going round the Cape. Yesterday at the Club dinner we drank his health at parting. I proposed it thus: "Gentlemen, I am reminded that we shall not again have with us for a year and a day our dear Agassiz, who sits there at the head of the table so joyous and unconcerned. I shall, therefore, for once break through our usual custom and propose his health. Wordsworth once said that he could have written the plays of Shakespeare if he had had a mind to. And I suppose that on an occasion like this I could make a speech, — if I had a mind to. But I shall do nothing of the kind; I shall limit myself to proposing 'The health of Agassiz: his deepest sea-soundings shall not be deeper than our love and admiration for him.

'Quis desiderio sit pudor aut modus
Tam cari capitis?'"

From Bayard Taylor.

KENNETT SQUARE, November 27, 1871.

MY DEAR LONGFELLOW, — *Now* all is clear! I can overlook your design from first to last, and see how each part grows in importance as it falls into its place. The closing of the Divine Tragedy with the Apostles' Creed somewhat puzzled me; and when I received your letter on Saturday, I could not guess how the New England Tragedies were to be connected. But the proofs of the Interludes and the Finale, which arrived this morning, give me the key to all. I do not feel that the meaning of any detail is doubtful, and each gains from the extent and beauty and altitude of the uniting design.

I know not who else before you has so wonderfully wedded Poetry and the Religious Sentiment. Milton, certainly, only half succeeded; and in spite of Klopstock's former popularity I must insist that he entirely failed. What in this completed work might seem simplest to the ordinary reader, is to me the greatest evidence of your success. In the Finale the familiar phrases meet me in a transfigured form: it is a new illustration of the power which perfect rhythm adds to language.

I congratulate you from my heart; and in doing so I congratulate myself: for each new achievement in Poetry is an indirect inspiration to me. I feel anew the capacity to rise when another rises. And I have not had for a long time such an influx of fresh hope and courage as within the past seven days.[1]

Always faithfully yours,
BAYARD TAYLOR.

December 1. Dined with Charles Perkins to meet Dr. Howson, Dean of Chester, England.

3d. Finished the 'Baron Castine of St. Castine.'

4th. Call on the Dean of Chester at Dr. Wharton's; and with him on Mrs. Stowe. We see her and her sister Miss Beecher, and Dr. Stowe, with his wild snowstorm of hair and beard.

5th. A year ago to-day I began the Divine Tragedy, and finished it on the 27th of January. To-day the thought comes back to my mind of a Tragedy of Judas Maccabeus, which I noted down as long ago as 1850. Went with the Dean and his daughters to the Library, to the Museum, to Dr. Palfrey's, to the Botanic Garden. They dined with us.

[1] Shortly before, Mr. Taylor had written: "I am full of renewed hope and courage this evening after your cordial words. But, as I have tried to say, I have never yet met you without some clear, strong, generous encouragement."

8th. Lunched at President Eliot's to meet the Grand Duke Alexis of Russia, a tall, handsome youth of twenty-one or two.

9th. At the dinner given by citizens of Boston to the Grand Duke. Winthrop presided, and there was much speech-making till midnight.

10th. At home all day. Began the Tragedy of Judas Maccabeus. The subject is a very striking one, — the collision of Judaism and Hellenism; I greatly wonder that it has not been treated before.

11th. By invitation of the Grand Duke, dine with him at the Revere. Besides his suite, the guests were Winthrop, Lowell, Holmes, President Eliot, Mr. Fox, Mr. Winlock, and Mr. Storer, the Russian consul.

12th. The Divine Tragedy is published to-day.

17th. Taylor's notice of Christus in the New York Tribune is very good, and shows the scope of the whole poem and the connection of its parts.

To G. W. Greene.

December 17, 1871.

It is not tobacco that brings upon the human race those evils whose long and dismal catalogue you send me; but, as Dr. Holland — not the author of 'Bitter-Sweet,' though I dare say the author of sweet bitters — once said, tapping a bottle at the dinner-table with his knife, "That is the fellow that does the mischief!"

I supposed that long ago you had gone from Cornell's Ithaca to your own; by your letter to-day I see that little Telemachus must still be looking for Ulysses.

The Divine Tragedy is very successful, from the bookseller's point of view, — ten thousand copies were published on Tuesday last, and the printers are already at work on three thousand more. That is pleasant, but that is not the main thing. The only question about a book ought to be whether it is successful in itself. Bayard Taylor, Lowell, and Fields dined with me yesterday.

18th. Finish Act third of Maccabeus, begun yesterday.

21st. Finish Judas Maccabeus, — begun on the 10th; the Acts are not long, but there are five of them. A new subject comes to my mind, — Hagar and Ishmael. But can it be wrought into a tragedy? It is tragic enough; but has it unity, and has it a catastrophe to end with?

22d. Read in Forster's Life of Dickens.

To G. W. Greene.

December 23, 1871.

The weather to-day has been Roman weather, that takes all manliness out of a man; and to-night the south wind is pelting hail, rain, and sleet against my study-windows. I feel, too, a little exhausted by work, for within the last fortnight I have written a tragedy, which hangs over your visit like a thunder-cloud. You will have to hear it, however sound you may sleep in the green chair. I have also many things to tell you of the dinner to the Grand Duke Alexis, at which I was present, sitting at the right hand of this amiable and handsome youth. On the whole, it was most successful; but two or three things were said in speeches that were amazingly funny. Have you seen Forster's Life of Dickens? It is very interesting, but it made me profoundly melancholy; perhaps I can tell you why, but I hardly care to write it.

With all good wishes for a happy, if not a merry, Christmas.

27th. Finished two scenes of 'Hagar.' It interests me; but whether I can make anything of it is doubtful.[1]

[1] Only a few fragments more were written.

29th. Read to Greene (who arrived last night) 'Baron Castine,' which he likes, and 'Judas,' which he does not dislike. Receive a highly complimentary letter from Rev. Dr. Bushnell on the Divine Tragedy.

From Horace Bushnell.

HARTFORD, December 28, 1871.

DEAR SIR, — Since it will be a satisfaction to me to express my delight in the success of your poem, you cannot well deny me the privilege. When I heard the first announcement of it as forthcoming, I said: "Well, it is the grandest of all subjects; why has it never been attempted?" And yet I said inwardly in the next breath: "What mortal power is equal to the handling of it?" The greater and the more delightful is my surprise at the result. You have managed the theme with really wonderful address. The episodes, and the hard characters, and the partly imaginary characters, you had your liberty in; and you have used them well to suffuse and flavor and poetize the story. And yet, I know not how it is, but the part which *finds* me most perfectly, and is, in fact, the most poetic poetry of all, is the prose-poem, — the nearly rhythmic transcription of the simple narrative matter of the gospels. Perhaps the true account of it may be that the handling is so delicately reverent, intruding so little of the poet's fine thinking and things, that the reverence incorporate promotes the words and lifts the ranges of the sentiment; so that when the reader comes out at the close, he finds himself in a curiously new kind of inspiration, born of modesty and silence.

I can easily imagine that certain chaffy people may put their disrespect on you for what I consider your praise. Had you undertaken to build the Christ yourself, as they would require of you, I verily believe it would have killed you, — that is, made you a preacher.

With many thanks, I am yours,

HORACE BUSHNELL.

30th. Receive from Routledge in London three notices of the Tragedy, all hostile.

CHAPTER X.

JOURNAL AND LETTERS.

1872.

January 4. Read Sheik Saadi's Gulistan, in Gladwin's translation, with preface by Emerson.

15th. Give the day to the reading of a novel of Tourgénief, — beautifully written, but painful.

16th. Read Mrs. [Emma] Marshall's Heights and Valleys, which the authoress sends me, — a well-written tale of the religious kind.

To G. W. Greene.

January 21, 1872.

Do not jump rashly at disagreeable conclusions. A newspaper writer is not infallible, any more than Pio Nono. So do not yield to despondency because Solomon proposes to cut the baby in two. Possibly he has no such intention.

A theological question has just risen in my mind. What right has a Calvinist to get married and beget children, when, according to his doctrine, the chances are that they will go into everlasting torment? Ought he not rather to go into a monastery or a Shaker brotherhood?

I return Professor F——'s letter, and am glad that he enjoyed the dinner. You did, and I did, and we all did; and it was very pleasant every way.

February 3. Read in Taine's History of English Literature, — a prodigiously clever book.

4th. Continue Taine. How does a Frenchman contrive to go out of himself and get such insight into things English?

11th. Read Voltaire's *Zaïre.* These two lines make me think of Sumner: —

> "Heureux à qui le ciel a donné le pouvoir
> De remplir comme vous un si noble devoir."

To C. E. Norton (in Europe).

February 20, 1872.

I was delighted to get your letter and to learn that you are all well, and particularly that your mother's health is quite restored. That is the best news you could send, and brightens up your letter, otherwise rather gloomy with the gigantic scoundrelism of your native land. And no wonder. At times it seems to me that we have the millstone round our neck, and that the rest is coming. Still, I have faith that the good will conquer, and do not fall upon my sword.

Thanks for the Uhland Catalogue, which is curious and worth keeping. But what a mouldy, mediæval collection of old armor! Quaritch has published a similar catalogue of valuable old rubbish, which if you have not seen I advise you to get. It is very curious; and for the moment one is seduced into believing that he really wants the books and must have them: but he lays the catalogue away, and the pleasing illusion soon vanishes. Still, I confess that of all the ways of spending money yet devised by man, this is to me the most fascinating.

I have requested Tauchnitz to send you a copy of his edition of my new book [The Divine Tragedy]. It is the first part of Christus. The three parts are to be joined by

Interludes of 'The Abbot Joachim' and 'Martin Luther,' and closed by a Finale, 'St. John,'—a counterpoise to the 'Introitus' of the present volume. This is an old, old design; twenty years old and more, and only now completed. In a certain sense one part explains and requires the others. . . .

Your cousin, S. Eliot, has begun his lectures in the University course, on the History of the present century. I hear that his audience is large, and young ladies abound in the class. I missed his introductory, but shall attend the rest. I rejoice in his success.—Appleton has a volume of poems in the press.

24th. Club dinner. Had as my guest the amiable Robert Dale Owen. On the other side of me sat Robert Collyer, the clergyman. Both men of mark.

25th. Read Schiller's *Don Carlos.* At dinner had Dr. Clement, of Hamburg,—a simple, sweet old man, very *naïf.* By birth he is a Frieslander, born on one of the islands in the North Sea.

26th. Hear Sophocles on Simon Magus, with some extracts from his writings and account of his doctrines that have not found their way into the Biblical Dictionaries. Very interesting and curious. Helen of Tyre he called his *Epinoia,* or self-consciousness.

I have more definitely conceived the idea of a dramatic poem on Michael Angelo and Vittoria Colonna, which has been vaguely hovering in my thoughts for some time. Can I accomplish it?

To G. W. Greene.

February 26, 1872.

I have been reading to-day Schiller's *Don Carlos.* It is more poetical than Alfieri's *Filippo,* but not so simply tragic. Alfieri's tragedy is the drop of deadly poison in a ring; Schiller's is the same, diluted and drunk from a silver-chased goblet. Schiller's is a very noble poem, affluent in thought and diction, but too long and too intricate for a tragedy. The real Tragic Muse hardly stops to pluck so many flowers by the way.

I went down this morning to hear Professor Sophocles lecture on Simon Magus. It was curious, — curt, sarcastic, learned. He has found some rather new material which the ready writers of the Biblical Dictionaries seem to have overlooked; but, virtually, it was the portrait I have given in the Divine Tragedy. There were some things, however, which I wish I had known before.

I am at this moment paying the penalty of exposure to the bitter wind. It has pierced me with a thousand spears, dried up my lungs, and parched my throat. Talk of the east wind! It is a benediction compared with this west wind out there now, howling like a wolf, — though, come to think of it, I never heard a wolf howl, only a dog.

I have been reading to-day Maffei's *Meropa*. An interesting subject; but such a style! The great Dryasdust himself could hardly surpass it. Schlegel is unjust to Alfieri; he emphasizes his defects, and seems not to see his merits, — his force, his directness, the "still river that runs deep" of his style.

27th. My sixty-fifth birthday, — and a bitter cold day it is, which keeps me close indoors. Read Schlegel's lectures on the German Drama; then a most interesting and charmingly written book, Hermann Grimm's Life of Michael Angelo.

28th. Indoors, reading Grimm. The book is very interesting, though I think too much space is given to the political history of the time; at all events, I should have been satisfied with less.

29th. Heard S. Eliot's lecture. He came home to dine with me, and it was very pleasant.

March 2. Keep indoors, looking over Vasari's Lives of the Painters. Write to Sumner and to Greene.

3d. Read in Vasari and Benvenuto Cellini and Mrs. Jameson's Italian Painters, and live in Italy in spirit, while my poor body suffers here with a dismal cold. — In the afternoon Howells came in with Bret Harte.

4th. Reading and making notes for Michael Angelo. The subject attracts me; but it is difficult to treat dramatically, for want of unity of action and plot in general.

15th. I have long neglected this record. The last ten days have been filled with Michael Angelo. I have made many notes, and written one Act, — the scenes between him and Benvenuto and Sebastian, — and sketched others. I shall have as hard a time in casting this statue as Benvenuto had in casting his Perseus; but it promises fair, and I am in no hurry. I want it for a long and delightful occupation. I have written the close, or epilogue.

17th. Have Ascanio Condivi's Life of Angelo; also Halford's, which has an engraving of Sebastian's portrait of Vittoria.

31st. This is a melancholy Easter Sunday. The ground is white with snow, the thermometer at freezing, the wind northeast, and a sleety rain falling. — In Michael Angelo I have now written [six scenes]; others are to be interspersed and added.

To G. W. Greene.

March 31, 1872.

What has put it into my head, I do not know, but I was thinking just now of Empoli, famous in Tuscan annals and *Storie Fiorentine.* We passed through it after dark. The station was ablaze with lights. It sounded strangely to hear the conductor of the train cry: "Empoli!" and a boy selling cakes and fruit repeat over and over again, "Aranci, cigari, paste, pane, mele!" What a contrast with Farinata's fiery speech in the days of old!

If you can tell by what possible association this comes to mind, you can do more than I can.

April 3. A wedding in St. John's Church, close by us. An April day of cloud and sunshine; but in the prayer, as the clergyman said "Send down thy blessing upon them," the sun burst from the clouds and poured through the high windows of the choir a flood of golden light upon the bride and bridegroom.

4th. Arranged my books upstairs. Governor Claflin called, with President Raymond of Vassar College, — a female college at Poughkeepsie.

5th. Went to town to give Ernest a sitting. Saw Hazeltine's bust of me, made in Rome in 1869, — a clever piece of work, I should say.

6th. Went to the Lifting Cure. Sat to Ernest.

10th. Field of Philadelphia, Fields of Boston, and Lowell dined with us at our Wednesday family dinner.

12th. Have put a balustrade on the bank in front of the house. Do not half like it.

18th. Finished 'San Silvestro,' in Michael Angelo. I have now written seven acts or parts of the work; but some of the most important are still to come. In the evening went with Mrs. F. to hear the German poet, Dr. Jordan, recite his *Nibelungen.*

May 4. The Three Books of Song is going to press at once. First edition to be ten thousand copies.

5th. A dreary day. Paced up and down the veranda,

but took no long walk. — Horace Greeley is nominated by the Cincinnati Convention as candidate for the Presidency in opposition to General Grant!

6th. I take this time of Greene's visit for a good rest, neither writing nor reading.

10th. A lovely day, full of sunshine, blossoms, and sweet, sad memories.

11th. Greene departs, and I am left solitary, to resume the old tasks.

12th. Wrote a short poem on 'Charlemagne' from a story in an old chronicle, *De Factis Caroli Magni*, quoted by Cantù, *Storia degli Italiani*, ii. 122. I first heard it from Charles Perkins in one of his lectures.

To G. W. Greene.

May 14, 1872.

After you left me on Saturday, I beguiled a part of the dull day by reading the last book of the Iliad in Cesarotti's translation. This reading confirms me in my theory of translation. In Cesarotti you see Homer, — the very man you are looking for. Sometimes his prose runs almost into hexameters.

Yesterday I received a beautiful bouquet of tea-roses from Mr. A—— and Miss W——, in memory of their visit. I also wrote a poem on the descent of Charlemagne into Italy, from an old Latin chronicle, — a very striking incident. It will find a place — indeed, has already found a place — in Michael Angelo; you will not see how nor where, but I do.[1] Soon after you were gone, came a note from Mrs. Fields, inviting us to dine with her after hearing Emerson on Monday.

[1] This poem, 'Charlemagne,' found a place, not in Michael Angelo, but in the third part of the Wayside Inn.

18th. Finished 'Santa Anna dei Funari' in Michael Angelo; and that finishes the poem, the third part being already written. So the poem in its first form is complete; but other scenes will be intercalated. I began it March 6.

19th. Read Miss Preston's translation of *Mireio*, a Provençal poem by Frédéric Mistral,—a truly lovely and wonderful poem. I wish I had the original. Why did no one put it into my hands in France? It is very pathetic and captivating.

25th. My Three Books of Song published to-day. Club dinner. Admiral Stedman, Julian Hawthorne, and Mr. Aldrich were the guests. In the evening J. O.

29th. The lilacs in full bloom, and a certain sadness in the air. Read Mr. Watt's *Fra Ægypternes Land.* In the afternoon heard Charles Perkins's closing lecture on Italian Art.

June 1. Read parts of Oehlenschläger's *Helge*, and also Mr. Watt's account of his visit to the Craigie House, "Et Besog hos Henry Longfellow," in *For Romantik og Historie*, with a portrait having the shoulders up to the ears. I confess I do not like to have my private conversations reported in print.

To G. W. Greene.

June 4, 1872.

On reading the line in your letter about your reluctance to touch an Italian theme, there came swimming into the twilight of memory, like a planet, a sentence from Locke, which I have remembered ever since my college days:

> "Thus the ideas, as well as the children, of our youth often die before us; and our minds represent to us those tombs to which we are approaching, where, though the brass and marble remain, yet the inscriptions are effaced by time, and the imagery moulders away."

That little flower of rhetoric blooms for me far back in my Junior year.

To C. E. Norton.

June 19, 1872.

As soon as I received your last letter I acted upon it without a moment's delay. I wrote a line or two in the evening to Karl Witte, and the next morning sent a large-paper copy of the Divine Comedy. . . . Your description of him is very interesting, and makes me regret that I did not go to Halle to visit him and see his Dante collection, as you did. — I suppose you have not yet seen Miss Rossetti's Shadow of Dante, — it is an excellent book, which you will like. Lowell has a review of it in the next North American. — Cambridge is now in its glory of leaves and blossoms, and awaits your return with impatience.

21st. Class-day, and very hot. A call from Rear-Admiral Polo de Bernabé, the Spanish Minister, and Antonio Flores, Minister of Ecuador; they stayed to dinner with me, and we had a good deal of pleasant chat. In the evening I walked with the girls in the College grounds to hear the music.

25th. Went with E., A. and B. to the Peace Jubilee in Gilmore's Coliseum, and heard the English, French, and Prussian bands. They all played beautifully.

July 2. At last an east wind! Welcome a thousand times!

5th. Came down to Nahant for the summer, — everything as of old. A lovely afternoon, the air perfect and most delightful.

6th. Get things to rights, and read *Les Nièces de Mazarin* [by Amédée Renée], — a very interesting book, which I read fifteen years ago, and have not looked at since.

From T. G. Appleton.

NEWPORT, July 19, 1872.

DEAR H., — Your last jolly letter has been received and appreciated. All you say of the little joker, the Mercury, is but too true. He has no station like his relative in 'Hamlet,' and he moves about under the finger of Apollo as he does under ours, ever dodging and elusive. But I have a little fellow here who has ways of his own, — a Mercury that cannot be got to go above 74°; and a quarrelsome couple that are ever reversing their orders, — the old fellow plunging out in fair weather, and the lady without an umbrella risking it in the rain. Evidently a German toy, made to sell, and one of the dark manœuvres of the Black Forest.

E. seemed much afflicted at my infidelity to Nahant.[1] But Nahant must have had an easy victory over Newport this year as to heat, — especially our delightful villa, with the fresh strike of the southwest from the water. But now it is much cooler, and I do not think we shall have broilers, as before; yet I am preparing to get out of these seas of sleep to the crisp dancing of our clearer water I do not now often go beyond Benton's Reef; once to Block Island, — to me always before an isle of mystery, and now known to be like many another, though so solitary and alone. We lounge up the Sound and see the sunsets, — often a splendid bonfire made from the remnants of a fog. Last evening we spent at Mrs. R. H——'s, with Miss [Charlotte] Cushman and the L——s. It is a pleasant thing sitting in the moonlight, with flats all about like opera decorations, and such good talk as Miss Cushman commands. Mrs. H—— told me that, to decorate her hemicycle and relieve her too much green, she painted

[1] Mr. Appleton had built himself a house in Newport.

some of her chairs red, herself; and presently a scarlet fever broke out among all the outdoor chairs of the country; and now in Connecticut they prepare them red by hundreds. Mrs. L—— is in constant delight contemplating the study Dante, which she has on a little table by itself. I hope you have secured [the pieces of] the Dante coffin, and I am curious to hear what you will do with them,—leave them as they are, or imprison them in gold and precious stones.[1]

Queer! I have had but one chowder this summer. It is like some Burgundies,—it must be tasted only where the codfish are plucked. I do not care for it in Boston, and here it has but a faint relish; but at Nahant—every day, and two helps! That will do for talk, now.

Yours affectionately,

T. G. Appleton.

25th. I always find the seaside a very idle, and therefore a very restless, place. I must have myself tied into my chair, as Alfieri used to do, or I can accomplish nothing.

30th. A northeastern storm is raging,—no steamboat, no possibility of going to the post-office. We are embargoed.

To J. T. Fields.

Nahant, August 22, 1872.

The masked batteries of the clouds have opened upon us again to-day, and I write this under fire. The house leaks like a friend to whom you have confided an important secret; and altogether the aspect of things is lugubrious.

[1] Some bits of the coffin, discovered in 1865, had been sent to Mr. Longfellow from Mr. T. B. Lawrence, United States Consul-General in Italy.

Sumner and Greene have both departed, each taking up his burden of care which he had laid down for a little while; and I have at length leisure to thank you for your letter of last week and Mr. Lea's of this. His communication is very interesting and curious. At all events it shows how old the song is, and quite cuts off the claims of the young Lochinvar of the West who wants to run away with the Muse.[1] Owen has found in Cambridge a lady who says that her mother taught her those lines in her childhood; and another who says they were written by — Abraham Lincoln!

September 1. Sumner comes down. He is quite overworked, and has made up his mind to go to Europe on Tuesday next.

To Mrs. J. T. Fields.

NAHANT, September 3, 1872.

The interruption of many visitors has prevented me from thanking you sooner for your beautiful poem. I have read it and re-read it with great pleasure. It is simple and tender, as an Idyl should be, particularly an 'Idyl of the Shakers.'

I have long thought that a poem could be drawn from their strange and unnatural lives of self-surrender and seclusion from the world. They are the Protestant Monks and Nuns. You have treated the theme with great deli-

[1] The communication had reference to the song put into the mouth of the Cobbler of Hagenau, in the second part of the Wayside Inn, —

"Our ingress into the world
Is naked and bare," etc.

A youth had written from the West to say that he was the author of the lines. They have been attributed to Franklin, and are found in print in an English work, Eccentricities of John Edwin, 1791.

cacy and sympathy, — the only way in which such a theme can be treated.

You must soon be going home. I wish I were; and yet, before closing this establishment, where the "sea-views are unrivalled, and charges moderate," I hope to be honored by your presence and that of your husband.

We remain here till that indefinite period known as "the middle of next week."

Till then, and afterwards,

Yours truly.

8th. Read some of Haweis's sermons. He is a very liberal divine of the Church of England. Also some parts of Buchner's Origin of Man, — a Darwinian book.

10th. T. and Kensett sail over to Taft's in the cold gray weather to dine on birds. Taft's and the hospital opposite and the gulf between them are an illustration of Dives and Lazarus, — Dives faring sumptuously every day, and the sea-tides coming and licking the sores of Lazarus.

14th. Return to Cambridge.

21st. Went to see the Mayor and intercede for the Whitfield elm, which is to be cut down.

22d. In the afternoon Fields comes, and Joaquin Miller, the California poet, — a rather wild, but to me very interesting, personality. They stay to dinner.

24th. Hear that the Whitfield elm has been cut down. Cambridge has an ill renown for destroying trees.

25th. Pleasant readings of Horace every morning with Edith and Greene.

28th. Christus published to-day, in three volumes.

October 1. Called on Dr. Hedge at his house on North Avenue to welcome him to Cambridge as Professor of German in the College.

2d. Hedge, Palfrey, Howells, and Robert Dale Owen to dinner.

3d. Signor Mario, the famous tenor, called, with Signor Marzo, of Naples.

To G. W. Greene.

October 8, 1872.

If you have forgotten it, you will be pleased to be reminded that Horace mentions the Craigie House in Ode XXI. of the First Book. He speaks of it as the *viridis Cragi,* in which Diana takes delight, — that is, on which the moonlight lingers. To-night her face is rather clouded as she looks across the meadows. How splendidly Autumn begins to tread his wine-press! The creepers round the seat in the old apple-tree have assumed the shape of two magnificent bay horses, or red-bronze horses rather; the eyes being formed by hollows in the old trunk. I delighted in them for an hour to-day, pacing the veranda after the rain.

Nothing from Sumner yet. He is as silent as Grant, and I am as garrulous as Greeley, having already written him three letters. Mr. [George] Macdonald is here, and lectures on Burns next Thursday at Cambridgeport.

10th. The evening at Mr. George Macdonald's lecture on Burns. After lecture he with his wife and son supped with me.

13th. Heard Dr. Hedge preach an excellent sermon on the Real and the Ideal. Looked over Eckermann's Conversations. Was pleased to find Goethe's hearty praise of Manzoni, particularly his *Promessi Sposi,* which I had forgotten.

16th. Went to Rubinstein's concert. He is a superb player on the pianoforte. Equally good on the violin was

Wieniowsky. Wonderful masters of their instruments both. Rubinstein looks like Beethoven.

19th. Called on Professor Tyndall; a very lively, agreeable man. He is lecturing on Light at the Lowell Institute. On my way out stopped to see Agassiz, who has just returned from the Pacific.

20th. *Sunday.* A walk in Mount Auburn, — a sad place. Then called upon Aldrich, who has Lowell's house [Elmwood] during his absence.

23d. The "Hecla" telegraphed. We ordered the carriage and drove in to the steamer. We were just in time. We drive home very happy.

To G. W. Greene.

October 24, 1872.

I forgot to say that Dr. S——'s object in writing to me, an "entire stranger," is to get a professorship at Cornell, or some other university, in order to pursue his studies in comparative philology "in the manner of Max Müller's method, without hindrance." He further says: "I should be happy to contribute to the sciential development of a country that produces men like James Gordon Bennett and Henry M. Stanley."

I received the other day a valuable and curious present from England, — namely, Coleridge's inkstand;[1] and only wish he had left some of his poems in it. It is an oblong ebony tray, with two glass *flacons* for the ink Inlaid between them is a small ivory plate, with the inscription, — *Samuel Taylor Coleridge, his inkstand.* I fear that the bronze owl which now adorns the centre of my study-table will have to give place to this interesting relic.

[1] A gift from Mr. S. C. Hall, of London, who had received it from Mr. Gilman, in whose house at Highgate Coleridge spent his last years. See page 444.

I have been reading lately Goethe's *Tag und Jahres Hefte,* and Schiller's Correspondence with Körner. Taken together, they give a very different view of Goethe from the one usually given, and show a man not holding himself apart from others, but longing for sympathy, and very lenient in his judgments. Schiller and Korner do not spare his weaknesses. Extracts from these and similar works would make the best life of Goethe. All that is tedious could be left out.

25th. Tyndall's closing lecture, on the invisible rays of the sun. Illustrated by brilliant experiments.

26th. An influenza is raging among the horses. They are all ill, and nearly all communication with Boston is cut off. We persuade the stable-keeper to let us have a carriage for town to-night. He promises the only two horses that are not disabled. Drive in with Agassiz and President Eliot to dine with Tyndall at Mr. Lowell's. A pleasant dinner.

27th. Try to read Festus. I cannot do it; it baffles, eludes, and tires me. It is too chaotic, too shapeless. Read Corneille's *La Place Royale;* and two *Proverbes* of Alfred de Musset,—*Un Caprice,* and *Il faut qu'une porte.*

To G. W. Greene.

October 27, 1872.

Here is a bold rhyme from a new poet. What would the Academy say to it,—if there were an Academy?

"A pencilled shade the sky doth sweep,
And transient glooms creep in to sleep
Amid the orchard;
Fantastic breezes pull the trees
Hither and yon, to vagaries
Of aspect tortured."

Hood and Horace Smith would have delighted in it. But you will think that Pegasus has caught the influenza now prevailing among the horses. This influenza has cut us off from Boston almost entirely. It has thrown Cambridge back to where it was forty years ago. Our city has become once more a remote and quiet village. To me the feeling is delightful. I think of the army of invaders unable to cross the bridge, and I enjoy their discomfiture and my repose. Alas, it is only a momentary triumph!

> "L'onde s'enfle dessous, et d'un commun effort
> Les Maures et la mer entreront dans le port."

For *Maures* read *Bores*, and by *port* understand *Cambridgeport*.

You will see by this quotation that I have just been reading Corneille's *Cid.* It is in the grand style,—a strong and effective tragedy. It made me think of Cooper by its rude power and a certain force and roughness.

28th. It is astonishing how all things are brought to a standstill by this horse-distemper. It would seem almost as if the world were turned by horse-power. Drove to Brookline with Mr. and Mrs. Agassiz to lunch at Mr. Winthrop's with Professor Tyndall. I sat next to Rev. Mr. Brooks, who has just returned from Sweden and Russia.

30th. It came into my head to-day to read Ossian. which I have not looked into for forty years or more,—the strange rhapsody, "Did not Ossian hear a voice? Or was it the sound of the days that are no more?" It is full of the figures of the mist and rain that shroud the northern shores of Scotland and Ireland, and cannot be wholly a forgery.

November 2. Passed the morning in hanging pictures, — changing them about; the afternoon in walking; the evening in reading Weber's analysis of the *Nibelungen Lied*, with translations, and Bonnet's *Olympia Morata*.

10th. W. comes in at breakfast, and says there was a great fire in Boston last night. It proves to be a terrible fire, and is still raging among the largest and finest warehouses in the city.

11th. A soft Indian-summer day; went to the funeral of my old friend Charles Folsom, in the chapel of Mount Auburn.

To G. W. Greene.

November 13, 1872.

This is a pretty serious calamity, this fire in Boston. Everybody seems to have lost something who had anything to lose. . . . You may depend upon it, there is nothing perfectly secure but poverty.

I had a letter yesterday from Sumner in London. He says he has not read an American newspaper since he went away; but some idiotic friend has sent him articles which stir him up to wrath. He will soon return to find — what? His party defeated,

"Et cuncta terrarum subacta,
Præter atrocem animum Catonis;"

that is to say, his own intrepid mind.

I lunched to-day at Winthrop's, to meet Froude [the historian], — a very quiet, pleasant gentleman, whom I like much. I have not yet heard any of his lectures.

23d. One of the loveliest mornings. There was rain in the night, and it is frozen on the veranda roofs in ferns and stars. The birds are singing as if they thought spring had come; the air is exhilarating. Greene arrives from Rhode Island. We dine with T.

24th. A quiet day at home. More talking than walking.

27th. Read Gibbon's Autobiography; also Fitzgerald's translation of the Hippolytus of Euripides. A modern application of this classic tale might be made effective.

30th. Too ill with cold to go to Club dinner, and so lost the opportunity of proposing Agassiz's welcome home with a speech.

December 1. Read Carlyle's account of Voltaire in the Frederic, — very amusing.

5th. Read Forster's Dickens, volume second. Very interesting. The most restless of mortals, — no repose in anything; always at full speed. It is a wonder that he lived so long.

7th. Read Nichol's Hannibal, — an historic drama; then, looking over the Publishers' Circular, I saw, in Longmans' list, Hannibal in Italy, an Historical Drama, by W. Forsythe. I have often noticed this kind of duality in literary work. Are thoughts and themes in the air, like an epidemic? Benedict, of London, and Paine, of Cambridge, have both just completed oratorios of St. Peter.

To G. W. Greene.

December 19, 1872.

Your letter of yesterday is like a bucket of water poured into a dry pump, and forthwith sets the valves at work again. The cold I took when you were here has lasted till now, and made me rather disinclined to do anything but read. I have only written to my enemies, — the worst of all enemies, the "entire strangers" who ask questions that it takes a day's research to answer. *Marforio* was here yesterday, and stayed three hours; but the day before, *Pasquino* stayed five: so I forgave *Marforio*, though he left all his sentences unfinished. It is my own fault, I know; and I seem to hear the words of Demosthenes: "How would you comport yourself in weightier concerns if you cannot turn off an impertinent babbler, but suffer the eternal trifler to walk over you without telling him, 'Another time, good sir; at present I am in haste!'"

Among my readings is that of Thorwaldsen's Life and Works, by Eugène Plon. Not very well written, but extremely interesting, and illustrated with thirty-five wood-engravings of the great master. It is like a dream of Rome. You will be afraid to read it; and yet you must.

23d. A snowstorm. Read, and write letters, — I begin to think I shall never write anything else.

24th. E. and A. go to Portland to pass the Christmas holidays with their cousins at Highfield. In the afternoon Carl Schurz calls, and stays to dinner.

To G. W. Greene.

CHRISTMAS, 1872.

Multos et felices! "Many happy returns!" as a young lady of your acquaintance here said to a friend who was just engaged, — not knowing what else to say. *Multos et felices!* — a coin pretty well worn, and somewhat wasted. One may say, as St. Peter in *Paradiso* says of Faith: —

"— assai bene è trascorsa
D' esta moneta già la lega e 'l peso."

And I reply, like Dante, —

" — I' ho si lucida e si tonda
Che nel suo conio nulla mi s' inforsa."

And such I send it to you. Unluckily no unsentimental grocer will receive it.

Carl Schurz came to see me yesterday, and stayed to dinner. He said a good deal about Sumner, and thinks he feels keenly the action of the Massachusetts Legislature.[1] Well he may; for it was vindictive and brutal. Schurz thinks that Sumner's health is in a perilous condition, and regrets that he brought forward his Battle-flag resolution just now, when not well enough to support it. The subject, he thinks, is sure to be called up immediately after the holidays. Sumner is writing a speech to sustain his motion, and Schurz offers to read it for him and fight the battle sure to follow. Once more, *multos et felices!*

To G. W. Greene.

December 28, 1872.

For two days past I have had trouble in my left eye,— a kind of network before it, or, as Dr. Johnson might say, "something reticulated or decussated at equal distances, with interstices between the intersections;"[2] moreover, a great display of fireworks, sparks, and shooting-stars,

> "Quante il villan . . .
> Vede lucciole giù per la vallea."

This is by no means pleasant; but it shall not prevent me from thanking you for your letter.

I rejoice that you agree with me about Sumner's motion on the Battle-flags. I shall let him know what you

[1] Mr. Sumner had introduced in the United States Senate a resolution providing that for the sake of "national unity and good-will," and in accordance with the usage of civilized nations, "the names of battles with fellow-citizens [in the recent Civil War] should not be placed upon the regimental colors" of the National Army. His position was misrepresented, and condemned in resolutions of the Massachusetts Legislature. These were subsequently rescinded, just before Mr. Sumner's death, in 1874.

[2] This is the definition of "network" given in Johnson's Dictionary.

think of it, as it will comfort him, and you have not time to write to him just now, I suppose. I saw the account of Putnam's death in the paper, but said nothing about it to you, not wishing to come with black sails, and thinking that you would see it in your journal. This cold weather is very disconsolate. Sitting at dinner yesterday, I thought of you, and wished we were both at Amalfi. I had a vision of sunshine and a sapphire sea, which sent the nimble Mercury up many rounds of his ladder in the thermometer.

30th. Resumed the Wayside Inn, and put in order the Prelude and First Tale of Part Third.

From T. G. Appleton.

[Without date.]

DEAR HENRY, — I met lately Mr. P. at my publishers', and he told me of a new book of his. I send you a New York review of it. It is nice to see these fellows venture into the ink-stream and get so spattered. The book is a good book, too, — following out those spider-threads of instinct which are lost in the sky, and not too much losing hold of his web. I dare say he will now, like poor ——, go into retirement among the *incompris* authors. The Duke of Somerset has a nice little book which I have got, — only about a hundred pages, snug and compact, and modest for a duke; also about the eternal subject. There seems great soreness in the world at the place where soul and body dovetail. An expression of Mr. T. Lyman to me, years ago: "The bother of the Yankee," said he, "is that he rubs badly at the junction of soul and body." As true a thing as was ever said; and he not much of a sayer of such things. Yours,

T. G. APPLETON

CHAPTER XI.

JOURNAL AND LETTERS.

1873–1874.

January 1. Dined at 39 Beacon Street. How the old days come back to me; terribly distinct! Every corner of the house has its memory.

3d. A thaw in the night. At four o'clock, drip, drip, drip. I got up two or three times, and finally dressed myself at five; lighted my study-lamp, and strangely enough some passages for 'Michael Angelo and Titian' came into my mind. What spirit was abroad at that hour dictating to me?

5th. Look into Victor Hugo's *Année Terrible.* It seems to me violent rather than forcible.

16th. Here are the first seven lines of the Iliad, which I have put into hexameters,—though with no intention of going farther:—

Sing, O Goddess, the wrath of Peleidean Achilles,
Baleful, that brought disasters uncounted upon the Achaians.
Many a gallant soul of heroes flung into Hades,
And the heroes themselves as a prey to the dogs and to all the
Fowls of the air; for thus the will of Zeus was accomplished;
From the time when first in wrangling parted asunder
Atreus' son, the monarch of men, and godlike Achilles.

21st. I have now three tales finished of the Third Part of the Wayside Inn, with Prelude and Interludes.

February 19. This morning I counted the letters to be answered on my table. They are fifty-two. Thus is my life riddled to pieces. Nevertheless, I have now completed six tales of the new volume.

27th. My sixty-sixth birthday. Finished the new volume of the Wayside Inn,[1] and close the book.

April 3. Translated from the Spanish of Castillejo the little ditty, *Alguna vez,* —

"Some day, some day,
O troubled breast,
Shalt thou find rest," etc.

5th. S. Eliot's lecture on European Revolutions of '48 and '49. Mr. S—— came out with Mr. and Mrs. Blackburn, of England. He gave me his book, Artists and Arabs.

To Ferdinand Freiligrath.

April 5, 1873.

I am deeply touched and grieved by the melancholy tidings you send me[2] These are the sorrows to which all others are as nothing. They change us. We can never be again what we were before, though we may seem so to the eyes of others. But we know that a part of ourselves is gone, and cannot come back again. I will not attempt to console you,—that is useless; but I suffer with you, and share your affliction.

Mrs. D—— and her daughters, to whom you have been so kind, and who are so grateful for all your kindness, write with the deepest sympathy, and speak of your son as "dear Otto Freiligrath." I never saw him; yet from this expression, and his photograph, and his brother Wolfgang, I have a picture of him in my mind, and feel what your loss must be.

All this will not comfort you; but I know you will be courageous, and bear the inevitable with resignation.

[1] It was begun December 30.

[2] Of the death of his son.

July 12. *Nahant.* I had a dream last night of meeting Tennyson at a hotel in some Italian town. He was elegantly dressed, and had the easy manners of a man of the world. He said he was going to the opera. While we were talking, C. came in, looking like a German boy of fourteen.

13th. Dreamed last night that I was at a dinner-party at Mr. W——'s. To reach the dining-room we had to pass through a carpenter's shop, climb out of a window, and go over a roof. Among the guests was the Rev. Mr. ——, dressed as a woman in white.

14th. Dreamed last night that I was talking to the Emperor Napoleon, who asked me if I remembered the portrait which the Princess Charlotte — his cousin, and wife of his brother Charles — drew of me in her album at Florence in 1828.

18th. A northeastern storm. A pigeon flew into my room and flapped round my head, then perched on my shoulder, then on the back of a chair, where it sat winking. When put out of the window it returned again. It is the lost pet of somebody.

September 17. Returned from Nahant.

18th. Mr. Charles Warren Stoddard, a young Californian poet, called.

25th. Three German professors called.

28th. Sumner at dinner. More nervous than at Nahant. I urge him not to lecture.

29th. A call from four Englishmen; [among them] Mr. Charles Read, M.P., and the Dean of Canterbury.

November 13. Wrote a sonnet on Milton.

15th. Wrote a sonnet on Shakespeare.

16th. Wrote a sonnet on Chaucer.

From Samuel Ward.

BREVOORT HOUSE, December 27, 1873.

DEAREST L., — The rain that fell when we parted yesterday has not yet dried upon your steps, which I have so often ascended with joy, and always gone down with regret; and here is "Monsieur Tonson come again."

The line I was trying to recall is the one about which Horace Walpole lost a bet of a guinea to Pulteney in the House of Commons. It is: —

> "Nil conscire sibi; nullâ pallescere culpâ."[1]

Walpole quoted it "nullæ pallescere culpæ;" Pulteney corrected him, won the wager, and the identical guinea is in the family of the winner.

Your lovely poem ['The Hanging of the Crane'] made music all night in the car. The omission of those dramatic contrasts which render the *Glocke* song [Schiller's 'Bell'] so exciting, makes your masterpiece soothing and tender, almost to idyllism.

I cannot tell you how your noble devotion to poor —— has warmed my heart. But for my physical health, which sustains my exertions, I should be as wretched as he is, without a tithe of the merit he possesses of conscientious work.

I think your poem will make people better and happier, and I long to see it a part and parcel of human possessions. I do not know what your terms are with the Atlantic; but I think my trotting friend Bonner, of the New York Ledger, would pay two guineas a line for it. I make the suggestion in view of your charities and the constant demand upon your purse.

[1] Horace, Epistles I. i. 61.

To Mrs. J. T. Fields.

December 28, 1873.

Accept, I beg you, my best thanks for your kind remembrance at Christmas, and the gift of Keats's photograph.[1] What a pathetic face! It is sad to see, and yet most interesting. Severn I saw in Rome in 1869, — a prosperous gentleman; with buff waistcoat and bright buttons. I dare say you knew him, — perhaps had the picture from him.

With all kinds of good wishes for endless Christmases and New Years.

January 1, 1874. The New Year's greetings, — the flowers and other presents. — Finish the scene, 'In Fra Bastiano's Garden,' for Michael Angelo. This will give variety.[2]

3d. Bought the beautiful edition of Milton, "carefully printed from the Author's copies," by Bickers & Son, 1851.

4th. Fields comes out, and I read to him 'The Hanging of the Crane.' He advises not to publish in any periodical, but to make a small illustrated volume of it.

5th. In the afternoon Mr. Boyesen calls. He is just returned from Europe, and is hurrying to his professorship at Cornell. He reports Hans Christian Andersen as very ill.

6th. Wrote 'In the Coliseum,' — a scene for Angelo. Read in the *Souvenirs* of Mme. Vigée le Brun, — a light, lively book by this beautiful artist.

7th. T. and N. A. at dinner, at which was served a Stilton cheese sent from Clifton, England.

[1] A copy of a head by Severn, Keats's friend.

[2] This scene was afterward rejected as "jarring with the tone of the poem." It introduced Rabelais.

9th. Cut down a great elm-tree at the carriage-gate, which seemed dangerous, and threatened to fall into the street. It was a pang to me.

14th. Wrote 'Michael Angelo and Titian.'

16th. Finished reading the *Divina Commedia* with E. Worked a little on the Monologues of Michael Angelo, and translated his sonnet on the death of Vittoria Colonna.

20th. The days are miserably like each other when one is shut up in the house. Read Hertz, the Danish poet's drama of *Svend Dyring's Huns*, which is very good.

22d. To-day I have been reading Rabelais, which, I confess, wearies me.

To G. W. Greene.

January 29, 1874.

I have submitted the 'Hanging of the Crane' to the microscopic eye of J. O. The result is, that "the sound of *sc* — as in scene, celestial, Ceylon, and so forth — occurs thirty-two times," so that the production may be called

"Il bel *poema* là dove il *si* suona."

Since you were here I have dined only once a week; all the rest is bread and milk, — a diet on which I thrive as if I were in my second childhood. I make the same apology for it that Michael Angelo did for writing sonnets in his old age: "Messer Giorgio, amico caro, voi direte ben ch' io sia vecchio e pazzo a voler far sonetti; ma poichè molti dicono ch' io son rimbambito, ho voluto far l' uficio mio." This reminds me that I have added a new scene to the Angelo, — namely, 'Messer Michele in the Street with Bindo Altoviti,' — and have interspersed several sonnets of M. A. in other parts, which I think has a good effect.[1]

[1] These were afterward omitted. The quotation from Michael Angelo is: "Master George, dear friend, you may well say that I am

30th. Translated another sonnet of M. A. Looked over Duparc's very interesting sketch of Regnault, the young French painter killed in the siege of Paris in 1871, "victime de la dernière heure et du dernier combat."

February 1. Comfortably indoors, reading Regnault's Correspondence, — a fiery genius, who did great things in painting, and promised greater.

6th. Lunched in town to meet Miss L——, an English lady devoted to hospitals. She is the most attractive philanthropist I ever met. In the evening completed the scene in Angelo in which he takes Vittoria's portrait. The work is now finished, saving always revision. I do not see what other scene can be added.[1]

17th. Called upon Charles Kingsley and his daughter.

19th. The Kingsleys dined with us.

I have forgotten to record Mr. Gill's elegant banquet to Wilkie Collins at the St. James Hotel.

20th. Dined with Mr. A—— in a new and elegant house in Marlborough Street. Young people, who gave an old dinner-party. None of the guests were under sixty. Looking down the table was like a distant view of the Alps from the Jura.

21st. Wilkie Collins and T. dined with us.

22d. Sam Ward came to lunch. He has negotiated with Bonner for the 'Hanging of the Crane' [for publication in the New York Ledger]. I am to have three thousand dollars. It is a great sum. It was not my asking, but his offer.

old and foolish to wish to make sonnets; but since so many people are saying that I am in my second childhood, I have chosen to fulfil my office."

[1] Michael Angelo was begun on the 6th of March, 1872. "I want it," he wrote, "for a long and delightful occupation." On the 18th of May in that year he says: "The poem *in its first form* is complete." But he continued to add new scenes from time to time. It was not published till after his death.

24th. Drove to town with my dear old friend Greene, who goes back to East Greenwich after a short visit. I am always glad when he comes, and sorry when he goes. In the afternoon Miss B—— called with a Turk

27th. My sixty-seventh birthday. These milestones are so many that they begin to look like a graveyard.

28th. Club dinner at Parker's. On my right I had Wilkie Collins, on my left the elder Dana, — the oldest of the American poets.[1]

March 1. Received two letters to-day, one from New York, one from Yonkers on the Hudson, each beginning, "Will you please tell me who was Evangeline, and what country did she belong to; also the place of her birth."

To G. W. Greene.

March 3, 1874.

I enclose you as pretty a piece of vituperation as one sees in a twelvemonth. If I had not ceased to wonder at anything in the newspapers, I should wonder that such astounding language as this should have found its way into the columns of the Tribune. I grieve over the bad news which your letter brings me. I know how you suffer when your children are ill. I trust, however, to hear soon that all cause of anxiety has passed away. I have written the new scene that you suggested for Angelo. I am not dissatisfied with it, and yet do not want to add it.[2] It seems to me better to leave the close a little vague, than to give a tragic ending, — though that may be the proper *finis* of the book.

What a debilitating day this has been! It is enough to take away the strength of a whole family of athletes.

[1] Then eighty-six years old. He died in 1879.

[2] The new scene was Angelo's Death, and was afterward rejected.

Here is a gloomy [newspaper] paragraph for you. See what barbarism may exist in the midst of culture and civilization! "The last of the Paddock elms fell at a quarter past nine o'clock yesterday morning, and there are now no signs left of the old trees, except the smoothly cut stumps, which are on a level with the sidewalk."[1] Paddock, who planted these elms, was a Tory in the days of the Revolution. Could that have had anything to do with it? I know not.

11th. Sad news from Washington, — of Sumner's sudden illness and death: seized at ten last night with *angina pectoris;* dead to-day at three!

To G. W. Greene.

March 11, 1874.

The fatal news has come at last. You doubtless saw, in your morning paper, the mention of Sumner's attack last night. I had a telegram from Sam Ward, saying he could not live through the day; and now comes another with the words: "Charles Sumner is dead."

I thought I was prepared by his frequent attacks for this final one; but I was not. It is terribly sudden and unexpected to me, as it will be to you. I cannot write more.

16th. Sumner's funeral. A bright morning. I heard the first bluebirds singing.

[1] The Paddock elms were ancient English elms in front of the Granary Burying-ground in Tremont Street, whose pleasant greenness and shade were long missed. They were cut down by the city authorities.

To J. B. Everhart.

March 31, 1874.

Many thanks for your beautiful poem, — beautiful notwithstanding its subject, for which I have no sympathy. I am so little of a sportsman that I rank fox-hunting with bull-fighting, and think them equally detestable. You will perhaps smile at this; but I never lose an opportunity of entering my protest against all pleasures that spring from the pain of dumb animals.

But I meant to thank you, not to preach to you; and again beg you to accept my thanks for your kindness in sending me your book.

April 2. I have been trying to write something about Sumner, but to little purpose. I cannot collect my faculties.[1]

15th. Received a Portuguese translation of 'Evangeline' by Franklin Doria, published at Rio de Janeiro, 1874.

To G. W. Greene.

April 18, 1874.

Who shall write the Life of Sumner?[2] That is the question that perplexes me. All his papers have arrived, and we have a room devoted to them in Pemberton Square. I am going in on Monday to examine them. I dread it, but it must be done. It seems strange that I must delegate to another the task of writing his life; but I feel that I cannot do it. Ah, if you were only well

[1] The first draft of the poem 'Charles Sumner' is dated March 30. It was printed in the volume with 'The Masque of Pandora.'

[2] It was afterward written, as is well known, by Mr. E. L. Pierce.

enough for the work! Motley, too, is incapacitated by ill-health, and has his own historic projects. Meanwhile we shall have the materials arranged, and ready for use.

May 13. The great tragedian Salvini and his brother, with Mme. Rudersdorff, dined with us. After dinner Salvini read some scenes from Alfieri's *Saul*, — to the delight of us all, especially of Greene, who was here and heard one of his favorite Italian authors beautifully interpreted.

From J. L. Motley.

HÔTEL BRISTOL, PARIS, May 16, 1874.

MY DEAR LONGFELLOW, — Your very kind letter of April 23d reached me on the day before we left Cannes. It was impossible for me, therefore, to reply sooner. Believe me that I am very deeply touched by your thinking of me on this sad occasion of our dear Sumner's death. That I should have been thought worthy by you and your co-trustees of his literary estate to write his Life, I regard as the highest honor that could be conferred on me. But having said this, I can only add that I am, alas! utterly incompetent to the task. The strange and sudden seizure which befell me at the end of last July has, I fear, put an end to my working power; at any rate, I have gained so little by my search for health and strength at Cannes this winter that it would be a fraud on my part to conceal from you the hopelessness of my undertaking to perform so noble a service. It is with great difficulty that I am writing this letter. I have but little use of my right hand and arm; and to employ them for a few minutes only exhausts my strength for the day. Pardon this egotism, which perhaps was necessary in order to show that it was not the will, but the power to comply with your request that is wanting. It is, indeed, a most bitter disappointment to me. Had I been able, however inadequately, to do this work, it would have been a high gratification as well as consolation to me in the grief which I feel for his loss, — if I have a right to speak of my personal share in a sorrow which is a national, and even wider than a national, one. The value to the country of so pure and noble a life, and of such magnificent and long-sustained labor to such lofty ends, can scarcely be exaggerated. The nation is honored which has given birth to such a man and kept him in the public councils for a quarter of a century.

Most sincerely and affectionately your friend,

J. L. MOTLEY.

29th. A lovely morning, just suited to the work I am doing; that is, selecting from various writers *poems of places*, to make a kind of poetic guide-book.

To G. W. Greene.

May 31, 1874.

I have been wanting to write to you for some time, but have not found the happy moment. Between —— and ——, the upper and nether millstones, I have been ground to powder. Moreover, I have given the bright mornings to the collection of Poems of Places, of which I once spoke to you; and a pleasant occupation it is, — travelling in one's easy-chair, and making one's own poetic guide-book. It is amazing what an amount of second and third rate poetry there is in the world. It would be more amazing if it were all first rate!

To G. W. Greene.

NAHANT, July 23, 1874.

In a late number of the *Revue des Deux Mondes* Laugel has a very good article on Sumner, — have you seen it?

You will hardly be satisfied with it, perhaps, when you come to the quarrel with the President [Grant], where he tries to hold the historic scales very evenly, but does not give weight enough to the provocation. I am glad you are getting steadily on with your History. I want that stone of Sisyphus rolled fairly over the hill, and thundering down the other side.

I have been amusing myself with reading the Spectator. How musical and sweet Addison is! Steele is a little more sinewy in style, but far less charming. Good reading, this, for a summer's day by the seaside, or a winter's day by the fireside. I find the blaze and glare of sunshine here not very good for the eyes. This I make an excuse for being idle. Professor Brunetta, of Verona, wishes to make an interlinear translation of 'Evangeline,' to be used as a school-book.

To G. W. Greene.

September 17, 1874.

What cheer? Here I am once more in the Craigie,—comparatively speaking, a happy man. But so many things lie in wait for me that I have hardly time to write you these lines; in fact, I had written only two of them last evening, when Nichols and Owen appeared with the Sumner proof-sheets,[1] and we worked away at them till half-past ten.

If, in your reading, you find any poems of places, do not fail to make a note of them for me. The printers are just beginning 'The Hanging of the Crane.' Some of the illustrations [by Mary Hallock] are charming; it will be a pretty picture-book. The poem will be read by Mr. Woollett on the 1st of October in the Bay State Course of Lectures, and published on the 15th by Osgood & Co.

[1] The proof-sheets of the collected Speeches, or Works, of Mr. Sumner.

This is all the news I have to tell you, except that Sumner's tenth volume is out. It closes with the speech on Art in the National Capitol. The last sentence is that pungent protest of Powers against giving great national works to mere beginners.

From T. G. Appleton.

HÔTEL DU JARDIN, PARIS, September, 1874.

DEAR HENRY, — Here am I again at the good little hotel we liked so well before. Our young couple are no longer here, — new people are in their place; but the house is as neat and well kept as before. Only you and the girls are missing. How I wish you were all here to see the new Paris since the war, and to enjoy the pictures and the lovely Tuileries garden! How pleasant it is to take one's nice bread and butter and *café au lait*, and an omelette such as only Paris prepares, and then go [into the garden] and read one's Galignani under the trees, with the children and birds all about, and the same old woman coming for her *sous!* And the weather is so soft and bright, and light with the same *légèreté* the people have, and which is perhaps the best thing about Paris.

I called, and found Marmier in. He was enchanted; and instantly presented me with a fine engraving and Ségur's work on 1812, and tore the map for me out of his Swiss Guide, thinking it better than Baedeker's. The Bretonne showed her teeth and her earrings, and inquired tenderly after you. I tried coffee and kirsch, and they had the good old taste Last evening he took me to see his inseparable brave, old M. Thiers. The old gentleman had been twenty-four hours the day before coming in the train; and arriving at 6 A. M., sent at once for Marmier, who found him as chipper as a bird. I was most kindly received, and stayed late, talking about everything, and he making many acute remarks. He spoke with regard of Sumner and Seward; and I ventured to describe the dinner with Sumner, and touched on Seward's mistake in saying that Mme. Thiers spoke English. "And so she does," he said; "but I do not." He is much pleased with the compliments he gets from America, and talked much about us. There were only a few present, so we two did all the talking. A lady, one of the household, is a great admirer of yours, and asked after you with interest. Thiers has taken a handsome house, 45 Faubourg St.-Honoré.

I am glad that C. enjoyed his cruise in the "Alice." I wish I had been of the party. Our yachting is much nicer than the European, and I have nothing to envy them. I wonder the girls don't write, and yet so fond of it; but the old are neglected for the young.

Ever affectionately yours,

T. G. APPLETON.

From T. G. Appleton.

CADENABBIA!! October 3, 1874.

DEAR HENRY, — Does not the very name look pretty? Yes, there is no mistake, it is lovely; and though now the melancholy days are come, and I see its beauties through rain like some lovely widow through her tears, the rain may veil but cannot spoil them. We have had this summer faultless weather; and now I fear that Aquarius is making up his average, and it may hold a month. But in a better sense I may say, "it never rains but it pours;" for I had all my letters sent here. And what a shower of them I found! I can only fire now one gun for a broadside. So I send this to you, to parcel with affection and remembrance among all. I have letters from all but A., and she must not be forgotten for that. The darlings, how I love them all! and my heart cries out for them as do their letters for me. The yearning is but accumulating fondness, and I mean to love them more than ever when I come back. "On recule pour mieux *aimer.*" And when will that be? I am now hunting for a companion to go to Egypt with me, and he does not turn up. Dear, good Gay has had his cake and eaten it, and he can't go. —— and —— are to go; but one is too cross, and the other too noisy, for me. So if I get nobody, — and my last chance will be in Paris, — I may bolt, and be [in Boston] before you can say "Jack Robinson." I do not promise, but it may be yet. I am never fonder of Boston than when I am farthest from it, — which shows what a pull it has. I miss the whip in the sky, as the liberated West India blacks did, who had, for form's sake, a slave-whip carried over them to remind them of the good old times. I miss you all *here*, as you can imagine. Yonder is our old balcony and its nest of rooms; the very boatmen are the same, and the olive-complexioned olive-wood women, and the pillared trees which Ernest painted so well, — and all these but make me miss my old party the more. They seem more present than the one I now have; they belong more to Cadenabbia, and loved it first. And yet my present party is a success. ——, who travels in search of a digestion, is always nice and clever, — rather prone to criticism, perhaps, and not with that big exclamation mark behind her eyes which American girls have; and Mlle. C—— is very practised and wise as a traveller, and pleasant in every way. To them we have added Miss H——, who is brave and bright, a good sketcher, and even a good climber, going up the Bel Alp and everywhere. She was never before in Italy, and is wild about it.

Yesterday we took our first row, — we arrived only the day before, — to Bellagio. There is a new hotel there; great bustle, — the carriages flying about (we have no carriages at Cadenabbia), and great show and bother, which made us the more prefer Cadenabbia. Our boatman was Achille, and he grinned the old Como grin through his five-days' beard. On Sunday, he says, he shaves for a penny; I think he cheats his barber. We inquired of him about the *agoni* and the fish-nets and the little bells, and found they were all right. The turn we took round the corner toward Lecco made me remember the lovely threatening rocks and their wealth of shrubbery. Putting back as we reached Villa Giulia, we found that a Viennese had bought it who would not let any one see it; and Achille denounced the *Tedesco* with the traditionary hatred of the Austrian. To-day is sheeted with rain, — soothing and quiet after so much sun. The hotel is much improved; what was the dining-room is now a noble vestibule, marble steps, with flowers rising from the other end. It is the perfection of comfort, without bother or display. But the miracle of hotels is at Varese, not far off. There we tarried for three days, and E. wanted to forever. It was princely, from the impressively majestic landlord to the clothes-brush, which seemed made only for royal shoulders. There are some seven salons *en suite*, one lovelier than the other; and over a vast garden the eye runs down to the Lago di Varese and the mountains beyond. If Mary Anne Starke could revisit the Italy she once wrote about, surely she would not recognize it.

I saw [in the papers] the death of Wyman,[1] and felt it much; he was a man of real value.

Affectionately,

T. G. Appleton.

October 25. Professor Bonamy Price, of Oxford, at dinner, — a man of sixty, and a man of a thousand; bright and elastic.

[1] Jeffries Wyman, the anatomist, Curator of the Peabody Museum of Archæology at Harvard University.

To G. W. Greene.

October 26, 1874.

I wish you could have been here for the last few days. I have had some curious experiences in national character. On Saturday came an English gentleman with a letter of introduction, and stayed to dinner. He was taciturn, reserved, fastidious, and appeared to take little pleasure in anything. He seemed to have no power of enjoyment. On Sunday came another Englishman to dine; but of a very different type, — expansive, hilarious, talking incessantly, laughing loud and long; pleased with everything. These were the two opposite poles of English character and manners.

This afternoon came Parkman, asking for your address, in order to send you his book, The Old Régime in Canada. I have just been reading Tasso's *Aminta* with E., who is delighted with it. I think of taking up, now, the *Pastor Fido* of Guarini, — unless you can suggest something better.

Pain never kills any one, but is a most uncomfortable bedfellow. But that, I trust, will soon be over, and you will enter that convalescent state which is so pleasant.

To G. W. Greene.

October 29, 1874.

I received this evening your wife's letter, and was debating whether I should answer it at once, or finish first a poem on the Terra di Lavoro ['Monte Cassino']; and while I was debating, a felicitous termination of the poem slid into my mind, and left me free to write to you without hindrance.

I know how a man feels with toothache, with rheumatism in the back, with neuralgia in the chest; but how he feels with his collar-bone broken, is to me a merciful mystery, which I hope I shall never comprehend. I am afraid that with all your morphine you will be in such a dreamy state that letters and newspapers will have a vague and far-off interest for you. Nevertheless, I write this, and send you a paper, in which a poor, abused author makes his melancholy complaint. He quotes all the unhandsome epithets that have been applied to him; and if you are "sitting clothed and in your right mind," you will be interested in his story. But why do I write in this light vein while I am suffering with you, and feeling deeply your distress? I know not, unless it be that the ferment of the mind sends up bubbles to the surface. You, who know my rather effervescent nature, will not be pained by it, though it is like laughing in church. But get well as soon as you can, and let me hear good news of you.

31st. Lord Dufferin dined with me at the Saturday Club.

To G. W. Greene.

October 31, 1874.

I am troubled to hear that you do not sleep. Better to sleep among the poppies than not to sleep at all, — a disagreeable alternative. But when your shoulder is once strong again, you can more easily give up the narcotic.

I had a call to-day from Miles Standish, — not the old hero, but one of his descendants; a tall, handsome youth from New York, who had been last evening at the Music Hall to hear Mr. Woollett recite the 'Courtship' of his ancestor. This afternoon Lord Dufferin dined with me at the Club. He is a charming person, and his wife more charming still. I wish you could have seen them. Old Mr. Dana was there, eighty-six years old, and apparently good for ten years more, — though that is saying a great deal. But I cannot keep my thoughts from you. Are physicians powerless to bring help? In one of Dr. Holmes's Essays, I find the enclosed prescription, which will amuse you.

November 2. Began reading Petrarca with Edith.

5th. Harvard Association Concert. The finest pieces were Chopin's Concerto in E minor and Beethoven's Seventh Symphony.

To G. W. Greene.

November 5, 1874.

I have been in town all day on business of various kinds, and have come home very tired, — or, as an Englishman called it, the other day, "very tarred." At first, I did not know what he meant; but when he used the expression a second time, it dawned upon me. Among other things, I went to see Mrs. Hamilton's portrait of Agassiz. She inquired particularly after you, and was very sorry to hear of your accident. In the afternoon I went to a concert, and had the inevitable cold draught let in upon me before it was over, spoiling the effect of the beautiful Allegro of Beethoven's Seventh Symphony. And, finally, here I am, where I have been wanting to be all day long. I really believe it will end in my never going out of sight of my own chimney-pots.

And now, good-night; and may the good physician Sleep comfort and console you. But such a sunrise as I saw two days ago was better than sleep to me!

To G. W. Greene.

November 10, 1874.

Howells and his brother-in-law, Mr. Mead, the sculptor, have been dining with me to-day. After dinner we went to a neighbor's to hear Mr. James read an Essay on Carlyle.[1] And now, at eleven o'clock, I am waiting for some people in the library to go home, that I may go to bed, where I much desire to be. I only wish that you could sleep half as soundly as I do.

Last evening I wrote a sonnet on the *Ponte Vecchio* of Florence, which I think you will like. You are one of the few who know what a sonnet is. I wrote last summer a good many; among them, a series of five entitled, 'Three Friends of Mine,' meaning Felton, Agassiz, and Sumner,— my small tribute to their memory. In the Atlantic for January will be the poem on Sumner I read to you when you were last here. Pardon me for thinking that such small items will amuse you.

14th. My classmate Benson writes urging me to prepare a poem for the class-meeting at next Commencement, — our fiftieth anniversary. Professor Ignaz Zingarle writes to ask that I will get up a subscription here to aid in erecting a statue of Walther von der Vogelweide at Botzen, in the Tyrol. Two equally difficult things to do.

To G. W. Greene.

November 14, 1874.

When one is hungry, and waiting for dinner, there is no better way of shortening the time than by writing letters. So I have just been writing one to Mr. Trowbridge on his volume of poems, and will write you one on nothing in particular. Your wife's letter this morning was very encouraging. You will come through triumphantly. But now that you sit in your library again, I must not write you any more nonsense. When you were morphined out of your wits, anything might pass. Now that you are in

[1] Henry James, the elder.

your right mind, I can no longer impose upon you. I saw to-day, for the first time, the Life and Letters of Cogswell. It is a large and handsome octavo, privately printed. I am sorry that I have not a copy. I think it must be a very interesting book. The young woman who writes the literary notices for the Advertiser informs me this morning that the 'Hanging of the Crane' will not add anything to my reputation. I am sorry for that; I thought perhaps it might! I hope the mustard-leaves reached you in safety; you will find them very potent. The dinner-bell rings. Farewell.

To G. W. Greene.

November 15, 1874.

Mindful of the French saying, *Il n'y a rien de certain que l'imprévu,* I often wonder what will be my next annoyance; for annoyances are as sure to come as the world is to turn round.

Last evening the unforeseen appeared in the shape of a letter from a German professor in Innsbrück, requesting me to act as agent for collecting funds to raise a bronze statue to Walther von der Vogelweide in Botzen. Good heavens! have we not enough to do in erecting equestrian statues of General Jackson, and in making the perpendicular steed stand on the tip of his tail? Have we not enough to do in adorning our streets with wooden Indians at the doors of tobacconists, and our ships with figure-heads of Hebe and Pocahontas? I do not believe there are a hundred men in the United States — except Germans — who ever heard of Vogelweide the Minnesinger, and not ten who would give ten cents toward raising a statue to him at Botzen.

I promised to write you no more nonsense; and lo! here are three pages of it, besides the enclosure, which is nonsense or not, as you please to regard it. Meanwhile get well as fast as you can, and do not be depressed by gloom of weather or anything else.

24th. Finished a Poem for the Fiftieth Anniversary of the Class of 1825 at Bowdoin College.

26th. This morning translated my Sonnet on the Ponte Vecchio at Florence into Italian.

To G. W. Greene.

November 29, 1874.

I am afraid you will get tired of my letters, and say they are too many. Nevertheless, I will wind up the month with another, though I have nothing in the world to tell you. I am not Baron Grimm, nor Mme. de Sévigné.

Yesterday, under the archway of the Marlborough, I found and bought a copy of Guicciardini, ten volumes in five, half-calf octavo, for the moderate price of fifty cents per volume!

I beg your pardon; I forgot. You "take no further interest in books." Still, I would not trust you alone under the archway for any length of time, nor down in the depths below, with the tempter Lovering. The passion for buying books must be one of the last to leave us. As to the *reading* of books, that is another matter. I am afraid that long ago I became an impatient reader. Perhaps I always was one. I early felt the despair that comes over the soul at the sight of a large library. I am very restless under the infliction of a diffuse style, and want everything said in as few words as possible.

I am sorry about your sleep. If you were here, I would read to you my last poem; that would do the business effectually!

30th. Wrote a sonnet on an unknown soldier's grave at Newport News.[1]

December 4. In the evening Owen and Nichols, with Sumner's proofs.

To G. W. Greene.

December 6, 1874.

I send you to-day a number of the Overland Magazine containing two articles which I think will interest you. One is on Stuart Mill; the other on Hubert Bancroft, the first volume of whose work on the Native Tribes of the Pacific Coast has just appeared. You will admire, as I do, his devotion to his work; it is a noble example. Thus are great things achieved; happy the man who has the will and the way to accomplish them!

An amiable critic in a New York paper says of the 'Hanging of the Crane' that everybody connected with the book "has done his duty except one, and that is the author himself." Among other equally flattering remarks, he repeats that old, old formula: "If this poem had been sent anonymously to any magazine in the country, it would have been instantly rejected." Howells says he wishes somebody would try the experiment on him.

So we drift along, buffeted by side-winds and flaws.

To G. W. Greene.

December 7, 1874.

I sent you yesterday an essay on Stuart Mill which I thought might have some interest for you. There is nothing new in it, but it may reawaken your slumbering love of reading. Stuart Mill is a kind of Petrarca in prose, and Mrs. Taylor a modern Laura de Sade. How strange

[1] A newspaper paragraph, "A soldier of the Union mustered out," had been sent him long before.

it is that after five centuries Avignon and Vaucluse should again become the scene of a romantic passion! Stranger still, but characteristic of the two different ages and nations, that the part of the Italian troubadour should be played by an English philosopher, and sonnets give place to essays on Political Economy. Yet the sweet old passion was the same, and as powerful in the philosopher as in the poet, and perhaps more sincere and lasting. Who knows?

I have had rather a rough week of it, this last. One evening, finding my room oppressively hot, I opened the window to breathe, and in two minutes was shot through and through by the arrows of the heavenly maid, Influenza.

Good heavens! what kind of style is this? Am I John Lilly writing Euphues?

Have you seen Howells's new novel, A Foregone Conclusion? The scene is in Venice, and the character of the priest Don Ippolito is very powerfully drawn. In that respect this book is a stride forward.

From T. G. Appleton.

THEBES, December 10, 1874.

I can add little to my address; that tells the whole story. Here we are at last at this supreme centre of the old civilization. I certainly shall not attempt to describe it to you,—the books must do that; but you at least will gladly hear that we are not disappointed. We have just returned from our first visit to the wonders. What shall I say of the grand old stones and tender cuttings? So clear and pure, yet telling about what we so little understand that, while everything is undisguised, the secret is still kept, or much of it. But I must not waste my paper in æsthetics. My party is a delightful one. All are cultivated and ardent admirers of beauty. I keep a little journal which I dictate to Miss Fletcher, and Eugene Benson is to illustrate it. I shall make a little book of it, that you all may see what a charming thing this Nile life is. Your letter and the lovely poem on Cadenabbia reached me last night. It seems, when reading your words, that I am stretching my hands from natron cerements over the centuries to young America. We have a consort boat, the "Clara," now rustling by us, and in it are a daughter of Praed the poet, and a *savant*, and Mr. and Mrs. P——, who are the heads of the party. Each boat does just what the other does, and we walk and shoot together. We stumbled, at Sioot, upon the Ghawazees, who were at a marriage, as dancing-girls are, and we all went in, thinking it was a café; but it was the Governor's house. But they are not proud in Egypt, and we had kindness and coffee, and especial dancing for us. The *howadji* can do anything here. A Prussian prince, too, was in our company; but he has run on, — probably here only for the shooting. The Prussian bloodthirstiness was shown by shooting doves into the river to die and drown. But he did get a magnificent eagle, who had indeed "the strength of pinion that the Theban eagle bare." We shall drink deep from these antique fountains here for three days, and then forward. We got up yesterday, as you did, to see the transit, and blacked our noses against the glass. It was as clear as possible, and I rejoice for the *savants* here, who had their *dahabeyah* illuminated last night. We daily have a cool bath, and the weather, when there is a breeze, is beyond belief. One hangs, in this bright sky, like a fly in amber. The evenings are incredible, — such tones, such gradations of splendor! Every night Eugene and I dash at our colors and shoot straight at the setting sun as at a target. Not often do I hit; but E. has a dozen dear bits, which he is to sink into an Arabian cabinet which we can get at Cairo. And what shall I say of Antonio, our cook? He is a magician; and such *mishmash*, such dates with almonds and sugar, such pigeon-pies, — we shoot our own pigeons, — such turkeys, always young ones! It is almost too much for us.

I hear the consorts firing away their guns; so another boat has come. I hope it is General McClellan. We had a *feu de joie* last evening, as we came in under a wing of gold from Thebes across the river; for we are now at Luxor. Our consul visited us, — an Arab, brown as a berry, and having no idea where America is, but speaking English well. Giving and taking coffee seems the sum of official duty. Imagine our coffee! direct from beyond yonder hills, and as aromatic as it is innocent. We have it three times a day; and our tea is delicious. Our library is a double one, — my own and the boat's, which is a private yacht in summer. George Curtis [Nile Notes] reads better than ever, so graceful and so refined. But Martineau is our favorite; she is a thinker. Lepsius and the colossal pair of England, Lane and Wilkinson, are never off our table. When there is no wind the flies descend like fiends; we are at their mercy. But they disappear when Zephyr comes.

Love to Craigie House and all dear ones. Need I tell A. that the hollow diamond[1] hangs from my yard sixty feet over head?

T. G. Appleton.

[1] The flag of his yacht, the "Alice."

CHAPTER XII.

JOURNAL AND LETTERS.

1875–1876.

January 14, 1875. Have got down into my study again, after being shut up in my chamber a fortnight with influenza and neuralgia. Greene has departed, and I feel quite strange and solitary.

To Miss K——.

January 15, 1875.

Not being a Spiritualist in the usual and popular sense of the word — that is to say, never having seen any manifestations that convinced me of the presence of spirits — I should deem it almost an act of dishonesty on my part to accept the compliment you offer.[1]

I must therefore, with many thanks for this mark of your consideration, beg leave to decline it.

22d. Began a Dramatic Idyl, — Epimetheus [afterward called Pandora].

To G. W. Greene.

February 5, 1875.

The pain in my head is somewhat assuaged, though the roar of "multitudinous seas" still continues in my ears. So far so good, looking for something better.

[1] Apparently an honorary membership in an English "Association of Spiritualists."

As I laid down the paper this morning, I wished that I could be, for a season at least, in a land where are no newspapers. What kind of a public are we, to be fed daily with such horrors of all kinds, and tolerate it? The low tone of everything disturbs and discourages me.

February 6.

The roar of the ocean has ceased, and now I have a sewing-machine in my head, turning out any amount of ready-made clothing. Such is my bulletin for to-day. What is yours? Whatever it may be, do not lose heart. Faith is half the battle; the spirit lifts the body.

I sent you this morning a portrait of Sam Ward in a newspaper as "King of the Lobby." I will send another paper with several interesting articles. Do not fail to read that on Sainte-Beuve, and what Ruskin says about critics and criticism.

Besides the ready-made clothing, the sewing-machine has turned out a poem on Amalfi. In this cold weather what can one do better than think of that lovely land, — and sing of it, if the song comes?

From T. G. Appleton.

MINEAH, EGYPT, February 13, 1875.

DEAR HENRY, — Behold me returned from a descent into Africa, where was no post and no railroad, but only Nature and History. I went as into a cloud; but, oh! the silver and gold lining of it, as the sun or the moon shone. It was weird and wonderful, and put me in relation with Speke and Grant and the other great travellers. I kept a faithful journal, and made endless sketches, all in water-color. My friend Mr. Benson was very active, and in oil has a store of beauties. He and his family have proved delightful companions, and enjoyed every moment; not a sunset nor a dish was thrown away upon them. Oh, that you had our spring instead of the sulky, reluctant visitor I so well remember! Before my eyes is a sheet of green, such as only Egypt knows, and set in the gold of sand and cliff which doubles its beauty. You must get Mr. Gay to tell you of these wonders; my space can do them no justice.

None but a goose can see this country and not feel as if he were saluting a mother. At Beni-Hassan yesterday I saw Homer and the Bible painted on the walls; and yet the life of to-day. These Egyptian children were indeed the fathers of all of us men since. Life here cannot escape from the old conditions. Our dethroned mast (for we row only, now) rests on a semicircle of iron identical with one I saw yesterday on a boat of five thousand years ago. To walk in the shadow of such a date gives grandeur to life. Would you were here, and we should have a poem with a fine old-crusty-port flavor. *I* have shut up my exuberant Muse in sonnets, and my brain is still spinning more. . . .

Faithfully,

T. G. APPLETON.

To G. W. Greene.

February 15, 1875.

By way of recreation, I am reading the *Fasti* of Ovid. What a curious coincidence there is between his legend of Flora and Zephyrus (book v. 201) and that of Winona and the West Wind in 'Hiawatha.' Ovid makes Flora tell her own story briefly and modestly in two lines. What a beautiful line is this, —

"Dum loquitur, vernas efflat ab ore rosas."

But why talk of Zephyr when Boreas is blowing? The winter intimidates me. Even in-doors I am cold. We have made a mistake in bringing into this severe climate our old English prejudices in favor of open fires. We need Russian stoves. I wish I had one this moment in my study.

A stranger in the West asks me to write for him two poems "on friendship, or a subject like that, for the album of a young lady who is a very particular friend." He asks me also to "send the bill with the articles."

February 20. Since Christmas I have been suffering the tortures of neuralgia in the head, fostered and augmented by the cold and bitter northwest wind that has been blowing for two months.

To Miss ——.

February 20, 1875.

If I had time I would write you a long letter in reply to yours, which has greatly interested me. But, alas! though, as the Indian said, I have all the time there is, it is not enough for the many claims made upon it. I can only send you and the boys and girls under your care a friendly salutation. To those who ask "how I can write so many things that sound as if I were happy as a boy," please say that there is in a neighboring town a pear-tree planted by Governor Endicott two hundred years ago, and it still bears fruit not to be distinguished from that of a young tree in flavor. I suppose the tree makes new wood every year, so that some parts of it are always young. Perhaps this is the way with some men when they grow old; I hope it is so with me. I am glad to hear that your boys and girls take so much interest in poetry. That is a good thing; for poetry is the flower and perfume of thought, and a perpetual delight, clothing the common-place of life with "golden exhalations of the dawn." Give them all my sympathy and good wishes.

To Mrs. J. T. Fields.

February 27, 1875.

How very kind you are to remember my birthday, and to crown it with such a lovely wreath of flowers! Sweeter than the flowers were the good wishes that came with them. How much I thank you!

A mysterious stranger came to me last evening; said that he had heard that I was suffering from neuralgia, and had brought me a wonderful belt which would cure me. As my mind is always hospitably open to empiricism and its "kindred delusions," I lent a willing ear to his suggestions; wore the belt at night; slept seven hours without waking; and to-day the cloud is lifted from my brain. It may be all imagination. If so, imagination is a good medicine. Should I be as much better to-morrow as I am to-day, I shall think it a reality.

March 3. Wrote a little poem, 'The Sermon of Saint Francis;' that is, his sermon to the birds. — Mr. White, the City Forester, called, and brought me several articles made of the Washington elm. Mr. Monti came to dinner, and in the evening read an interesting paper on Brigandage in Calabria and Sicily.

5th. Have nearly finished the first draft of Epimetheus [Pandora]. To-day wrote the Chorus beginning, —

"What the Immortals
Confide to thy keeping," etc.

6th. Mrs. Sargent and Whittier, the poet, came to see me.

To H. A. Bright.

March 19, 1875.

I beg you to accept my thanks for your kind remembrance, and for the pretty little volume on the Glenriddel MSS. of Burns.

Burns's own estimate of these verses seems to me just, and it seems also strange to me that he should have copied some of them, even for a friend. But the account you give of them is curious, and valuable as a bit of literary history.

I always recall with pleasure our drive to Ashfield before your house was built. The grounds and gardens were hardly yet in order, — hardly more than a promise and a prophecy. I dare say both promise and prophecy have been fulfilled, and the place has that comfortable and elegant look which England expects as a duty. Long may you live to enjoy it!

Let me thank you also for your hospitable invitation to show my friends the pathway to your door. That would be a great pleasure to me, should the occasion present itself.

From T. G. Appleton.

JERUSALEM, March 24, 1875.

DEAR HENRY, — We are back again at our old camping-ground; and I must tell you something of our excursion to the Pools of Solomon and the Dead Sea. We went through Bethany, — a hamlet of twenty houses, just out of sight of Jerusalem, on the hill's farther side. When, coming thence, the Saviour turned a point of the hill, Jerusalem burst upon him and drew forth the passionate apostrophe. We now know the way he came; for though there are three roads, only one is large enough for the multitude which followed and met him. On we went down, down, thirteen hundred feet, till we reached the plain, with the Mountains of Moab just opposite, — a long, even line, hazy with purple lights and shadows, and the Dead Sea on our right. We camped near Elisha's Well, and enjoyed our gypsying famously. After dinner, by the light of the moon we had a Bedouin dance, — some fifty men, women, and children. It was weird and savage, and their cries just like our Indians' war-whoop. We had to pay them well for their civility; but it was better than being robbed, — their usual business. We took as a protector a famous Bedouin chief, who thundered about on horseback at full speed, and drawing his sword, looked like a first-rate circus-rider. He haggled much for his *backsheesh*, but finally presented me with his photograph! Imagine Barak or Sisera presenting his photograph to visitors! The next day we pricked over the plains two hours to the Dead Sea. Soon we were hunting for pebbles and shells, with biggish waves breaking at our feet, and a feeling of the sea as the salt was blown in our faces. On our way we had skirted the Jordan and drunk of it. It is a lively little river, like the Tiber for color and size, but with oleanders and terebinth and rich variety of trees and flowers. The flowers accompany us wherever we go, crimsoning our lunch places and drawing us in fond pursuit round many a rock and swell. The sky was veiled, but pure and tender; the weather quite perfect, and no insects. Then we turned from the sea; and up, up we went, as by a torrent-bed of loose stones, swinging round inaccessible heights, and getting stuck at times; but up, up, till the vast chasms of limestone in circular scoops drew us, giddy at their edge, suddenly in sight of the famous Convent of Masaba, — the oldest convent in the world, and by far the most picturesque. It half clings to, and half soars above, the cliff, and has zigzag walls to protect it from the Bedouins. It was more like a dream than a reality, or one of Gustave Doré's most daring grotesques; and as we rode to the top and I saw an incredible tower, with a citizen in a *chapeau* leaning over the wall, and a telegraphic wire hanging out of the sky, I was sure I was asleep. But a little bird sat on the wire and chirped, "Come up; don't be afraid! Don't you see I am not?"

and then we swept into camp. The next day we spent an hour in chatting with the drowsy monks about St. Saba and the lovely blue birds who comfort these recluses, and in eating the good coarse bread and spitting out the uncooked beans they eat (for flesh they will not touch), and in sketching the one palm-tree which waves them heavenward. Then we glided down to the three Pools of Solomon, — of the size of our Boston reservoir, — and there we reposed, thinking of the Song of Solomon and rebuilding his garden bowers, indolent after our ten hours' ride of the day before; and then, in two more hours, we were at Bethlehem. Instead of talking about this sacred place, I send you some flowers, as better than words.

Affectionately,

T. G. Appleton.

To G. W. Greene.

March 30, 1875.

The neuralgia still rages in my head with unabated violence. What a discipline of pain!

I am glad that no college class can have more than one semi-centennial anniversary. It makes me nervous to think of it. I do not like to hear the subject spoken of; and when I look at the poem, it gives me a shudder.[1]

But what nonsense this is! I have no doubt everything will go off well; and if it does not, there will be no great harm done. Wednesday, the seventh of July, is the appointed day.

[1] With characteristic promptness, he had written the poem some months before, and had had a few copies printed and carefully guarded. In November he had written to Mr. Greene: "After telling my classmates that I could not write a poem for the anniversary, I have gone to work and written one, — some two or three hundred lines in all, and quite long enough. Whether I shall have the courage to read it in public when the time comes, is another question."

April 14. A very bad day for neuralgia; suffered intensely.

16th. Read in the London Publishers' Circular that "Professor Longfellow has almost ready for the press a translation of the *Nibelungen Lied* in verse, and a sacred Tragedy, conceived in the spirit of his Judas Maccabeus, which extends to no less than fifteen acts." There is not one word of truth in this.

17th. Mr. Nadal, one of the literary editors of the New York Evening Post, dines with me; also Lowell.

18th. Bad day for me; neuralgia raging. In the evening my girls drive over to Prospect Hill to see the lighting of Paul Revere's lanterns in the belfry of the old North Church.[1]

To G. W. Greene.

April 22, 1875.

I wish I could write you oftener and more fully; but it is impossible. This constant pain is very debilitating, and takes away all pleasure in writing or doing anything one is not absolutely obliged to do. You must not, however, be troubled about me; I shall worry through it.

My girls all went up to Concord on Monday, and enjoyed the celebration heartily. I could not go, but was glad they should have this historic memory. You of course have read the orations of Curtis and Dana; they are very different, and both very good. So is Lowell's Ode, which is not yet published. He read it to me beforehand. He has a gift for that kind of composition.

For the next few years we shall have centennial celebrations all over the country. I hope they will do some good; and I think they may, in holding up the noble lives of other days as examples.

[1] This was one of the many "centennial" incidents of this and the following years.

From T. G. Appleton.

PARIS, June 3, 1875.

My dream is now over; the pearly gates of the Orient are shut, and the prosy comforts of civilization take their place. And great is our relish of them after the barbaric deficiencies of the winter! Never did order, did art, did literature, look more charming; and we take our full draught of all. I am at the Hôtel du Jardin, well up and in front, and the lovely [Tuileries] garden is in front. The trees, I think, were never so beautiful. And yet, gaping and grim with unhealed wounds, just beside, is the home of France's kings.[1] Along the ruined front is written *République Française*, as in mockery, seeming to say: "You see how we look after France's monuments."

The *Salon* is open, and so big that it swallows us like a sea-monster. We come out dishevelled and undone, and I refuse for days to look on a picture. How I wish Ernest were here to enjoy it with us! It is full of talent, and has far less of the cultivated brutal than there used to be. One huge canvas of Rizpah protecting the corpses of Saul's sons, is quite enough for one morning. The young Americans look well. Some sporting scenes by a Philadelphian, Eakins, and two Egyptian scenes by Bridgman, are capital. Healey is strong in portraits; but I missed them in my battle with the hosts of canvases. I have a gallery of my own,—my one hundred and sixty sketches. I am proud of my industry, and forever I shall have what will recreate for me at a glance Syria and Egypt.

I have dined with the Laugels to meet Renan; and you may imagine how we talked of Syria and the lovely fields around Galilee. I renounced talking Spiritualism with

[1] The palace of the Tuileries, burned by the Communists, who feared the restoration of the monarchy.

him the moment I saw him. He is jolly and clever, and allowed to the hated Germans the best scholarship of Europe. He thought they had the best death-weapon the world ever saw, and he wished not to run against it, but let it rust and consume itself. This I hold to be wisdom. We saw *La Fille de Roland* at the Français, — every line an allusion to Prussia and the war.

How I long to kiss the dear nieces! Love to them overflowing. Tell Charles if he is sure to wish for the "Alice" to put her at once in commission.

T. G. APPLETON.

June 17. The centennial of the Battle of Bunker Hill.

18th. A call from the "Confederate" General Fitzhugh Lee.[1] In the afternoon General Sherman and his staff came.

July 7. Read before my Class at Brunswick a poem on our fiftieth anniversary, entitled 'Morituri Salutamus.'[2]

From Benjamin Pierce.[3]

July 8, 1875.

MY VERY DEAR FRIEND, — I have read your poem twice this morning, — once aloud to my wife and sister. It is new, it is true, it is touching, it is beautiful. Worthily of your youth have you used the opportunity of age. It seems to me the most spiritual of all your immortalities.

Your sincere friend and admirer,

BENJAMIN PIERCE.

[1] Some of the Southern generals and a military company from South Carolina came on to attend the celebration at Bunker Hill, in friendly token of restored peace and amity.

[2] The poem was published the next day in Harper's Magazine.

[3] The distinguished mathematician, for many years professor in Harvard College.

To G. W. Greene.

July 18, 1875.

I reached home on Thursday last, and found on my table between thirty and forty letters, in addition to ten which I brought with me from Portland unanswered. What shall I do? What can I do? And echo answers What? Ah, if it would only answer the letters?

I wish you could have been in Brunswick on the memorable seventh. I think you would have been well satisfied with my reception and with the thing in general. The story is too long for a letter. I will tell it to you when we meet. As soon as you can tear yourself from the arms of your beloved Windmill, I hope you will come to Cambridge. To-morrow I shall put the 'Legend of Epimetheus' [Pandora] into the printer's hands. I want you to go over the proofs with me. It shall not tax your eyes, for I will read them to you.

I am not well yet; but I come back from Brunswick better than I went. The excitement did me good.

To G. W. Greene.

July 30, 1875.

The cars go jingling by, but your form is not seen emerging from them and passing under the lilac arch at the gate. I wait in vain.

The printers are slow. They have had my manuscript for a week, and have not yet sent me the first proof. How impatient young authors are! Proof-reading is just the work for this weather.

I am getting slowly better. So long as I keep perfectly quiet I feel pretty well. Patience and Nux Vomica are my two sheet-anchors.

And the Windmill with its folded wings, and the stones

that grind no more! That was a happy thought, if it makes you happy.

To-morrow I try dining with the Club, and hope that Motley will be there. He is at Nahant.

October 5. Lord Houghton[1] called, and sat an hour. He is tormented with neuralgia, as I am.

7th. Lord Houghton lunched with us. No other guests but Lowell and Greene.

11th. Went with Lowell to see Motley, who goes back to England on Saturday.

14th. Call from the Governor of Victoria in Australia, and afterward from old Admiral Coffin, of the British Navy.

16th. In the afternoon Anthony Trollope, the novelist, calls.

25th. Drove with the Horsfords to Wellesley to see Mr. Durant's Female College. A fine building overlooking Lake Waban; three hundred pupils. After dinner we had a row on the lake in the College boat, the "Evangeline," with a crew of eight girls and the handsome captain, Miss E——. It was like sailing with the nine Muses.

To G. W. Greene.

October 29, 1875.

On page 32 of Pandora there is an unlucky false quantity, — Cybe'le for Cyb'ele. This is all owing to my Lord Byron, with his

"She looks a sea Cybele fresh from ocean,"

which has familiarized our ears to a wrong accentuation, — as Louis XIV. is said to have changed the gender of the word *carrosse*.

[1] Known in literature as Richard Monckton Milnes.

C. is out yachting in this rather rude and rough weather. What different tastes there are in this world!

November 1. Dr. Charles Appleton, of London, editor of the Academy, passed the evening with us. A very intelligent and agreeable young man.

To O. W. Holmes.

December 6, 1875.

Credo quia impossibile est. We take our feeble vision for the gauge of Nature. What we see, we believe; what we do not see, we doubt: and how foolish we are! I will never hereafter doubt the impossible possibilities of the unseen. These revelations of the microscope are perfectly astounding. Some day you must show them to me.

Ah! my dear Doctor, if you would only apply these lenses to the *materia medica*, perhaps the microscopic dose might be magnified into some importance in your eyes. Secrets of Nature discovered in one direction suggest secrets discoverable in all directions.

With all my absurd credulities and incredulities,

Always affectionately yours.

To G. W. Greene.

December 25, 1875.

A Merry Christmas to all in the Windmill Cottage!

Houghton has just sent me your new book [The German Element in the Revolution], and a very handsome book it is, — paper, page, type, and binding. This is an outside view; alas! I have not yet had time to take an inside one. Had I foreseen the labor of getting the Poems of Places through the press, I should never have had the courage to undertake it. Making the selections was pleasant, and not fatiguing. To get it all printed correctly is quite another matter. I might have given the time to Michael Angelo. Now he must wait, — which is a pity.

January 29, 1876. Translated a poem of Gustave Le Vavasseur, *Vire et les Virois.*

30th. Translated a poem of Méry, *Sur la terrasse des Aygalades.*

To Isaac McLellan.

February 6, 1876.

You will pardon me, I know, for not sooner thanking you for your letter and pamphlet, when I tell you that I have again been suffering from my old enemy, neuralgia. It damages my correspondence and throws everything into confusion. I have to begin every letter with an apology. Mr. Lossing's pamphlet on the surrender of Detroit I read with great interest. He makes out a very strong case; and I am glad to see the old General Hull, your grandsire, so ably vindicated. I hope you are having as fine a winter on your [Shelter] Island as we have. I see you in imagination tramping with your gun and dogs over the frozen marshes, eager for any birds that have not been wise enough to migrate southward at this season. "Straight a short thunder breaks the frozen sky," and the beautiful creatures "fall and leave their little lives in air."

Meanwhile, I sit here by the fire, busy with the reading and the making of books, — not so healthy a recreation as yours, perhaps, but more congenial to my tastes.

February 7th. Mr. Winter and Mr. McCulloch, the tragedian, called in the afternoon.

8th. At lunch Miss M —— and Mme. Teresa Careño Sauret, the pianist, — a handsome Spanish woman from Caraccas in Venezuela.

13th. A wonderful winter day: the air soft and windless; thermometer at 60°; the river at its best and fullest, as in an Indian summer.

To Mrs. J. T. Fields.

February 27, 1876.

In presence of the prettiest wreath of flowers ever wreathed by human hands, I hasten to thank the donor.

All this morning the well-known lines of Willis, 'I'm twenty-one, I'm twenty-one,' have been running through my mind, intermingled with Hood's 'I remember, I remember,' and a strange confusion of figures; so that I hardly know whether I am sixty-nine years old, or only ninety-six! Nobody remembers when he was born, consequently we never know when we have grown old. When somebody said of Ducis, "Le vieux Ducis est tombé en enfance," a friend replied, "Non, il est rentré en jeunesse." I hope I shall have some friend to say the same of me.

So the years are mingled and woven together like the white and red flowers of this beautiful garland, for which thanking you most cordially, I am

Your young and old friend.

To G. W. Greene.

February 28, 1876.

Pray don't let those unpleasant thoughts haunt and torment you. Dismiss them from your mind as disagreeable guests. Not the wrongs done to us harm us, only those we do to others. You cannot afford to make yourself unhappy by brooding over this matter. One's only chance of quietude is in banishing all things that disturb and annoy.

I send you enclosed an advertisement which will interest you. You remember Wiggin and his books. I think we once went together to look at his collection in School Street. Drake's library is also to be sold a little later. I will send you Catalogues as soon as I get them. You can then do as I do, — mark the books you think you want, close the Catalogue, and forget all about it. To imagine you have bought the books is, in nine cases out of ten, as good as buying them. Such is my philosophy at the age of threescore years and ten, save one. I am startled to think how old I am, and cannot believe it. There must be a mistake. My birthday yesterday was a very pleasant one; I am surrounded with flowers as if I were going to be married, or buried. I send you a sonnet I wrote on the occasion; being an *Arcadian*, of course I write sonnets.[1]

29th. A call from Madame Titjens. Wrote a sonnet, 'Midnight.'

To Miss E. S. Phelps.

March 12, 1876.

I fear that I cannot establish by any historic proof the identity of the old building you speak of in your kind letter with that in which Evangeline found Gabriel.[2] A great

[1] When he was in Italy in 1869 Mr. Longfellow had been made a member of the *Arcadia*, — a literary Society founded in 1690 by Crescimbeni and others. In this Society each member assumes some classic pastoral name.

[2] The "Quaker almshouses," the remains of which were taken down at this time, were not the scene which the author of 'Evangeline' had in his mind.

many years ago, strolling through the streets of Philadelphia, I passed an old almshouse within high brick walls, and with trees growing in its enclosure. The quiet and seclusion of the place — "the reserve," as your poor woman so happily said — impressed me deeply. This was long before the poem was written and before I had heard the tradition on which it was founded. But remembering the place, I chose it for the final scene. . . . The cottage I do not remember; only an enclosure, with tall trees and brick walls, — just enough for the imagination to work upon.

March 28. There are unlucky days, and this is one of them. After breakfast a lot of unpleasant letters. Then an old nurse who had been here in sickness came and laid her hand too roughly on a wound that will never heal. Then I went to the printing-office to hunt up a book which they have lost, and cannot find; then to see Osgood about publishing John Neal's 'Seventy-six,' and find he has gone to New York; then to a tailor's, and read on his door, "Removed to 290," — which number cannot be found. Then I returned home to find a clamorous woman with a book to sell; I can stop her only by buying the book, which I do not want. All this before five o'clock, and interspersed with hand-organs![1]

To J. R. Lowell.

May 4, 1876.

I shall be delighted to dine with you on Saturday at six, and to meet your guest from Baltimore, whose name suggests the Hesperides, as I doubt not her presence does.

[1] Nevertheless, the hand-organists were never sent away without due pennies, — perhaps, in part, because they came from Italy.

I understand perfectly your mood of mind in revising your poems for a new edition.[1] You were looking after "crimes and misdemeanors," like a policeman with a dark lantern, determined to arrest somebody. I hope you will be sparing of omissions and corrections. As a general rule, I think that poems had better be left as they were written; their imperfections are often only imaginary.

Do not fail to have an index to the new volume.

May 16–21. A week with Mr. Childs at Philadelphia, and a week in the country at Rosemont, near Bryn Mawr. A charming vacation, with all the wonders of the Centennial Exhibition.[2]

June 10. Dom Pedro II., Emperor of Brazil, dined with us. The other guests were Emerson, Holmes, Agassiz, and Appleton. Dom Pedro is the modern Haroun-al-Raschid, and is wandering about to see the great world we live in, as simple traveller, not as king. He is a hearty, genial, noble person, very liberal in his views.

[1] Mr. Lowell had written to him, "I had such a pleasure yesterday that I should like to share it with you, to whom I owed it. Osgood and Co. sent me a copy of your Household Edition, to show me what it was, as they propose one of me. I had been reading over with dismay my own poems, to weed out the misprints, and was awfully disheartened. Then I took up your book, to see the type; and before I knew it I had been reading two hours and more. I never wondered at your popularity, nor thought it wicked in you; but if I had wondered, I should no longer, for you sang me out of all my worries. To be sure, they came back when I opened my own book again, — but that was no fault of yours."

[2] Mr. Longfellow had been invited to read an ode at the opening of the Exhibition. He declined, being always unwilling to write for public occasions. The ode was written by Mr. Sidney Lanier; and Mr. Whittier wrote the hymn which was sung.

To G. W. Greene.

June 11, 1876.

Yesterday, Dom Pedro of Brazil, the modern Haroun-al-Raschid, did me the honour to dine with me, naming the persons he would like to meet, — Emerson, Lowell, and Holmes. Lowell was out of town; but the other two came, and the dinner was very jovial and pleasant.

The first volume of Poems of Places is printed; but I see no notice yet of its publication, and do not know when it will appear. It is to come out volume by volume, and not all at once.[1]

I hope you are enjoying the summer weather as much as I am. I should be deliciously idle, were it not for the incessant letter-writing forced upon me. That embitters my existence, and I suppose will to the end. I mean now to have an amanuensis, and only sign my name. I must come to it, though it is almost as bad as using spectacles, which I have not yet come to.

To G. W. Greene.

June 21, 1876.

I send for your amusement some nonsense-verses on a servant who had just broken two beautiful Japan vases in her headlong hurry.

EPITAPH

On a Maid-of-all-Work.

Hic jacet ancilla
  Quae omnia egit,
Et nihil tetigit
  Quod non fregit.[2]

[1] It extended to thirty-one small volumes.

[2] For those who have "forgotten their Latin," this version must suffice: —

This afternoon the girls give W., the graduating senior, a garden-party. The house is full of his friends already.

Have you seen a book by H. M. Dexter, just published in Boston, entitled, As to Roger Williams? It might be of use to you in your work.

What do you and the Governor think of the Presidential nomination at Cincinnati? Does he know Mr. Hayes personally?

This letter is only a column of items. I am so interrupted and distraught, I can do no better.

To G. W. Greene.

June 28, 1876.

Rather exhausting than otherwise is this hot weather; it always comes in June. The longest days will assert their right to be the hottest. But it will soon be over. If the thermometer would only keep pace with our years after sixty, it would be very comfortable; for I suppose a man of ninety would not have any serious objections to keep his thermometer at that level.

To-day I attended Commencement in the new theatre. It was a strange sensation to be walking with Lowell, who wore my old professorial gown!

For the last fortnight we have had the house brimful of people. It is very pleasant, but something of an interruption to one's every-day pursuits.

Reading yesterday the *Briefe von Johann Heinrich Voss*, the poet, I came upon a sketch of André when he was a lieutenant and a student at Göttingen. Voss wrote a

Here a maid-of-all-work
Her rest doth take;
When alive, she touched nothing
She did not break.

And those who have forgotten their Goldsmith may be reminded of the "nullum quod tetigit non ornavit" in his epitaph by Dr. Johnson.

poem to him, and calls him "der liebenswürdigste und edelste Jüngling, und einer meiner besten Freunde. . . . Er nahm mit Thränen Abschied von mir;" being suddenly called away, "weil sein Regiment nach America geht." [1]

August 31. The son and daughter of the Bishop of Carlisle at dinner.

September 3. Mr. Black, author of the Princess of Thule, and other novels, called; and Dr. Lauder Brunton; also Mr. E. Lyulph Stanley, with his sister and two gentlemen.

To G. W. Greene.

September 10, 1876.

"Sweet is it to write the end of any book," says the old Transcriber. I am glad you are so near the end of yours. When it is finished, take a long vacation.

In regard to ether, and the inhalation thereof, I beg you not to "listen with credulity to the whispers of fancy." It will not do me any harm, — for I am not taking it.

A foolish man in Elmira has done me the honor of writing what he calls a "Paraphrase of the Courtship of Miles Standish," — which paraphrase consists in altering the lines enough to make them rhyme! I suggested to him that perhaps he might have employed his time and talent more profitably in writing an original work.

To G. W. Greene.

September 29, 1876.

The Poems of Places plod slowly on and on. We have reached Lammermoor, in Scotland, and I shall be glad

[1] "The most lovable and noble youth, one of my best friends. He took leave of me with tears when his regiment was ordered to America."

when Her Majesty's dominions are finished, and we can go to the Continent. Have you been able to get out of Rhode Island, or are you still a prisoner? I hope no future historian, reading these lines, will imagine that we are defaulters trying to evade the Extradition Treaty!

I have a letter from Tennyson, enclosing a paragraph from the Times, which says that he and his publishers had refused their permission to insert any of his poems in my collection.

The letter is as follows: —

"Here in a little country town in Suffolk I came upon this in the Times. I have had no word from yourself or Messrs. King and Co. about your forthcoming publication. They have my copyright in England for two years longer; but in America I give you full leave, and shall be honored by your insertion of anything of mine in your collection."

At present I am overwhelmed with visitors, some with letters of introduction, more without. Luckily I am pretty well; but, alas! I cannot sleep.

October 11. At Wellesley College. Read to the girls 'The Descent of the Muses' [a sonnet].

To Mrs. Marshall (in England).[1]

November 18, 1876.

. . . It may comfort you to know that I have had twenty-two publishers in England and Scotland, and only four of them ever took the slightest notice of my existence, even so far as to send me a copy of the books. Shall

[1] Whose books had been republished in America without permission or compensation. For want of an international copyright Mr. Longfellow himself is believed to have been a loser by some forty thousand dollars. This measure of simple justice to the writers of both countries is still delayed.

we call that "chivalry," — or the other word? Some good comes of it, after all; for it is an advertisement, and surely helps what follows. It gives you thousands of readers instead of hundreds.

In November of this year there appeared in the International Review a full and discriminating critique upon Mr. Longfellow's writings, by the Rev. Ray Palmer. Dr. Palmer communicated to Mr. Longfellow this extract from a letter written to him by Mr. Bryant: —

"I think that you have done a service to American literature in your admirable review of Longfellow's Poetical Works. You have given a more perfect analysis of their character than I have before seen, and you have praised them, as they deserve to be praised, generously and warmly. It is delightful to see a poet of such eminent merits, and such freedom from the faults that infect the poetry of the day, commended with so much emphasis and decision. I am glad that you entered so emphatic a protest against criticising, as many do, by comparison, — which is the easy resort of those who have no standard of judgment in their own minds."

This cordial tribute of the elder poet seemed of sufficient interest to be preserved here. Somewhat later in the year Mr. Longfellow wrote to Mr. Tennyson of the pleasure he had received from reading his drama, Harold. In reply Mr. Tennyson wrote: —

"Thanks for your generous letter. I have had many congratulatory ones about Harold, but scarce any that I shall prize like yours. [You ask] 'What old ancestor spoke through you?' I fear none of mine fought for England on the hill of Senlac, for, as far as I know, I am part Dane, part Norman. When are you — or are you ever — coming to England? We are both getting old, — I am, I believe, the older of the two; but I hope that we shall come together again before we pass away forever."

CHAPTER XIII.

JOURNAL AND LETTERS.

1877.

January 1. At the Boston Theatre to see the first representation of the Scarlet Letter, dramatized from Hawthorne's story. Mrs. Lander as Hester Prynne.

2d. Snow, deep snow. A lovely sunset. Winter sunsets are more delicate than any others.

4th. Martin Farquhar Tupper at lunch. Asked him to dinner on Saturday.

To Mrs. J. T. Fields.

January 14, 1877.

I have to thank you for three things. The first is the beautiful poem, which is simple, tender, and true; the second is your kindness in writing to Mrs. Thaxter, from whom I have, in consequence, a letter; and the third is your amiable conduct in promising to come to supper with Miss Doria, after her concert on Wednesday.

In return for these three things I will tell you a pleasant piece of news.

Now, I might keep you waiting and guessing through three long pages, as Madame de Sévigné did her daughter when she announced to her the engagement of the *Grande Mademoiselle*. But I am not Madame de Sévigné, and I will not do it. I will only lead you gently down to the bottom of this page, as down a hillside covered with snow in which some one is fast making footprints, and say that Richard Dana is the youth. . . .

To G. W. Greene.

January 14, 1877.

I have a pleasant bit of news to send you from Craigie House, which I know will interest you. . . . And so there is to be a new 'Hanging of the Crane,' —

> "with dexter auguries,
> And all the wing'd good omens of the skies."

I say no more, having learned the great art of leaving off in time. You cannot improve a sonnet by making it more than fourteen lines long.

And speaking of sonnets reminds me to send you this on the Rhone, and with it some lines on the River Yvette. They were written to fill blank pages in Poems of Places. Perhaps you will think the pages had better have been left blank. The printer thinks otherwise, and feebly flatters me, so that I may be ready to meet other emergencies of the kind.

Welch [the gardener] on America: "This is not a good country, sorr! One half the year you are an icicle, and the other half you are boiled." This is not so conciliatory and flattering as the Proverbial Philosopher, who says we are improving.

To G. W. Greene.

January 15, 1877.

I went into my library this morning and found three damsels sitting by the fire; one of them was reading aloud from a volume on her knee. I asked what book it was, and she answered, "The Life of General Greene." It was a pretty picture, and would have pleased the author, had he seen it. This is the only thing of importance that has occurred in our household since I wrote you last. But as that was yesterday, and as to-day we have a snowstorm, there has been little chance for anything to happen. All our adventures, like the Vicar of Wakefield's, have been by the fireside.

Dr. Johnson said that the tragedy of Coriolanus was one of the author's most amusing performances. Were he now living, he could say the same of "Washington, a Drama in Five Acts." It is truly an amusing performance, — or will be if it is ever performed.

And the History, — is all going on smoothly? A young publisher, with few books to care for, is better than an old one with many. The terms he offers are much better than I get. It is half-past ten; so good-night.

To G. W. Greene.

January 24, 1877.

Do you remember our visit to Ischia, in 1829, — nearly fifty years ago? I never think of that island without thinking of you; and when I saw it last, in 1869, I remembered our being there together. Therefore I hope you will like the enclosed lines ['Vittoria Colonna'] which I have written for Poems of Places. If you see how and where they can be mended, let me know it. Inarimé was one of the old names of Ischia.

My turtle-doves are as happy as we used to be under similar circumstances. It is a pleasure to see them so joyous and free from care.

To G. W. Greene.

January, 1877.

Have you begun printing your History [of Rhode Island]? I imagine you sitting in your study, wrapped in your dressing-gown and reading proof-sheets with that gentle feeling of complacency with which an artist sees his plaster cast put into marble. I have just taken my morning draft of the Daily Advertiser, and send you a mouthful. It is a notice of Baron de Worms's book on the Eastern Question, and gives a simple, straightforward view of the whole matter, — the best I have yet seen. The remainder of this day I intend to devote to writing a poem on the French fleet that sailed from Brest in 1746 to ravage the New England coast and avenge Louisbourg. So farewell.[1]

February 1. A call from Mr. Dennett, author of Louisiana as it is. He gave me a fascinating account of the State. A day of spring; the icy fetters fall off.

To R. H. Dana, Jr.[2]

February 26, 1877.

I certainly would, if it were possible, but I do not see how it can be done. There is not time. If I were an Italian *improvisatore,* I might do it; but as I am only an American *professore,* I cannot. Anything to reach Ger-

[1] The Rev. E. E. Hale had written to Mr. Longfellow: "You told me that if the spirit moved, you would try to sing us a song for the Old South Meeting-house. I have found such a charming story that I think it will really tempt you. I want at least to tell it to you. . . . The whole story of the fleet is in Hutchinson's Massachusetts, ii. 384, 385. The story of Prince and the prayer is in a tract in the College Library, which I will gladly send you, or Mr. Sibley will. I should think that the assembly in the meeting-house in the gale, and then the terror of the fleet when the gale struck them, would make a ballad — if the spirit moved!" This ancient building, with its historic memories, was in danger of being demolished.

[2] Mr. Longfellow had been asked to write something to be read at a meeting in Stutgard for the purpose of erecting a monument to Ferdinand Freiligrath. He sent a handsome contribution to this memorial of his friend.

many by the middle of March should leave here by the first. I should be unwilling to present myself with a poor production on such an occasion, and it would be poor enough if written between now and the first of March.

27th. My seventieth birthday. My study is a garden of flowers; salutations and friendly greetings from far and near. I have a whole box full of letters and poems.

To G. W. Curtis.

February 28, 1877.

I hasten to respond to your cordial and affectionate greeting on my birthday, and to say how delightful it was to hear such words from you. It was almost as good as seeing you; but not quite.

It is a strange feeling, this of being seventy years old. I cannot say precisely what the feeling is, — but you will know one of these days. It is something like that of a schoolboy who has filled one side of his slate with the figures of a very long sum, and has to turn the slate over to go on with it.

Poor T.! it is really sad to see him so disabled. He keeps, however, very merry for the most part, and has written by dictation one or two little books while lying on his back.[1]

March 10. Greene, who came for my birthday, went home this afternoon. He is my oldest friend living, and always a welcome guest.

13th. A snow-storm. Good for writing letters. I have too many to write. Sometimes a single mail brings me

[1] It was while lamed by a fall upon the ice that Mr. Appleton wrote in this way his Syrian Sunshine, and his Windfalls.

fifteen. My time is taken up in answering them. I no sooner sit down to meditate upon something I have in mind, than I am haunted by the spectre of some unanswered letter, and start up, exclaiming: "Ha, ha, boy! say'st thou so? Art thou there, truepenny?"

To G. W. Childs.

March 13, 1877.

You do not know yet what it is to be seventy years old. I will tell you, so that you may not be taken by surprise when your turn comes. It is like climbing the Alps. You reach a snow-crowned summit, and see behind you the deep valley stretching miles and miles away, and before you other summits higher and whiter, which you may have strength to climb, or may not. Then you sit down and meditate and wonder which it will be. That is the whole story, amplify it as you may. All that one can say is, that life is opportunity.

April 1. Easter. If the sun is "dancing in the heavens," he is doing it behind the clouds. Only one level gleam at sunset lit up the landscape for a moment.

2d. Almost a pleasant day, after much rain. A visit from Fields, always cheery and cheering.

6th. A visit from Professor Packard, the only survivor of my old instructors and colleagues. With him his son, a naturalist.

7th. In the afternoon Charles Norton called. We talked of Ruskin and Carlyle, and of Lowell's having the English mission.

10th. Two Scotch ladies called. Then Mr. Clark brought me a copy of Prang's splendid portfolio of the "Yellowstone National Park,"—a wonderful region, looking more like fairy-land than anything on earth. Then a pleasant call from Miss ——, who has chosen the medical profession for her career, and is going to Germany, as the Harvard Medical School does not admit women.

12th. Lieutenant Arseniew, of the Russian Navy, at lunch. A pleasant, modest youth. He gave me some poems in English by his sister. How these Russians master foreign tongues! They are taught in their childhood.

19th. Evening at the Opera. Beethoven's *Fidelio*, with Mme. Pappenheim as Fidelio. The music splendid, but the subject of the most lugubrious and dismal kind. The scene passes wholly in a prison. Fidelio helps to dig her husband's grave in an old cistern in a dungeon.

21st. In the morning arranging Poems of Places for Syria. In the evening read over again Chodzko's Persian Poetry, and designed a poem, 'The Leap of Kurroglou.'

To Benjamin Alvord.

April 26, 1877.

I hasten to thank you for your letter and for the number of "Nature" containing the article on the compass-plant. In quoting from 'Evangeline,' the writer has used the earlier editions; in the later ones the passage has been somewhat changed. As soon as I saw the compass-plant [in the Cambridge Botanical Garden] I saw my error, and for "delicate plant" substituted "vigorous plant," and for "on its fragile stalk" the words "in the houseless wild." This puts the matter right, botanically speaking.

I hope that you are also the vigorous plant I remember, though so many years have gone since we met. I am sorry not to have seen you at Philadelphia. Do not let your good resolve to write a paper on the compass-plant slumber too long. It could not fail to be interesting and valuable.[1]

[1] An article by General Alvord will be found in the American Naturalist for August, 1882.

27th. Mrs. —— calls to talk with me about the 'Building of the Ship;' she is going to read it in public. She is German, and has a strong accent; she calls it "The Lunch of the Sheep."

To G. W. Greene.

April 29, 1877.

To-day I have been reading Sumner's letters from Italy. They are full of enthusiasm, and exhibit the softer and more poetical side of his character, — a side so little known or dreamed of by most people. He speaks of you often, and never without a caress.

What a devourer of books he was! It amazes me to see the extent of his reading in four summer months. He brought away from Italy a vast amount of knowledge; while I brought away little more than memories and impressions, — a kind of golden atmosphere, which has always illuminated my life. Perhaps we were both wiser than we knew. Each assimilated to himself what best served his purpose afterward.

May 1. It is pleasant to write the name of May, though one may have nothing more to say about it.

2d. Ole Bull, with his wife and her brother, dined with us.

7th. Trying to write a poem on the Potter's Wheel, — a poem of Ceramic Art.

8th. A day of musical dissipation. In the afternoon at Mme. Essipoff's concert; and in the evening at Miss Amy Fay's.

9th. A very tardy and reluctant spring. A letter from William Allingham.

10th. My holiday, with all its memories of thirty-four years! Wrote a sonnet on 'Holidays.'

11th. A lovely spring day. A mist and shadow of tender leaves over all the landscape.

12th. The lovely weather continues, and makes me as lazy as Maxentius, who could not, or would not, walk even in the shade of his own portico.

To G. W. Greene.

May 28, 1877.

What a dripping month of May we have had! But today the Spring comes out with all her lilacs in bloom, and all her horse-chestnut tapers lighted.

When you come to Cambridge, you will find George Washington[1] brought down from his station on the stairs, and standing in the hall below, where he can be better seen. In his place you will see an old Dutch clock, whose silver chimes will lull you to sleep at night. At the half-hours it strikes the coming hour, to give timely warning. The hours are struck on a larger bell, and the chimes "shiver the air into a mist of sound." On top is a figure of Time, with scythe and hour-glass, attended by four other figures, representing the seasons, — all beautifully carved in wood. This is my latest plaything.

Fields was here yesterday. When you come, we are to have a dinner at the Brunswick, with yourself, Emerson, Holmes, and Appleton.

June 1. In the afternoon a beautiful basket of flowers from pupils of the Lasell Seminary at Auburndale, in return for an autograph copy of a Sonnet.

2d. Reading the Frogs of Aristophanes, I was struck with the thought that it was a good introduction for the second part of *Faust*.

[1] A cast from Houdon's bust.

19th. Sophocles at dinner, bringing with him two bottles of Greek wine.

July 19 to 28. In Portland.[1]

August 1. Proofs of Poems of Places; Germany. A letter from Dr. Kohl, of Bremen.

2d. Drove to Longwood to call upon Hillard. In the afternoon a call from two ladies, school-teachers in Cincinnati.

3d. Received from Harper and Brothers one thousand dollars for the poem 'Kéramos;' that is, for the right of first publication in their Magazine.

To J. T. Fields.

August 3, 1877.

When you played your first card, I was in Portland, and could not send you the Sonnet. Your second finds me here; and as it is a trump, it takes the Sonnet, which you will find enclosed. Let the last line read, "And lovely as a landscape in a dream."

The poem 'Kéramos' has gone to the Harpers, who will harp it in one hundred and fifty thousand households, or say half a million ears, — if they will listen to such music as comes from a potter's wheel.

I am too busy to come to Manchester, or even to think of it. I must get these Poems of Places finished with all possible speed; and if I go away, it stops the machinery. When you next come to town, try to come as far as Cambridge.

Driving through Charles Street yesterday, I looked out

[1] "In Portland," he wrote a friend, "I bought a copy of Plutarch's Lives, in Latin, printed in Venice in 1496. I believe this is my first purchase of a book on account of its age. I already begin to suspect that the date has been altered from 1596. The 4 has a doubtful look."

for you, but did not see you, — because, like the Spanish fleet, you "were not in sight."

To G. W. Greene.

August 5, 1877.

The article you send me is certainly written with *malice prepense.* But Seneca says that malicious people have to drink most of their own venom. The way to make them drink all of it is to take no notice of them whatever. Your reply is dignified and conclusive, and I know you would not have made it except for the sake of justice and fair dealing. I hope you will adhere to your resolution not to be dragged into a newspaper controversy. The book is its own defender, and will fight its own battles if need be; therefore do not let your peace of mind be disturbed. The clock is striking half past five. I will take a walk in the garden before dinner, and add a postscript after.

P. S. — Result of the walk in the garden: I find that some unknown vagabonds have been in the summer-house.

6th. Finished 'The Leap of Kurroglou [Roushan Beg].'

8th. A lovely summer day; I wanted to be in many places at once.

10th. I called to see my old friend Palfrey, the historian. Found him, as ever, cordial and genial, but very feeble.

11th. A letter from Mr. ——, of Washington, a fierce and "un-reconstructed" rebel, and an entire stranger, asking me to defray the expense of publishing his Analytical Essays on the Great Poets, which some of his friends tell him are "the most eloquent and beautiful compositions in the English language."

September 2. A splendid autumn day. Miss Sara Jewett, the actress, called.

3d. Mr. —— called, with another Englishman. Speaking of the weather, he said: "It is quite equal to anything we have in England, if not superior."

5th. At lunch, the Rev. W. A. S., of New College, Oxford, with his father, and the Rev. Mr. T., son of the Archbishop of Canterbury [introduced by Dean Stanley], and Mr. W., a young barrister.

6th. Dr. Playfair, M.P. for St. Andrews.

To J. T. Fields.

September 9, 1877.

I am so busy reading your new book that I cannot find a moment to thank you for it. I stop midway in the reading to say it is charming. I hardly know which Essay I like the best. Yes, I do; it is My Friend's Library, — the longest, and yet not long enough. It might be drawn out like an extension-table; and I advise you to do it.

Thanks and congratulations. The book will be a favorite, and you will incur the penalty pronounced in Scripture when all men speak well of you.

Do you know how to apply properly for an autograph?[1] Here is a formula which I have just received on a postal card: —

DEAR SIR, — As I am getting a collection of the autographs of all honorable and worthy men, and as I think yours such, I hope you will forfeit by next mail.

When are you coming back from your cottage on the

[1] At one time Mr. Longfellow, burdened with these demands, had a slip of paper printed, which he enclosed with his autograph, for the benefit of others: "In applying for an autograph, always inclose a stamped and addressed envelope."

cliff? The trees on the Common and the fountains are calling for you.

> "Thee, Tityrus, even the pine-trees,
> Thee the very fountains, the very copses, are calling."

Perhaps, also, your creditors. At all events I am, who am your debtor.

21st. Fourteen callers in the afternoon.

22d. Arrange Poems of Places; Russia. They are more numerous than I thought they would be.

26th. To-day, sirocco. I feel as limp as Somebody's poetry.

27th. Arranging poems for a new volume; this time my own. In the evening Dr. Asa Gray with Sir J. D. Hooker, another botanist, and President of the Royal Society.

29th. Monti and music.

October 1. Dined with Agassiz to meet Sir Joseph Hooker, a very agreeable man.

2d. The weather continues superb. A wild Texan herd broke into the front field. The leader, a huge bull, was shot. The rest of the herd at once grew quiet.

4th. Called on Sir Joseph Hooker at the Botanical Garden. Evening at the theatre; Madame Janauschek as Brunhild.

10th. A young Westerner and his wife called. He asked me how old I was. "Seventy," I answered. He replied, "I have seen a good many men of your age who looked much younger than you."

To Mrs. J. T. Fields.

October 16, 1877.

You command me to be silent, and say nothing of your beautiful poem till I see you. Nevertheless I cannot be quite silent. I must at least say that it is beautiful, and sweet with the breath of meadows, and simple in its treatment, as an Idyl should be. A great deal of the poetry I read is hot and feverish, and makes me long for shade and coolness. Your little book is like a grotto, cool and refreshing. I am particularly struck by some of the choruses. But as I am not to speak of the book till I see you, I will hold my peace.

Will you ask Sir James to lend me Landor's Hellenics? I am sorely in want of his poems 'Ida' and 'Ithaca,' being now engaged upon Greece.

18th. Dined with the Rev. Dr. Gray to meet Bishops Stevens of Pennsylvania, Dudley of Tennessee, and Eliot of Texas.

19th. Evening at Mr. Haskins's, where I met sundry other bishops. — Emerson was there.

20th. Last night I dreamed of Emerson. He said: "The spring will come again; but shall we see it, or only the eternal spring up there?" lifting both his hands on high. — At dinner Joaquin Miller and Monti.

24th. Opera; Wagner's *Lohengrin*.

30th. Read Miss Phelps's novel, the Story of Avis. A fresh, original style of writing, very interesting and peculiar.

To G. W. Greene.

October 30, 1877.

Pierce's Life of Sumner will be published on the 7th of November. Last evening I received a copy in advance. I read in it, here and there, and a profound sorrow came over me, — much like what I felt when I heard of Sumner's death. We are all there in our youth; and the Past is too powerful for me. Too many things are touched upon that send a quiver through the nerves. I shall never be able to read the book, except in fragments at long intervals.

Osgood has sold or given and conveyed the North American into the hands of the Appletons. Henceforth it will be edited, printed, and published in New York. Mr. Clarke, at the printing-office, said: "It is like parting with the New England Blarney-Stone." He might have said, in more classic language: "Troy has lost her Palladium."

31st. A hazy autumn day. W. W. Story, the sculptor, called.

November 26. Dark and wet as London. Copied for the "Old South" Committee the 'Ballad of the French Fleet.'

From John Weiss.

Boston, December 1, 1877.

Dear Mr. Longfellow,—As you desired, I send you herewith some verses of Places. Perhaps, if you care to receive those from the famous Naushon, you will think that a footnote or curt introduction may be needed; that can be easily provided. The Island Book, in several volumes, contains some most interesting traces of the distinguished men who have been guests there. I have thought you would like to see the following by Daniel Webster,—one of his rare ventures into the domain of verse-writing:

"'T is not the capture of the finny race,
'T is not the exciting pleasure of the chase,
But hospitality, that gives the grace
And sweetest charm to this enchanting place.
Though skies and stars and seas unite their power,
And balmy airs their softest influence shower,
To gild the outspread wings of every hour,
Yet oft nor eye nor ear these objects seeks,
Drawn both away while Beauty smiles and speaks."

Mr. Webster used to be keen for the venison, and a very good shot, bagging his game as he used to do ideas succinctly in a paragraph. But when Mr. E—— was down there, the Governor (Mr. Swain) gave him a favorite stand, with injunction to take the deer when it emerged into the open. The deer did well enough; but when it came through, Mr. E——, shaking his double-barrelled Manton wildly in the air, capered about, shouting: "There she goes! there she goes!"

Excuse me; the reminiscences of Naushon are too alluring. But some of the little poems in its Album are better than most of those which stray into German *Andenken.*

Very truly yours,

J. WEISS.

December 3. A letter from Lowell in Madrid. He is a little homesick; but on the whole, I should say well pleased with his place as minister.[1]

17th. The "Atlantic" dinner at the Brunswick Hotel, to celebrate the thirtieth anniversary of the Magazine, and Whittier's seventieth birthday.

[1] Mr. Lowell wrote to him: "I have just had a visit from the Perpetual Secretary of the Royal Spanish Academy, who came to tell me that you had just been nominated a foreign member of that venerable body. When your name was proposed, he said, there was a contest as to who should second the nomination, 'porque tiene muchos apasionados aqui el Señor Longfellow.' You may conceive how pleasant it was to me to hear this, and likewise your name perfectly pronounced by a Spaniard. I told the Secretary that one of your latest poems had recorded your delightful memories of Spain. It made me feel nearer home to talk about you, and I add that to many debts of friendship I owe you. I wish I could walk along your front walk, and drop into your study. However, I shall find you there when I come back; for you looked younger than ever when I bade you good-by. Your diploma will be sent to me in a few days, and I shall take care that you receive it."

CHAPTER XIV.

JOURNAL AND LETTERS.

1878–1879.

From W. C. Bryant.

NEW YORK, January 3, 1878.

DEAR MR. LONGFELLOW, — The Goethe Club of this city numbers as many admirers of your writings as it has members. They are desirous of seeing you among them in person, and of taking by the hand one whom they have long held in reverence. You will have a formal invitation to that effect, and I have been asked to accompany it with a few words of entreaty that you will give it a favorable consideration. You will certainly nowhere meet with those who more delight in what you have written, or who would receive greater pleasure from your visit. If you do not care to come on your own account, let me beg you to consider whether you will not come for their sakes. I am, dear sir,

Faithfully yours,

W. C. BRYANT.

To J. T. Fields.

January 25, 1878.

Behold the song "from beginning to end." I am glad you like it well enough to ask for it in this shape.

I have answered the letter of the young lady of Cincinnati. Her request was for a poem for her class. I could not write it, but tried to say *No* so softly that she would think it better than *Yes.*

When I remember that it is less than half an hour from my door to yours, I am ashamed not to see you oftener. I think the reason is that while you are on the wing it is in vain to seek you. And then the days are so short! It seems to me they are only twelve hours long, instead of twenty-four, as they used to be.

I hope Mrs. Fields is quite well again. I have taken her cold, or somebody-else's, and should like to find the owner.

February 1. Mme. Modjeska and her son, with Mrs. Fields and Miss Phelps, author of Avis, at lunch.

2d. Begin again on proof-sheets [of Sumner's Works] with Nichols and Owen.

3d. Translated Ovid's *Tristia,* book iii. Elegy 12, for Poems of Places.

To G. W. Greene.

February 24, 1878.

You tell me nothing of your Southern journey, — whom you saw and what you did, only that you went and came back. I heard of you through my neighbor Horsford, who left you feasting with the grandees of Washington. What a humiliating spectacle was that presented by the Senate on the passage of the Silver Bill! To this have we come? *Quousque tandem?* Still there remains a "land of pure delight," — the land of letters, in which you and I can take refuge. My new volume of poems ['Kéramos,' etc.] is all in type. I hesitate about inserting the Virgilian Eclogue. What do you think? Will it not be considered rather a school-boy performance? And the Poems of Places: Europe is finished, and I am now in Syria. In

Russia the material falls short. Is there any poetic translation of Ovid's *Tristia?* His lamentations from the shores of the Black Sea would help me, and give a classic flavor to the otherwise rather barbaric volume.

To G. W. Greene.

April 29, 1878.

How have you got through this rainy week, in which all nature, except human nature, has been rejoicing and exulting? Here, Poems of Places have shut out the dull weather. I have been in India and China and Japan, and am now in Africa, where it is hot and dry enough. I think Africa will be one of the most interesting volumes. There are no new books here just now except my own. 'Kéramos' is out; but I no longer feel *la procellosa e trepida gioja* of sending out a book into the world.

May 1. Bought Champeaux's Handbook of Tapestry. A poem might be written on this subject. A lovely May day after a week of rain.

4th. Afternoon at the Boston Theatre, to see Jefferson in Rip Van Winkle.

5th. A wild south wind blowing. Cherry-trees in full bloom, and dandelions in the grass.

25th. Dined at Mr. Winthrop's to meet Lord and Lady Dufferin.

28th. Lord and Lady Dufferin drove over from Brookline to breakfast with us. They are both charming people, very simple and cordial.

To G. W. Greene.

May 31, 1878.

This is sad news about Bryant; I fear he will not survive. Two reporters, or interviewers, have been to me already, for any incidents or anecdotes I could furnish concerning him. I had little or nothing to say, and said less. What they will say I said remains to be seen.

In Poems of Places I have travelled all the world over, except America. That remains, and will probably fill several volumes. Even the final volume, Oceanica, is in type. That will complete the series, and embrace much interesting matter on seas and islands, not given before.

"Dulce est cujusvis libri finem scribere."

July 10–16. In Portland.

August 5. Went with Fields down to his cottage by the sea [in Manchester], — a lovely place.

6th. Drove with Mr. and Mrs. F. to Gloucester to see Miss Phelps in her cottage [the Sea Shell], just as large as my study, — twenty feet square.

18th. Alfred Dommett sends me his 'Ranolf and Amohia,' — a New Zealand poem, with splendid descriptions of scenery.

19th. A day when everything went wrong, till evening, when a Nova Scotian artist came, and by way of compensation gave me a sketch of Grand Pré in oils.

To Miss E. S. Phelps.

August 21, [1878].

Your letter fills me with regret. I am sorry that I did not stay long enough at East Point to see the fog lift and Norman's Woe rise to view. I have never seen those fatal rocks. I have a vision of you speeding away with your swift steed, and the white cloud floating in the wind as you turned the corner and vanished out of sight. We got safely back to Thunderbolt Hill[1] before the rain came on. But what a wet afternoon it was!

[1] Mr. Fields's place.

I thank you for the paragraph on Co-education. That is a difficult problem to solve. I know that life, like French poetry, is imperfect without the feminine rhyme. But I remember how much time I lost at the Academy, in my boyhood, looking across the schoolroom at the beautiful rhyme. Perhaps, after all, it was not time lost, but a part of my education. Of what woman was it said that "to know her was a liberal education," and who said it?[1] Certainly there is something more in education than is set down in the school-books. Whittier has touched the point very poetically in that little lyric of his called 'In School Days.'

To G. W. Greeene.

August 21, 1878.

As I have written only eight letters to-day, I may as well add another, and give you what is left in the ink-stand. Not that I have anything in particular to say, but my pen has got such headway upon it that I cannot stop it.

I have just been looking over Mr. Cushing's Index to the North American Review, recently published. It is like walking through a graveyard and reading the inscriptions on head-stones. So many familiar names, so many old associations! Bowen is the largest contributor; Edward Everett the next largest; then his brother Alexander. You wrote twenty articles; Charles Sumner three; George Sumner only one.[2] I am struck by the great variety of subjects treated, and the prevalence of those purely literary; and my regret is rendered more

[1] It was Steele, who said of Lady Elizabeth Hastings, under the name of Aspasia, that "to love her was a liberal education." — *The Tatler*, No. 49.

[2] Mr. Longfellow himself wrote eleven.

keen than ever that the old Review should have slipped its moorings in Massachusetts Bay and drifted down to the mouth of the Hudson. It must be towed back again, and safely anchored in our harbor.

To J. T. Fields.

August 25, 1878.

I am sorry to hear that you are not quite yourself. I sympathize with you, for I am somebody else. It is the two W's — Work and Weather — that are playing the mischief with us. I ought to have stayed longer with you; I ought to have stayed longer at Portland and at Nahant, — in fine, ought not to have come home so soon. You must not open a book; you must not even look at an inkstand. These are both contraband articles, upon which we have to pay heavy duties. We cannot smuggle them in; Nature's custom-house officers are too much on the alert.

I should be delighted to make you another visit before the season is over, and will if possible, — but not for the gayeties of the hotel; they do not tempt me. What I want is rest. Greene writes in very poor spirits; he says he cannot walk half a mile. Are we all crumbling to pieces? I trust not.

To G. W. Greene.

August 30, 1878.

You need not be afraid of Hop Bitters; they will never do you any harm, — because you will never take them. Here at the Craigie House everything goes on as usual. We debate the errors in the Sumner proof-sheets. Poems of Places drag their length from volume to volume. Mrs. McD. has gone back to Holly Springs to face and fight the pestilence. It is very noble in her to do so. She could not resist the maternal instinct to protect her child, and her desire to share the fate of her family. She will be a great support and comfort to them with her courage and cheerfulness. What a terrible devastation this is at the South! What a terror in the air! The laws of Nature are inexorable. Truly, cleanliness *is* next to godliness. Have your cellar whitewashed. The inside of the platter must be kept clean, as well as the outside, — and this sounds like a sermon, of which you stand in no need.

September 1. A soft rain; then sunshine intense and pitiless. E. and R. are staying here. A. and A. are in the forests of Maine.

11th. Went to town to see Mrs. ——. She is in great grief, and almost despair. I could not help recalling the lines of Keats: —

> "There was a listening fear in her regard
> As if calamity had but begun,
> As if the vanward clouds of evil days
> Had spent their malice, and the sullen rear
> Was with its storèd thunder laboring up."

17th. Dean Stanley called, with Dr. Harper and Mr. Grove, editor of Macmillan's Magazine, escorted by Governor Rice.

25th. At the theatre to see Olivia, — a play made from the Vicar of Wakefield.

To G. W. Greene.

September 25, 1878.

I went yesterday to the theatre to see the Vicar of Wakefield, and was struck with the immense superiority of dramatic representation over narrative. Dr. Primrose and his daughter were living realities. Sophy was perfectly lovely, and it would have delighted Goldsmith's heart to have seen her. Dr. Primrose was very well done by Warren, and Olivia by Miss Clarke. Mrs. Primrose was represented by Mrs. Vincent. It was all very pathetic, and half the audience were in tears, — the present writer among the rest.

To-day I am paying the penalty of my dissipation, having taken a heavy cold from the ladies' fans behind me, and the invariable theatrical custom of flooding a heated audience with cold air from open doors and windows. I might have foreseen it, and did foresee it; and get no consolation from Molière's "Tu l'as voulu, George Dandin," or his "Que diable allait-il faire dans cette galère?"

I suppose you have seen by the papers that Dean Stanley has been here. He came to see me, and I afterwards dined with him at Winthrop's. He is very pleasant and animated in conversation, and full of anecdote. I wish you had been here; I think you would have enjoyed seeing him.

Did I tell you of a request I had from Chattanooga to write one hundred autographs for a Fair in behalf of Southern sufferers? It was like fighting the battle over again; but I did it!

To J. T. Fields.

October 6, 1878.

"Affable Archangel," — have you written to Chicago for reinforcements of those stout little "men in buckram"?

I rather like that sentence beginning with Milton, who, as —— thinks, was no poet, and going back to Shakespeare, of whom your travelling companion at Stratford-on-Avon entertained the same opinion. Let us try again. Have you summoned those "spirits from the vasty" West?

Let me take this opportunity to recommend to you the Family Library of British Poetry. It is an excellent work, and not only a body of British poetry, but the very soul thereof. You will like it as well as I do.[1]

All things here have resumed their wonted aspect. Poems of Places, also an excellent work, "drags at each remove a lengthening chain." Don Jorge Nichols and Don Juan Owen come with the Sumner proof-sheets, and we sit together, like the three wise men in a bowl, all at sea. If I were not an enemy to quotations, I should say it is enough to "make the judicious grieve" to see us three sitting and sifting, and weighing and measuring with endless iteration. Meanwhile you look serenely down from the heights of Thunderbolt Hill, like Lucretius in his second book, or Lord Bacon in his beautiful paraphrase of the same in his Essay "Of Truth": "It is a pleasure to stand upon the shore and to see ships tossed upon the great sea;" and so forth.

Did you read in the papers of Mr. ——'s recitation of The Spanish Student at the Hawthorne Rooms? I understand that he appeared in a complete suit of red, like Mephistopheles in *Faust!*

October 9. Sam Ward came with young Lord Ronald Gower, a younger brother of the Duchess of Argyll.

15th. Went to Portland for B.'s wedding, — and a very pretty wedding it was.

18th. Returned home. Found sixteen letters.

23d. Lunched with Professor Pierce to meet Dr. Lyon Playfair, M. P.

[1] The book was compiled by Mr. Fields and Mr. Whipple.

To G. W. Greene.

October 27, 1878.

I shall be delighted to see you and your wife whenever you can come. Let me know the day and the hour, and I will send in for you. If I do not come myself, it is because the coupé holds but two.

Mr. Henry W. Holland, of Cambridge, has published a very handsome book entitled "William Dawes, and his Ride with Paul Revere," in which he convicts me of high historic crimes and misdemeanors. The book will interest you; and I can already see you sitting by your favorite southern window reading its attractive pages.

"New England" makes two volumes of Poems of Places; they are among the best. The "Middle States" are in type, and the "Southern" ready for the printer. I begin at last to see the end.

To W. M. Green.

October 29, 1878.

I hasten to thank you for your kind remembrance and for your excellent address to the Board of Trustees of the "University of the South." I have read it with deep interest. Certainly your forcible and timely words need no indorsement of mine; and yet at all times the response and sympathy of others is comforting, and in a certain sense upholds our hands.

I have always, my dear sir, the pleasantest remembrance of your visit here, and I have learned with great sorrow of the affliction that has come upon you.[1] When I hear of a young man's death, I instinctively recall that touching picture of a father's grief, where David goes

[1] Bishop Green's son, a clergyman, had died at his post of duty and mercy during the prevalence of the yellow fever.

up to the "chamber over the gate" and weeps; and I hear the cry of his soul: "O Absalom, my son, my son!"

30th. Wrote 'The Chamber over the Gate.' It was suggested by writing to the Bishop of Mississippi on the death of his son.

November 4. Met Dr. Holmes at the printer's. He is putting to press his Memoir of Motley.

To Miss K——.

November 13, 1878.

I am glad you take interest enough in Hyperion to ask any questions about it, and I answer them with pleasure. St. Gilgen is a real place. The churchyard is there, and the chapel and the funeral tablet, and the inscription. Perhaps you would like to have it in German. It reads as follows: —

"Blicke nicht traurend in die Vergangenheit. Sie kommt nicht wieder. Nütze weisse die Gegenwart. Sie ist dein. Der düstern Zukunft geh ohne Furcht mit männlichen Sinne entgegen."

No author's name is given, for no one signs funeral inscriptions, and I do not suppose this was taken from anybody's writings. In the Gazetteer you may possibly find "Sanct Wolfgangs See." This is the same lake as St. Gilgen, St. Wolfgang being at the other end of the lake.

December 21. Edward Reményi, the famous violinist, passed the evening with us, with Mr. Ducken to accompany him. Their music was charming.

24th. Mr. Guest and Mrs. Gaskell, of England.

28th. Wrote some verses on Bayard Taylor, for the memorial meeting.

January 2, 1879. Evening at the Opera, Mme. Gerster as Lucia. An exquisite soprano voice and an excellent actress.

3d. A bitter wind howling and whistling. A Catholic priest, who has left his Church, calls. He looks frightened. Write many letters.

To G. W. Greene.

January 3, 1879.

Last night I was at the opera of *Lucia*. I thought of you. How delighted you would have been with the music, and how tired with sitting on those *ci-devant* red velvet cushions, now changed by Time into layers of red sandstone!

Mme. Gerster's pure, young, fresh soprano voice is exquisite; the other singers all good; chorus and orchestra good, — a rare completeness in voices and instruments. The *sestetto* at the end of the second act was "splendid."

There is to be a meeting at the Music Hall next week to commemorate the death of Bayard Taylor. I have written some verses for the occasion, which I hope you will like; I will send them to you in a few days.

This is my sixth letter this morning, — a fact which will account for its meagreness. I do not wish to say the same things over too often; you might think me growing old, — which would be a great mistake; I have done that already.

A. calls at the door, "Papa, dear, will you come to lunch?" "In a moment." And then to the printer's to prove —

> "Come è duro calle
> Lo scendere e 'l salir le sue scale."

You cannot have forgotten them; if you have, I have not. I send you to-day a paper with an article on copyright. *E pur si muove!*

4th. At the Opera. The *Sonnambula* of Bellini, with Mme. Gerster as Amina. It was beautiful throughout.

5th. Fed the sparrows and wrote a sonnet on 'The Voice of a Singer.' In the afternoon Minnie Hauk called, with her mother.

7th. Afternoon at Mrs. S ——'s; music. Señora Carmen Pisani, a Spanish singer of the opera, and a little French girl of five years, who played wonderfully well some fugues of Bach! Evening at the Opera. Minnie Hauk in *Carmen*, — a rather brilliant opera by a French composer, Bizet, who died before it was performed.

8th. Curtin comes in the evening and reads parts of a wild Russian story of Cossacks, lawless in their lives and fierce in their religion. Their blind zeal makes one understand better the phrase, "Holy Russia." It is the spirit of the Crusaders.

To G. W. Greene.

January 10, 1879.

I think you will feel that I have done wisely in making up my mind not to venture going in to the Taylor memorial meeting to-night. I could not bear the exposure and the excitement of the occasion, without too much strain; so I have sent my poem to be read by Dr. Holmes. I am now enjoying a little leisure. All the work is done on Poems of Places, except reading proofs, which will last some time longer. I wish I could send your mother the lovely roses that are blooming and breathing out their little lives on the table before me. As I cannot, I send the wish to do so. You shall have the poem in a day or two; it is coming out in the next Atlantic.

14th. T. and Mr. and Mrs. Waring at lunch. In the afternoon Louise and Jeanne Douste, the wonderful musicians of eight and ten years, came with their father. They played pieces from Bach, Beethoven, Mozart, Chopin, and Brahms. Dear little girls, both of them! In the midst of the music came Mrs. Clara Doria Rogers.

To G. W. Curtis.

January 15, 1879.

I have just received, and have read with unabated interest and delight from beginning to end, your Discourse on Bryant. It is admirable; very just and very eloquent. It is not a painting of the man, but his statue, which may be seen from all sides, and represents him as he was and will be in the minds of his countrymen. There is something very noble and grand in his attitude and aspect.

Many thanks. In return I send you some verses which I wrote for the Bayard Taylor meeting.

16th. In the evening comes Mr. Balch, who agrees to let me have the sole charge of the three remaining volumes of Sumner's Works.[1]

To G. W. Greene.

January 17, 1879.

Have you any faith in the mystery and meaning of numbers, as Dante had, and Cowley, and other poets? Last night, as I lay awake, thinking of many things, the number eighteen came into my mind, and I was amazed to find what a part it has played in my life.

I was eighteen years old when I took my college degree; eighteen years afterward, I was married for the second time; I lived with my wife eighteen years, and it

[1] Mr. Francis Balch, Mr. E. L. Pierce, and Mr. Longfellow were named by Mr. Sumner as his literary executors.

is eighteen years since she died. These four eighteens added together make seventy-two, — my age this year. And then, by way of parenthesis or epicycle, I was eighteeen years professor in the College here, and have published eighteen separate volumes of poems.

This is curious; the necromancers would make a good deal out of it: I cannot make anything at all.

18th. Send the last copy of Poems of Places to the printer. That stone is rolled over the hill.

To Jules Marcou.

January 23, 1879.

I should have written you long ago to thank you for your kind remembrance and for the *Chants Populaires de la Franche Comté.* I promised your son to do so when he brought me the book, but have been prevented by many engagements, — those numberless nothings that break the smooth current of life like pebbles in a stream. It is a very curious and interesting collection of popular songs; and I can say to you, as does Victor Hugo to the editor: "Je vous remercie, monsieur; vous m'avez fait connaître la Franche Comté." I wish I had some pleasant news to send you from Cambridge. You know what a New England winter is, and I need not enlarge upon it. Two handmaidens, Influenza and Neuralgia, sent from that intelligence-office which is generally supposed to furnish us with cooks, make me as wretched as a Mormon with two wives.

28th. Among my letters to-day are two from old people, — one signed "M. T., seventy-eight years old;" the other, "S. H., eighty-one years old, and nearly blind." Why do old people like to boast of their age?

February 1. Received from Mantua *Canti Inglesi*, by Luigi Carnevali, containing excellent translations of some of my lyrics.

27th. My seventy-second birthday. A present from the children of Cambridge of a beautiful armchair, made from the wood of the Village Blacksmith's chestnut-tree.

To G. W. Greene.

March 7, 1879.

I had a note this morning from Miss P——, of Andover, in which she sends me the following: —

"I just now heard of a little girl (*very* little), who has begun to go to Sunday-school, and was asked by her teacher the question: 'What book do good people like best to read?' Loud her answer rang: 'Longfellow's Poems!'"

Of the birthday-chair I hear nothing farther; but no doubt shall hear soon, and have written a poem in reply to anything which may come. That is my only achievement since you left me. A more important achievement is the translation of Heine's Poems into Italian by Bernadino Zendrini, — a volume of over four hundred pages, sent me by the translator, "desideroso di un suo giudizio." As far as I have examined it, he has done his work well. And what a difficult work! There is evidently a great and strange fascination in translating. It seizes people with irresistible power, and whirls them away till they are beside themselves. It is like a ghost beckoning one to follow.

Last night I went to an opera at the *Teatro dell' Arsenale*, composed by a gentleman of Cambridge, and sung by amateurs. Very clever, both in composition and performance.[1]

[1] An amateur company for several years gave very spirited performances in one of the buildings of the disused Arsenal in Cambridge, which they fitted up for the purpose.

To Mrs. J. T. Fields.

March 12, 1879.

Pardon me for not writing sooner to thank you for the lovely glass jar you sent me on my birthday. I never saw anything of the kind so beautiful. It stands on my study table; whenever I raise my head I see it, and whenever I see it, it gives me a fresh delight. It is a golden sun that lights the room. I hope soon to have the pleasure of showing you my elbow-chair. I cannot send it to you, but it shall wait your coming; meanwhile I send you some verses which I have written to the children by way of thanks for their present. Please do not show them to any one out of your own house before the end of the week, as they are to appear first in the Cambridge papers, as is right and proper. With renewed thanks,

Yours faithfully.

March 31. Winter has come back in great force, — a whirling snowstorm to end the month. Have been this morning at the City Hospital in Boston to see Miss H., the reader, who is dying of consumption.

To G. W. Greene.

May 26, 1879.

Your letter, with its pleasant tidings, has just reached me, and I hasten to send you my cordial congratulations. As girls will grow up and get married, and there is no power on earth to prevent it, all we have to do is — to let them. We, who are on the western side of life, must forget ourselves a little, and see with their eyes, who are looking out at the eastern windows; there it is all sunshine.

I am glad that you are satisfied with K——'s choice; that is the main point. Everything else will take care of itself. We all join in felicitations and good wishes. No wonder you are still somewhat anxious about your mother; though I suppose that any ill effects of the accident, if any were to be, would have shown themselves before now.[1]

The visit of the school-girls passed off very pleasantly; and such a pretty girl presented the pen![2] The teacher asked after you, and remembered that you were here last year.

To Mrs. J. T. Fields.

June 25, 1879.

. . . I went to town to see you, but you had already gone to the seaside. You have escaped the stir and noise of Class-Day and Commencement-Day week. I think the Duke of Argyll must be in town, for the Lancers have just ridden by, the band playing lustily, "The Campbells are coming." I shall probably find him at the Commencement dinner, to which I am going presently. For the last ten days I have had Mr. Kitson, the sculptor, staying with me, making my bust. It is very good; so say "all the crowned heads" of Cambridge. "Two or three sittings!"—that is the illusory phrase. Two or three sittings have become a standing joke. . . . Give my love to your patient, and tell him to be of good cheer.

July 11. The Duke of Argyll and his daughters dined with us. Other guests,—R. H. Dana and his son, Mrs. L——, and Charles Norton.

[1] Mr. Greene's mother died in 1886, at the age of one hundred and two.

[2] The "iron pen," afterward celebrated in his verse. It was made from a bit of iron from the prison of Bonnivard at Chillon, the handle of oak-wood from the frigate "Constitution," set with three precious stones from Siberia, Ceylon, and Maine.

To G. W. Greene.

PORTLAND, August 7, 1879.

My principal reason for "not giving you an account of my narrow escape from shipwreck" was that no such thing ever happened to me. The last place in which you would ever look for me would be out at sea in a cat-boat. I was not there. It was C. and A. coming from Nahant; and they reached their landing before the storm came on. Their only danger was that they were run into by a yacht, with one man and four women on board; and one of the women flew into a passion and cried out: "I wish they had been drowned!" Ten minutes later the yacht was capsized, and the four women perished!

I am here on my annual visit to the old house, inhaling health with every breath of sea-air; I shall stay here ten days longer, and then go home to welcome Ernest and his wife, who leave Liverpool on Tuesday next.

I am "as idle as a painted ship upon a painted ocean." I only sit here at this upper window and see the people go by, and commit to memory the signs on the opposite side of the street.

The seaside laziness overwhelms me like a tide. I close my letter and my eyes.

To J. T. Fields.

PORTLAND, August 10, 1879.

As soon as I received your note, I sent the poem ['Kéramos'] to Mr. Alden. Many thanks to you, my noble friend and financier; I hope the Harpers will be as well satisfied with the transaction as I am.[1]

Church-bells ringing; clatter of church-going feet on the pavement; boys crying, "Boston Herald!" voices of

[1] The *honorarium* was one thousand dollars.

passing men and women, — these are the sounds that come to me at this upper window, looking down into the street. I contrast all this with last Sunday's silence at Manchester-by-the-Sea, and remember my delightful visit there. Then comes the thought of the moonlight and the music, and Shelley's verses,

> "As the moon's soft splendor
> O'er the faint, cold starlight of heaven
> Is thrown ;"

and so on, to

> "Some world far from ours,
> Where moonlight and music and feeling
> Are one."

How beautiful this song would sound if set to music by Mrs. B ——, and chanted by her in the twilight !

Portland is a pleasant place. So are other places, — as may be seen by certain poems written about them. It is a pity that we cannot be in more than one at a time.

August 22. As I was standing at my front door this morning, a lady in black came up and asked : "Is this the house where Longfellow was born ?"

"No, he was not born here."

"Did he die here ?"

"Not yet."

"Are you Longfellow ?"

"I am."

"I thought you died two years ago."

25th. I went to Boston to call on Dr. Acland, of Oxford.

26th. I received the diploma of the Spanish Academy.

28th. Dr. Acland called. He took me aside to speak of his beautiful wife, who lately died. He is overwhelmed with grief and bewildered by the rush of events, but tries to rise above it all into

"that blessed mood
In which the burden of the mystery,
In which the heavy and the weary weight
Of all this unintelligible world
Is lightened."

September 1. Born in the southwest chamber of the Craigie House, at ten o'clock, a new Richard Henry Dana; my first grandchild.

2d. Mr. and Mrs. Leycester, of Knutsford, Cheshire, England, called. Charming people; I remember meeting her on the Roman Campagna in 1869.

22d. Dr. Plumptre, Professor in King's College, London, and translator of Sophocles and Æschylus, with his wife and the Rev. J. Cotton Smith, came to lunch. She is sister of the late Rev. F. D. Maurice. In the afternoon Miss T., a charming reader.

To G. W. Greene.

October 7, 1879.

The seventh of October, and the thermometer in my study, with doors and windows open, at seventy-four! But out of doors the scene is splendid, and the house is walled about with bronze and gold. It is just the same with you; and I will not dilate upon it. Nor do I see how I am ever to get to Windmill Cottage and see the mill at work. One thing after another prevents; and I regret it all the more because, the house here being full, I cannot ask you to come to me.

This autumn my time has been more than ever broken in upon and devastated. It goes from bad to worse.

"Ach! ich bin des Treibens müde!
Wozu all dies Leid und Lust?
Süsse Friede,
Komm, O komm in meine Brust!"

How often I repeat these lines of Goethe! And then, the letters — the daily inundation of letters! Luckily, some require no answer; as, for instance, this from a teacher in a Western college: "Please inform me whether or not your *feelings* were in sympathy with your immortal thought when you wrote 'The Bridge.'"

However, I have said enough on that subject, and will never allude to it again, if I can help it.

October 9. This forenoon fourteen callers; thirteen of them English.

To his Sister A.

November 20, 1879.

Thanks for your note of last evening. I hasten to answer it, and send you a correct list of the personages of 'The Wayside Inn.'

The precious stones in the "Iron Pen" are a white Phenacite from Siberia, a yellow Zircon from Ceylon, a red Tourmaline from Maine.

The "little Dana boy" is thriving, and begins to notice things about him. Every afternoon I give him a music-lesson. He sits attentively listening while I play to him on the piano, and evidently thinks me equal to Rubinstein or Perabo.

To-day we have a fall of snow, but without wind, — which makes the landscape beautiful. The trees are all in full blossom with snowflakes.

To J. T. Fields.

December 17, 1879.

Thanks for this pretty little volume of Verses for a Few Friends, — the prettiest of Christmas gifts. This morning I have been reading all the comic poems, and have enjoyed them extremely, and particularly my old favorite, 'The Owl Critic.' Thanks again and again!

What do you know of the proposed dinner in New York on Burns's birthday? I have received the most tremendous invitation from a gentleman, — in authority, I suppose, — in which he says: "It will be, in fact, as it were not merely a meeting of mental and moral giants, but, metaphorically speaking, a council of literary giants."

Only think of it! What a dinner-party![1]

[1] Mr. Longfellow of course did not attend this dinner, if it ever was given. But the invitation turned his thoughts toward Burns; and we probably owe to it the poem which he wrote some months later, and which was printed in Ultima Thule. Its publication brought him two letters from Scotland, in which there is something more singular than that they should have reached him on the same day. Here is the first: —

THORNLIEBANK, GLASGOW, July 18, 1880.

MASTER, — Permit me to thank you for your wonderful verses, which I have just read to-day, on Robert Burns. They will touch the heart of every true Scotsman; and, as one, I cannot refrain from expressing my gratitude.

I am your humble servant,

R. L.

The second reads thus: —

JAMES SQUARE, EDINBURGH, July 19.

DEAR SIR, — Hoping that the information conveyed herein may be a sufficient warrant for the intrusion of a stranger. Your new poem about Robert Burns has created a melancholy interest. When Burns was on his death-bed, in Dumfries, one of the Baillies of the town went to his bedside and endeavored to get him to express a belief of, and trust in, Christ. Instead of doing so, Burns replied: "In a hundred years they will be worshipping me." Of the truth of these facts there is no room for doubt, as the Baillie told the foregoing to a Miss H ——, of Dumfries, who was an elderly lady in my young days, and she told it to me. Burns had no personal experience of the human soul created anew in Christ Jesus, without which there can be no entrance into heaven. But Burns had extensive knowledge of fallen human nature. It was this that led him to prophesy that in a hundred years men would be worshipping him, — a prophecy which is being fulfilled in many quarters. Your poem is an instance of it. These facts having been brought before you, it will not surprise you that the last verse of your poem made me feel that it was an effort to hold fellowship and friendly intercourse with one in the place of eternal woe.

One may imagine a way of presenting the theological dogma which might have awakened the poet's impatient reply But it must be permitted, under the circumstances, to doubt whether Burns's words are exactly quoted. Still, they would not mean anything very bad if by "worship" he intended only such homage as "the last verse" is "an instance of:" —

"His presence haunts this room to-night,—
A form of mingled mist and light,
From that far coast.
Welcome beneath this roof of mine!
Welcome! this vacant chair is thine,
Dear guest and ghost!"

CHAPTER XV.

THE LAST YEARS.

1880–1882.

January 1. I begin the year with a Folk-song. Have written to-day 'The Maiden and the Weathercock,' to keep company with 'The Sifting of Peter,' written some weeks ago.

2d. Six Pennsylvanians and one Bostonian called, in a body.

To G. W. Greene.

February 25, 1880.

R—— was here this morning, and said that he had some new ideas on the hexameter. I told him I thought the rules of that metre were pretty well established already; but he blandly insisted that he had his own views on the subject.

Day after to-morrow will be my birthday. As the Spaniards say, "Mis setenta y tres años, no hay quien me los quite."[1] I heartily wish the day were over; for such a multitude of letters as I receive from schoolboys and schoolgirls who are going to celebrate the day, is quite amazing. If I were Briareus, or a disembodied echo,

[1] "My seventy-three years, there is no one who can take them from me."

I could not answer them. You will say that Briareus could not write,—which is highly probable; and that echo never answers anything, but only repeats what is said,—and that is certainly true.

We have a charming actress here,—Miss Neilson. I have seen her in Twelfth Night and in Cymbeline; and she is admirable in both.

To G. W. Greene.

April 18, 1880.

I have written several poems of late; one of which, 'The Windmill,' I send you. You will see at a glance it is not *your* windmill; for yours is like a butterfly with its wings pulled off. I think this is the first poem ever written on the subject.

I have a little volume in press, to appear early in the autumn. I call it Ultima Thule; and the motto is from Horace:—

"precor, integrâ
Cum mente, nec turpem senectam
Degere, nec citharâ carentem."[1]

I am anxious to read the whole to you. When will you and your wife come? E. has moved to Boston, and the vacant room awaits you. The weather is not all you could wish, but the welcome will be.

May 19. Our opinions are biassed by our limitations. Poets who cannot write long poems think that no long poems should be written.

[1] "My prayer is, that with mind unshattered I may pass an old age neither unworthy nor without song."—*Odes*, I. xxxi.

The volume was dedicated to Mr. Greene, in a poem.

June 13. Yesterday I had a visit from two schools; some sixty girls and boys, in all. It seems to give them so much pleasure, that it gives me pleasure.

21st. The Brazilian Consul-General called, with a message of friendly remembrance from his Emperor, Dom Pedro, who invites me to be his guest at Rio for a month. Also Mrs. N——, and Miss S—— of New York, who gave me a fan curiously made of fibres of Indian corn, and resembling a great sunflower. Then Mr. Henry Hudson, of Shakespeare fame, with three young ladies.

September 15. Ultima Thule published.[1]

To Mrs. J. T. Fields.

September 29, 1880.

Thanks for your kind and most amiable letter; as many thanks as there are poems in the book you so generously praise. Each of them shall thank you.

I regret more than ever that I could not come to Manchester this summer. I was pulled about in the most extraordinary manner, — first to Nahant, then to Portland, then back again to Nahant, then to East Greenwich, then Nahant once more; finally bringing up here, and coming to anchor in the old Snug Harbor. The visit to Greenwich was to attend the wedding. And a beautiful wedding it was; an ideal village wedding, in a pretty church; — the Windmill Cottage of our friend Greene

[1] Mr. Lowell wrote him from London: "I have just been reading, with a feeling I will not mar by trying to express it, your Ultima Thule. You will understand the pang of pleasurable homesickness it gave me. It is like you, from the first line to the last. Never was your hand firmer. If Gil Blas had been *your* secretary, he need never have lost his place. If I could drop in on you as I used, . . . I should tell you that you had misreckoned the height of the sun, and were not up with *Ultima Thule* by a good many degrees yet. Do such fruits grow there?"

resplendent with autumnal flowers. In one of the rooms was a tea-kettle hanging on a crane in the fireplace. So begins a new household.

Yesterday Mrs. Horsford came with letters from Norway, giving particulars of Ole Bull's last days, his death, and burial. The account is very touching. All Bergen's flags at half-mast; telegram from the King; funeral oration by the poet Björnsen. The dear old musician was carried from his island to the mainland in a steamboat, followed by a long line of others. No viking ever had such a funeral.

October 11. It is not the possession of a thing, but the use of it, which gives it value.

To G. W. Greene.

November 23, 1880.

I hope you will be here when the Mapleson Italian Opera comes; you will hear fine music.

But the new operas, — ah! I do not think you would care much for them. For my own part, I confess, I like the music of the past better than the music of the future. At present, we are ground between the upper and nether millstones of the two; and rather a pleasant grind it is, after all.

The other night I went to hear Boito's *Mefistofele;* very powerful, but wild and weird beyond conception. Boito, you know, is called "the Wagner of Italy."

December 4. A censorious critic is often like a boy sharpening a penknife. The blade suddenly closes and cuts his fingers.

8th. I have often had great joy in little things, — and often little joy in great things.

To Miss B——.

December 9, 1880.

In reply to your letter received this morning, I would inform you that in the poem of 'The Singers' I intended to indicate schools or classes only, — the Lyric, the Epic, and the Devotional or Didactic. I had no reference whatever to individual poets, except so far as they are types or representatives of these classes.

From Lord Houghton.

ELMETE HALL, 1880.

DEAR MR. LONGFELLOW, — Mr. Henschel, our chief bass-singer, desires to be introduced to you. It is pleasant to present singer to singer. Mr. H. is a German by origin, but has made himself half an Englishman, and is going, in a very short time, to make himself, for the other and better half, an American, by marrying a Boston lady. I write from the great Musical Festival at Leeds, my neighboring town, which has had this peculiarity, that its two most successful pieces have been good music applied to good poetry. Music is usually married to such very wretched verse that to hear Milman's 'Martyr of Antioch' and your 'Building of the Ship' set to harmony and admirably sung, has been a rare æsthetic pleasure. I am too glad of this and every opportunity to express to you my deep regard, and to hope that your *Ultima Thule* may turn out to be no more true than the Britannic one of the old Roman poet.[1]

I am yours very truly,

HOUGHTON.

[1] The reference, of course, is to the chorus in Seneca's *Medea*, ending, —

"Nec sit terris
Ultima Thule."

"And no more shall Thule be the last of the lands."

25th. In the forenoon General Sherman called, with his son-in-law, Lieutenant Thackara, of the Navy, Colonel Bacon, his aide-de-camp, and Mr. ——, of Boston. Then Sam Ward and ——, who reminds me of the Baroness in *Wilhelm Meister*. In the evening, music.

January 1, 1881. Bitter cold weather. With fire and furnace in full blast, impossible to warm the house.

3d. Seventeen letters received to-day; all but three asking some favor!

6th. Salvini and Monti at lunch.

8th. Monti at dinner. In the evening he played to us from the *Sonnambula*.

13th. After all, great writers, even the greatest, illumine but a small space round them,—at most, a little hemisphere of light. Egypt, Arabia, Turkey, Persia, China, know nothing of Dante or Shakespeare or Milton.

February 21. Some forty or more schools in the West are preparing to celebrate my seventy-fourth birthday; and all write me letters and request letters. I send to each some stanza, with signature and good wishes.

22d. A gentleman writes me for "your autograph in your own handwriting."

23d. Two women in black called to-day. One of them said she was a descendant of the English philosopher, John Locke; and that she was going to establish a society for the suppression of cruelty to letter-carriers. A lady in Ohio sends me one hundred blank cards, with the request that I will write my name on each, as she wishes to distribute them among her guests at a party she is to give on my birthday.

24th. Am receiving from ten to twenty letters daily with all kinds of questions and requests.

25th. Letters, letters, letters! Some I answer, but many, and most, I cannot.

26th. A birthday dinner in advance, at Mr. Houghton's. Holmes, Howells, Aldrich, Miss Bates, and Miss Jewett, author of Deephaven.

27th. My seventy-fourth birthday. I am surrounded by roses and lilies. Flowers everywhere, —

> "And that which should accompany old age,
> As honor, love, obedience, troops of friends."

March 1. I like fog, it is so mysterious, transfiguring all things. The wind drives it like a smoke. The brown branches of the trees against the dusk of the sky.

To G. W. Greene.

March 27, 1881.

I hasten to answer your questions as well as I can, and as briefly.

My first French teacher in my boyhood was, I think, an Italian [Nolcini]. The second, also in Portland, a German. In college, plodding on by myself, I remember reading Mme. de Genlis's *Siège de Rochelle.* I never knew how the professorship [at Bowdoin] was brought about; only that it was offered to me, to my great surprise and delight. I made no acquaintances in Paris [in 1826] among the French, but Lafayette and Mme. de Sailly, sister of Berryer the orator.[1] I worked at French with Levizac's Grammar, the Dictionary of Boniface, and the

[1] And daughter of Berryer the advocate. Mr. Longfellow had forgotten, after so many years, two French gentlemen of whom he speaks in one of his letters from Paris in 1826. A detailed account has been published of an acquaintance made at that time with Jules Janin ; but there is certainly some mistake about this, as Mr. Longfellow nowhere mentions it in any journal or letter at the time or afterward. He could not well have forgotten it ; and when he describes his visit to Janin in 1842 there is no hint of any previous acquaintance.

Mémoires de Sully, among other books no longer remembered. I did not much frequent the theatres or operas, but went once or twice to all the principal ones. Nor was I much of a sight-seer. My chief companions in Paris were Pierre Irving, David Berdan, and my cousin, Dr. Storer.

April 1. A pleasant beginning of the month after a week of snow and rain, which have kept me prisoner. Have read with much interest Abel Stevens's Life of Mme. de Staël.

To G. W. Greene.

April 3, 1881.

The bad weather of last week, and a bad cold of my own, made me give up my intended trip to Germantown, which I believe I mentioned in my last letter.

The famous French actress, Sara Bernhardt, has been again in Boston, but I did not see her. The fame of her extreme thinness has reached far and wide. A common man, driving by here in a cart, with a poor lank horse, gave him a cut with his whip, crying, "Get up! Sara Bernhardt!"

As an offset to this, here is a portrait of me, as I seemed to a compositor in the summer of 1851, when he was setting up The Golden Legend. He is now an editor in Lansing, and thus paints me in his paper: "He was then a hale, portly, fine-looking man, nearly six feet in height, well-proportioned, with a tendency to fatness; brown hair and blue eyes, and bearing the general appearance of a comfortable hotel-keeper." This surpasses the Newport bookseller, who exclaimed, "Why! you look more like a sea-captain than a poet!"

I send you to-day, an English publisher's circular, with some remarks on international copyright.

6th. There is great pleasure in doing without things; quite as much sometimes, I think, as in having them.

18th. At the Globe, to see Salvini in Othello. He in Italian; the rest in English.

10th. Salvini came this afternoon, and read me a paper he has written on Hamlet, Othello, and Macbeth.

To G. W. Greene.

April 25, 1881.

I told you some time ago that Fields was suffering from *angina pectoris*. He seemed to recover, and was here a week ago, not quite well, but in his usual merry mood.

Last night, about ten o'clock, sitting among his friends, a sudden alarm of fire startled him; he sprang up and rushed to the window, and then sank into a chair, rallied for a moment, and died. His funeral will be to-morrow, at noon; very private, to avoid a crowd.

Another friend gone! It is a great shock to me, as it will be to you.

29th. A sorrowful and distracted week. Fields died on Sunday, the 24th, and was buried on Tuesday. Dr. Palfrey died on Tuesday, and will be buried to-day Two old and intimate friends in one week!

To G. W. Greene.

May 16, 1881.

A book by the window is the best medicine. I have been trying Walpole's Letters, which are always a remedy for a dull hour.

Edith and her boys are with me, and bring back the Golden Age to the old house.

"Jam nova progenies caelo demittitur alto,"

and child-voices are heard again from the upper chambers, and footsteps of the coming generation.

I have written some lines in memory of Fields, which you will find on the last page of the June Atlantic.[1]

To G. W. Greene.

June 22, 1881.

I have not written to you of late, because I have a lame wrist, and writing is painful. But I will try to answer your questions as well as I can.

During my first visit to Europe, I wrote no verses, save the few lines preserved in Outre-Mer. In France, my reading was mostly prose; in Spain, it was about equally divided between poetry and prose; in Italy mostly poetry; and in Germany the same.

I do not remember translating anything before going to Brunswick. I think I began with the poem of Luis de Gongora, 'Let me go warm.' You will find it in Poets and Poetry of Europe, page 695. This was in 1829 or 1830. Then followed various pieces in the North American Review articles, and finally, the *Coplas de Manrique.*

I am sorry you are feeling depressed. But we must neither of us hope to be as strong as we were fifty years ago. I am also sorry I could not have you this month of

[1] 'Auf Wiedersehen: in memory of J. T. F.'

June, though you would have shivered with cold. After all, it may be lucky you did not come. Immediately after the noisy and patriotic Fourth, I shall run to Portland for a week, and then go to Nahant.

I send you some autographs for your mother, with my kindest regards.

To G. W. Greene.

PORTLAND, July 12, 1881.

Portland has lost none of its charms. The weather is superb, and the air equal to that of Newport or East Greenwich or any other Rhode Island seashore. I shall remain here a week or two longer, and think of running up to North Conway and to Sebago, to see the winding Songo once more. If I carried out all my plans, I should be a great traveller. The end of this month and the month of August I shall devote to Nahant; then back to the Craigie House,—if it is n't burnt down, as I always fancy it will be when I am away.

It is very pleasant sitting here and dictating letters. It is like thinking what one will say, without taking the trouble of writing it. I have discovered a new pleasure.

To G. W. Greene.

September 20, 1881.

Since learning the sad news from Long Branch this morning [of President Garfield's death], Dante's line has been running in my mind:—

"E venni dal martirio a questa pace." [1]

And what a martyrdom! Twelve weeks of pain and struggle for life at last are ended.

[1] *Paradiso* xv. 148: "I came from martyrdom unto this peace." So closes the sonnet which he wrote on Garfield's death.

Let us turn to some other subject. You will be glad to know that we are having a copy made in Florence of Benvenuto da Imola's Commentary on the *Divina Commedia.* Within a year we shall have the first volume ready for the press, and if we can get subscribers enough, it will be published without delay.

I send back the foolish verses to which some wag has appended your name; I hope you will take no notice of the matter. If nothing is said, it will soon be forgotten. Only you might leave a disavowal of the authorship among your papers, so that no one can say you never denied it.

I am rather busy with answering schoolgirls.

To G. W. Greene.

September 26, 1881.

What splendid weather is this! It is truly Virgil's "alienis mensibus aestas," or as Harriet Preston so gracefully translates it, —

"Summer days
In months that are not summer's."

I am glad there should be so resplendent a morning as this for the funeral of our President. Let us hope that our new King Arthur may have inherited the virtues of his illustrious namesake, and will not undervalue or neglect his great opportunity.

I have lately received from the Duca di Sermoneta, his *Tre Chiose,* on certain passages of the *Commedia.* He thinks that the angel who opens the gates of the City of Dis by a touch of his rod, was not an angel at all, but — who do you think? Simply Æneas! I have also received from Holland translations in Dutch of Outre-Mer, Kavanagh, and Hyperion.

Ah me! how dark the discipline of pain,
Were not the suffering followed by a sense
Of infinite rest and infinite release!
This is our consolation; and again
A great soul cries to us in our suspense,
"I came from martyrdom unto this peace!"

Henry W. Longfellow.

My summer-scattered family are slowly gathering together again. Nichols comes with his proof-sheets. *Redeunt Saturnia regna!*

A year ago, —— was engaged to make an Index to Sumner's Works. At the last accounts he had completed six pages of the first volume. At this rate, he will not finish his work before the middle of the next century! I am making the Index myself, and have already reached the tenth volume.

October. This month and all November and December I was confined to my room by a violent attack of vertigo, followed by nervous prostration.

To G. W. Greene.

October 28, 1881.

I am creeping along slowly, but have not yet left my room. I amuse myself as well as I can, by looking out of the window and seeing the leaves fall. Then I take a turn at Miss Berry's Journal and Correspondence, — Walpole's Miss Berry, — which I find very amusing.

I go to bed early and get up late, and like it so well that I mean to stay in my room a long while yet, — perhaps all winter. I see no one as yet, and find something rather pleasant in having the world shut out. This freedom from callers is a great relief.

> "'Shut, shut the door, good John,' fatigued, I said,
> "'Tie up the knocker, — say I'm sick, I'm dead.'"

Miss Berry says, "I suffer from what I am, from what I have been, from what I might have been, and from what I never shall be." Very well said. I suppose every one suffers at times from some such fleeting fancy as this.

Whittier writes me that he dreads the coming winter. I do not; the thought brings with it a sense of rest and seclusion.

To G. W. Greene.

[Enclosing a printed circular.]

November 28, 1881.

I have come to this at last, and find it an immense relief: —

"On account of illness, Mr. Longfellow finds it impossible to answer any letters at present.

"He can only acknowledge their receipt, and regret his inability to do more.

"CAMBRIDGE, MASS."

Of course it is n't meant for you and other friends, but for those who begin their letters with the words, "Though an entire stranger."

I will attend to your request about Ultima Thule, as soon as I am well enough. I am getting better slowly from day to day; no perceptible difference, only from week to week. To-day I am better than I have been at any time.

I do not know who is to write a Life of Fields. Mrs. Fields has already published her Reminiscences, which are very interesting, and written with good taste and judgment, — a difficult task well done.

To G. W. Greene.

December 25, 1881.

I begin by wishing you a Merry Christmas! Mine, I am sorry to say, is not a very merry one. I don't get strength yet, and consequently, don't get well. *Pazienza!*

I agree with you about the North American Review. There is a bit of the romance of our youth connected with it. If we were young, we should probably want to get possession of it. It should return, like the Prodigal Son, to its father's house, and become again a solid and respectable quarterly.

I send you a little cutting from a newspaper, which will gratify you. I was sorry not to see the French delegation when it was here.[1]

To William Senter (Mayor of Portland).

January 12, 1882.

I have had the pleasure of receiving your letter, with its enclosed copy of the Resolutions of the city authorities of Portland in reference to my seventy-fifth birthday. I hasten to thank you and them for the honor conferred upon me. I hardly need assure you, dear sir, that this mark of consideration from my native city is very gratifying to me; and I regret extremely that, on account of my ill-health, I am forced to decline the public reception offered me. My physician has prescribed absolute rest; and I do not see any chance of my being able to go to Portland in February, so slow is recovery from nervous prostration.

I am, dear sir, with great regard, yours faithfully.

To Samuel Ward.

January 23, 1882.

"Whom the gods love, die young," because they never grow old, though they may live to fourscore years and upward. So say I whenever I read your graceful and sportive fancies in the papers you send me or in those I

[1] A party of French officers and civilians, among them a grandson of Lafayette, had, by invitation, come over to attend the centennial celebration of the Surrender of Cornwallis at Yorktown, which closed the War of the Revolution. They visited Craigie House, but Mr. Longfellow was not well enough to see them.

send you. I am now waiting for the last announced in your letter of yesterday, but not yet arrived.

Pardon my not writing sooner and oftener. My day is very short, as I get up late, and go to bed early, — a kind of Arctic winter's day, when the sun is above the horizon for a few hours only.

Yes, the 'Hermes' went into the Century.[1]

I come back to where I began, — the perpetual youth of some people. You remember the anecdote of Ducis. When somebody said of him, "Il est tombé en enfance," a friend replied, "Non, il est rentré en jeunesse." That is the polite way of putting things.

To Bessie M——.[2]

March 16, 1882.

My dear Miss Bessie, — I thank you very much for the poem you wrote me on my birthday, a copy of which your father sent me. It was very sweet and simple, and does you great credit. I do not think there are many girls of your age who can write so well. I myself do not know of any. It was very good of you to remember my birthday at all, and to have you remember it in so sweet a way is very pleasant and gratifying to me.

[1] The poem 'Hermes Trismegistus.' After this, Mr. Longfellow wrote but four poems, — 'Mad River,' 'Possibilities,' 'Decoration Day,' and 'The Bells of San Blas.'

[2] This note, addressed to a young girl in Pennsylvania, was probably the last letter written by Mr. Longfellow. Two days later he was seized with the illness which proved fatal.

CHAPTER XVI.

THE LAST DAYS.

1882.

After the note in his journal which speaks of his illness in October and the following months, there are but very few, and those trifling, entries. He was able to leave his bed in a few weeks, but remained quietly in his chamber, enjoying its seclusion as he began to recover from his prostration. He read a little, saw a few friends, wrote a very few letters, and played backgammon with his daughter, and sometimes played at playing it with his little grandson, who was staying in the house, and in whose society he took great pleasure. He was well enough at Christmas to go into Boston. On the day after, he wrote the touching sonnet, 'My Books,' in which he compares himself, as he looked at them on his study walls, to an old knight looking at the arms which he can no longer wield.

So I behold these books upon their shelf, —
  My ornaments and arms of other days,
  Not wholly useless, though no longer used;
For they remind me of my other self,
  Younger and stronger, and the pleasant ways
  In which I walked, now clouded and confused.

In January he wrote the poem 'Mad River,' and the sonnet 'Possibilities;' and in February, the verses for Decoration Day, — a dirge of tender and calm memory for the soldiers who had died in defence of their country. The letter to a little girl who had sent him some verses for his birthday is dated the 16th of March. In the number of Harper's Magazine for that month he read, in an article on Mexico, a few lines speaking of the bells of the destroyed convent of San Blas on the Pacific coast. They touched his imagination; and on the 15th of March he wrote the closing stanza of the poem which they had suggested. Had he known that they were to be the last verses he would write, could he have chosen any more fitting close?

Out of the shadow of night
The world moves into light;
  It is daybreak everywhere!

Those friends who saw him on his seventy-fifth birthday had remarked how well and cheerful he appeared. He had exchanged telegrams with the Historical Society of Maine, which was celebrating it in Portland, little thinking how soon they would be meeting to mourn his death. On the forenoon of the 18th of March — it was Saturday — there came four schoolboys from Boston, who had asked permission to visit him. He received them with his wonted kindness and courtesy, showed them the objects of interest in his study and the view of the Charles from its windows, and

B. of S. B.

O Bells of San Blas, in vain
Ye call back the Past again;
The Past is deaf to ~~It will never heed~~ your prayer;
Out of the shadows of night
The world rolls into light;
It is daybreak everywhere.

March 15. 10

wrote his name in their albums. In the afternoon he walked for exercise upon the eastern veranda, wrapped in his long Italian fur-lined coat; for the air was chill, — alas, fatally chill! Mr. Monti, as was his wont on Saturdays, came to dine with him, noticed that he seemed unwell, and took his leave immediately after dinner, begging his friend to retire early. "I think I will," Mr. Longfellow answered, "for I do not feel well;" then, shaking his friend's hand, "God bless you! I hope I shall be better next Saturday." Mr. Monti, waiting a few moments outside for the car to Boston, saw the light in the study put out, and heard his friend's steps as he went up the stairs.

In the night, Mr. Longfellow was seized with violent pain, but, with characteristic consideration, was unwilling to disturb the household. A physician was called in the morning, and the disease proved to be *peritonitis*. The pain being very severe, ether and opiates were administered. When not under their influence, his mind was clear; but he spoke little. When his sister arrived from Portland, he said, "Now I know that I must be very ill, since you have been sent for." His sufferings were less on Wednesday, and his friends were encouraged. On Friday afternoon, the 24th, he sank quietly in death. The bells of Cambridge tolled the sorrowful news to the anxious, waiting people, whose sympathies had been so deeply touched by his illness that even the school-boys had hushed their voices as they passed his door.

The long, busy, blameless life was ended. The loneliness of separation was over. He was dead. But the world was better and happier for his having lived.

Early on Sunday afternoon the funeral services were held in the home, very quietly, in accordance with his own well-known feeling. The family circle and a few of his most intimate friends met in the library, where the body lay in its coffin, upon whose lid was placed a palm-branch and a spray of passion-flower, — symbols of victory and the glory of suffering. Four voices sang, in low tones, a hymn. Then were read some verses of the poet, and some Scripture sentences, followed by a prayer; and the body was borne to Mount Auburn, under the gently falling snow. Later in the afternoon there was a public funeral service in the college chapel, closing with a eulogy by Professor C. C. Everett.

From the life that has been spread upon these pages, as much as possible in the words of him who lived it, it can hardly be needful to draw out the threads of character everywhere interwoven, in order to name them or to exhibit them by themselves. The *man* cannot fail to have been seen through what he did and what he wrote, — the good son, devoted husband, affectionate father; the generous, faithful friend; the urbane and cultivated host; the lover of children; the lover of his country; the lover of liberty and of peace. The key to his character was *sympathy*. This made him the gentle and courteous receiver of every visitor, however obscure, however tedious; the ready responder to every appeal to his pity and his purse; the kindly encourager of literary aspirants, however unpromising; the charitable judge of motives, and excuser of mistakes and offences; the delicate yet large liker; the lenient critic, quick to see every merit beyond every defect. This gave to his poetry the *human* element, which made thousands feel as if this poem or that verse was written for each of them especially, and made in thousands of hearts in many lands a shrine of reverence and affection for his name. Through this sympathy thousands of grateful hearts had been touched, comforted, and lifted, — made more gentle, more courageous, more full of holy trust in God, of faith in immortality.

The gratitude of many of England's best and noblest has placed his marble image among her own honored dead in the shadowed seclusion of Westminster's Poets' Corner. In the city in which he was born, and in that in which he lived and died, his statues will keep alive his features and his fame. But his works are his lasting monument, and his memory is in the keeping of those whom his song has charmed and blessed.

CHAPTER XVII.

TRIBUTES.

After the burial at Mount Auburn on the 26th of March, 1882, a funeral service was held in the College Chapel, at which the Rev. Professor C. C. Everett made the following address: —

In this service of sympathy and reverent sorrow it is a comforting and inspiring thought that the feeling which has drawn us here is shared by multitudes wherever the English tongue is spoken. Many, indeed, share it to whom the songs of our poet are known only in what is to them a foreign speech. It shows our civilization in one of its most interesting aspects, that a feeling so profound, so pure, so uplifting, should unite such a large portion of the world to-day. Here is no dazzling position; here is no startling circumstance: a simple life has uttered itself in song, and men have listened, rejoiced, and loved, and now they mourn. Yet for us there is a deeper sorrow. While others mourn the poet who is gone, we mourn the man. He was our townsman, he was our neighbor, he was our friend. We knew the simple beauty of his life; we knew its truth, its kindness, its helpfulness, its strength. We could not, indeed, separate from our thought of him the knowledge of his fame and of his genius; but even this showed only his heart in its true beauty. We saw him wear the honors of the world more easily than many bear the small triumphs of our ordinary life. Thus we knew and loved him, and thus we sorrow for him.

But this difference of which I speak is, after all, one chiefly of degree. He poured himself into his songs, and wherever they went he was found with them; and in them others found the beauty of that spirit which was revealed to us in its nearer presence. Thus he drew very near to many hearts; thus many, who never looked upon his face, feel to-day that they, too, have lost a friend. You remember how sweetly and gracefully he greets these unseen and unknown friends in the dedication of one of his books. He feels their presence, though he sees them not. He enters their households sure of a welcome. Thus he cries: —

> "I hope as no unwelcome guest
> At the warm fireside, when the lamps are lighted,
> To have my place reserved among the rest."

The kindly request was heeded; he found a place in many households which he had never seen. And now by many a fireside it is almost as though there was one more "vacant chair."

I have said he poured his life into his work. It is singular that the phase of life and experience which forms so large a portion of poetry, which many sing if they sing nothing else, he was content to utter in prose, — if prose we must call the language of his romances. He seems content to have scattered unbound the flowers of romantic love at the doors of the temple of his song. There is something strange, too, in the fascination which the thought of death has for so many generous youth. You remember that Bryant first won fame by a hymn to death; and so, I think, the first fame of Longfellow which won recognition for him was that translation of those sounding Spanish lines which exalt the majesty of death and sing the shortness of human life. But the first song of his own which won the recognition of the world was not a song of death, it was a psalm of life. That little volume, the Voices of the Night, formed an epoch in our literary history. It breathed his whole spirit, — his energy, his courage, his tenderness, his faith; it formed the prelude of all which should come after; and henceforth we find his whole life imaged in his verse. I do not mean that he tore open the secrets of the heart or the home; but all is there, — transfigured, enlarged, made universal, máde the common property of all. We wander with him through foreign lands; he takes us with hiṁ into his studies, and in his translations he gives us their fairest fruits. We hear with him the greeting of the new-born child; we are taken into the sacred joy of home; the ṁerry notes of the children's hour ring upon our ears; we feel the pains of sorrow and of loss; we hear the prayer of elevated trust. And when age draws near at last, when the shadows begin to fall, then we share with him the solemnity and sublimity of the gathering darkness.

The life which is thus imaged in these songs was one that was fitted for such use. I think we may look at it as one of the most rounded lives that ever has been lived upon earth, so that we can say there seems little that was lacking to its perfect completeness. I do not mean there was no sorrow in it. What life can be made perfect without that? What poet's life can be made complete without the experience of suffering? But from the very first his life flowed on its calm and even way. His first songs received the applause of the world, and the sympathy of men moved with him as he moved forward in his work. Travel in foreign lands enlarged his sympathies and added a picturesqueness to his poems which they otherwise might have lacked. The literature of all ages and nations was open to him, and he drew from all. It is said, I know, that thus he represents the culture of the past and of foreign lands; that he is not our poet, not

American. But what is the genius of our country, what is American? Is it not the very genius of our nation to bring together elements from far-off lands, fusing them into one, and making a new type of man? The American poet should represent the genius of all lands. He must have no provincial Muse. He must sing of the forest and of the sea; but not of these alone. He must be "heir of all the ages." He must be a representative of all the culture of all time. He must absorb all things into himself, and stand free, strong, able, a man as simple as though he had never strayed beyond his native woods. He must, in other words, be like our Longfellow. When what we may call his preparation was completed, his life flowed on its course, gathering only greater and calmer feelings as it flowed. His age was as beautiful as his manhood and his youth. 'Morituri Salutamus,' that marvellous poem, is perhaps the grandest hymn to age that was ever written. Death is no distant dream, as it was when those sounding Spanish lines fell from his pen; he feels its shadows; he feels that the end is drawing near. But there he stands, strong and calm, with sublime faith as at first; he greets the present as he greeted the past; he gathers from the coming of age, from approaching night, not a signal for rest, but a new summons to activity. He cries:—

> "It is too late! Ah, nothing is too late
> Till the tired heart shall cease to palpitate."

And so he takes up his glad work again; and I think some of his sweetest and deepest songs date from this latest period, — such as that graceful poem to Tennyson, that chivalrous greeting from one son of song to another, and that tender message that he sent to Lowell across the seas in 'Elmwood Herons.' There comes in a little playfulness, too, of which there was not much in his earlier songs.

His was a calm, loving age, full of activity, confidence, and peace. He writes upon his latest volume those words that mark the end of his career, and his labors are at an end. The Ultima Thule has been reached. The world's love gathered about him as he lived, and its homage was breathed into his ear. On his last birthday there was paid to him an ovation given to few living. From the home of his youth in Maine came greetings; children's voices, those which were ever most welcome to his ear, joined in the acclaim. Thus the story of his life was completed. His last book had been written, and marked by him as his last; the final greeting of the world had been uttered to him, and he passed away.

"He passed away!" I think we have not yet learned the meaning of those words. I think we do not yet quite feel them. We still half think we may sometimes meet him in his familiar haunts. Does not this protest of the heart contain a truth? His spirit, as we trust, has been called to higher service; yet he had given himself unto the world, he had breathed himself into his songs: in them he is with us still. Wherever they go, as they wander over the world, he will be with them, a minister of love; he will be by the side of youth, pointing to heights as yet unscaled, bidding him have faith and courage; he will be with the wanderer in foreign lands, making the beauty that he sees more fair; he will be with the mariner on the seas; he will be in the quiet beauty of home; he will be by the side of the sorrowing heart, pointing to a higher faith. When old age is gathering about the human soul, he will be there still, to cry that "age is opportunity no less than youth itself." Thus will he inspire faith and courage in all, and point us all to those two sources of strength that never fail, — "Heart within, and God o'erhead."

At a meeting of the Massachusetts Historical Society, of which Mr. Longfellow had been for twenty-five years a member, Dr. Oliver Wendell Holmes addressed the Society as follows: —

It is with no vain lamentations, but rather with profound gratitude, that we follow the soul of our much-loved and long-loved poet beyond the confines of the world he helped so largely to make beautiful. We could have wished to keep him longer; but at least we were spared witnessing the inevitable shadows of an old age protracted too far beyond its natural limits. From the first notes of his fluent and harmonious song to the last, which comes to us as the "voice fell like a falling star," there has never been a discord. The music of the mountain stream, in the poem which reaches us from the other shore of being,[1] is as clear and sweet as the melodies of the youthful and middle periods of his minstrelsy. It has been a fully rounded life, beginning early with large promise, equalling every anticipation in its maturity, fertile and beautiful to its close in the ripeness of its well-filled years.

Until the silence fell upon us we did not entirely appreciate how largely his voice was repeated in the echoes of our own hearts. The affluence of his production so accustomed us to look for a poem from him at short intervals that we could hardly feel how precious that was which was so abundant. Not, of course, that every single poem reached the standard of the highest among them all. That could not be in Homer's time, and mortals must occasionally nod now as then. But the hand of the artist shows itself unmistakably in everything which left his

[1] The poem 'Mad River in the White Mountains' appeared in the Atlantic Monthly after Mr. Longfellow's death.

desk. The O of Giotto could not help being a perfect round, and the verse of Longfellow is always perfect in construction.

He worked in that simple and natural way which characterizes the master. But it is one thing to be simple through poverty of intellect, and another thing to be simple by repression of all redundancy and overstatement; one thing to be natural through ignorance of all rules, and another to have made a second nature out of the sovereign rules of art. In respect of this simplicity and naturalness, his style is in strong contrast to that of many writers of our time. There is no straining for effect, there is no torturing of rhythm for novel patterns, no wearisome iteration of petted words, no inelegant clipping of syllables to meet the exigencies of a verse, no affected archaism, rarely any liberty taken with language, — unless it may be in the form of a few words in the translation of Dante. I will not except from these remarks the singular and original form which he gave to his poem of 'Hiawatha,' — a poem with a curious history in many respects. Suddenly and immensely popular in this country, greatly admired by many foreign critics, imitated with perfect ease by any clever schoolboy, serving as a model for metrical advertisements, made fun of, sneered at, abused, admired, but, at any rate, a picture full of pleasing fancies and melodious cadences. The very names are jewels which the most fastidious Muse might be proud to wear. Coming from the realm of the Androscoggin and of Moosetukmaguntuk, how could he have found two such delicious names as Hiawatha and Minnehaha? The eight-syllable trochaic verse of 'Hiawatha,' like the eight-syllable iambic verse of 'The Lady of the Lake,' and others of Scott's poems, has a fatal facility, which I have elsewhere endeavored to explain on physiological principles. The recital of each line uses up the air of one natural expiration, so that we read, as we naturally do, eighteen or twenty lines in a minute, without disturbing the normal rhythm of breathing, which is also eighteen or twenty breaths to the minute. The standing objection to this is, that it makes the octosyllabic verse too easy writing and too slipshod reading. Yet in this most frequently criticised composition the poet has shown a subtle sense of the requirements of his simple story of a primitive race, in choosing the most fluid of measures, that lets the thought run through it in easy sing-song, such as oral tradition would be sure to find on the lips of the story-tellers of the wigwam. Although Longfellow was not fond of metrical contortions and acrobatic achievements, he well knew the effects of skilful variation in the forms of verse and well-managed refrains or repetitions. In one of his very earliest poems — 'Pleasant it was when woods were green' — the dropping a syllable from the last line [but one] is an agreeable surprise to the ear, expecting only the common monotony of scrupulously balanced lines. In 'Excelsior' the repetition of the aspiring exclamation which gives its name to the poem lifts every stanza a step higher than the one which preceded it. In the 'Old Clock on the Stair' the solemn words, "Forever, never, never, forever," give wonderful effectiveness to that most impressive poem.

All his art, all his learning, all his melody, cannot account for his extraordinary popularity, not only among his own countrymen and those who in other lands speak the language in which he wrote, but in foreign realms, where he could only be read through the ground glass of a translation. It was in his choice of subjects that one source of the public favor with which his writings, more especially his poems, were received, obviously lay. A poem, to be widely popular, must deal with thoughts and emotions that belong to common, not exceptional character, conditions, interests. The most popular of all books are those which meet the spiritual needs of mankind most powerfully,—such works as the Imitation of Christ and the Pilgrim's Progress. I suppose if the great multitude of readers were to render a decision as to which of Longfellow's poems they most valued, the 'Psalm of Life' would command the largest number. This is a brief homily, enforcing the great truths of duty and of our relation to the unseen world. Next in order would very probably come 'Excelsior,'—a poem that springs upward like a flame and carries the soul up with it in its aspiration for the unattainable ideal. If this sounds like a trumpet-call to the fiery energies of youth, not less does the still small voice of that most sweet and tender poem, 'Resignation,' appeal to the sensibilities of those who have lived long enough to know the bitterness of such a bereavement as that out of which grew the poem. Or take a poem before referred to, 'The Old Clock on the Stair;' and in it we find the history of innumerable households told in relating the history of one, and the solemn burden of the song repeats itself to thousands of listening readers, as if the beat of the pendulum were throbbing at the head of every staircase. Such poems as these—and there are many more of not unlike character—are the foundation of that universal acceptance his writings obtain among all classes. But for these appeals to universal sentiment, his readers would have been confined to a comparatively small circle of the educated and refined. There are thousands and tens of thousands who are familiar with what we might call his household poems who have never read the Spanish Student, 'The Golden Legend,' 'Hiawatha,' or even 'Evangeline.' Again, ask the first schoolboy you meet which of Longfellow's poems he likes best, and he will be very likely to answer, 'Paul Revere's Ride.' When he is a few years older he might perhaps say, 'The Building of the Ship,'—that admirably constructed poem, beginning with the literal description, passing into the higher region of sentiment by the most natural of transitions, and ending with the noble climax, —

> "Thou, too, sail on, O Ship of State,"

which has become the classical expression of patriotic emotion.

Nothing lasts like a coin and a lyric. Long after the dwellings of men have disappeared, when their temples are in ruins and all their works of art are shattered, the ploughman strikes an earthen vessel holding the golden and silver disks on which the features of a dead monarch — with emblems, it may be, betraying the beliefs or the manners, the rudeness or the finish of art, and all which this implies — survive an extinct civilization. Pope has expressed this with his usual Horatian felicity in the letter to Addison on the publication of his little Treatise on Coins, —

> "A small Euphrates through the piece is rolled,
> And little eagles wave their wings in gold."

Conquerors and conquered sink in common oblivion; triumphal arches, pageants the world wonders at, all that trumpeted itself as destined to an earthly immortality, pass away; the victor of a hundred battles is dust; the parchments or papyrus on which his deeds were written are shrivelled and decayed and gone, —

> "And all his triumphs shrink into a coin."

So it is with a lyric poem. One happy utterance of some emotion or expression, which comes home to all, may keep a name remembered when the race to which the singer belonged is lost sight of. The cradle-song of Danaë to her infant as they tossed on the waves in the imprisoning chest, has made the name of Simonides immortal. Our own English literature abounds with instances which illustrate the same fact so far as the experience of a few generations extends; and I think we may venture to say that some of the shorter poems of Longfellow must surely reach a remote posterity, and be considered then, as now, ornaments to English literature. We may compare them with the best short poems of the language without fearing that they will suffer. Scott, cheerful, wholesome, unreflective, should be read in the open air; Byron, the poet of malecontents and cynics, in a prison-cell; Burns, generous, impassioned, manly, social, in the tavern-hall; Moore, elegant, fastidious, full of melody, scented with the volatile perfume of the Eastern gardens, in which his fancy revelled, is pre-eminently the poet of the drawing-room and the piano; Longfellow, thoughtful, musical, home-loving, busy with the lessons of life, which he was ever studying, and loved to teach others, finds his charmed circle of listeners by the fireside. His songs, which we might almost call sacred ones, rarely if ever get into the hymn-books. They are too broadly human to suit the specialized tastes of the sects, which often think more of their differences from each other than of the common ground on which they can agree. Shall we think less of our poet because he so frequently aimed in his verse not simply to please, but also to impress some elevating thought on the minds of his readers? The Psalms of King David are burning with religious devotion and full of weighty counsel; but they are not less valued, certainly, than the poems of Omar Khayam, which cannot be accused of too great a tendency to find a useful lesson in their subject. Dennis, the famous critic, found fault with the 'Rape of the Lock' because it had no moral. It is not necessary that a poem should carry a moral, any more than that a picture of a Madonna should always be an altar-piece. The poet himself is the best judge of that in each particular case. In that charming little poem of Wordsworth's, ending, —

> "And then my heart with rapture thrills,
> And dances with the daffodils,"

we do not ask for anything more than the record of the impression which is told so simply, and which justifies itself by the way in which it is told. But who does not feel with the poet that the touching story, 'Hart-leap Well,' must have its lesson brought out distinctly, to give a fitting close to the narrative? Who would omit those two lines? —

> "Never to blend our pleasure or our pride
> With sorrow of the meanest thing that lives."

No poet knew better than Longfellow how to impress a moral without seeming to preach. Didactic verse, as such, is no doubt a formidable visitation; but a cathedral has its lesson to teach as well as a school-house. These beautiful medallions of verse which Longfellow has left us might possibly be found fault with as conveying too much useful and elevating truth in their legends, having the unartistic aim of being serviceable as well as delighting by their beauty. Let us leave such comment to the critics who cannot handle a golden coin, fresh from the royal mint, without clipping its edges and stamping their own initials on its face.

Of the longer poems of our chief singer, I should not hesitate to select 'Evangeline' as the masterpiece; and I think the general verdict of opinion would confirm my choice. The German model which it follows in its measure and the character of its story was itself suggested by an earlier idyl. If Dorothea was the mother of Evangeline, Luise was the mother of Dorothea. And what a beautiful creation is the Acadian maiden! From the first line of the poem, from its first words, we read as we would float down a broad and placid river, murmuring softly against its banks, heaven over it and the glory of the unspoiled wilderness all around,

"This is the forest primeval."

The words are already as familiar as

"Μῆνιν ἄειδε, θεά,"

or

"Arma virumque cano."

The hexameter has been often criticised; but I do not believe any other measure could have told that lovely story with such effect, as we feel when carried along the tranquil current of these brimming, slow-moving, soul-satisfying lines. Imagine for one moment a story like this minced into octosyllabics. The poet knows better than his critics the length of step which best befits his Muse.

I will not take up your time with any further remarks upon writings so well known to all. By the poem I have last mentioned, and by his lyrics, or shorter poems, I think the name of Longfellow will be longest remembered. Whatever he wrote, whether in prose or poetry, bore always the marks of the finest scholarship, the purest taste, fertile imagination, a sense of the music of words, and a skill in bringing it out of our English tongue, which hardly more than one of his contemporaries who write in that language can be said to equal.

The saying of Buffon, that the style is the man himself, — or of the man himself, as some versions have it, — was never truer than in the case of our beloved poet. Let us understand by "style" all that gives individuality to the expression of a writer; and in the subjects, the handling, the spirit and aim of his poems, we see the reflex of a personal character which made him worthy of that almost unparalleled homage which crowned his noble life. Such a funeral procession as attended him in thought to his resting-place has never joined the train of mourners that followed the hearse of a poet, — could we not say of any private citizen? And we all feel that no tribute could be too generous, too universal, to the union of a divine gift with one of the loveliest of human characters.

Dr. Holmes was followed by Mr. Charles Eliot Norton, who said: —

I could wish that this were a silent meeting. There is no need of formal commemorative speech to-day, for all the people of the land, the whole English-speaking race, — and not they alone, — mourn our friend and poet. Never was poet so mourned, for never was poet so beloved.

There is nothing of lamentation in our mourning. He has not been untimely taken. His life was "prolonged with many years, happy and famous." Death came to him in good season, or ever the golden bowl was broken, or the pitcher broken at the cistern. Desire had but lately failed. Life was fair to him almost to its end. On his seventy-fourth birthday, a little more than a year ago, with his family and a few friends round his dinner-table, he said, "There seems to me a mistake in the order of the years: I can hardly believe that the four should not precede the seven." But in the year that followed he experienced the pains and languor and weariness of age. There was no complaint; the sweetness of his nature was invincible.

On one of the last times that I saw him, as I entered his familiar study on a beautiful afternoon of this past winter, I said to him, "I hope this is a good day for you?" He replied, with a pleasant smile, "Ah! there are no good days now." Happily, the evil days were not to be many. . . .

The accord between the character and life of Mr. Longfellow and his poems was complete. His poetry touched the hearts of his readers because it was the sincere expression of his own. The sweetness, the gentleness, the grace, the purity of his verse were the image of his own soul. But beautiful and ample as this expression of himself was, it fell short of the truth. The man was more and better than the poet.

Intimate, however, as was the concord between the poet and his poetry, there was much in him to which he never gave utterance in words. He was a man of deep reserves. He kept the holy of holies within himself inviolable and secluded. Seldom does he admit his readers to even its outward precincts. The deepest experiences of life are too sacred to be shared with any one whatsoever. "There are things of which I may not speak," he says in one of the most personal of his poems.

> "Whose hand shall dare to open and explore
> Those volumes closed and clasped forevermore?
> Not mine. With reverential feet I pass."

It was the felicity of Mr. Longfellow to share the sentiment and emotion of his coevals, and to succeed in giving to them their apt poetic expression. It was not by depth of thought or by original views of nature that he won his place in the world's regard; but it was by sympathy with the feelings common to good men and women everywhere, and by the simple, direct, sincere, and delicate expression of them, that he gained the affection of mankind.

He was fortunate in the time of his birth. He grew up in the morning of our Republic. He shared in the cheerfulness of the early hour, in its hopefulness, its confidence. The years of his youth and early manhood coincided with an exceptional moment of national life, in which a prosperous and unembarrassed democracy was learning its own capacities and was beginning to realize its large and novel resources; in which the order of society was still simple and humane. He became, more than any one else, the voice of this epoch of national progress, — an epoch of unexampled prosperity for the masses of mankind in our New World, prosperity from which sprang a sense, more general and deeper than had ever before been felt, of human kindness and brotherhood. But, even to the prosperous, life brings its inevitable burden. Trial, sorrow, misfortune, are not to be escaped by the happiest of men. The deepest experiences of each individual are the experiences common to the whole race. And it is this double aspect of American life — its novel and happy conditions, with the genial spirit resulting from them, and, at the same time, its subjection to the old, absolute, universal laws of existence — that finds its mirror and manifestation in Longfellow's poetry.

No one can read his poetry without a conviction of the simplicity, tenderness, and humanity of the poet And we who were his friends know how these qualities shone in his daily conversation. Praise, applause, flattery, — and no man ever was exposed to more of them, — never touched him to harm him. He walked through their flames unscathed, as Dante through the fires of purgatory. His modesty was perfect. He accepted the praise as he would have accepted any other pleasant gift, — glad of it as an expression of good-will, but without personal elation. Indeed, he had too much of it, and often in an absurd form, not to become at times weary of what his own fame and virtues brought upon him. But his kindliness did not permit him to show his weariness to those who did but burden him with their admiration. It was the penalty of his genius, and he accepted it with the pleasantest temper and a humorous resignation. Bores of all nations, especially of our own, persecuted him. His long-suffering patience was a wonder to his friends; it was, in truth, the sweetest charity. No man was ever before so kind to these moral mendicants. One day I ventured to remonstrate with him on his endurance of the persecutions of one of the worst of the class, who to lack of modesty added lack of honesty, — a wretched creature; and when I had done, he looked at me with a pleasant, reproving, humorous glance, and said, "Charles, who would be kind to him if I were not?" It was enough. He was helped by a gift of humor which, though seldom displayed in his poems, lighted up his talk and added a charm to his intercourse. He was the most gracious of men in his own home; he was fond of the society of his friends, and the company that gathered in his study or round his table took its tone from his own genial, liberal, cultivated, and refined nature.

> "With loving breath of all the winds his name
> Is blown about the world; but to his friends
> A sweeter secret hides behind his fame,
> And love steals shyly through the loud acclaim
> To murmur a *God bless you!* and there ends."

His verse, his fame, are henceforth the precious possessions of the people whom he loved so well. They will be among the effective instruments in shaping the future character of the nation. His spirit will continue to soften, to refine, to elevate the hearts of men. He will be the beloved friend of future generations as he has been of his own. His desire will be gratified, —

> "And in your life let my remembrance linger,
> As something not to trouble and disturb it,
> But to complete it, adding life to life.
> And if at times beside the evening fire
> You see my face among the other faces,
> Let it not be regarded as a ghost
> That haunts your house, but as a guest that loves you.

LONGFELLOW IN ENGLAND, 1868.

An English greeting to the Bard who bears
His chaplet of sweet song from that far West
Where pine-woods, with their branches low depress'd,
Cease not lamenting to the scented airs
For Hiawatha as he disappears,
Swift sailing to the Islands of the Blest,
And for Evangeline, who, now at rest,
With our own Gertrude's self the amaranth shares.

Glad greeting! for in many an English home
The poet's voice has pierced the silent night
With chants of high resolve, and joys that come
At Duty's summons; then Hope's answering light,
Clear as the red star watching o'er the earth,
Glows forth afresh on life's rekindled hearth.

H. A. Bright.

CHAPTER XVIII.

THE MEMORIAL IN WESTMINSTER ABBEY.[1]

On Saturday, March 2, 1884, at midday, the ceremony of unveiling a bust of Longfellow took place in Poets' Corner, Westminster Abbey. It is the work of Mr. Thomas Brock, A. R. A., and was executed by the desire of some five hundred admirers of the American poet. It stands on a bracket near the tomb of Chaucer, and between the memorials to Cowley and Dryden.

Before the ceremony took place, a meeting of the subscribers was held in the Jerusalem Chamber. In the absence of Dean Bradley, owing to a death in his family, the Sub-Dean, Canon Prothero, was called to the chair.

Mr. Bennoch having formally announced the order of proceeding, Dr. Bennett made a brief statement, and called upon Earl Granville to ask the Dean's acceptance of the bust.

Earl Granville then said: "Mr. Sub-Dean, ladies and gentlemen, . . . I am afraid I cannot fulfil the promise made for me of making a speech on this occasion. Not that there are wanting materials for a speech; there are materials of the richest description. There are, first of all, the high character, the refinement, and the personal charm of the late illustrious poet, — if I may say so in the presence of those so near and so dear to him. There are also the characteristics of those works which have secured for him not a greater popularity in the United

[1] From an English paper.

States themselves than in this island and in all the English-speaking dependencies of the British Empire. There are besides very large views with regard to the literature which is common to both the United States and ourselves, and with regard to the separate branches of literature which have sprung up in each country, and which act and react with so much advantage one upon another; and there are, above all, those relations of a moral and intellectual character which become bonds stronger and greater every day between the intellectual and cultivated classes of these two great countries. I am happy to say that with such materials there are persons here infinitely more fitted to deal than I could have been even if I had had time to bestow upon the thought and the labor necessary to condense into the limits of a speech some of the considerations I have mentioned. I am glad that among those present there is one who is not only the official representative of the United States, but who speaks with more authority than any one with regard to the literature and intellectual condition of that country. I cannot but say how glad I am that I have been present at two of the meetings held to inaugurate this work, and I am delighted to be present here to take part in the closing ceremony. With the greatest pleasure I make the offer of this memorial to the Sub-Dean; and from the great kindness we have received already from the authorities of Westminster Abbey, I have no doubt it will be received in the same spirit. I beg to offer to you, Mr. Sub-Dean, the bust which has been subscribed for."

The American Minister, Mr. Lowell, then said: "Mr. Sub-Dean, my lord, ladies and gentlemen, I think I may take upon myself the responsibility, in the name of the daughters of my beloved friend, to express their gratitude to Lord Granville for having found time, amid the continuous and arduous calls of his duty, to be present here this morning. Having occasion to speak in this place some two years ago, I remember that I then expressed the hope that some day or other the Abbey of Westminster would become the Valhalla of the whole English-speaking race. I little expected then that a beginning would be made so soon, — a beginning at once painful and gratifying in the highest degree to myself, — with the bust of my friend. Though there be no Academy in England which corresponds to that of France, yet admission to Westminster Abbey forms a sort of posthumous test of literary eminence perhaps as effectual. Every one of us has his own private Valhalla, and it is not apt to be populous. But the conditions of admission to the Abbey are very different. We ought no longer to ask why is so-and-so here, and we ought always to be able to answer the question why such a one is not here. I think that on this occasion I should express the united feeling of the whole English-speaking race in confirming the choice which has been made, — the choice of one whose name is dear to them all, who has inspired their lives and consoled their hearts, and who has been admitted to the fireside of all of them as a familiar friend. Nearly forty years ago I had occasion, in speaking of Mr. Longfellow, to suggest an analogy between him and the English poet Gray; and I have never since seen any reason to modify or change that opinion. There are certain very marked analogies between them, I think. In the first place, there is the same love of a certain subdued splendor, not inconsistent with transparency of diction; there is the same power of absorbing and assimilating the beauties of other literature without loss of originality; and above all there is that genius, that sympathy with universal sentiments and the power of expressing them so that they come home to everybody, both high and low, which characterize both poets. There is something also in that simplicity, — simplicity in itself being a distinction. But in style, simplicity and distinction must be combined in order to their proper effect; and the only warrant perhaps of permanence in literature is this distinction in style. It is something quite indefinable; it is something like the distinction of good-breeding, characterized perhaps more by the absence of certain negative qualities than by the presence of certain positive ones. But it seems to me that distinction of style is eminently found in the poet whom we are met here in some sense to celebrate to-day. This is not the place, of course, for criticism; still less is it the place for eulogy, for eulogy is but too often disguised apology. But I have been struck particularly — if I may bring forward one instance — with some of my late friend's sonnets, which seem to me to be some of the most beautiful and perfect we have in the language. His mind always moved straight toward its object, and was always permeated with the emotion that gave it frankness and sincerity, and at the same time the most ample expression. It seems that I should add a few words — in fact I cannot refrain from adding a few words — with regard to the personal character of a man whom I knew for more than forty years, and whose friend I was honored to call myself for thirty years. Never was a private character more answerable to public performance than that of Longfellow. Never have I known a more beautiful character. I was familiar with it daily, — with the constant charity of his hand and of his mind. His nature was consecrated ground, into which no unclean spirit could ever enter. I feel entirely how inadequate anything that I can say is to the measure and proportion of an occasion like this. But I think I am authorized to accept, in the name of the people of America, this tribute to not the least distinguished of her sons, to a man who in every way, both in public and in private, did honor to the country that gave him birth. I cannot add anything more to what was so well said in a few words by Lord Granville, for I do not think that these occasions are precisely the times for set discourses, but rather for a few words of feeling, of gratitude, and of appreciation."

The Sub-Dean, in accepting the bust, remarked that it was impossible not to feel, in doing so, that they were accepting a very great honor to the country. He could conceive that if the great poet were allowed to look down on the transactions of that day he would not think it unsatisfactory that his memorial had been placed in that great Abbey among those of his brothers in poetry.

The Chancellor of the Exchequer moved a vote of thanks to the honorary secretary and the honorary treasurer, and said he thought he had been selected for the duty because he had spent two or three years of his life in the United States, and a still longer time in some of the British colonies. It gave him the greater pleasure to do this, having known Mr. Longfellow in America, and having from boyhood enjoyed his poetry, which was quite as much appreciated in England and her dependencies as in America. Wherever he had been in America, and wherever he had met Americans, he had found there was one place at least which they looked upon as being as much theirs as it was England's, — that place was the Abbey Church of Westminster. It seemed, therefore, to him that the present occasion was an excellent beginning of the recognition of the Abbey as what it had been called, — the Valhalla of the English-speaking people. He trusted this beginning would not be the end of its application in this respect.

The company then proceeded to Poets' Corner, where, taking his stand in front of the covered bust,

The Sub-Dean said: "I feel to-day that a double solemnity attaches to this occasion which calls us together

There is first the familiar fact that to-day we are adding another name to the great roll of illustrious men whom we commemorate within these walls, that we are adding something to that rich heritage which we have received of national glory from our ancestors, and which we feel bound to hand over to our successors, not only unimpaired, but even increased. There is then the novel and peculiar fact which attaches to the erection of a monument here to the memory of Henry Longfellow. In some sense, poets — great poets like him — may be said to be natives of all lands; but never before have the great men of other countries, however brilliant and widespread their fame, been admitted to a place in Westminster Abbey. A century ago America was just commencing her perilous path of independence and self-government. Who then could have ventured to predict that within the short space of one hundred years we in England should be found to honor an American as much as we could do so by giving his monument a place within the sacred shrine which holds the memories of our most illustrious sons? Is there not in this a very significant fact; is it not an emphatic proof of the oneness which belongs to our common race, and of the community of our national glories? May I not add, is it not a pledge that we give to each other that nothing can long and permanently sever nations which are bound together by the eternal ties of language, race, religion, and common feeling?"

The reverend gentleman then removed the covering from the bust, and the ceremony ended.

CHAPTER XIX.

REMINISCENCES.

THROUGH the kindness of the writers I have been permitted to include in this volume some personal recollections which have already appeared in print. The first of these in point of date is from the pen of Mr. William Winter.

The least of us who have recollections of such a man as Longfellow may surely venture, now, to add them to the general stock of knowledge without incurring the reproach of intrusiveness. My remembrance of him goes back to a period about thirty years ago, when he was a professor in Harvard University. I had read every line he had then published; and such was the affection he inspired, even in a boyish mind, that on many a summer night I have walked several miles to his house, only to put my hand upon the latch of his gate, which he himself had touched. More than any one else among the many famous persons whom, since then, it has been my fortune to know, he aroused this feeling of mingled tenderness and reverence. I saw him often — walking in the streets of Cambridge, or looking at the books in the old shop of Ticknor and Fields at the corner of Washington and School streets in Boston — long before I was honored with his personal acquaintance; and I observed him closely, — as a youth naturally observes the object of his honest admiration. His dignity and grace, and the beautiful refinement of his countenance, together with his perfect taste in dress and the exquisite simplicity of his manners, made him the absolute ideal of what a poet should be. His voice, too, was soft, sweet, and musical, and, like his face, it had the innate charm of tranquillity. His eyes were blue-gray, very bright and brave, changeable under the influence of emotion (as, afterward, I often saw); but mostly calm, grave, attentive, and gentle. The habitual expression of his face was not that of sadness; and yet it was pensive. Perhaps it may be best described as that of serious and tender thoughtfulness. He had conquered his own sorrows thus far; but the sorrows of others threw their shadow over him, — as he sweetly and humanely says in his pathetic ballad of 'The Bridge.' One day (after he had bestowed on me the honor and blessing of his friendship, which, thank God, I never lost) he chanced to stop his carriage just in front of the old Tudor Building in Court Street, Boston, to speak to me; and I remember observing then the sweet, wistful, half-sad, far-away look in his sensitive face, and thinking he looked like a man who had suffered, or might yet suffer, great affliction. There was a strange touch of sorrowful majesty and prophetic fortitude commingled with the composure and kindness of his features.

It was in April, 1854, that I became personally acquainted with Longfellow; and he was the first literary friend I ever had, — greeting me as a young aspirant in literature, and holding out to me the hand of fellowship and encouragement. He allowed me to dedicate to him a volume of my verses, published in that year, being the first of my ventures. . . . His spontaneous desire, the natural instinct of his great heart, was to be helpful, — to lift up the lowly, to strengthen the weak, to bring out the best in every person, to dry every tear, and make every pathway smooth. It is saying but little to say that he never spoke a harsh word, except against injustice and wrong. He was the natural friend and earnest advocate of every good cause and right idea. His words about the absent were always considerate, and he never lost a practical opportunity of doing good.

For the infirmities of humanity he was charity itself, and he shrank from harshness as from a positive sin. "It is the prerogative of the poet," he once said to me, in those old days, "to give pleasure; but it is the critic's province to give pain." He had, indeed, but a slender esteem for the critic's province. Yet his tolerant nature found excuses for even as virulent and hostile a critic as his assailant and traducer, Edgar Allan Poe, of whom I have heard him speak with genuine pity. His words were few and unobtrusive, and they clearly indicated his consciousness that Poe had grossly abused and maligned him; but instead of resentment for injury, they displayed only sorrow for an unfortunate and half-crazed adversary. There was a little volume of Poe's poems — an English edition — on the library table; and at sight of this I was prompted to ask Longfellow if Poe had ever personally met him, — "because," I said, "if he had known you, it is impossible he could have written about you in such a manner." He answered that he had never seen Poe. . . . Then, after a pause of musing, he added, very gravely: "My works seemed to give him much trouble, first and last; but Mr. Poe is dead and gone, and I am alive and still writing — and that is the end of the matter. I never answered Mr. Poe's attacks; and I would advise you now, at the outset of your literary life, never to take notice of any attacks that may be made upon you. Let them all pass." He then took up the volume of Poe, and, turning the leaves, particularly commended the stanzas entitled 'For Annie' and 'The Haunted Palace.' Then, still speaking of criticism, he mentioned the great number of newspaper and magazine articles, about his own writings, that were received by him, — sent, apparently, by their writers. "I look at the first few lines," he said; "and if I find that the article has been written in a kindly spirit, I read it through: but if I find that the intention is to wound, I drop the paper into my fire, and so dismiss it. In that way one escapes much annoyance."

Longfellow liked to talk of young poets, and he had an equally humorous and kind way of noticing the foibles of the literary character. Standing in the porch, one summer day, and observing the noble elms in front of his house, he recalled a visit made to him, long before, by one of the many bards, now extinct, who are embalmed in Griswold. Then suddenly assuming a burly, martial air, he seemed to reproduce for me the exact figure and manner of the youthful enthusiast, who had tossed back his long hair, gazed approvingly on the elms, and in a deep voice exclaimed: "I see, Mr. Longfellow, that you have many trees — I love trees!!" "It was," said the poet, "as if he gave a certificate to all the neighboring vegetation." A few words like these, said in Longfellow's peculiar dry, humorous manner, with a twinkle of the eye and a quietly droll inflection of the voice, had a certain charm of mirth that cannot be described. It was that same demure playfulness which led him, when writing, to speak of the lady who wore flowers "on the congregation side of her bonnet," or to extol those broad, magnificent Western roads, which "dwindle to a squirrel-track and run up a tree." He had no particle of the acidity of sparkling and biting wit; but he had abundant, playful humor, that was full of kindness, and that toyed good-naturedly with all the trifles of life. That such a sense of fun should be amused by the ludicrous peculiarities of a juvenile bard was inevitable.

I recall many talks with him about poetry, and the avenues of literary labor, and the discipline of the mind in youth. His counsel was always summed up in two words,— calmness and patience. He did not believe in seeking experience, or in going to meet burdens. "What you desire will come, if you will but wait for it," — that he said to me again and again. "My ambition once was," he remarked, "to edit a magazine. Since then the opportunity has been offered to me many times — and I did not take it, and would not." . . .

His sense of humor found especial pleasure in the inappropriate words that were sometimes said to him by persons whose design it was to be complimentary; and he would relate, with a keen relish of their pleasantry, anecdotes to illustrate this form of social blunder. Years ago he told me, at Cambridge, about the strange gentleman who was led up to him and introduced at Newport, and who straightway said, with enthusiastic fervor: "Mr. Longfellow, I have long desired the honor of knowing you! Sir, I am one of *the few* men who have read your 'Evangeline.'" . . .

About poetry he talked with the earnestness of what was a genuine passion, and yet with no particle of self-assertion. Tennyson's 'Princess' was a new book when first I heard him speak of it, and I remember Mrs. Longfellow sitting with that volume in her hands and reading it by the evening lamp. The delicate loveliness of the little lyrical pieces that are interspersed throughout its text was, in particular, dwelt upon as a supreme merit. Among his own poems his favorite at that time was 'Evangeline;' but he said that the style of versification which pleased him best was that of 'The Day is Done;' nor do I wonder, reading this now, together with 'The Bridge,' 'Twilight,' 'The Children's Hour,' and 'The Open Window,' and finding them so exquisite both in pathos and music. He said also that he sometimes wrote poems that were for himself alone, that he should not care ever to publish, because they were too delicate for publication. One of his sayings was that "the desire of the young poet is not for applause, but for recognition." He much commended the example, in one respect, of the renowned Italian poet Alfieri, who caused himself to be bound into his library chair and left for a certain period of time, each day, at his library table — his servants being strictly enjoined not to release him till that time had passed: by this means he forced himself to labor. No man ever believed more firmly than Longfellow did in regular, proportioned, resolute, incessant industry. His poem of 'The Builders' contains his creed; his poem of 'The Ladder of St. Augustine' is the philosophy of his career. Yet I have many times heard him say "the mind cannot be controlled;" and the fact that he was, when at his best, a poet of pure inspiration, is proved beyond possibility of doubt by such poems as 'Sandalphon,' 'My Lost Youth,' 'The Beleaguered City,' 'The Fire of Drift-wood,' 'Suspiria,' 'The Secret of the Sea,' 'The Two Angels,' and 'The Warden of the Cinque Ports.' Either of them is worthy of the brightest name that ever was written on the scroll of the lyric Muse.

The two writers of whom he oftenest spoke, within my hearing, were Lowell and Hawthorne. Of Lowell he said, "He is one of the manliest and noblest men that ever lived." "Hawthorne often came into this room," he said, "and sometimes he would go there, behind the window curtains, and remain in silent revery the whole evening. No one disturbed him; he came and went as he liked. He was a mysterious man." With Irving's works he was especially familiar, and he often quoted from them in his talk to me. One summer day at his cottage at Nahant I found him reading Cooper's sea-stories, and had the comfort of hearing from his lips a tribute to that great writer, — the foremost novelist in American literature, unmatched since Scott. . . . Longfellow was in fine spirits that day, and very happy; and I have always thought of him as he looked then, holding his daughter Edith in his arms, — a little child, with long, golden hair, and lovely, merry face, — and by his mere presence making the sunshine brighter and the place more sacred with kindness and peace.

The best portrait of Longfellow is the one made by Samuel Lawrence; and it is the best because it gives the noble and spirited poise and action of his head, shows his clean-cut, strong, yet delicate features unmasked with a beard, and preserves that alert, inspired expression which came into his face when he was affected by any strong emotion. I recall Mrs. Longfellow's commendation of it in a fireside talk. It was her favorite portrait of him. We discussed together Thomas Buchanan Read's portrait of him and of his three daughters, when those pictures were yet fresh from the easel. I remember speaking to him of a fancied resemblance between the face of Mrs. Longfellow and the face of 'Evangeline' in Faed's well-known picture. He said that others had noticed it, but that he himself did not perceive it. Yet I think those faces were alike, in stateliness and in the mournful beauty of the eyes. It is strange what trifles crowd upon the memory when one thinks of the long ago and the friends that have departed. I recollect his smile when he said that he always called to mind the number of the house in Beacon Street, Boston, — which was Mrs. Longfellow's home when she was Miss Appleton, — "by thinking of the Thirty-nine Articles." I recollect the gentle gravity of his voice when he showed me a piece of the coffin of Dante, and said, in a low tone, "That has touched his bones." I recollect the benignant look in his eyes and the warm pressure of his hand when he bade me good-by (it was the last time), saying, "You never forget me; you always come to see me." There were long lapses of time during which I never saw him, being held fast by incessant duties, and driven far away by the gales of life from the old moorings of my youth. But as often as I came back to his door his love met me on the threshold and his noble serenity gave me comfort and peace. It is but a little while ago since, in quick and delicate remembrance of the old days, he led me to his hearthstone, saying, "Come and sit in the Children's Chair." What an awful solemnity, and yet what a soothing sense of perfect nobleness and beneficent love, must hallow now that storied home from which his earthly and visible presence has forever departed!

Let us turn to his own words, and take comfort once more from that loving heart which was always so ready to give it: "Death is neither an end nor a beginning. It is a transition, not from one existence to another, but from one state of existence to another. No link is broken in the chain of being, any more than in passing from infancy to manhood, from manhood to old age. . . . Death brings us again to our friends. They are waiting for us, and we shall not long delay. They have gone before us, and are like the angels in heaven. They stand upon the borders of the grave to welcome us, with the countenance of affection which they wore on earth, — yet more lovely, more radiant, more spiritual."

The reminiscences that follow are from the hand of an intimate friend of many years, Mrs. J. T. Fields.[1]

There was always a striking contrast between the perfect modesty and simplicity of Longfellow and the blare of

[1] Reprinted from The Century, April, 1886, by permission of the publishers.

popularity which beset him. Though naturally of a buoyant disposition and fond of pleasure, he lived as far as possible from the public eye, especially during the last twenty years of his life. The following note gives a hint of his natural gayety, and details one of the many excuses by which he always declined to speak in public, — the one memorable exception being that beautiful occasion at Bowdoin when he returned in age to the scenes of his youth and read to the crowd assembled there to do him reverence his poem entitled 'Morituri Salutamus.' After speaking of the reasons which must keep him from the Burns festival [in 1859], he adds: —

"I am very sorry not to be there. You will have a delightful supper, or dinner, whichever it is; and human breath enough expended to fill all the trumpets of Iskander for a month or more.

I behold as in a vision a friend of ours, with his left hand under the tails of his coat, blowing away like mad; and, alas! I shall not be there to applaud. All this you must do for me; and also eat my part of the haggis which I hear is to grace the feast. This shall be your duty and your reward."

The reference in this note to the "trumpets of Iskander" is the only one in his letters regarding a poem which was a great favorite of his, by Leigh Hunt, called 'The Trumpets of Doolkarnein.' It is a poem worthy to make the reputation of a poet, and is almost a surprise even among the varied riches of Leigh Hunt. Many years after this note was written, Longfellow used to recall it to those lovers of poetry who had chanced to escape a knowledge of its beauty.

In spite of his dislike of grand occasions, he was a keen lover of the opera and theatre. He was always the first to know when the opera season was to begin, and to plan that we might have a box together. He was always ready to hear *Lucia* or *Don Giovanni*, and to make a festival time at the coming of Salvini or Neilson. There is a tiny notelet among his letters, with a newspaper paragraph neatly cut out and pasted across the top, detailing the names of his party at a previous appearance at a theatre, — a kind of notoriety which he particularly shuddered at; but in order to prove his determination, in spite of everything, he writes below: —

> "Now for 'Pinafore,' and another paragraph! Saturday afternoon would be a good time."

He easily caught the gayety of such occasions, and in the shadow of the box-curtains would join in the singing or the recitative of the lovely Italian words with a true poet's delight. . . .

Day by day he was besieged by every possible form of interruption which the ingenuity of the human brain could devise; but his patience and kindness, his determination to accept the homage offered him in the spirit of the giver, whatever discomfort it might bring himself, was continually surprising to those who watched him year by year. Mr. Fields wrote: "In his modesty and benevolence I am reminded of what Pope said of his friend Garth: 'He is the best of Christians, without knowing it.'" . . .

He was distinguished by one grace which was almost peculiar to himself in the time in which he lived — his tenderness toward the undeveloped artist, the man or woman, youth or maid, whose heart was set upon some form of ideal expression, and who was living for that. Whether they possessed the power to distinguish themselves or not, to such persons he addressed himself with a sense of personal regard and kinship. When fame crowned the aspirant, no one recognized more keenly the perfection of the work; but he seldom turned aside to attract the successful to himself. To the unsuccessful he lent the sunshine and overflow of his own life, as if he tried to show every day afresh that he believed noble pursuit, and not attainment, to be the purpose of our existence. . . .

His kindness and love of humor carried him through many a tedious interruption. He generously overlooked the fact of the subterfuges to which men and women resorted in order to get an interview, and to help them out made as much of their excuses as possible. Speaking one day of the people who came to see him at Nahant, he said: "One man, a perfect stranger, came with an omnibus full of ladies. He descended, introduced himself, then returning to the omnibus took out all the ladies, one, two, three, four, and five, with a little girl, and brought them in. I entertained them to the best of my ability, and they stayed an hour. They had scarcely gone when a forlorn woman in black came up to me on the piazza and asked for a 'dipper of water.' 'Certainly,' I replied, and went to fetch her a glass. When I brought it she said, 'There is another woman just by the fence who is tired and thirsty; I will carry this to her.' But she struck her head as she passed through the window and spilled the water on the piazza. 'Oh! what have I done?' she said. 'If I had a floor-cloth, I would wipe it up.' 'Oh! no matter about the water,' I said, 'if you have not hurt yourself.' Then I went and brought more water for them both, and sent them on their way, at last, refreshed and rejoicing." Once Longfellow drew out of his pocket a queer request for an autograph, saying, "that the writer loved poetry in 'most any style, and would he please copy his 'Break, break, break!' for the writer?" He also described in a note a little encounter in the street, on a windy day, with an elderly French gentleman in company with a young lady, who introduced them to each other. The Frenchman said: —

"'Monsieur, vous avez un fils qui fait de la peinture.'
'Oui, Monsieur.'
'Il a du mérite. Il a beaucoup d'avenir.'
'Ah!' said I, 'c'est une belle chose que l'avenir.'

The elderly French gentleman rolled up the whites of his eyes and answered, —

'Oui, c'est une belle chose; mais vous et moi, nous n'en avons pas beaucoup!'

Superfluous information!"

It would be both an endless and unprofitable task to recall many more of the curious experiences which Longfellow's popularity brought down upon him. There is a passage among Mr. Fields's notes, however, in which he describes an incident during Longfellow's last visit to England which should not be overlooked. Upon his arrival the Queen sent a graceful message and invited him to Windsor Castle, where she received him with all cordiality; but he told me no foreign tribute touched him deeper than the words of an English hod-carrier, who came up to the carriage-door at Harrow and asked permission to take the hand of the man who had written the Voices of the Night.

There are many letters belonging to the phase of Longfellow's life dwelt upon in this sketch, but they belong more properly to his biography. There is a brief note, however, written in 1849, which gives a pleasant idea of the close relation already existing between him and his publisher. He writes: —

"MY DEAR FIELDS, — I am extremely glad you like the new poems so well. What think you of the inclosed, instead of the sad ending of 'The Ship'? Is it better?[1] . . . I send you also 'The Lighthouse' once more; I think it is improved by your suggestions. See if you can find anything more to re-touch. And finally, here is a letter from Hirst. You see what he wants; but I do not like the idea of giving my 'Dedication' to the 'Courier.' Therefore I hereby give it to you, so that I can say it is disposed of.

Am I right, or wrong?"

[1] The original ending of 'The Building of the Ship' will be found on page 443.

There was no break nor any change in this friendship during the passing of the years; but in 1861 there is a note containing only a few words, which shows that a change had fallen upon Longfellow himself, — a shadow which never could be lifted from his life. He writes:

"My dear Fields, — I am sorry to say No instead of Yes; but so it must be. I can neither write nor think; and I have nothing fit to send you but my love, which you cannot put into the magazine."

For ever after the death of his wife he was a different man. His friends suffered for him and with him, but he walked alone through the valley of the shadow of death. They were glad when he turned to his work again, and still more glad when he showed a desire for their interest in what he was doing.

It was not long before he began to busy himself continuously with his translation of the *Divina Commedia*, and in the journal of 1863 I find: —

"*August.* A delightful day with Longfellow at Nahant. He read aloud the last part of his new volume of poems, in which each one of a party of friends tells a story. Ole Bull, Parsons, Monti, and several other characters are introduced."

"*September* 1. A cold storm by the sea-shore; but there was great pleasure in town in the afternoon. Longfellow, Paine, Dwight, and Fields went to hear Walcker play the great new organ in the Music Hall for the first time since its erection. Afterward they all dined together. Longfellow comes in from Cambridge every day, and sometimes twice a day, to see George Sumner, who is dying at the Massachusetts General Hospital."

"*September* 19. Longfellow and his friend George W. Greene, Charles Sumner, and Dempster, the singer, came in for an early dinner. A very cosey, pleasant little party. The afternoon was cool, and everybody was in kindly humor. Sumner shook his head sadly when the subject of the English ironclads was mentioned. The talk prolonged itself upon the condition of the country. Longfellow's patriotism flamed. His feeling against England runs more deeply and strongly than he can find words to express. There is no prejudice nor childish partisanship, but it is hatred of the course she has pursued at this critical time. Later, in speaking of poetry and some of the less-known and younger poets, Longfellow recalled some good passages in the poems of Bessie Parkes and Jean Ingelow. As evening approached we left the table and came to the library. There in the twilight Dempster sat at the piano and sang to us, beginning with Longfellow's poem called 'Children,' which he gave with a delicacy and feeling that touched every one. Afterward he sang the 'Bugle Song' and 'Turn, Fortune,' which he had, shortly before leaving England, sung to Tennyson; and then, after a pause, he turned once more to the instrument and sang 'Break, break, break!' It was very solemn, and no one spoke when he had finished, only a deep sob was heard from the corner where Longfellow sat Again and again, each time more uncontrolled, we heard the heart-rending sounds. Presently the singer gave us another and less touching song, and before he ceased, Longfellow rose and vanished from the room in the dim light without a word."

"*September* 27. Longfellow and Greene came to town in the evening for a walk and to see the moonlight in the streets, and afterward to have supper. . . . He was very sad, and seemed to have grown an old man since a week ago. He was silent and absent-minded. On his previous visit he had borrowed Sidney's 'Arcadia' and Christina Rossetti's poems, but he had read neither of the books. He was overwhelmed with his grief, as if it were sometimes more than he could endure."

"*Sunday, October.* Took five little children to drive in the afternoon, and stopped at Longfellow's. It was delightful to see their enjoyment and his. He took them out of the carriage in his arms and was touchingly kind to them. His love for children is not confined to his poetic expressions or to his own family; he is uncommonly tender and beautiful with them always."

I remember there was one little boy of whom he was very fond, and who came often to see him. One day the child looked earnestly at the long rows of books in the library, and at length said,—

"Have you got Jack the Giant-Killer?"

Longfellow was obliged to confess that his library did not contain that venerated volume. The little boy looked very sorry, and presently slipped down from his knee and went away; but early the next morning Longfellow saw him coming up the walk with something tightly clasped in his little fists. The child had brought him two cents, with which he was to buy a Jack the Giant-Killer to be his own.

He did not escape the sad experiences of the War. His eldest son was severely wounded, and he also went, as did Dr. Holmes and other less famous but equally anxious parents, in search of his boy. . . .

In the year 1865 began those Wednesday evenings devoted to reading the new translation of Dante. They were delightful occasions. Lowell, Norton, Greene, Howells, and such other Dante scholars or intimate friends as were accessible, made up the circle of kindly critics. Those evenings increased in interest as the work went on; and when it was ended, and the notes were written and read, it was proposed to re-read the whole rather than to give up the weekly visit to Longfellow's house. In 1866 he wrote to Mr. Fields:—

"Greene is coming expressly to hear the last canto of *Paradiso* to-morrow night, and will stay the rest of the week. I really hoped you would be here; but as you say nothing about it, I begin to tremble. Perhaps, however, you are only making believe, and will take us by surprise; so I shall keep your place for you.

This is not to be the end of all things. I mean to begin again in September with the dubious and difficult passages; and if you are not in too much of a hurry to publish, there is still a long vista of pleasant evenings stretching out before us. We can pull them out like a spy-glass. I am shutting up now, to recommence the operation."

In December of the same year he wrote: —

"The first meeting of the Dante Club Redivivus is on Wednesday next. Come and be bored. Please not to mention the subject to any one yet awhile, as we are going to be very quiet about it."

"*January*, 1867. Dante Club at Longfellow's again. They are revising the whole book with the minutest care. Lowell's accuracy is surprising, and of great value to the work; also Norton's criticisms. Longfellow sits at his desk, taking notes and making corrections, — though of course no one can know yet what he accepts." . . .

He was seldom stimulated to external expression by others. Such excitement as he could express again was always self-excitement; anything external rendered him at once a listener and an observer. For this reason it is peculiarly difficult to give any idea of his lovely presence and character to those who have not known him. He did not speak in epigrams. It could not be said of him:

"His mouth he could not ope,
But out there flew a trope."

Yet there was an exquisite tenderness and effluence from his presence which was more humanizing and elevating than the eloquence of many others.

Speaking one day of his own reminiscences, Longfellow said, "that however interesting such things were in conversation, he thought they seldom contained legitimate matter for bookmaking; and ——'s life of a poet, just then printed, was, he thought, peculiarly disagreeable, chiefly because of the unjustifiable things related of him by others. This strain of thought brought to his mind a call he made [in 1842], with a letter of introduction, upon Jules Janin. The servant said her master was at home, and he was ushered immediately into a small parlor, in one corner of which was a winding stairway leading into the room above. Here he waited a moment while the maid carried in his card, and then returned immediately to say he could go up. In the upper room sat Janin under the hands of a barber, his abundant locks shaken up in wild confusion, in spite of which he received his guest quite undisturbed, as if it were a matter of course. There was no fire in the room, but the fire-place was heaped with letters and envelopes, and a trail of the same reached from his desk to the grate. After a brief visit Longfellow was about to withdraw, when Janin detained him, saying: 'What can I do for you in Paris? Whom would you like to see?'

'I should like to know Madame George Sand.'

'Unfortunately that is impossible! I have just quarrelled with Madame Sand!'

'Ah! then, Alexandre Dumas; I should like to take him by the hand!'

'I have quarrelled with him also; but no matter! *Vous perdriez vos illusions.*'

"However, he invited me to dine the next day, and I had a singular experience; but I shall not soon forget the way in which he said, 'Vous perdriez vos illusions.'

"When I arrived on the following day I found the company consisted of his wife and himself, a little red-haired man who was rather quiet and cynical, and myself. Janin was amusing and noisy, and carried the talk on swimmingly, with much laughter. Presently he began to say hard things about women; when his wife looked up reproachfully, and said, 'Déjà, Jules!' During dinner a dramatic author arrived with his play, and Janin ordered him to be shown in. He treated the poor fellow brutally, who in turn bowed low to the great power. He did not even ask him to take a chair. Madame Janin did so, however, and kindly too. The author supplicated the critic to attend the first appearance of his play. Janin would not promise to go, but put him off indefinitely; and presently the poor man went away. I tingled all over with indignation at the treatment the man received; but Janin looked over to his wife, saying, 'Well, my dear, I treated this one pretty well, did n't I?'

'Better than sometimes, Jules,' she answered."

Altogether it was a strange scene to the American observer.

"*July*, 1867. Passed the day at Nahant. As Longfellow sat on the piazza, wrapped in his blue cloth cloak, he struck me for the first time as wearing a venerable aspect. Before dinner he gathered wild roses to adorn the table, and even gave a careful touch himself to the arrangement of the wines and fruits. He was in excellent spirits, full of wit and lively talk. Speaking of the use and misuse of words, he quoted Chateaubriand's mistake (afterward corrected) in his translation of 'Paradise Lost,' where he rendered

'Siloa's brook that flowed
Fast by the oracle of God,'

as

'Le ruisseau de Siloa qui coulait rapidement.'"

In talking about natural differences in character and temperament, he said of his own children that he agreed with one of the old English divines who said, "Happy is that household wherein Martha still reproves Mary!"

In February, 1868, it was decided that Longfellow should go to Europe with his family. He said that the first time he went abroad it was to see places alone, and not persons; the second time he saw a few persons, and so pleasantly combined the two; he thought once that on a third visit he should prefer to see people only. But all that was changed now. He had returned to the feeling of his youth. He was eager to seek out quiet places and wayside nooks where he might rest in retirement and enjoy the beautiful country sights of Europe undisturbed.

The following year found him again in Cambridge, refreshed by his absence. The diary continues: "He has been trying to further the idea of buying some of the low lands in Cambridge for the College. If this can be done, it will save much future annoyance to the people from wretched hovels and bad odors, besides holding the land for a beautiful possession forever. He has given a good deal of money himself. This might be called 'his latest work.'"

"*January*, 1870. Longfellow and Bayard Taylor came to dine. Longfellow talked of translators and translating. He advanced the idea that the English, from the insularity of their character, were incapable of making a perfect translation. Americans, French, and Germans, he said, have much larger adaptability to and sympathy in the thought of others. He would not hear Chapman's Homer or anything else quoted on the other side, but was zealous in enforcing this argument. He anticipates much from Taylor's version of *Faust*. All this was strikingly interesting, as showing how his imagination wrought with him, because he was arguing from his own theory of the capacity of the races, and in the face of his knowledge of the best actual translations existing to-day, the result of the scholarship of England. . . .

"His account of Sainte-Beuve during his last visit to Europe was an odd little drama. He had grown excessively fat, and could scarcely move. He did not attempt to rise from his chair as Longfellow entered, but motioned him to a seat by his side. Talking of Chateaubriand and Lamartine, 'Take them for all in all, which do you prefer?' asked Longfellow.

"'Charlatan pour charlatan, je crois que je préfère Monsieur de Lamartine,' was the reply.

"Longfellow amused me by making two epigrams:

'What is autobiography?
It is what a biography ought to be.'

And again: —

'When you ask one friend to dine,
Give him your best wine!
When you ask two,
The second best will do!'

"He brought in with him two poems translated from Platen's Night-Songs. They are very beautiful." . . .

When Longfellow talked freely, as at this dinner, it was difficult to remember that he was not really a talker. The natural reserve of his nature made it sometimes impossible for him to express himself in ordinary intercourse. He never truly made a confidant of anybody except his Muse. . . .

His sympathetic nature was ever ready to share and further the gayety of others. He wrote one evening:

"I have been kept at home by a little dancing-party to-night. . . . I write this arrayed in my dress-coat, with a rose in my button-hole, — a circumstance, I think, worth mentioning. It reminds me of Buffon, who used to array himself in his full dress for writing Natural History. Why should we not always do it when we write letters? We should, no doubt, be more courtly and polite, and perhaps say handsome things to each other. It was said of Villemain that when he spoke to a lady he seemed to be presenting her a bouquet. Allow me to present you this postscript in the same polite manner, to make good my theory of the rose in the button-hole."

How delightful it is to catch the exhilaration of the little festival in this way! In his endeavor to further the gayeties of his children he had received again a reflected light and life which his love for them had helped to create.

"*December* 14, 1870. Taylor's *Faust* is finished, and Longfellow is coming with other friends to dinner to celebrate the ending of the work. . . .

"A statuette of Goethe was on the table. Longfellow said Goethe never liked the statue of himself by Rauch, from which this copy was made. He preferred above all others a bust of himself by a Swiss sculptor, a copy of which Taylor owns. He could never understand, he continued, the story of that unpleasant interview between Napoleon and Goethe. Eckermann says Goethe liked it; but Longfellow thought the Emperor's manner of address had a touch of insolence in it. The haunts of Goethe in Weimar were pleasantly recalled by both Longfellow and Taylor, to whom they were familiar; also that strange portrait of him, taken standing at a window, and looking out over Rome, in which nothing but his back can be seen.

"I find it impossible to recall what Longfellow said, but he scintillated all the evening. It was an occasion such as he loved best. His *jeux d'esprit* flew rapidly right and left, often setting the table in a roar of laughter, — a most unusual thing with him." . . .

"*January*, 1871. Dined at Longfellow's, and afterward went upstairs to see an interesting collection of East Indian curiosities. Passing through his dressing-room, I was struck with the likeness of his private rooms to those of a German student or professor, — a Goethean aspect of simplicity and space everywhere, with books put up in the nooks and corners and all over the walls. It is surely a most attractive house!"

Again I find a record of a dinner at Cambridge: "The day was spring-like, and the air full of the odors of fresh blossoms. As we came down over the picturesque old staircase, he was standing with a group of gentlemen near by, and I heard him say aloud unconsciously, in a way peculiar to himself, 'Ah, now we shall see the ladies come downstairs!' Nothing escapes his keen observation — as delicate as it is keen."

And in the same vein the journal rambles on

"*Friday.* Longfellow came in to luncheon at one o'clock. He was looking very well; . . . his beautiful eyes fairly shone. He had been at Manchester-by-the-Sea the day before to dine with the Curtises. Their truly romantic and lovely place had left a pleasant picture in his mind. Coming away by the train, he passed in Chelsea a new soldiers' monument, which suggested an epigram to him that he said, laughingly, would suit any of the thousand of such monuments to be seen about the country. He began somewhat in this style: —

'The soldier asked for bread;
But they waited till he was dead,
And gave him a stone instead,
Sixty and one feet high!'

"We all returned to Cambridge together, and being early for our own appointment elsewhere, he carried us into his library and read aloud 'The Marriage of Lady Wentworth.' E., with pretty girlish ways, and eyes like his own, had let us into the old mansion by the side-door, and then lingered to ask if she might be allowed to stay and hear the reading too. He, consenting, laughingly lighted a cigar and soon began. His voice in reading was sweet and melodious, and it was touched with tremulousness; although this was an easier poem to read aloud than many others, being strictly narrative. It is full of New England life, and a beautiful addition to his works. He has a fancy for making a volume, or getting some one else to do it, of his favorite ghost-stories, — the Flying Dutchman, Peter Rugg, and a few others."

On another occasion the record says: —

"Passed the evening at Longfellow's. As we lifted the latch and entered the hall-door, we saw him reading an old book by his study-lamp. It was the *Chansons d'Espagne*, which he had just purchased at what he called the 'massacre of the poets;' in other words, at the sale that day of the library of William H. Prescott. He was rather melancholy, he said, — first, on account of the sacrifice and separation of that fine library; also because he is doubtful about his new poem, the one on the life of our Saviour. He says he has never before felt so cast-down.

"What an orderly man he is! — 'well-ordered,' I should have written. Diary, accounts, scraps, books, — everything where he can put his hand upon it in a moment."

"*December*, 1871. Saturday Mr. Longfellow came in town and went with us to hear twelve hundred school children sing a welcome to the Russian Grand Duke in the Music Hall. It was a fine sight, and Dr. Holmes's hymn, written for the occasion, was noble and inspiring. Just before the Grand Duke came in I saw a smile creep over Longfellow's face. 'I can never get over the ludicrousness of it,' he said. 'All this array and fuss over one man!' He came home with us afterward, and lingered awhile by the fire. He talked of Russian literature, — its modernness, — and said he had sent us a delightful novel by Tourgénief, *Liza*, in which we should find charming and vivid glimpses of landscape and life like those seen from a carriage-window. We left him alone in the library for a while, and returning, found him amusing himself over the Ingoldsby Legends. He was reading the 'Coronation of Victoria,' and laughing over Count Froganoff, who 'could not get prog enough,' and was found eating underneath the stairs. He wants to have a dinner for Bayard Taylor, whose coming is always the signal for a series of small festivities. His own Divine Tragedy is just out, and everybody speaks of its simplicity and beauty."

"*April.* In the evening Longfellow came into town for the purpose of hearing a German gentleman read an original poem, and he persuaded me to go with him. The reader twisted his face up into frightful knots, and delivered his poem with vast apparent satisfaction to himself, if not to his audience. It was fortunate, on the whole, that the production was in a foreign tongue, because it gave us the occupation at least of trying to understand the words, — the poem itself possessing not the remotest interest for either of us. It was in the old sentimental German style familiar to the readers of that literature. Longfellow amused me as we walked home by imitating the sing-song voice we had been following all the evening. He also recited in the original that beautiful little poem by Platen, *In der Nacht, in der Nacht,* in a most delightful manner. 'Ah!' he said, 'to translate a poem properly it must be done into the metre of the original; and Bryant's Homer, fine as it is, has this fault, — that it does not give the music of the poem itself.' He came in and took a cigar before walking home over the bridge alone. . . .

"Emerson asked Longfellow at dinner about his last visit to England, of Ruskin and other celebrities. Longfellow is always reticent upon such subjects; but he was eager to tell us how very much he had enjoyed Mr. Ruskin. He said it was one of the most surprising things in the world to see the quiet, gentlemanly way in which Ruskin gave vent to his extreme opinions. It seems to be no effort to him, but as if it were a matter of course that every one should give expression to the faith that is in him in the same unvarnished way as he does himself not looking for agreement, but for conversation and discussion. 'It is strange,' Ruskin said, 'being considered so much out of harmony with America as I am, that the two Americans I have known and loved best, you and Norton, should give me such a feeling of friendship and repose.'"[1] . . .

"Longfellow came in to an early dinner to meet Mr. Joseph Jefferson, Mr. William Warren, and Dr. Holmes He said he felt like one on a journey. He had left home early in the morning, had been sight-seeing in Boston all day, was to dine and go to the theatre with us afterward. The talk naturally turned upon the stage. Longfellow said he thought Mr. Charles Mathews was entirely unjust in his criticisms upon Mr. Forrest's King Lear. He considered Mr. Forrest's rendering of the part as very fine, and close to nature. He could not understand why Mr. Mathews should underrate it as he did. Longfellow showed us a book given him by Charles Sumner. In it was an old engraving (from a painting by Giulio Clovio) of the moon, in which Dante is walking with his companion. He said it was a most impressive picture to him. He knew it in the original; also there is a very good copy in the Cambridge Library among the copies of illuminated manuscripts."

There is a little note, belonging to this period, full of poetic feeling, and giving more than a hint at the wearifulness of interrupting visitors:—

"I send you the pleasant volume I promised you yesterday. It is a book for summer moods by the seaside, but will not be out of place on a winter night by the fireside. . . . You will find an allu-

[1] Mr. Ruskin had written to Mr. Longfellow: "I had many things to say about the sense I have of the good you might do this old world by staying with us a little, and giving the peaceful glow of your fancy to our cold, troubled, unpeaceful spirit. Strange, that both you and Norton come as such *calm* influences to me and others."

sion to the 'blue borage flowers' that flavor the claret-cup. I know where grows another kind of bore-age that embitters the goblet of life. I can spare you some of this herb, if you have room for it in your garden or your garret. It is warranted to destroy all peace of mind, and finally to produce softening of the brain and insanity.

'Better juice of vine
Than berry wine!
Fire! fire! steel, oh, steel!
Fire! fire! steel and fire!'"

The following, written in the spring of the same year, gives a hint of what a festival season it was to him while the lilacs which surround his house were in bloom: —

"Here is the poem, copied for you by your humble scribe. I found it impossible to crowd it into a page of note-paper. Come any pleasant morning, as soon after breakfast, or before, as you like, and we will go on with the 'Michael Angelical' manuscript. I shall not be likely to go to town while the lilacs are in bloom."

The rambling diary continues: "To-day Longfellow sent us half a dozen bottles of wine, and after them came a note saying he had sent them off without finding time to label them. 'They are wine of Avignon,' he added, 'and should bear this inscription, from Redi: —

'Benedetto
Quel Claretto
Che si spilla in Avignone.'"

About this period Longfellow invited an old friend, who had fallen into extreme helplessness from ill health, to come and make him a visit. It was a great comfort to his friend, a scholar like himself, "to nurse the dwindling faculty of joy" in such companionship, and he lingered many weeks in the sunshine of the old house. Longfellow's patience and devoted care for this friend of his youth was a signal example of what a true and constant heart may do unconsciously, in giving expression and recognition to the bond of a sincere friendship. Long after his friend was unable to rise from his chair without assistance, or go unaccompanied to his bedroom, Longfellow followed the lightest unexpressed wish with his sympathetic vision, and performed the smallest offices for him. "Longfellow, will you turn down my coat-collar?" I have heard him say in a plaintive way; and it was a beautiful lesson to see the quick and cheerful response which would follow many a like suggestion.

In referring to this trait of his character, I find among the notes made by Mr. Fields on Longfellow: "One of the most occupied of all our literary men and scholars, he yet finds time for the small courtesies of existence, — those minor attentions that are so often neglected. One day, seeing him employed in cutting something from a newspaper, I asked him what he was about. 'Oh,' said he, 'here is a little paragraph speaking kindly of our poor old friend Blank. You know he seldom gets a word of praise, poor fellow, nowadays; and thinking he might not chance to see this paper, I am snipping out the paragraph to mail to him this afternoon. I know that even these few lines of recognition will make him happy for hours, and I could not bear to think he might perhaps miss seeing these pleasant words so kindly expressed.'"

"*May Day*, 1876. Longfellow dined with us. He said during the dinner, when we heard a blast of wintry wind howling outside, 'This is May Day enough; it does not matter to us how cold it is outside.' He was inclined to be silent, for there were other and brilliant talkers at the table, one of whom said to him in a pause of the conversation, 'Longfellow, tell us about yourself; you never talk about yourself.' 'No,' said Longfellow gently, 'I believe I never do.' 'And yet,' continued the first speaker eagerly, 'you confessed to me once——' 'No,' said Longfellow, laughing, 'I think I never did.'"

And here is a tiny note of compliment, graceful as a poet's note should be: —

"I have just received your charming gift, — your note and the stately lilies; but fear you may have gone from home before my thanks can reach you.

How beautiful they are, these lilies of the field; and how like American women! Not because 'they neither toil nor spin,' but because they are elegant and 'born in the purple.'"

There is a brief record in 1879 of a visit to us in Manchester-by-the-Sea. Just before he left he said, "After I am gone to-day, I want you to read Schiller's poem of the 'Ring of Polycrates,' if you do not recall it too distinctly. You will know then how I feel about my visit." He repeated also some English hexameters he had essayed from the first book of the Iliad. He believes the work may be still more perfectly done than has ever yet been achieved. We drove to Gloucester wrapped in a warm sea-fog. His enjoyment of the green woods and the sea-breeze was delightful to watch. "Ay me! ay me! woods may decay," but who can dare believe such life shall cease from the fair world!

Seeing the Portland steamer pass one night, a speck on the horizon, bearing, as he knew, his daughter and her husband, he watched it long; then said: "Think of a part of yourself being on that moving speck!" . . .

Already in 1875 we find Longfellow at work upon his latest collection of poems, which he called Poems of Places. It was a much more laborious and unrewarding occupation than he had intended, and he was sometimes weary of his self-imposed task. He wrote at this period: —

No politician ever sought for Places with half the zeal that I do. Friend and foe alike have to give Place to,

Yours truly,

H. W. L.

Again he says: —

"What evil demon moved me to make this collection of Poems of Places? Could I have foreseen the time it would take, and the worry and annoyance it would bring with it, I never would have undertaken it. The worst of it is, I have to write pieces now and then to fill up gaps."

More and more his old friends grew dear to him as the years passed and "the goddess Neuralgia," as he called his malady, kept him chiefly at home. . . .

And here the extracts from letters and journals must cease. It was a golden sunset, in spite of the increasing infirmities which beset him; for he could never lose his pleasure in making others happy, and only during the few last days did he lose his own happiness among his books and at his desk. The influence his presence gave out to others, of calm good cheer and tenderness, made those who knew him feel that he possessed, in larger measure than others, what Jean Paul Richter calls "a heavenly unfathomableness which makes man godlike, and love toward him infinite." Indeed this "heavenly unfathomableness" was a strong characteristic of his nature, and the gracious silence in which he often dwelt gave a rare sense of song without words. Therefore, perhaps on that day when we gathered around the form through which his voice was never again to utter itself, and heard his own words upon the air, saying: "Weep not, my friends! rather rejoice with me; I shall not feel the pain, but shall be gone, and you will have another friend in heaven," — it was impossible not to believe that he was with us still, the central spirit, comforting and uplifting the circle of those who were most dear to him.

CHAPTER XX.

OTHER REMINISCENCES.

In Chapter IV. is given an account of the Dante Club by Mr. C. E. Norton. The following sketch of a single evening, in the winter of 1867, will interest the reader:[1] —

The final revision of the proof-sheets was then going on, and the Wednesday evenings were devoted to the last "cabinet councils" on them before they were dismissed for publication. To my delight, the next day brought me a pleasant invitation from Longfellow to accompany Professor Lowell to the Dante gathering that evening, and to attend these meetings as long as I remained at Cambridge. It was of course accepted; and in the evening we walked through the snow to the well-known Longfellow home, and were met at the door by the poet himself, who had from the window seen us approaching. It is hardly necessary to repeat the description of Longfellow's appearance, and his kindly courtesy of manner, which has become familiar to every one. He was then approaching his sixtieth birthday; but his white hair and beard gave him a patriarchal appearance more in keeping with twenty years' greater age. That was, however, the only sign of advanced years. His complexion was fresh, his eyes softly

[1] This sketch, by Mr. J. H. A. Bone, of Cleveland, Ohio, is copied from the Life by Mr. Austin.

bright, and his manner so courteous and winning that the question of real or apparent age was at once forgotten. The visitor felt himself at ease immediately, as if he had always belonged to the inner circle of the poet's friends; and the secret of the strong affection felt toward Longfellow by his literary neighbors — and some might think rivals — was explained.

After a few minutes' pleasant conversation in the poet's well-appointed study, James T. Fields, the poet's publisher, who was also a poet-publisher, walked briskly up the snowy path from the old-fashioned gateway, and was warmly greeted. William D. Howells, then assistant-editor of the Atlantic Monthly, and a great favorite with both the older Cambridge poets, quickly followed. There was a lively conversation for a short time, a remark concerning the unusual absence of Charles Eliot Norton, — "snowed in," some one suggested, — and then Longfellow, glancing at the clock, said, "School-time!" To each of the visitors was handed a copy of Dante in the original, with which to follow the translation as read from the printed sheets. I pleaded my insufficient acquaintance with the Italian; but the "schoolmaster" would not let me off thus. "All scholars must work," said Longfellow; and he handed me a volume containing a prose literal translation, with the injunction that any marked difference in the rendering of a word or construing the sense of a passage must be noted, if a doubt as to its propriety arose. Then all settled down to close study.

As a preliminary, Longfellow took from a drawer the sheets which had been passed upon at the previous meeting, and on which he had noted the suggestions, objections, and doubts of the "scholars" made at that time. These had all been carefully considered, some amendments accepted, others rejected, and the doubtful passages thoroughly examined. Where the translator still preferred his own rendering to that suggested by his critics, he gave his reasons. This done, the sheets were replaced, the new set taken up, and the poet began reading the lines slowly, and at the same time watchful of any indication of dissent or doubt on the part of his hearers.

The reading commenced with Canto XIII. of the *Inferno,* where Dante and his guide enter the marvellous wood:—

> "Not foliage green, but of a dusky color,
> Not branches smooth, but gnarled and intertangled,
> Not apple-trees were there, but thorns with poison."

The reading continued without interruption until the thirtieth line was reached:—

> "Therefore the Master said, 'If thou break off
> Some little spray from any of those trees,
> The thoughts thou hast will wholly be made vain.'"

Longfellow appeared to be not quite satisfied with his rendering, and invited suggestions of improvement; but these were hesitatingly given. All the suggested emendations were noted for after-consideration, and the reading continued. Sometimes one of the listeners checked the reader to interpose a question or a doubt; at other times the poet himself stopped to explain the reason for his selection of a word. In either case discussion generally followed, authorities were examined and cited; and after all the information obtainable had been brought out and the net result noted on the margin of the proof, the reading was resumed.

One stop was at the incident of the shades of the unfortunate Lano of Siena and Jacopo of Sant' Andrea rushing through the ghastly wood, chased by "black she-mastiffs, ravenous, and swift of foot as greyhounds who are issuing from the chain;" the ghosts—

"Naked and scratched, fleeing so furiously
That of the forest every fan they broke.
He who was in the advance, 'Now help, Death, help!'"

A question was raised as to the exact meaning in that connection of *accorri*. Dante says the foremost of the fleeing shapes cried, "*Ora accorri, accorri, morte.*" Cary, with some other translators, renders the word in its sense of haste:—

"'Haste now,' the foremost cried, 'now haste thee, Death!'"

After some discussion Longfellow's choice of meaning was approved, and the line retained without change. The fourteenth canto was read with fewer interruptions. One of these was at the passage describing the rain of fire upon the naked spirits stretched or crouched upon the burning sand:—

"Thus was descending the eternal heat,
Whereby the sand was set on fire, like tinder
Beneath the steel, for doubling of the dole."

One of the listeners looked up quickly, as if to offer a remark; but immediately returned to the open book. Longfellow noticed the movement, and interpreted its meaning. "I prefer 'dole' to 'suffering,' 'sorrow,' or 'sadness,'" he said, "because it is more poetic in this place, as well as better expressing the exact shade of meaning. A poet's license might well be pleaded for such a word," he added with a smile, "although our friends the dictionary-makers mark it as obsolete."

"Tennyson uses the word," I ventured to remark.

"Tennyson restores to literature many words that are under the ban of the dictionary-makers as obsolete," said Fields; "and the use to which he puts them justifies the act." . . .

"'Dole,' in the sense of pain, mental suffering, sadness, or sorrow," remarked Lowell, "was a frequently used and expressive word in the hands of Chaucer and Spenser and their contemporaries, and did not disappear until after Shakespeare's time. The dramatist Ford used 'dolent,' in the sense of sad and sorrowful, in his play of Perkin Warbeck, where the 'passionate duke,' after a mishap, is spoken of as 'effeminately dolent.'"

At the end of the fourteenth canto Longfellow dropped the last sheet into an open drawer, and rising, with a light laugh said, "Now, gentlemen, school is over, and we will have some refreshment after our labors." The books were closed, and the "scholars" adjourned to the dining-room, where a supper, charmingly served, was in waiting. One or two other guests joined the circle; and for about an hour there was a lively interchange of pleasant chat, piquant remarks, and gossipy anecdotes. The host of the evening was not talkative, but was attentive to every one, and had the tact to keep the conversation lively and general. Mr. Fields had brought some interesting bits of publishers' gossip out from Boston with him, which afforded material for comment and pleasant raillery. . . .

Before the repast was ended, one of Longfellow's sons came in,—a slim young fellow, full of boyish vivacity and ready talk. It was pleasant to note the attention paid by the father to his account of what he had been doing and how he had enjoyed himself during the visit from which he had just returned, and the interest manifested by questions he put to draw the young man out.

All pleasures come to an end at some time. The guests rose, prepared themselves for the wintry night air; and after a warm hand-clasp, and cordial invitation to repeat the evening's experience, each took his homeward way. . . .

Three or four months later, the first volume of 'The Divine Comedy,' containing the *Inferno*, was published, and I prepared a review of it. A marked copy was sent to the publishers, as customary. Very soon after, I was both surprised and gratified by the receipt of the following letter: —

CAMBRIDGE, May 14, 1867.

MY DEAR SIR, — I have had the pleasure of receiving the Cleveland Herald containing your most friendly and sympathetic notice of my translation of the Divine Comedy, and I hasten to thank you for your great kindness.

The notice is excellent, bringing forward just the points I should wish to have touched upon. It is positive and not negative; and will not fail to do the work much good.

It is difficult to thank one for praise; so let me thank you rather for telling your readers what I have tried to do, and how far, in your opinion, I have succeeded.

Our pleasant Wednesday evenings are now ended, for the present at least; but I hope in the autumn, on some pretext or other, we shall begin again; and that we may once more have the pleasure of seeing you among us.

Lowell is well; and we are urging him to take up the Canzoni, which I really hope he will do.

In 1882 a lady wrote to Mr. Longfellow, sending him a sketch which Thackeray had drawn one morning in 1856 in her father's library. It was on the cover of a number of Putnam's Magazine, which was adorned, as the readers of that day will recall, with two tall palm-trees extending from the bottom to the top of the page. On the upper part of this cover was a lunette, drawn with pen and ink, of a negro hoeing in a cotton field, and under it was the legend: "Am I not a man and a brother?" On the lower part of the page a similar lunette showed a Turk sitting cross-legged, smoking a narghile. On the border of the cover was sketched a tremendously elongated man, about as tall as the palm-tree by which he stood, ogling a tiny bird drawn on one of its branches. Under this figure Thackeray had written "Longfellow," — a pun fresher in 1856 than now.

A writer in the Washington Post gives this account of a visit to the poet: [1]—

Provided with a letter of introduction, I entered the gate of the grounds, which is ever hospitably open; and standing on the piazza was the gray-haired poet himself. He advanced, and saluted his visitor with a gracious courtesy that would have put the most timid at their ease and kept the most presumptuous in check. He has [a native] kindliness and a beautiful simplicity in manner, — that which the French have aptly called the "politeness of the heart," —

> "His eyes diffuse a venerable grace,
> And charity itself was in his face."

. . . A young enthusiast exclaimed, after seeing him, "All the vulgar and pretentious people in the world ought to be sent to see Mr. Longfellow, to learn how to behave." He led the way to his study, a sunny corner room, and wheeling up a comfortable chair for his visitor, seated himself in his own especial chair.

"Now," said he in the kindest voice, "tell me what you have written."

He listened with an admirable attention to the story, old but always interesting to a veteran, of the struggles of a literary beginner. Then he said impressively, "Always write your best," — repeating it, with his hand

[1] I have drawn this and the two passages which follow from Mr. W. S. Kennedy's biography.

upraised — "remember, *your best.* Keep a scrap-book, and put in it everything you write. It will be of great service to you."

He spoke of Thackeray with admiration; "he was so great, so honest a writer." In speaking of the saints whom the Roman Catholics revere, he said: "I too have a favorite saint, — St. Francis of Assisi." . . .

He agreed with his visitor in a dislike for the modern verse that makes sense subservient to sound, and turns poetry into an elaborate arrangement of ornate phrases. In response to a quotation on the question, from Macaulay, to the effect that literary style should not only be so clear that it can be understood, but so clear that it cannot be misunderstood, he said: "I like simplicity in all things, but above all in poetry."

He spoke with strong aversion of the crude skepticism of the day, explaining, however, that the term "skeptic" was habitually misapplied, as it means not necessarily an unbeliever, but a seeker after truth. I remarked that the first order of mind was not skeptical, — Shakespeare, Dante, Milton, Bacon, Pascal, as compared with minds of the calibre of Voltaire and Gibbon; following with a quotation of Thackeray's noble lines: "O awful, awful Name of God! Light unbearable! Mystery unfathomable! Vastness immeasurable! O Name that God's people did fear to utter! O Light that God's prophet would have perished had he seen! who are they who now are so familiar with it?" He seemed much struck. "That," he said, "is a very grand sentence."

He took down two magnificent volumes of Dante. "This is my latest present," said he. I opened one, and exclaimed: "Why, this is Dutch!" "Yes, it is Dutch," said Mr. Longfellow, smiling; "and do you know there is no language in the world in which Dante can be so successfully translated as Dutch, owing to the formation of the participle?" And he gave a short explanation of the differences and difficulties of translating Dante into English verse.

A correspondent of the Chicago Times wrote thus of his visit: —

My thoughts revert to a bright day in last September, when, with a friend, I passed the morning and the greater part of the afternoon in Longfellow's home with the poet and his daughters. Over the door of the old-fashioned and very interesting house hung the American flag, half furled, and draped in mourning for President Garfield, who had died but two days before. I lifted the brass knocker with nervousness, thinking of the many distinguished people who had sought admittance there; and at once it was answered by a neat maid-servant, who ushered us into the quaint old drawing-room, the walls of which were hung with light-colored paper with vines of roses trailing over it, — a style of many years ago. We had no time for further observation; for almost immediately Mr. Longfellow came in, greeting us most kindly, saying, "Come into my room, where we shall be more at ease; I cannot make strangers of you!" How gladly we followed him, but without a word of reply; for, to acknowledge the truth, my heart at least was beating too painfully with the realization that I was in the presence of the poet beloved from my childhood. In person he was smaller than I had fancied him, — only of medium height; but his face, made familiar by his portraits, seemed that of an old friend. His silvery hair was carelessly thrown back from his forehead, the full beard and mustache partially concealed the pleasant mouth; but his mild blue eyes expressed the kindliness of his heart and his quick reading of the hearts of others. He wore a Prince Albert coat of very dark brown cloth, with trousers of a much lighter shade, and a dark-blue necktie. In his study we sat some hours, listening to his low, musical voice as he talked on many interesting topics, and read aloud to us from his beautiful 'Evangeline,' and selections from other poets. . . . In everything he read he found some new beauty, and spoke of it with almost boyish pleasure. We listened with delight to all; then he said: "You will tire of me and my nonsense. Come and meet my daughters. I shall not let you go; you must drink a cup of tea with us." Then we were led into the large, cheerful dining-room, where was spread a delicious luncheon. Miss Alice presided; Miss Annie being engaged in superintending the meal laid on a tiny table out on the broad porch, where two little children were being made happy. Mr. Longfellow was called, and we followed, to look upon the pretty scene; and when the children saw him they dropped their "goodies" and ran to climb up and receive his kiss and beg him to play with them. Then we gathered around the table, the copper kettle singing merrily; and Mr. Longfellow made the tea with his own hands, and poured it from the antique silver teapot for our enjoyment. While many dishes were offered us, the poet took simply his tea and Graham biscuit. There was no ostentatious ceremony, but all was served with quiet ease, as if only the family circle were gathered there. After lunch Mr. Longfellow led us through the house, pointing out his favorite pictures and treasures, relating interesting incidents as we passed from room to room. . . . Then we nestled upon the broad east porch, while the poet smoked a cigarette and chatted the while of many books and authors. . . . When the hour arrived for our departure, the venerable poet walked with us to the gate; and under the beautiful lilac hedge which surrounds the place we said good-by.

A neighbor of Mr. Longfellow wrote to the New York Independent as follows: —

The poet was never more attractive than in unexpected interviews with absolute strangers. He received them with gentle courtesy, glided readily into common topics, but carefully warded off all complimentary references to his works. This was his invariable custom in general conversation. I was present when a distinguished party from Canada was introduced, and remember, when a charming lady of the party gracefully repeated a message of high compliment from the Princess Louise, how courteously he received it, and how instantly he turned the conversation in another direction. I remember, at another of these introductions, a stranger lady distrustfully asked Mr. Longfellow for his autograph. He assured her by at once assenting, while he remarked: "I know some persons object to giving their autographs; but if so little a thing will give pleasure, how can one refuse?"

Mr. Longfellow often amused his friends with humorous accounts of some of these visits. I recall his account of one which seemed to delight him hugely. An English gentleman thus abruptly introduced himself without letters: "In other countries, you know, we go to see ruins and the like; but you have no ruins in your country, and I thought," growing embarrassed, "I thought I would call and see *you*." . . .

I recollect his telling me that the Duke of Argyll, a persistent ornithologist, troubled him considerably by asking him names of birds whose notes they heard while sitting on his veranda. Mr. Longfellow was no naturalist; he did not know our birds specifically, and flowers are sometimes found blooming at extraordinary seasons in his poetry. He remarked to me once upon the flaming splendor of the *Cydonia Japonica* (red-flowering quince), and asked the name of that familiar shrub, saying, "I know nothing about flowers." Yet he saw in Nature what no mere naturalist could ever hope to see.

Another says: —

I was in his library last fall with a young girl from California. She had been the wide world over, but stood shy and silent in his presence, moved to tears by his kindly welcome. It was touching to see the poet's appreciation of this, and his quick glance over his table that he might find something to interest her and make her forget her embarrassment. Taking up a little box covered with glass, he put it into her hand, and said: "This is a mournful thing to put into the hands of a bright girl; but think of it! six hundred years ago the bit of wood in that box touched Dante's bones;" and he related how this piece of Dante's coffin had come into his possession. He led her to his piano, and asked her to play for him. He told her anecdotes of Coleridge and Moore as he showed her their inkstands. . . . Soon his young visitor was chatting with him as freely as if she had not entered his door with a timidity amounting almost to fear. After that he turned to us. I hope he understood how this act had been silently appreciated by us; yet I think he was all-unconscious of the picture he created, — a picture never to be forgotten by those of us who witnessed it.

A young man writes: —

I remember my visit to Mr. Longfellow in 1881 as well as if it were an event of yesterday. Having received a box of oranges from a young lady in Florida (for whom I had, through Mr. Owen, obtained an autograph of the poet), I carried a basket of them to Cambridge as a sort of thank-offering. Many a time I had paused in front of the old house on Brattle Street and longed to enter and tell what pleasure and comfort I had found in reading the poems that had been written there. My brother and I stood in awe as we waited on the doorstep for somebody to answer our timid summons. The maid who came said that Mr. Longfellow was in, and ushered us into his presence. This embarrassed us, for we felt that he should first have been asked whether he could spare even a moment to see us. It seemed hardly possible that I was actually in the company of the poet at last, where I had so often wished I might be for a moment.

Our errand was soon stated, and Mr. Longfellow appeared much pleased to accept our gift. "This basket is so pretty that I must not deprive you of it," he said; and he rang for a maid to empty it of the fruit. And then he talked to us about Florida, and about the pleasure of visiting new scenes; talked about schools, "the old clock," and other matters. We probably stayed only ten minutes; yet it seemed a long time to us, for Mr. Longfellow spoke so pleasantly on every subject on which we touched. As we left the house he picked up the Transcript from the doorstep, and I went away, hoping that some little paragraph which I had written might interest him for a moment in the evening.

I suppose everybody has his idols. In a humble way I had long worshipped Mr. Longfellow, and it gratified me beyond expression to find him as I had pictured him, — the ideal of a kind, sympathetic, noble man. "I can never forget that call," said I to my brother as we walked down the street with light hearts; "it is the most memorable in my life." And my brother echoed the sentiment. To have been in the poet's study, to have seen him and heard his voice, made us completely happy.

A few months later, a quantity of fresh jasmine buds came to me from Mandarin; and as they had been gathered near Mrs. Stowe's house, it seemed to me that they might please Mr. Longfellow, they having retained much of their fragrance and something of their beauty. And so I sent some of them to him; and to my surprise and joy I received an acknowledgment in his own handwriting.

Mr. F. H. Underwood, in a recent number of Good Words, writes thus:—

His work was done in morning hours. Doubtless, he had his bright and his dull days, but he never gave way to idleness or ennui. When the inspiration came he covered a large space with verses; but he had the power to go back, and to forge anew or retouch before the fire had cooled. His methods were careful to the last degree; poems were kept and considered a long time, line by line; and he sometimes had them set up in type for better scrutiny. They were left so perhaps for months, and when they appeared it was after rigorous criticism had been exhausted.

He was not without business knowledge and tact, but he spent his income generously, and much of it in secret charity. I knew of an instance when an author, in no way intimate with him, was ill and destitute, and was about to sell his library; and greatly to his surprise, he received one day Longfellow's cheque for five hundred dollars. He was continually doing such acts of kindness.

His shrewdness and humor sometimes took the same road. When 'Hiawatha' appeared, it was sharply attacked in certain newspapers, and Fields, his publisher, after reading something particularly savage, went out in a state of excitement to see Longfellow. The poet heard the account, and then in a casual way said, "By the way, Mr. Fields, how is the book selling?" "Enormously; we are running presses night and day to fill the orders." "Very well," said Longfellow quietly, "then don't you think we had better let these critics go on advertising it?"

At a social gathering a poem recently published was picked to pieces amid shouts of laughter, in which it was observed Longfellow did not join. A few minutes later, taking up the despised poem and selecting here and there a good line or phrase, like one looking for flowers rather than nettles, he said, "After all, young gentlemen, the man who has thought these beautiful things cannot be wholly ridiculous!"

On festive occasions he was only shyly, delicately humorous, and rarely attempted an epigrammatic sally, still less to take part in a passage-at-arms; but his enjoyment of the gay skirmishes between others was evident. His voice, countenance, and manner conveyed one harmonious impression. His gray-blue eyes were tender rather than sad, and they were sometimes lighted by sweet smiles. His dignified bearing made him appear tall, though he was not above the medium height. A Frenchman who had visited him described him as being six feet. His simple and beautiful courtesy made every caller think himself a friend. In no ignoble sense, there was something caressing in his address.

Mr. Moncure Conway recalls these incidents:

On one occasion he met an English friend in Boston on the street. It was just after the return of a fugitive slave. While the two were conversing, a policeman came up and told the Englishman, who had a cigar, that smoking was not allowed in the street. "This policeman is right," said Longfellow; "Boston sends men into slavery, but allows no smoking in the street."

Once when some politician had made a speech in which he identified the *honor* of America with some national injustice, Longfellow said it reminded him of Gil Blas saying to the horse-dealer "that he would trust to his honesty." The horse-dealer replied, "When you appeal to my honesty, you touch my weak point."

Agassiz one day began half playfully trying to persuade Longfellow to write a poem on the great revelations of science concerning the earth. He grew eloquent depicting the successive periods of primeval rock, vast forests of fern, strange, huge creatures, etc. "There ought to be an epic written about it," cried Agassiz. Longfellow said he had no doubt there ought to be, and might be; but he was not the man to do it.

A lady relates that, passing one day a jeweller's window in New York, her attention was arrested by hearing from a crowd gathered before it a voice in unmistakable brogue saying, "Shure, and that 's for Hiawatha." The speaker was a ragged Irish laborer, unshaven and unshorn. She looked, and saw a silver boat with the figure of an Indian standing in the prow. "That must be," continued the speaker, "for a prisintation to the poet Longfellow; thim two lines cut on the side of the boat is from his poethry." "That is fame," said the friend to whom she told the story.

The two following simple incidents, occurring, one in the English, and the other in the American,

Cambridge, thrown by their observers into verse, may close this chapter: —

We plunged this morning into country lanes,
Talking and walking at our ease along,
When suddenly a distant sound of song
Stole down the hedgerow to us. No, no wains
With reapers chanting over harvest gains,
For this is Christmas. Then the sound grew strong,
And presently a rosy-cheeked child-throng
Tripped round the road-bend, shrilling rhymèd strains; —
A dozen cottage children, brown as birds,
With wild high voices and a fund of glee,
Their whole hearts in their singing, and their words
Thine own, gray poet! come from over sea.
We thought it would have made you very glad
If you had met the little choir we had.

I saw a boy beside a poet's gate
Coaxing from wheezy pipes a doleful strain,
And seeming some kind answer to await:
"Ah, boy!" I said, "your discord is in vain."

I saw a poet a window open wide,
And smile, and toss down pennies to the boy;
The great sun pushed the April clouds aside,
A tiny bird looked up and sang for joy.

Poet of all time! Beggar of to-day!
For me, unseen, this benison you leave, —
In God's great world there is no lonely way;
Humblest and highest may give and may receive.[1]

[1] It was on one such occasion that he said to his companion, "I always like to pay the musicians; they have to work hard." And smiling, added, "Did you ever carry a burden on your back?"

CHAPTER XXI.

THE STUDY AT CRAIGIE HOUSE.[1]

I PASSED an hour or two lately within the familiar walls of Longfellow's study. The room is on the ground floor at the right of the entrance. It is large and square, and the walls on three sides are covered above the white wainscot with paper of a soft brown tint. The fourth side is wainscoted to the ceiling in the "colonial" style, and in the spacious panel above the fireplace is a fine old round convex mirror with two sconces, reflecting in miniature all the interior and much even of what lies without beyond the dark-red curtains that shade the deep windows. Through these one looks across the open field and the meadows where winds, with an occasional gleam of flashing water, the Charles, the "Silent River" of the poet's song, to the long, low hills of Brighton and Brookline. It was this quiet view that met the poet's eye if he but turned his head while he wrote at the high desk which has always stood upon the table near the corner front window. Here many of the familiar lines were first put upon paper, many letters written, and a considerable part of the translation of Dante. On this desk stands a plaster statuette of Goethe, representing him in a long great-coat, with his hands folded behind him. Near by, on the seat in the window, is a plain little wicker basket that was once Thomas Moore's waste-paper basket; and

[1] By W. M. Fullerton, reprinted, with revision, from the Boston Sunday Record.

close at hand in the corner ticks the tall old-fashioned Willard clock. In the other front window stands an orange-tree, guarded by a bronze stork. Between the two windows is a carved oaken bookcase of antique style, surmounted by a bust of Shakespeare, and containing perhaps a hundred books. These are the earliest and latest editions of Mr. Longfellow's works, with some others; and, in thirty bound volumes, all Mr. Longfellow's manuscripts just as they came back from the printer. Over these one might spend hours tracing the development of the poet's thought in his additions, corrections, and erasures. One that I took up at random contained the review of Hawthorne's first book, Twice-Told Tales, and is written, with few corrections, in that easy, flowing back-hand which was characteristic of the poet during almost his entire life.

There are four other bookcases in the study, of the same massive style, besides the shelves that fill the recess of a window on the left-hand side of the room and contain, for the most part, the English poets and dramatists. Two of the bookcases stand on either side of the door as one enters from the hall, and two are at the back of the room, with the fireplace and the round mirror between them. They all contain fine editions of familiar authors in handsome bindings, but do not afford, either in number or character, more than a suggestion of the large and valuable collection of books which the house contains from bottom to top, and in almost every room.

In the study itself there are several extremely interesting first editions and authors' copies which the bibliophile would delight in. Here, for example, is the first edition of "Poems by Mr. Gray," the rare 1832 edition of Tennyson's poems, and the slender volume in board covers of "Poems by William Cullen Bryant," printed in 1821 at Cambridge, and containing in its forty-four pages so much that is really best in Bryant's work, — the lines 'To a Waterfowl,' the 'Inscription for the Entrance into a Wood,' 'Green River,' and 'Thanatopsis.' Here, also, is the first edition of Coleridge's "Sibylline Leaves," with many manuscript notes by himself and by his nephew. This volume contains the fine poem 'America to Great Britain,' with this note in Coleridge's hand: "By Washington Allston, a Painter born to renew the fifteenth century."

In the bookcase at the left of the door as one enters from the hall stand the three handsome octavos of the Works of Chatterton, — the first fine book which the poet owned. They represented the recompense of a year's writing of verse while he was a student at Bowdoin. A small ante-room, in the left-hand corner opposite the door, holds a notable collection of splendid vellum-bound folios of the Italian poets, some of them in the superb Bodoni type. Here also are the three great volumes of Lord Vernon's famous critical edition of Dante's *Inferno*, with its abundant illustrations, and the Dutch translation of the *Divina Commedia* in two large volumes. A bookcase in this ante-room is filled with various editions of Mr. Longfellow's works, including over thirty translations in different languages.

On the right of the fireplace is the well-known chair given to the poet by the children of Cambridge; and opposite, across the rug in front of the fire, is the deep arm-chair in which, without eyes, in the evening, much of 'Evangeline' was written in pencil, in an almost illegible hand, to be copied out next morning. This chair was a favorite seat of Charles Sumner also, to whose length of limb its depth was well fitted. In the bookcase in front of which it stands are the Works of Sumner in fifteen volumes, and his Life; above hangs his portrait in crayon. This is one of five portraits drawn in 1846 by Eastman Johnson, at the beginning of his career, at Mr. Longfellow's request. The thoughtful refined face of Sumner gazes pensively down upon the chair at the centre-table, where his friend most often sat. Opposite, over a bookcase in which is a photograph of the Severn portrait of Keats, hangs the picture of Emerson's clearly cut features, with the sweet smile about the mouth. Beyond, on the side wall, is the face of Hawthorne, — not so successfully portrayed, perhaps, as the rest, but still looking much as he must have looked as a young author, with the high, broad forehead, the mass of hair, and the great, open eyes. Then, on the same wall, beyond the books and the window near to the corner, comes the portrait of Felton, with a happy and scholarly expression, — the very face of him whom Dickens called "heartiest of Greek professors." Longfellow's own portrait is at the right of the door leading into the hall, near the orange-tree. These fine crayons are most interesting, from the fact that they show the faces of all in their earlier manhood. Sumner seems to have changed most of all, in the conflict of the bravely fought battle of his life. A portrait of Longfellow in oils, by his son Ernest, stands upon an easel in one corner.

On the eastern wall, high up on a bracket at the top of an ancient mirror, is a statuette of Dante. Below is an old-fashioned table, on which stands Crawford's bust of the poet's life-long friend, George W. Greene. The lower part of it is hidden by a small Italian casket, which contains some fragments of the coffin of Dante in a little glass box, and a minute edition of the *Divina Commedia.* Seen through the window at the right, is the spacious veranda, where the poet speaks often, in his journal, of walking. On the round table in the centre of the room, among the books and pamphlets, is the inkstand that once belonged to Coleridge, beside that of Thomas Moore and Longfellow's own; and by the side of the last are four or five quill pens — he used no other kind — that once were eloquent with song.

Here, then, is the room sacred to the Muses almost above all others on American soil. Here may be breathed the "still air of delightful studies." The favorite motto of the poet, *Non clamor, sed amor,* seems to be the burden of every tick of the clock. Time lingers within these walls as it does along the ridges of the hills in an August afternoon, and every suggestion is one of restfulness and peace. And in this quiet it may be fitting to read, from this white-covered volume on the table, Austin Dobson's tribute to

HENRY WADSWORTH LONGFELLOW.

Nec turpem senectam
Degere, nec cithara carentem.[1]
HORACE.

"Not to be tuneless in old age!"
Ah! surely blest his pilgrimage
Who, in his Winter's snow,
Still sings, with note as sweet and clear
As in the morning of the year
When the first violets blow!

Blest! — but more blest whom Summer's heat,
Whom Spring's impulsive stir and beat,
Have taught no feverish lure;
Whose Muse, benignant and serene,
Still keeps his Autumn chaplet green
Because his verse is pure.

Lie calm, O white and laureate head!
Lie calm, O Dead, that art not dead,
Since from the voiceless grave
Thy voice shall speak to old and young
While song yet speaks an English tongue
By Charles' or Thamis' wave!

[1] This is the motto of Ultima Thule.

CHAPTER XXII.

TABLE-TALK.

Mr. Longfellow, like other writers, was in the habit of jotting down thoughts upon scraps of paper. Many of these he used in his books, as in Hyperion, and especially in Kavanagh, — where, indeed, he has given a page or two of them, as written by Mr. Churchill on the panels of the old pulpit in his study. Others are printed as "Table-Talk" in Drift-wood. A few of the unpublished ones have been given in the previous pages under the dates which were attached to them. Others are inserted here.

Too many enthusiasts think all is safe because they head right, — not mindful that the surest way of reaching port is by following the channel, and not by going straight across the sandbanks and the breakers.

He who carries his bricks to the building of every one's house, will never build one for himself.

When looking for anything lost, begin by looking where you think it is not.

Many critics are like woodpeckers, who, instead of enjoying the fruit and shadow of a tree, hop incessantly around the trunk, pecking holes in the bark to discover some little worm or other.

All authors have some very judicious friends, who are fearful they will get more than their due; and when they see the measure of applause heaped and running over, dexterously sweep it down to a level.

There are conversations which make us suddenly old, or rather, by which we discover ourselves to have moved onward, far onward. Where we played in sunshine, we sit in shadow. There are revelations made in moments of intimacy which show us how great the changes of life are, — flashes of lightning revealing to careless travellers the precipice upon whose brink they stand.

Velocity and weight make the momentum of mind as well as of matter. Velocity without weight is a melancholy condition of the human brain.

Sometimes a single felicitous expression or line in a poem saves it from oblivion. There are other poems in which no individual lines or passages predominate. Like Wagner's music, they are equally sustained throughout, and depend for their effect upon their impression as a whole, and not on particular parts. Which of these kinds is the better is a question that should neither be asked nor answered. Each is good in its way. We should be thankful for both.

Perseverance is a great element of success. If you only knock long enough and loud enough at the gate, you are sure to wake up somebody.

There are but few thinkers in the world, but a great many people who think they think.

A great part of the happiness of life consists not in fighting battles, but in avoiding them. A masterly retreat is in itself a victory.

A young critic is like a boy with a gun; he fires at every living thing he sees. He thinks only of his own skill, not of the pain he is giving.

Amusements are like specie-payments. We do not much care for them, if we know that we can have them; but we like to know they may be had.

In old age our bodies are worn-out instruments, on which the soul tries in vain to play the melodies of youth. But because the instrument has lost its strings, or is out of tune, it does not follow that the musician has lost his skill.

Truths that startled the generation in which they were first announced become in the next age the commonplaces of conversation; as the famous airs of operas which thrilled the first audiences come to be played on hand-organs in the streets.

In the intellectual world, as in the physical, the rays that give light are not those that give heat.

Our "friends" are oftener those who seek us, than those whom we seek.

Love makes its record upon our hearts in deeper and deeper colors as we grow out of childhood into manhood; as the Emperors signed their names in green ink when under age, but when of age, in purple.

Shall there be no repose in literature? Shall every author be like a gladiator with swollen veins and distended nostrils, as if each encounter was for life or death?

The spring came suddenly, bursting upon the world as a child bursts into a room, with a laugh and a shout and hands full of flowers.

The years come when the mind, like an old mill, ceases to grind; when weeds grow on the wall; and through every crack and leak in dam and sluice, spouts the useless water.

Do the white marbles in churchyards mean that the day of death has been marked by a white stone?

So innate and strong is the love of liberty in all human hearts that, even against our better judgment, we instinctively sympathize with criminals escaping from prison.

The utility of many useful things is not at first very manifest, — as poetry, for instance. Yet its uses are as many and as sweet as those of adversity. When the first kettle boiled, who imagined the manifold uses of steam?

There are people in the world whom we like well enough when we are with them, but whom we never miss when they are gone. There are others whose absence is a positive pain. There are people whose society we enjoy for an hour, and never care to see again; others who cannot come too often, nor stay too long.

The happy should not insist too much upon their happiness in the presence of the unhappy.

After all definitions and descriptions, there remains in every book a certain something which defies analysis, and is to it what expression is to the human face, — the best part of it, which cannot be given by words.

Ferber, in his Travels through Italy, has observed that "the stones employed in buildings, decorations, and pavings are hints of the nature of the neighboring hills and quarries." So an author's style, language, and illustrations are hints of his surroundings, his favorite pursuits and studies.

Every man is in some sort a failure to himself. No one ever reaches the heights to which he aspires.

In childhood all unaccustomed things fascinate us; but there comes a period in our lives when the unusual is disagreeable and burdensome.

The imagination walks bravest, not in clouds, but on the firm green earth. It conquers worlds by the sinewy arms of thoughts that have been trained by sage reason and common-sense, — as Alexander conquered Asia with troops which his father Philip had disciplined.

Every village has its great man, who represents nobility, who walks down the village street with a cane, and stands very erect as the stage-coach or the train passes, and thinks the passengers are all looking at him and saying to themselves, "Who can that remarkable-looking man be? Surely there must be good society in this place!"

Nothing is more dangerous to an author than sudden success. The patience of genius is one of its most precious attributes.

"It is not enough to be a great man," says the French proverb, "but you must come at the right time." This is particularly true of authors.

Every author has the whole past to contend with; all the centuries are upon him. He is compared with Homer, Dante, Shakespeare, Milton.

Fame grows like a tree if it have the principle of growth in it; the accumulated dews of ages freshen its leaves.

It is a great mystery to many people that an author should reveal to the public secrets that he shrinks from telling to his most intimate friends.

Youth wrenches the sceptre from old age, and sets the crown on its own head before it is entitled to it.

Signs of old age are,—a tendency to cross your hands on the top of a cane; a tendency to pick up pins from the carpet; a tendency in your hat to come down on the back of your head; a disposition to sit still. When a young man sees a mountain he says: "Let us climb it." The old man says: "Let us stay down here."

A disposition to wear old clothes is one of the signs of old age.

Old men should not climb ladders, even in their libraries. The Marques de Morante, a famous book-collector of Spain, was killed by a fall from a ladder in his library.

The sentence of the first murderer was pronounced by the Supreme Judge of the universe. Was it death? No, it was life. "A fugitive and a vagabond shalt thou be in the earth;" and "Whosoever slayeth Cain, vengeance shall be taken on him sevenfold."

Some sorrows are but footprints in the snow, which the genial sun effaces, or, if it does not wholly efface, changes into dimples.

More and more do I feel, as I advance in life, how little we really know of each other. Friendship seems to me like the touch of musical-glasses,—it is only contact; but the glasses themselves, and their contents, remain quite distinct and unmingled.

If a woman shows too often the Medusa's head, she must not be astonished if her lover is turned into stone.

Unmarried men are not columns, only pilasters, or half-columns.

As oaks shoot up where pine-woods have been burned, so great resolves spring up when youthful passions have burned out, or where the ceasing of overshadowing cares lets in the sunshine upon the buried seed.

How sudden and sweet are the visitations of our happiest thoughts; what delightful surprises! In the midst of life's most trivial occupations, — as we are reading a newspaper, or lighting our bed-candle, or waiting for our horses to drive round, — the lovely face appears; and thoughts more precious than gold are whispered in our ear.

Some poets ought to be punished by the laws of the land for the contamination of their verses, — as Pheres, son of Medea, was stoned to death by the Corinthians for giving poisonous clothes to Creon's daughter.

Those poets who make vice beautiful with the beauty of their song are like the Byzantine artists who painted the Devil with a nimbus.

Each day is a branch of the Tree of Life laden heavily with fruit. If we lie down lazily beneath it, we may starve; but if we shake the branches, some of the fruit will fall for us.

When an author is entering the dreary confines of old age, and the critics begin to cry, "Go up, bald head!" it is not strange that he should want to let the bears loose upon them.

The highest exercise of imagination is not to devise what has no existence, but rather to perceive what really exists, though unseen by the outward eye, — not creation, but insight.

Genius is all-embracing. When at full speed on its winged courser, like the wild Arab, it stoops to pick up a pebble.

Style is the gait of the mind, and is as much a part of a man as his bodily gait is.

Silence is a great peacemaker.

Some poems are like the Centaurs, — a mingling of man and beast, and begotten of Ixion on a cloud.

The difference between a man of genius seen in his works and in person, is like that of a lighthouse seen by night and by day, — in the one case only a great fiery brain, in the other only a white tower.

There are no critics who resemble the old Florentine judge, Lotto degli Agli; for he hung himself in despair for having pronounced an unjust sentence.

"Be it known to each one," says Dante in his *Convito*, i. 7, "that nothing harmonized by a musical bond can be transferred from its native language into another without breaking all its sweetness and harmony." Of the same opinion was Cervantes, when he makes the Curate say of the Spanish translator of Ariosto: "He took from him much of his natural value; and all will do the like who endeavor to translate books of verse into another language: for however great the care taken and the ability displayed, they will never reach the point they have in their first birth." — *Don Quixote*, i. 6.

The difficulty of translation lies chiefly in the *color* of words. Is the Italian "ruscelletto gorgoglioso" fully rendered by "gurgling brooklet"? Or the Spanish "pájaros vocingleros" by "garrulous birds"? Something seems wanting. Perhaps it is only the fascination of foreign and unfamiliar sounds; and to the Italian or Spanish ear the English words may seem equally beautiful.

Translating the first line in the Divine Comedy is like making the first move in a game of chess; nearly every one does it in the same way.

The business of a translator is to report what his author says, not to explain what he means; that is the work of the commentator. What an author says and how he says it, — that is the problem of the translator.

We *know* that we are old before we *feel* it. The language of those around us betrays to us the secret. Life is a landscape without hedge or fence. We pass from one field to another, and see no boundary-line.

When I recall my juvenile poems and prose sketches, I wish sometimes that they were forgotten entirely. They however cling to one's skirts with a terrible grasp. They remind me of the "plusieurs enfants" in *M. de Pourceaugnac*, clinging to him in the street and crying, "Ah! mon papa! mon papa! mon papa!"

The breath of an audience is very apt to blow one's thoughts quite away, as a gust through an open window does the loose papers on a table.

How often it happens that after we know a man personally, we cease to read his writings. Is it that we exhaust him by a look? Is it that his personality gives us all of him that we desire?

A story or a poem should be neither too short nor too long; it should be enough to satisfy, but not enough to satiate. I have always aimed to have my books small.

A volume of poems ought never to be large. Real estate on Mount Parnassus should be sold by the foot, not by the acre.

There are many landscapes which fascinate us at first sight, and suggest a long stay, a lifelong sojourn; causing us to say, "It is good for us to be here; let us build."

I have always looked upon the writing of autobiography as a harmless occupation, and have never felt that it implied any excess of self-conceit in the writer. In the lives of most men there are many things which, if truthfully stated, partake of the nature of confessions, and tend rather to mortify than to flatter their self-conceit.

When we walk towards the sun of Truth, all shadows are cast behind us.

I have many opinions in Art and Literature which constantly recur to me in the tender guise of a sentiment. A clever dialectician can prove to me that I am wrong. I cannot answer him. I let the waves of argument roll on; but all the lilies rise again, and are beautiful as before.

Rather cheerless is the aspect of our early history. The stern old puritanical character rises above the common level of life; it has a breezy air about its summits, but they are bleak and forbidding.

In youth all doors open outward; in old age they all open inward.

The Americans are not thrifty, but spendthrifty.

A great sorrow, like a mariner's quadrant, brings the sun at noon down to the horizon, and we learn where we are on the sea of life.

Each new epoch of life seems an encounter. There is a tussle and a cloud of dust, and we come out of it triumphant or crest-fallen, according as we have borne ourselves.

The mission of some people on earth is not that of the sunshine, but of the twilight,—the twilight, with its reveries, its reflections, its ghosts.

What discord should we bring into the universe if our prayers were all answered! Then *we* should govern the world, and not God. And do you think we should govern it better? It gives me only pain when I hear the long, wearisome petitions of men asking for they know not what. As frightened women clutch at the reins when there is danger, so do we grasp at God's government with our prayers. Thanksgiving with a full heart,—and the rest silence and submission to the Divine will!

CHAPTER XXIII.

FRAGMENTS OF VERSE.

In this chapter are gathered some unpublished bits of verse and a few translations from the Greek Anthology, etc.

GREAT AND SMALL.

The Power that built the starry dome on high,
And groined the vaulted rafters of the sky,
Teaches the linnet with unconscious breast
To round the inverted heaven of her nest.
To that mysterious Power which governs all,
Is neither high nor low, nor great nor small.

THOUGHT AND SPEECH.

Sudden from out the cannon's brazen lips
The level smoke runs shining in the sun,
While the invisible and silent ball
Outruns it in its speed, and does its work
Unseen and far away. So from the sound
And smoke of human speech the thought runs forward,
Doing its work unseen and far away.

REFORMERS.

Something must be forgiven to great Reformers, —
The prophets of a fair new-world to be.
They cannot see the glory of the Past,
As men who walk with faces to the East
See not the glory of the setting sun.

EGYPT.

I see it in a vision, in the dark, —
The river, the great river, flowing, flowing
Forever through the shadowless, white land.
Upon its banks the gods of Abou Simbel
Sit patient, with their hands upon their knees,
And listen to the voice of cataracts,
And seem to say: "Why hurry with such speed?
Eternity is long; the gods can wait;
Wait, wait like us!" Along the river shores
The red flamingoes stand; and over them
Against the sky dark caravans of camels
Pass underneath the palm-trees, and are gone.

LEAVES.

Red leaves! dead leaves! that from the forest-trees,
Cradled in air a moment, fall and die,
Or float upon the surface of a brook, —
O Songs of mine! what are ye more than these?
What are ye more than Autumn leaves that lie
Gathered and pressed together in a book?

QUATRAIN.

Why waste the hours in idle talk,
When life is short, and time is flying?
Why interrupt my work or walk,
Since while we 're living, we are dying?

TWELFTH-NIGHT.[1]

Last night this room was full of sport,
For here, amid her train advancing,
The Queen of Twelfth-Night held her court,
With music, merriment, and dancing.

[1] In his Journal, March 6, 1857, Mr. Longfellow speaks of "a Twelfth-Night party for H. and her schoolmates, — a sleigh full of

Upon this Spanish convent chair
  The lovely maiden queen was seated;
A crown of flowers was in her hair,
  And kneeling youths their sovereign greeted.

The busts of Grecian bards sublime
  Smiled from their antique oaken cases,
As if they saw renewed the time
  Of all the Muses and the Graces.

And the old Poets on their shelves,
  Awaking from their dusty slumbers,
Recalled what they had sung themselves
  Of Youth and Beauty in their numbers.

And round the merry dancers whirled
  Beneath the evergreens and holly, —
A world of youth, a happy world,
  That banished care and melancholy.

Now all is changed; the guests have fled,
  The joyous guests, the merry-hearted.
Ah, me! the room itself seems dead,
  Since so much youth and life departed!

FROM THE ANTHOLOGY.

III. 100.

Here Dionysius of Tarsus, the Sexagenarian, lieth;
  He never married a wife, — would that my father had not!

schoolgirls, and young men from college. The evening passed pleasantly with dances, and rings in the cake, and king and queen." The party was given in the library of Craigie House, which is described in the verses above.

IV. 150.

Eros, beholding the bolts of the thunder, broke them in pieces;
Showing that Love is a fire, stronger than fire itself.

FROM PLATO.

Lookest thou at the stars, O Stella? Were I but the heaven,
With all the eyes of heaven would I look down upon thee.

FROM PLATO.

Thou as the morning star among the living resplendent.
Dead among the dead, shinest as Hesperus now.

FROM SAPPHO.

Over the grave of Pelágon the fisher, his father Meniscos
Hung his net and his oar, — signs of his wearisome life.

FROM

Take, O friendly Earth, old Amintikos into thy bosom,
Mindful of all the fatigue that he hath suffered for thee;
For he hath cultured for thee unceasing the trunks of the olive,
And with Bromius' vines hath he embellished thee oft.
Clothed thee hath he with grain, and digging channels for water,
Made thee fit for the plough, made thee the bearer of fruits.
Therefore, for what he hath done for thee, do thou too, benignant,
Cover his hoary head; blossom with flowers of spring.

FROM CALLIMACHUS.

Here in a holy sleep the son of Akanthian Dicon,
Saon, slumbers in peace; say not the good ever die.

ARABIC PROVERBS.

Not the stream that has passed, but only that which is passing,
Turns the wheel of the mill, grinds for the miller his corn.

If thy friend is of honey, thou should'st not wholly devour him.

Many things bitter as gall in this bitter life I have tasted;
But the most bitter of all is of a miser to beg.

Studious age at best but writes on the sand of the desert;
But a studious youth carves his inscription on stone.

When a word has been uttered, it straightway becometh thy master;
While it unspoken remains, thou art the master of it.

If in this life thou must serve as an anvil, endure and be patient;
If the hammer thou art, strong be thy blows and direct.

APPENDIX.

APPENDIX.

I.

GENEALOGY.

The name of Longfellow is found in the records of Yorkshire, England, as far back as 1486, and appears under the various spellings of Langfellay, Langfellowe, Langfellow, and Longfellow. The first of the name is James Langfellay, of Otley. In 1510 Sir Peter Langfellowe is vicar of Calverley. In the neighboring towns of Ilkley, Guiseley, and Horsforth lived many Longfellows, mostly yeomen: some of them well-to-do, others a charge on the parish; some getting into the courts and fined for such offences as "cutting green wode," or "greenhow," or "carrying away the Lord's wood," — wood from the yew-trees of the lord of the manor, to which they thought they had a right for their bows. One of the name was overseer of highways, and one was churchwarden, in Ilkley.

It is well established, by tradition and by documents, that the poet's ancestors were in Horsforth. In 1625 we find Edward Longfellow (perhaps from Ilkley) purchasing "Upper House," in Horsforth; and in 1647 he makes over his house and lands to his son William. This William was a well-to-do clothier who lived in Upper House, and, besides, possessed three other houses or cottages (being taxed for "4 hearths"), with gardens, closes, crofts, etc.

He had two sons, Nathan and William, and four or five daughters. William was baptized at Guiseley (the parish church of Horsforth), Oct. 20, 1650.

The first of the name in America was this William, son of William of Horsforth. He came over, a young man, to Newbury, Massachusetts, about 1676. Soon after, he married Anne Sewall, daughter of Henry Sewall, of Newbury, and sister of Samuel Sewall, afterward the first chief-justice of Massachusetts. He received from his father-in-law a farm in the parish of Byfield, on the Parker River.[1] He is spoken of as "well educated, but a little wild," or, as another puts it, "not so much of a Puritan as some." In 1690, as ensign of the Newbury company in the Essex regiment, he joined the ill-fated expedition of Sir William Phipps against Quebec, which on its return encountered a severe storm in the Gulf of St. Lawrence. One of the ships was wrecked on the Island of Anticosti, and William Longfellow, with nine of his comrades, was drowned. He left five children. The fourth of these, Stephen (1), left to shift for himself, became a blacksmith. He married Abigail, daughter of the Rev. Edward Tompson, of Newbury, afterward of Marshfield. Their fifth child, Stephen (2), born in 1723, being a bright boy, was sent to Harvard College, where he took his first degree in 1742, and his second in 1745. In this latter year (after having meanwhile taught a school in York) he went to Portland in Maine (then Falmouth), to be the schoolmaster of the town.[2] He gained

[1] In 1680 Samuel Sewall wrote to his brother in England: "Brother Longfellow's father W^{m} lives at Horsforth, near Leeds. Tell him bro. has a son William, a fine likely child, and a very good piece of land, and greatly wants a little stock to manage it. And that father has paid for him upwards of an hundred pounds to get him out of debt." In 1688 William Longfellow is entered upon the town-records of Newbury as having "two houses, six plough-lands, meadows," etc. The year before, he had made a visit to his old home in Horsforth.

[2] This was the letter from the minister of the town inviting him: —

FALMOUTH, November 15, 1744.

SIR, — We need a school-master. Mr. Plaisted advises of your being at liberty. If you will undertake the service in this place, you may be depend upon our being gener-

the respect of the community to such a degree that he was called to fill important offices; being successively parish clerk, town clerk, register of probate, and clerk of the courts. When Portland was burned by Mowatt in 1775, his house having been destroyed, he removed to Gorham, where he resided till his death in 1790. It was said of him that he was a man of piety, integrity, and honor, and that his favorite reading was history and poetry. He had married Tabitha, daughter of Samuel Bragdon of York. Their oldest son Stephen (3) was born in 1750, inheriting the name and the farm; and in 1773 he married Patience Young, of York. He represented his town in the Massachusetts legislature for eight years, and his county for several years after as senator. For fourteen years (1797–1811) he was Judge of the Court of Common Pleas, and is remembered as a man of sterling qualities, great integrity, and sound common-sense. His second child, Stephen (4), born in Gorham in 1776, graduated at Harvard College in 1798; studied law in Portland, and in 1801 was admitted to the Cumberland Bar, at which he soon attained and kept a distinguished position. In 1814, as a member of the Federalist party, to whose principles he was strongly attached, he was sent as representative to the Massachusetts legislature. In 1822 he was elected representative to Congress, which office he held for one term. In 1828 he received the degree of LL.D. from Bowdoin College, of which he was a Trustee for nineteen years. In 1834 he was elected President of the Maine Historical Society. He died in 1849, highly respected for his integrity, public spirit, hospitality and generosity. In 1804 he had married Zilpah, daughter of General Peleg Wadsworth, of Portland.

ous and your being satisfied. I wish you'd come as soon as possible, and doubt not but you'll find things much to your content.

Your humble ser't,

THOS. SMITH.

P. S. I write in the name and with the power of the selectmen of the town. If you can't serve us, pray advise us per first opportunity.

The salary for the first year was £200, in a depreciated currency.

Of their eight children, Henry Wadsworth was the second. He was named for his mother's brother, a gallant young lieutenant in the Navy, who on the night of Sept. 4, 1804, gave his life before Tripoli in the war with Algiers. Henry Wadsworth Longfellow was born on the 27th February, 1807; graduated at Bowdoin College in 1825; in 1829 was appointed Professor of Modern Languages in the same College; was married in 1831 to Mary Storer Potter (daughter of Barrett Potter, of Portland), who died in 1835; in 1836 was appointed Professor of Modern Languages and Belles-Lettres in Harvard College, which office he held till 1854. He was again married, in July, 1843, to Frances Elizabeth Appleton, daughter of Nathan Appleton, of Boston. She died in 1861. Their children were Charles Appleton, Ernest Wadsworth, Frances (who died in infancy), Alice Mary, Edith, and Anne Allegra. He died on the 24th March, 1882.

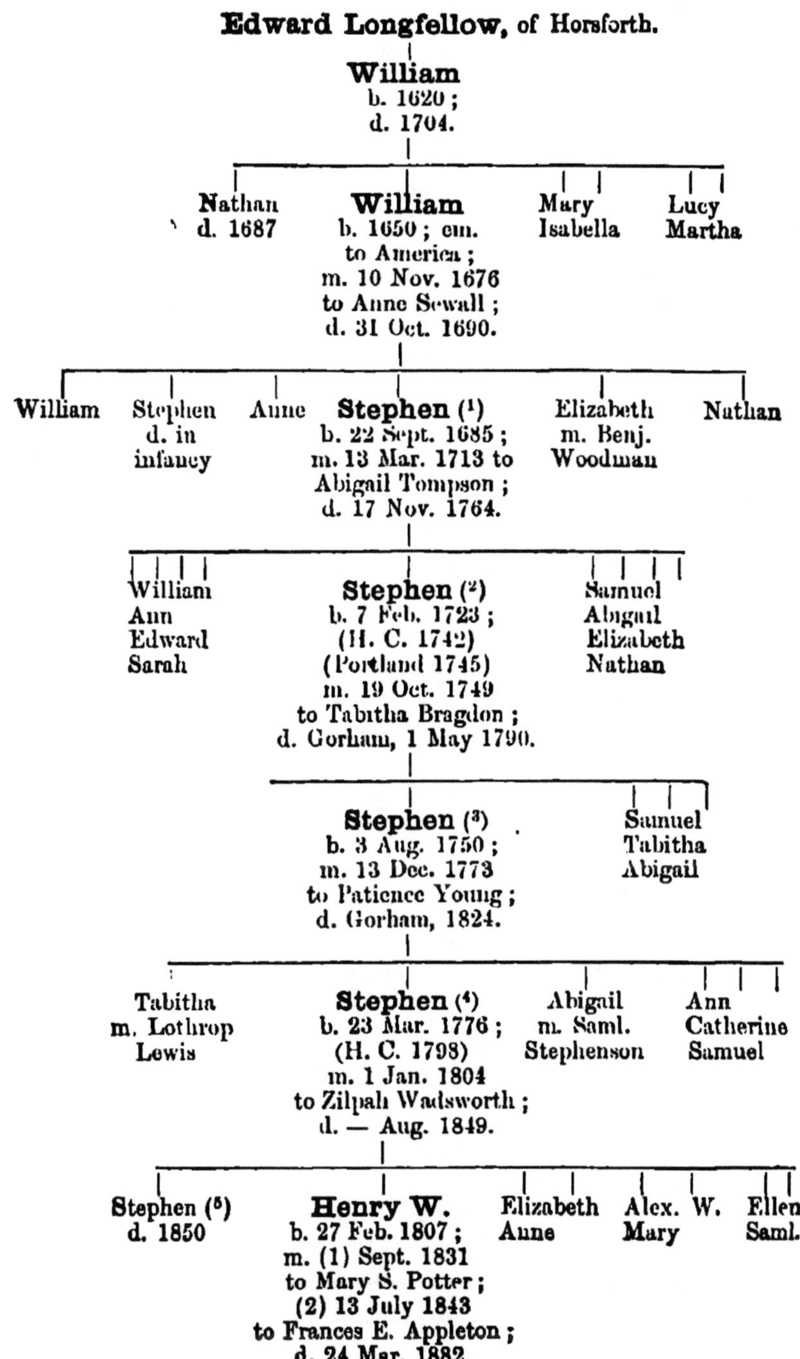
Edward Longfellow, of Horsforth.
William
b. 1620;
d. 1704.
Nathan
d. 1687
William
b. 1650; em.
to America;
m. 10 Nov. 1676
to Anne Sewall;
d. 31 Oct. 1690.
Mary
Isabella
Lucy
Martha
William
Stephen
d. in
infancy
Anne
Stephen (1)
b. 22 Sept. 1685;
m. 13 Mar. 1713 to
Abigail Tompson;
d. 17 Nov. 1764.
Elizabeth
m. Benj.
Woodman
Nathan
William
Ann
Edward
Sarah
Stephen (2)
b. 7 Feb. 1723;
(H. C. 1742)
(Portland 1745)
m. 19 Oct. 1749
to Tabitha Bragdon;
d. Gorham, 1 May 1790.
Samuel
Abigail
Elizabeth
Nathan
Stephen (3)
b. 3 Aug. 1750;
m. 13 Dec. 1773
to Patience Young;
d. Gorham, 1824.
Samuel
Tabitha
Abigail
Tabitha
m. Lothrop
Lewis
Stephen (4)
b. 23 Mar. 1776;
(H. C. 1798)
m. 1 Jan. 1804
to Zilpah Wadsworth;
d. — Aug. 1849.
Abigail
m. Saml.
Stephenson
Ann
Catherine
Samuel
Stephen (5)
d. 1850
Henry W.
b. 27 Feb. 1807;
m. (1) Sept. 1831
to Mary S. Potter;
(2) 13 July 1843
to Frances E. Appleton;
d. 24 Mar. 1882.
Elizabeth
Anne
Alex. W.
Mary
Ellen
Saml.

The Rev. Robert Collyer, who has made a study of the records of his native Yorkshire, thus brings together two names well known in poetry: —

"There is a curious last chapter to my story, for which I am indebted to the Boston Athenæum. Into this nook of the North [Ilkley], a good while ago, the Hebers came, and lived in an old gabled house that is still standing a mile out of the town. They were the ancestors in the direct line of that good Heber, bishop of Calcutta, who left us two or three of our noblest hymns; and the Reginald Heber of the days of the Ilkley Longfellow was a man of great charity, who left the interest of a good sum of money to be given forever to the poor of the place. But in a book in the Athenæum I found an account of one of these Hebers, — the son, I think, of this early Reginald, — who seems to have been a great scamp. He turns up in two or three places, always to his discredit; and what should he do at last but get himself brought up before Walter Hawksworth, the local magistrate of that day, on a charge of breaking into the house of a poor old man, together with two lewd companions, and robbing him of two pounds ten shillings in money, and a piece of beef. Heber stood over the old man with an axe, and threatened murder if he made any noise. It was one o'clock in the morning, and quite dark; but the old man said, 'I fear God, and not man,' seized the axe also, until he came to the hand that held it, felt it was a very soft hand, and could discern that the burglar was tall. They left a crowbar and a wedge, which were proven to belong to this Heber, and a woman sleeping in another room heard Heber's voice, which she well knew. But the main witness against him was Elizabeth Longfellow, who got somehow from the confederates the whole truth. To whom also Heber came on the Thursday after the robbery, and said it would not have been done if they had known there was no more money in the house than was found. So ends this old bit of violence and wrong. A note to the narrative says the thing was not followed any farther, but must have been hushed up by the gentlemen of the West Riding, for the sake of the *good* Hebers. Here is this curious conjunction of two names that have since become famous in two worlds. The trees that in this new time reach so beautifully toward heaven in the Missionary Hymn and the Psalm of Life, are blown together for a moment in that nook in the North by that lawless wind of midnight evil-doing at old Sandie Squire's little home, to touch no more, perhaps, forever."

The Wadsworths, Longfellow's ancestors on the mother's side, also go back to Yorkshire, where the name is found under the forms of Waddisworth, Waddesworth, and Wordesworth, — suggesting a possible connection with another famous poet. Longfellows are also found in the registers of Kendal, Westmoreland, from 1580 to 1705.

The relation of the poet to John Alden, of 'Miles Standish's Courtship,' is in this wise. John Alden married Priscilla Mullens (otherwise spelled Molines and Moleyns); their daughter Elizabeth married William Peabody, whose daughter Ruth married Benjamin Bartlett, whose daughter Priscilla married John Sampson, whose daughter Susanna married Deacon Peleg Wadsworth, whose son, General Peleg, was Longfellow's grandfather.

II.

BIBLIOGRAPHY.

[Revised and enlarged from the *Literary World*.]

I.

The Published Writings of Mr. Longfellow.

Elements of French Grammar. Translated from the French of C. F. L'Homond. Portland: 1830.

[Editor.] Manuel de Proverbes Dramatiques. Portland: 1830. With a long Preface in French by the Editor.

[Editor.] Novelas Españolas. Portland: 1830. With an original Preface in Spanish.

Origin and Progress of the French Language. Article in *North Am. Rev.*, **32**. 277. April, 1831.

Defence of Poetry. *North Am. Rev.*, **34**. 56. January, 1832.

History of the Italian Language and Dialects. *North Am. Rev.*, **35**. 283. October, 1832.

SYLLABUS DE LA GRAMMAIRE ITALIENNE. Written in French. Boston: 1832.

[Editor.] COURS DE LANGUE FRANÇAISE. Boston: 1832.

I. Le Ministre de Wakefield.

II. Proverbes Dramatiques.

[Editor.] SAGGI DE' NOVELLIERI ITALIANI D' OGNI SECOLO: Tratti da' più celebri Scrittori, con brevi Notizie intorno alla Vita di ciascheduno. Boston: 1832. With Preface in Italian by the Editor.

Spanish Devotional and Moral Poetry. *North Am. Rev.*, **34**. 277. April, 1832.

COPLAS DE MANRIQUE. A Translation from the Spanish. Boston: Allen & Ticknor, 1833.

Jorge Manrique was a Spanish poet of the fifteenth century. His *Coplas* is a funeral poem on the death of his father, extending to five hundred lines. Mr. Longfellow's volume is prefaced with the above essay on the moral and devotional poetry of Spain, from the *North Am. Rev.*, **34**. 277; and included in it are translations of Sonnets by Lope de Vega and others.

Spanish Language and Literature. *North Am. Rev.*, **36**. 316. April, 1833.

Old English Romances. *North Am. Rev.*, **37**. 374. October, 1833.

OUTRE MER; a Pilgrimage beyond the Sea. 2 vols. New York: Harpers, 1835.

A series of prose descriptions of foreign travel; a sort of "Sketch-book." Reviewed by O. W. Peabody in *North Am. Rev.*, **39**. 459; in *Am. Month. Rev.*, **4**. 157. Its publication was begun in numbers, of which only two were issued. [Boston: 1833.]

The Great Metropolis. *North Am. Rev.*, **44**. 461. April, 1837.

A lively review of a new work on London.

Hawthorne's Twice-Told Tales. *North Am. Rev.*, **45**. 59. July, 1837.

Tegnér's Frithiofs Saga. *North Am. Rev.*, **45**. 149. July, 1837.

Anglo-Saxon Literature. *North Am. Rev.*, **47**. 90. July, 1838.

HYPERION; a Romance. 2 vols. New York: 1839.

This was the first of Mr. Longfellow's works written in his Cambridge home, — in the Washington chamber of the Craigie House. Reviewed by C. C. Felton in *North Am. Rev.*, **51**. 145; in *So. Lit. Mess.*, **5**. 839.

VOICES OF THE NIGHT. Cambridge: 1839.

Mr. Longfellow's first volume of poems, containing "The Psalm of Life," "The Reaper and the Flowers," and six other poems, many of which were originally published in the *Knickerbocker Magazine;* also seven "Earlier Poems," as follows, all of which were composed before the author was nineteen, — "An April Day," "Autumn," "Woods in Winter," "Hymn of the Moravian Nuns at Bethlehem," "Sunrise on the Hills," "The Spirit of Poetry," "The Burial of the Minnisink."

Reviewed in *North Am. Rev.*, **50** 266; *Christ. Ex.*, **28**. 242.

The French Language in England. *North Am. Rev.*, **51**. 285. October, 1840.

BALLADS AND OTHER POEMS. Cambridge: 1841.

Including "The Skeleton in Armor," "The Wreck of the Hesperus," "The Village Blacksmith," "God's Acre," "To the River Charles," and "Excelsior." Reviewed by C. C. Felton in *North Am. Rev.*, **55**. 114; *Monthly Review*, **160**. 249.

POEMS ON SLAVERY. 1842.

Composed during a return voyage from Europe, in 1842. Reviewed by W. Ware in *Christ. Ex.*, **33**. 352; *Monthly Review*, **161**, 64.

THE SPANISH STUDENT. A Play in Three Acts. 1843.

In this may be found the serenade beginning, "Stars of the summer night." Reviewed in *Athenæum*, 1844, 8; in *Irish Quart. Rev.*, June, 1855, 202; in Poe's *Literati;* in Whipple's *Essays and Reviews*, **1**. 66.

[Editor.] THE WAIF: a Collection of Poems. Cambridge: 1845. With Proem by the Editor.

[Editor.] THE POETS AND POETRY OF EUROPE. Philadelphia: 1845.

A collection of poems, translated from a large number of European poets, with introductions and biographical and critical notices. The introductions and many of the translations are by Mr. Longfellow. A new edition, revised and enlarged, was published in 1871. Reviewed by F. Bowen in *North Am. Rev.*, **61**. 199; by C. C. Felton in *Christ. Ex.*, **39**. 225; *Am. Whig Rev.*, **4**. 496.

THE BELFRY OF BRUGES, and Other Poems. Boston: 1846.

[Editor.] THE ESTRAY: a Collection of Poems. Boston: 1847. With Proem by the Editor.

EVANGELINE: a Tale of Acadie. Boston: 1847.

Reviewed by C. C. Felton in *North Am. Rev.*, **66**. 215; *Am. Whig Rev.*, **7**. 155; *New Englander*, **6**. 518; *Eclectic Mag.*, **15**. 96; by T. S. King in *Univ. Quart. Rev.*, **5**. 104; by W. Whewell in *Fraser's Mag.*, **37**. 295; *Brownson's Quart. Rev.*, **7**. 56; *Pioneer*, **4**. 211; *Christ. Ex.*, **44**. 143; by Philarète Chasles in *Revue des Deux Mondes*, April, 1849. (See also J. G. Whittier's Prose Works, ii. 63.)

KAVANAGH; a Tale. Boston: 1849.

Reviewed by J. R. Lowell in *North Am. Rev.*, **69**. 196; by T. S. King in *Christ. Ex.*, **47**. 153.

THE SEASIDE AND THE FIRESIDE. Boston: 1850.

Contains "The Building of the Ship," "Resignation," and twenty-one other poems.

THE GOLDEN LEGEND. Boston: 1851.

This was the second part of the Trilogy of Christus, though first written.

Reviewed in *Blackwood*, **5**. 71; in *Eclectic Mag.*, 4th s., **31**. 455; in the *New Englander*, **10**. 90; *British Quart.*, **39**. 31; *Fraser's Mag.*, **47**. 367; *Christ. Ex.*, **52**. 141.

THE SONG OF HIAWATHA. Boston: 1855.

Reviewed by Rev. E. E. Hale in *North Am. Rev.*, **82**. 272; *Dublin Univ. Mag.*, **47**. 90; *Putnam's Monthly*, **6**. 578; *London Quart. Rev.*, **5**. 35; *Colburn's New Monthly*, **106**. 242; *Irish Quart.*, **6**. 1; *Christ. Ex.*, **60**. 133.

THE COURTSHIP OF MILES STANDISH. Boston: 1858.

With "Birds of Passage," twenty-two poems, including "My Lost Youth," "The Two Angels," "Sandalphon," and "The Fiftieth Birthday of Agassiz." Reviewed by A. P. Peabody in *North Am. Rev.*, **88**. 275.

TALES OF A WAYSIDE INN. Boston: 1863.

"First Day," with "Birds of Passage, Flight the Second," seven poems, including "The Children's Hour" and "The Cumberland." Reviewed in *British Quart.*, **39**, 31.

FLOWER-DE-LUCE. Boston: 1867.

Twelve poems.

THE NEW ENGLAND TRAGEDIES. Boston: 1868.

I. John Endicott.

II. Giles Cory of the Salem Farms.

Reviewed by W. F. Poole in *North Am. Rev.*, **108**, 395; by E. J. Cutler in *North Am. Rev.*, **108**. 669.

DANTE'S DIVINE COMEDY. A Translation. Boston: 1867–70.

Three vols. I. Inferno. II. Purgatorio. III. Paradiso. The same in 1 vol.

Reviewed by C. E. Norton in *North Am. Rev.*, **105**. 125; by G. W. Greene in *Atlantic Monthly*, **20**. 188.

THE DIVINE TRAGEDY. Boston: 1871.

Reviewed by J. H. Allen in *Christ. Ex.*, **83**. 291; *Dublin Rev.*, **79**. 331.

CHRISTUS: a Mystery. Boston: 1872.

Collecting, for the first time into their consecutive unity
I. The Divine Tragedy.
II. The Golden Legend.
III. The New England Tragedies.

THREE BOOKS OF SONG. Boston: 1872.

Contents: "Tales of a Wayside Inn, Second Day;" "Judas Maccabæus" (a dramatic poem in five acts); and "A Handful of Translations," eleven in number.

AFTERMATH. Boston: 1874.

Contents: "Tales of a Wayside Inn, Third Day," and "Birds of Passage, Flight the Third."

THE MASQUE OF PANDORA, and Other Poems. Boston: 1875.

Containing "The Hanging of the Crane;" "Morituri Salutamus," the Bowdoin College poem for the semi-centennial of the author's class of 1825; "Birds of Passage, Flight the Fourth;" and "A Book of Sonnets," fourteen in all. (An operatic version of "The Masque of Pandora" was produced on the Boston stage in January, 1881.)

[Editor.] POEMS OF PLACES. 31 vols. Boston: 1876–1879.

KÉRAMOS; and Other Poems. Boston: 1878.

Contents: A "Fifth Flight" of "Birds of Passage," sixteen in all, among which is the tribute to James Russell Lowell entitled "The Herons of Elmwood;" a second "Book of Sonnets," nineteen of them, including the tributes to Whittier, Tennyson, Irving, and Cleaveland; and fifteen translations, eight from Michael Angelo.

ULTIMA THULE. Boston: 1880.

Containing the poems to Bayard Taylor and to Burns; and those on the Children's Chair, the Iron Pen, and Old St. David's.

IN THE HARBOR. Boston: 1882.

Published after the author's death, and containing the tributes to J. T. Fields and President Garfield, seven personal poems, and the "Bells of San Blas," the last poem written by Mr. Longfellow.

MICHAEL ANGELO. Boston: 1883.

Printed after the Author's death in the *Atlantic Monthly*, and afterward in an illustrated volume.

A COMPLETE EDITION OF MR. LONGFELLOW'S POETICAL AND PROSE WORKS, in 11 volumes, with introductions and notes, was published by Houghton, Mifflin, & Co. Boston: 1886.

GENERAL REVIEWS.

London Quart., **2**. 440. — (A. Trollope) *North Am. Rev.*, **132**. 383. — (R. H. Stoddard) *Scribner's Monthly*, **17**. 1. — (F. F. Browne) *Dial* (Chicago), **2**. 275. — *National Review*, **8**. 198; same article, *Littell's Living Age*, **60**. 399. — *National Magazine*, **3**. 1. — (E. P. Whipple) *North Am. Rev.*, **58**. 22. — (C. C. Felton) *North Am. Rev.*, **55**. 114. — (W. D. Howells) *North Am. Rev.*, **104**. 531. — *London Quart.*, **17**. 45. — *Dublin Univ. Mag.*, **35**. 461. — *Eclectic Rev.*. **90**. 710. — *Am. Whig Rev.*, **13**. 359. — *Dublin Rev.*, **34**. 359. — *Chambers's Journal*, **22**. 310; same article, *Littell's Living Age*, **43**. 522. — *Irish Quart.*, **5**. 193; **8**. 915. — (C. Clarkson) *New Dominion Monthly*, **18**. 97. — *De Bow*, **26**. 357. — (J. F. Rusling) *Methodist Quart.*, **19**. 568. — With portrait, *Eclectic Mag.*, **49**. 566; **84**. 246. — *Sharpe's London Mag.*, **39**. 199. — *Victoria Mag.*, **12**. 41. — *So. Lit. Mess.*, **8**. 150; **11**. 92. — *Littell's Living Age*, **19**. 481. — (G. W. Curtis) *Atlantic Monthly*, **12**. 769. — (E. Montégut) *Revue des Deux Mondes*, Oct. 15, 1849. — (Ray Palmer) *International Rev.*, November, 1875. — (O. B. Frothingham) *Atlantic Monthly*, **49**. 819. — *Atlantic Monthly*, **57**. 702. — *Quarterly*, October, 1886. — *London Quart.*, October, 1886.

II.

Translations of Mr. Longfellow's Works.

GERMAN.

Longfellow's Gedichte. Übersetzt von Carl Böttger. Dessau: 1856.

Balladen und Lieder von H. W. Longfellow. Deutsch von A. R. Nielo. Münster: 1857.

Longfellow's Gedichte. Von Friedrich Marx. Hamburg und Leipzig: 1868.

Longfellow's ältere und neuere Gedichte in Auswald. Deutsch von Adolf Laun. Oldenburg: 1879.

Der Spanische Studente. Übersetzt von Karl Böttger. Dessau: 1854.

The Same. Von Marie Hélène Le Maistre. Dresden: n. d.

The Same. Übersetzt von Häfeli. Leipzig: n. d.

Evangeline. Aus dem Englischen. Hamburg: 1857.

The Same. Aus dem Englischen, von P. J. Belke. Leipzig: 1854.

The Same. Mit Anmerkungen von Dr. O. Dickmann. Hamburg: n. d.

The Same. Eine Erzählung aus Acadien. Von Eduard Nickles. Karlsruhe: 1862.

The Same. Übersetzt von Frank Siller. Milwaukee: 1879.

The Same. Übersetzt von Karl Knortz. Leipzig: n. d.

Longfellow's Evangeline. Deutsch von Heinrich Viehoff. Trier: 1869.

Die Goldene Legende. Deutsch von Karl Keck. Wien: 1859.

The Same. Übersetzt von Elise Freifrau von Hohenhausen. Leipzig: 1880.

Das Lied von Hiawatha. Deutsch von Adolph Böttger. Leipzig: 1856.

Der Sang von Hiawatha. Übersetzt von Ferdinand Freiligrath. Stuttgart und Augsburg: 1857.

Hiawatha. Übertragen von Hermann Simon. Leipzig: n. d.

Der Sang von Hiawatha. Übersetzt, eingeleitet und erklärt von Karl Knortz. Jena: 1872.

Miles Standish's Brautwerbung. Aus dem Englischen von F. E. Baumgarten. St. Louis: 1859.

Die Brautwerbung des Miles Standish. Übersetzt von Karl Knortz. Leipzig: 18—.

Miles Standish's Brautwerbung. Übersetzt von F. Manefeld. 1867.

Die Sage von König Olaf. Übersetzt von Ernst Rauscher.

The Same. Übersetzt von W. Hertzberg.

Gedichte von H. W. L. Deutsch von Alexander Neidhardt. Darmstadt: 1856.

Hyperion. Deutsch von Adolph Böttger. Leipzig: 1856.

Pandora. Übersetzt von Isabella Schuchardt. Hamburg: 1878.

Morituri Salutamus. Übersetzt von Dr. Ernst Schmidt. Chicago: 1878.

The Hanging of the Crane. Das Kesselhängen. Übersetzt von G. A. Zündt. n. d.

The Same. Einhängen des Kesselhakens, frei gearbeitet von Joh. Henry Becker. n. d.

Sämmtliche Poetische Werke von H. W. L. Übersetzt von Hermann Simon. Leipzig: n. d.

DUTCH.

Outre Mer en Kavanagh. Haar het Engelisch, B. T. L. Weddik. Amsterdam: 1858.

Het Lied van Hiawatha. In het Nederduitsch overgebragt door L. S. P. Meijboom. Amsterdam: 1862.

Miles Standish. Nagezongen door S. J. Van den Bergh. Haarlem: 1861.

Longfellows Gedighten. Nagezongen door S. J. Van den Bergh. Haarlem: n. d.

SWEDISH.

Hyperion. På Svenska, af Grönlund. 1853.

Evangeline. På Svenska, af Alb. Lysander. 1854.

The Same. Öfversatt af Hjalmar Erdgren. Göteborg: 1875.

The Same. Öfversatt af Philip Svenson. Chicago: 1875.

Hiawatha. På Svenska af Westberg. 1856.

DANISH.

Evangeline. Paa Norsk, ved Sd. C. Knutsen. Christiania: 1874.

Sangen om Hiawatha. Oversat af G. Bern. Kjöbenhavn: 1860.

Den Gyldne Legende, ved Thor Lange. Kjöbenhavn: 1880.

FRENCH.

Evangeline; suivie des Voix de la Nuit. Par le Chevalier de Chatelain. Jersey, London, Paris, New York: 1856.

The Same. Conte d'Acadie. Traduit par Charles Brunel. Prose. Paris: 1864.

The Same. Par Léon Pamphile Le May. Québec: 1865.

La Légende Dorée, et Poëmes sur l'Esclavage. Traduits par Paul Blier et Edward Mac-Donnel. Prose. Paris et Valenciennes: 1854.

Hiawatha. Traduction avec notes par M. H. Gomont. Nancy, Paris: 1860.

Drames et Poésies. Traduits par X. Marmier. (The New England Tragedies.) Paris: 1872.

Hyperion et Kavanagh. Traduit de l'Anglais, et précédé d'une Notice sur l'Auteur. 2 vols. Paris et Bruxelles: 1860.

The Psalm of Life, and Other Poems. Tr. by Lucien de la Rive in *Essais de Traduction Poétique.* Paris: 1870.

ITALIAN.

Alcune Poesie di Enrico W. Longfellow. Traduzione dall' Inglese di Angelo Messedaglia. Padova: 1866.

Lo Studente Spagnuolo. Prima Versione Metrica di Alessandro Bazzini. Milano: 1871

The Same. Traduzione di Nazzareno Trovanelli. Firenze: 1876.

Poesie sulla Schiavitù. Tr. in Versi Italiani da Louisa Graco Bartolini. Firenze: 1860.

Evangelina. Tradotta da Pietro Rotondi. Firenze: 1856.

The Same. Traduzione di Carlo Faccioli. Verona: 1873.

La Leggenda d' Oro. Tradotta da Ada Corbellini Martini. Parma: 1867.

Il Canto d' Hiawatha. Tr. da L. G. Bartolini. Frammenti. Firenze: 1867.

Miles Standish. Traduzione dall' Inglese di Caterino Frattini. Padova: 1868.

PORTUGUESE.

El Rei Roberto de Sicilia. Tr. by Dom Pedro II., Emperor of Brazil. Autograph MS.

Evangelina. Traduzida por Franklin Doria. Rio de Janeiro: 1874.

The Same. *Poema de Henrique Longfellow.* Traducido por Miguel Street de Arriaga. Lisbon: n. d.

SPANISH.

Evangelina. *Romance de la Acadia.* Traducido del Ingles por Carlos Mórla Vicuña. Nueva York: 1871.

POLISH.

Zlota Legenda. The Golden Legend. Tr. into Polish by F. Jerzierski. Warszawa: 1857.

Evangelina. Tr. into Polish by Felix Jerzierski. Warszawa: 1857.

Duma o Hiawacie. (The Song of Hiawatha.) Tr. into Polish by Feliksa Jerzierskiego. Warszawa: 1860.

OTHER LANGUAGES.

Excelsior, and Other Poems, in Russian. St. Petersburg: n. d.

Hiawatha, rendered into Latin, with abridgment. By Francis William Newman. London: 1862.

Excelsior. Tr. into Hebrew by Henry Gersoni. n. d.

A Psalm of Life. In Marathi. By Mrs. H. I. Bruce. Satara: 1878.

The Same. In Chinese. By Jung Tagen. Written on a fan.

The Same. In Sanscrit. By Elihu Burritt and his pupils. MS.

III.

Mr. Longfellow's Poems, under their Dates of Composition.

[Those marked (*) were not included by him in his works. Translations are omitted.]

1820. *The Battle of Lovell's Pond.
1824. *To Ianthe.
*Thanksgiving.
*Autumnal Nightfall.
*Italian Scenery.
An April Day.
Autumn.
Woods in Winter.
1825. *The Lunatic Girl.
*The Venetian Gondolier.
*The Angler's Song.
Sunrise on the Hills.
Hymn of the Moravian Nuns.
*Dirge over a Nameless Grave.
*A Song of Savoy.
*The Indian Hunter.
*Ode for the Commemoration of Lovewell's Fight.
*Jeckoyva.
*The Sea-Diver.
*Musings.
The Spirit of Poetry.
Burial of the Minnisink.
1826. *Song, "Where, from the eye of day."
*Song of the Birds.
1837. Flowers.
1838. A Psalm of Life.
The Reaper and the Flowers.
The Light of Stars.
1839. The Wreck of the Hesperus.
The Village Blacksmith.
Prelude to Voices of the Night.
Hymn to the Night.
Footsteps of Angels.
The Beleaguered City.
Midnight Mass for the Dying Year.
L'Envoi to Voices of the Night.
1840. It is not always May.
The Spanish Student.
The Skeleton in Armor
1841. Endymion.
The Rainy Day.
God's Acre.
To the River Charles.
Blind Bartimeus.
The Goblet of Life.
Maidenhood.
Excelsior.
1842. Mezzo Cammin.
To William E. Channing.
The Slave's Dream.
The Good Part.
The Slave in the Dismal Swamp.
The Slave singing at Midnight.
The Witnesses.
The Quadroon Girl.
The Warning.
The Belfry of Bruges.
1844. A Gleam of Sunshine.
The Arsenal at Springfield.
Nuremberg.

The Norman Baron.
Rain in Summer.
Sea-weed.
The Day is Done.
1845. To a Child.
The Occultation of Orion.
The Bridge.
To the Driving Cloud.
Carillon.
Afternoon in February.
To an Old Danish Song-Book.
Walter von der Vogelweid.
Drinking Song.
The Old Clock on the Stairs.
The Arrow and the Song.
The Evening Star (sonnet).
Autumn (sonnet).
Dante (sonnet).
Curfew.
Birds of Passage.
The Haunted Chamber.
Evangeline (begun).
1846. The Builders.
Pegasus in Pound.
Twilight.
1847. Tegnér's Drapa.
Evangeline (finished).
1848. Hymn for my Brother's Ordination.
The Secret of the Sea.
Sir Humphrey Gilbert.
The Fire of Drift-Wood.
The Castle-Builder.
Resignation.
Sand of the Desert.
The Open Window.
King Witlaf's Drinking-Horn.
1849. Dedication to the Seaside and the Fireside.
The Building of the Ship.
Chrysaor.
The Challenge of Thor (Wayside Inn).
The Lighthouse.
Gaspar Becerra.
Sonnet on Mrs. Kemble's Readings from Shakespeare.
Children.
The Singers.
The Brook and the Wave.
Suspiria.
1850. The Golden Legend (begun).
The Ladder of St. Augustine.
The Phantom Ship.
1851. In the Churchyard at Cambridge.
The Golden Legend (finished).
1852. The Warden of the Cinque Ports.
Haunted Houses.
The Emperor's Bird's-Nest.
Daylight and Moonlight.
The Jewish Cemetery at Newport.
1853. The Two Angels.
1854. The Ropewalk.
The Golden Milestone.
Becalmed.
Catawba Wine.
Prometheus.
Epimetheus.
Hiawatha (begun).
1855. Hiawatha (finished).
Oliver Basselin.
Victor Galbraith.
My Lost Youth.
1856. John Endicott (begun).
1857. John Endicott (finished).
Santa Filomena.
The Discoverer of the North Cape.
Daybreak.
The Fiftieth Birthday of Agassiz.
Sandalphon.
The Courtship of Miles Standish (begun).
1858. The Courtship of Miles Standish (finished).
1859. The Children's Hour.
*Twelfth Night.
Enceladus.
Snow-Flakes.
The Bells of Lynn.
1860. Paul Revere's Ride (Wayside Inn).

The Saga of King Olaf (Wayside Inn).
A Day of Sunshine.
1861. Interlude, 'A Strain of Music' (Wayside Inn).
1862. Prelude: The Wayside Inn.
The Legend of Rabbi Ben Levi (Wayside Inn).
King Robert of Sicily (Wayside Inn).
Torquemada (Wayside Inn).
The Cumberland.
1863. Five Interludes to the First Part of Tales of a Wayside Inn.
The Falcon of Ser Federigo (Wayside Inn).
The Birds of Killingworth. (Wayside Inn).
Finale to Part First of Tales of a Wayside Inn.
Something Left Undone.
Weariness.
1864. Palingenesis.
The Bridge of Cloud.
Hawthorne.
Christmas Bells.
The Wind over the Chimney.
Divina Commedia (Sonnets I., II.).
Noël (To Agassiz).
Kambalu (Wayside Inn).
1865. Divina Commedia (Sonnet III.).
1866. Flower-de-Luce.
Killed at the Ford.
Giotto's Tower (sonnet).
To-morrow.
Divina Commedia (Sonnets V., VI.).
1867. Divina Commedia (Sonnet IV.).
1868. Giles Corey of the Salem Farms.
1870. Prelude to Part II. of Wayside Inn.
The Bell of Atri (Wayside Inn).
Fata Morgana.
The Meeting.
Vox Populi.
Prelude to Translations.
The Divine Tragedy (begun).
1871. The Cobbler of Hagenau (Wayside Inn).
The Ballad of Carmilhan (Wayside Inn).
Lady Wentworth (Wayside Inn).
The Legend Beautiful (Wayside Inn).
The Baron of St. Castine (Wayside Inn).
Judas Maccabæus.
The Abbot Joachim (Christus).
Martin Luther (Christus).
St. John (finale to Christus).
The Divine Tragedy (finished).
1872. Introitus to Christus.
Interludes and Finale to Part II. of Wayside Inn.
Michael Angelo (first draft).
Azrael (Wayside Inn).
Charlemagne (Wayside Inn).
Emma and Eginhard (Wayside Inn).
1873. Prelude, Interludes, and Finale to Part III. of Wayside Inn.
Elizabeth (Wayside Inn).
The Monk of Casal-Maggiore (Wayside Inn).
Scanderbeg (Wayside Inn).
The Rhyme of Sir Christopher (Wayside Inn).
Michael Angelo (monologue).
The Last Judgment: Palazzo Cesarini: The Oaks of Monte Luca.
The Challenge.
Aftermath.
The Hanging of the Crane.
Chaucer (sonnet).
Shakespeare (sonnet).
Milton (sonnet).
Keats (sonnet).
1874. Charles Sumner.
Travels by the Fireside.
Cadenabbia.

Autumn Within.
Monte Cassino.
Morituri Salutamus.
Three Friends of Mine (sonnets).
The Galaxy (sonnet).
The Sound of the Sea (sonnet).
The Tides (sonnet).
A Summer Day by the Sea.
A Shadow (sonnet).
A Nameless Grave (sonnet).
The Old Bridge at Florence.
Il Ponte Vecchio di Firenze.
Michael Angelo; Vittoria Colonna: Palazzo Belvedere: Bindo Altoviti: In the Coliseum (Michael Angelo).

1875. Amalfi.
The Sermon of St. Francis.
Belisarius.
Songo River.
The Masque of Pandora.
Sleep.

1876. Parker Cleaveland.
The Herons of Elmwood.
To the Avon.
A Dutch Picture.
The Revenge of Rain-in-the-Face.
To the River Yvette.
A Wraith in the Mist.
Nature (sonnet).
In the Churchyard at Tarrytown (sonnet).
Eliot's Oak (sonnet).
The Descent of the Muses (sonnet).
Venice (sonnet).
The Poets (sonnet).
The Harvest Moon (sonnet).
To the River Rhone (sonnet).
The Two Rivers (sonnets).
Boston (sonnet).
St. John's, Cambridge (sonnet).
Moods (sonnet).
Woodstock Park (sonnet).
The Four Princesses at Wilna (sonnet).
The Broken Oar (sonnet).
The Four Lakes of Madison.
Victor and Vanquished (sonnet).

1877. Kéramos.
Castles in Spain.
Vittoria Colonna.
A Ballad of the French Fleet.
The Leap of Roushan Beg.
Haroun al Raschid.
King Trisanku.
The Three Kings.
Song, "Stay, stay at home."
The Three Silences of Molinos (sonnet; to Whittier).
Holidays (sonnet).
Wapentake (sonnet; to Tennyson).

1878. The Emperor's Glove.
The Poet's Calendar; March.
The White Czar.
Delia.
The Chamber over the Gate.
Moonlight.
Bayard Taylor.

1879. The Cross of Snow (sonnet).
From my Arm-chair.
Jugurtha.
The Iron Pen.
Helen of Tyre.
The Sifting of Peter.
The Tide rises, the Tide falls.
My Cathedral (sonnet).
The Burial of the Poet (sonnet; R. H. Dana).
Night (sonnet).
The Children's Crusade.
Sundown.
Chimes (sonnet).
Robert Burns.

1880. Dedication to Ultima Thule.
Elegiac.
Old St. David's at Radnor.
Maiden and Weathercock.
The Windmill.
Four by the Clock.
The Poet and his Songs (Envoi).
The Poet's Calendar (parts).
Elegiac Verse.

1881. Elegiac Verse.
The Poet's Calendar (parts).
Auf Wiedersehen (J. T. Fields).
The City and the Sea.
Memories (sonnet).
My Books (sonnet).
President Garfield (sonnet).
Hermes Trismegistus.
1882. Possibilities (sonnet).
Mad River.
Decoration Day.
The Bells of San Blas.

III.

HONORARIUM.

Some interest is attached in literary history to the payment received by authors. For his early poems, published during the last year of his college course, in the United States Literary Gazette, Mr. Longfellow received sometimes one dollar, sometimes two, according to their length; this was in 1825. In 1840–1841, 'The Village Blacksmith,' 'Endymion,' and 'God's Acre,' brought him $15 each; 'The Goblet of Life' and 'The River Charles,' $20 each. Then, in 1844, for 'The Gleam of Sunshine,' 'The Arsenal,' and 'Nuremberg,' he received $50 each. This remained the price up to 'The Ladder of Saint Augustine' and 'The Phantom Ship,' in 1850. After this there is no record; but later on he began to receive $100 or $150 for a poem. The Harpers paid $1,000 for 'Kéramos,' and the same for 'Morituri Salutamus;' Bonner, of the Ledger, $3,000 for 'The Hanging of the Crane.' Mr. Longfellow noted his income from his writings in 1840 as $219; in 1842 it was $517; in 1845 (the year of the Poets and Poetry of Europe), $2,800; in 1846, $1,800; the next year, $1,100; in 1850, $1,900; then $2,500 and $1,100; and there the record stops.

IV.

A JEU D'ESPRIT.

The following are the verses mentioned on page 68 as sent to Mr. Lowell when he excused himself from a Dante Club meeting on account of a sore throat: —

ALL' ILLUSTRISSIMO SIGNOR PROFESSORE LOWELL:

PRESCRIZIONE PER IL MAL DI GOLA.

"Benedetto
Quel Claretto
Che si spilla in Avignone,"
Dice Redi;
Se non, vedi
La famosa sua Canzone.

Questo vino
L' Aretino
Loda certo con ragione;
Ma sta fresco
Ser Francesco
Se 'l migliore lo suppone.

Con qualunque
Vino, dunque,
Tinto che dall' uvo cola,
Mescolato
Ed acquato,
Gargarizza ben la gola.

T' assicuro
E ti giuro,
(Uomo son di mia parola)
Il dolore,
Professore,
Tutto subito s' invola.

RISPOSTA DEL SIGNOR PROFESSORE.

Ho provato
Quest' acquato
Vino tinto della Francia,
E s' invola
Dalla gola
Il dolore alla pancia!

Such *jeux d'esprit* hardly bear translation. Those who do not read Italian may put up with the following: —

PRESCRIPTION FOR A SORE THROAT.

"Benedight
That claret light
Which is tapped in Avignone;"
Redi said it;
Who don't credit,
Let him read the famed Canzone.

This same wine
The Aretine
Justly praises as he drinks it;
And yet but poor
His taste, I 'm sure,
If the best of wines he thinks it.

Take this or another
(Make no bother),
Any red wine in your bottle,
Mixed with water
Of any sort or
Kind; then gargle well your throttle.

I assure you
It will cure you
(Me a man of my word you'll own);
Your distress or
Pain, Professor,
All of a sudden will have flown.

ANSWER OF THE PROFESSOR.

Quite delighted,
Quick I tried it,—
Your red wine of Avignon';
When, like a bullet,
Out of my gullet
Into my paunch the pain has flown!

V.

THE FIRST CLOSE OF THE 'BUILDING OF THE SHIP.'

The original ending of the 'Building of the Ship,' referred to on page 363, was this:—

How beautiful she is! How still
She lies within these arms that press
Her form with many a soft caress!
Modelled with such perfect skill,
Fashioned with such watchful care!
But, alas! oh, what and where
Shall be the end of a thing so fair?

Wrecked upon some treacherous rock,
Or rotting in some noisome dock, —
Such the end must be at length
Of all this loveliness and strength.

They who with transcendent power
Build the great cathedral tower,
Build the palaces and domes,
Temples of God and princes' homes,
These leave a record and a name.
But he who builds the stately ships,
The palaces of sea and air,
When he is buried in his grave
Leaves no more trace or mark behind
Than the sail does in the wind,
Than the keel does in the wave.
He whose dexterous hand could frame
All this beauty, all this grace,
In a grave without a name
Lies forgotten of his race!

VI.

THE TWO INKSTANDS.

Mention has been made (on p. 208) of the inkstand once belonging to the poet S. T. Coleridge, and bearing his name on a small ivory plate inserted in the black wood.

To General James Grant Wilson, who brought it from England, Mr. Longfellow wrote: —

"Your letter and the valuable present of Mr. S. C. Hall have reached me safely. Please accept my best thanks for the great kindness you have shown in taking charge of it and bringing from the Old World a gift so precious as the inkstand of the poet who wrote the 'Rime of the Ancient Mariner.' Will you be so good as to send me the present address of Mr. Hall? . . ."

This was in 1872. Mr. Hall wrote to Mr. Longfellow in 1878: —

"It rejoices me to know that you value so much the common inkstand of Coleridge, which I had the honor to give you. I have another inkstand, — the one to which Moore wrote some very beautiful lines, 'To the Inkstand of the poet George Crabbe.' It was bequeathed to me by Moore's widow, and I have, in Moore's handwriting, a copy of the poem. On Crabbe's death his son presented it to Moore. I do not like to part with it before we die, for Mrs. Hall uses it daily; but I shall bequeath it to you."

After Mrs. Hall's death the inkstand was sent to Mr. Longfellow. Mr. Hall wrote, "I send you the poem in Moore's handwriting;[1] also I send you a letter from the son of Crabbe, presenting the inkstand to Moore." It is in bronze, handsomely chased, and surmounted by a cupid, much more in keeping with the songs of Moore than with the sober and often sombre Tales of Crabbe. Both these inkstands Mr. Longfellow kept upon his study table, but he did not use them. His own

[1] These are the lines beginning: —

"All as he left it! ev'n the pen
So lately at that mind's command,
Carelessly lying, as if then
Just fallen from his gifted hand."

There are eighteen stanzas, the last half of them written in pencil. It is the first draft, written in a notebook.

was of French china, with a screw-top for raising or lowering the ink. His pens — he used only quills — were in a glass of water close by.

Mr. Hall also sent Mr. Longfellow the waste-paper basket which had been in Moore's use, — a small basket to be placed upon, not under, a writing table.

VII.

THE MOTTO.

Upon one of Mr. Longfellow's book-plates was engraved the motto "Non clamor sed amor." It was taken from the following stanza which he had found, without any author's name, in one of his books: —

"Non vox sed votum,
Non chorda sed cor,
Non clamor sed amor,
Clangit in aure Dei."

Not voice but vow,
Not harp-string but heart-string,
Not loudness but love,
Sounds in the ear of God.

VIII.

THE CHILDREN'S CHAIR.

When Brattle Street was widened in 1876, the horse-chestnut tree under which the "village smithy" of Cambridge had stood in the days when *The Village Blacksmith* was written, was cut down. Some portions of its wood were, however, saved. As the poet's seventy-second birthday approached, it occurred to his friends and neighbors, Mr. and Mrs. E. N. Horsford, that an appropriate gift for the occasion would be a chair made from the wood of the tree, to be presented in the name of the children of Cambridge. Some seven hundred of the children in the public schools contributed their dimes, and their elders supplied what was lacking. The artistic design of the chair was by the poet's nephew, Mr. W. P. P. Longfellow. Upon the seat beneath the cushion is a brass plate with this inscription: —

TO THE AUTHOR OF THE VILLAGE BLACKSMITH

This chair made from the wood of the spreading chestnut tree is presented as an expression of grateful regard and veneration by the children of Cambridge, who with their friends join in best wishes and congratulations on this anniversary.

February 27, 1879.

Around the base of the chair are carved in Gothic letters four lines: —

And children coming home from school
  Look in at the open door
And catch the burning sparks that fly
  Like chaff from a threshing floor.

Mr. Longfellow wrote to the children in acknowledgment of their gift, which gave him great pleasure as coming from them, a poem which closes thus: —

Only your love and your remembrance could
  Give life to this dead wood
And make these branches, leafless now so long,
  Blossom again in song.

Mr. Longfellow explained these last lines in a note, March 11, 1879, to Miss C. F. Bates: —

I am very glad you like the poem, and hope it will give pleasure to the dear children for whom it was written, and who have taken, as I hear, the liveliest interest in the arm-chair.

The last line of the poem, "Blossom again in song," alludes to a stanza of *The Village Blacksmith* running round the chair in Gothic letters.

And what a beautiful chair it is! As I look at it now, the brass nails along its arms shine like the street lights of Brighton opposite, or the double line of lights on the Cambridge bridge.

Of this poem he had a large number printed, and gave a copy to each of the children who came to see, and sit in, the chair.

In connection with this gift of the Cambridge children, mention may be made of what was to the poet a very interesting event, the celebration of his birthday in the following year by the public schools of Cincinnati. The superintendent of the schools, Mr. John B. Peaslee, had written to Mr. Longfellow in the previous December that he was making preparation for such a celebration, in which some fifteen thousand pupils, from the primary to the high schools, would take part, with addresses, biographical sketches, and recitation of poems or stanzas from the poet's works, and singing of his songs. It was part of a larger plan, to introduce into the schools a series of celebrations of author's birthdays, with the view of creating and educating a love of literature among the youth. Mr. Longfellow wrote to him in reply: —

I have had the pleasure of receiving your very interesting letter and wish it were in my power to comply with your request to send you some lines to be read on the occasion you mention. But want of time and numerous avocations render it impossible. I can only send you my Christmas and New Year's greeting to the grand army of your pupils, and ask you to tell them, as I am sure you have often told them before, to live up to the best that is in them; to live noble lives, — as they all may, in whatever condition they may find themselves.

The next year the idea spread through the country; and especially in the West, the celebrations were numerous, and numerous the letters from teachers and pupils which came to the poet. With patient good-nature he replied to a great many of them so far as to send an autograph stanza "with Mr. Longfellow's good wishes." The thought of the children evidently touched him; for he gathered into a scrap-book a multitude of the newspaper accounts of these celebrations.

INDEX.